Praise for *Entity Modelling*

'This book is a welcome deep dive into the background and [illegible] of a paradigm shift in standards for bibliographic metadata concepts and content.'
Gordon Dunsire, retired, and recipient of the IFLA Medal 2016 for 'enhancing the field of bibliographic data, linked data and the semantic web'

'This book, with its essential and extensive introductory essays, is a concise, yet complex, description of the most advanced state at the present time of cataloging, and thus discovery, for library collections using Linked Open Data, of which BIBFRAME is a variant. *Entity Modelling* demonstrates the progress made to a theoretical construct for the new and more flexible approach to library cataloging, that is also apropos to cataloging and thus discovery in other cultural heritage organizations, especially museums, for their collections, whether virtual or analog, or both. *Entity Modelling* is highly endorsed!'
Michael A. Keller, Vice Provost and University Librarian, Stanford University, USA

'This book presents a deep, philosophical investigation into the somewhat elusive notion of entity modelling as applied in cataloguing practice. It convincingly demonstrates how issues grappled with in everyday bibliographical work lead back to the age-old, big questions of being and identity, and by that, enables readers to form independent thoughts on practical solutions. Anyone intrigued by the conceptual underpinnings of bibliographical work – cataloguers and terminologists alike – should read this book. So should anyone dismissing cataloguing as a mere mechanical activity.'
Oddrun Pauline Ohren, Metadata Specialist, National Library of Norway

'Tiziana Possemato's *Entity Modelling* offers a compelling case for reimagining cataloging in the digital era. Arguing that traditional methods are insufficient, Possemato introduces entity modelling as the next generation of cataloging, leveraging semantic web principles to represent bibliographic resources through real-world entities and their relationships. This insightful work explores theory and implementation, revealing how entity modelling enhances access, interoperability, and research. It is essential reading for librarians, archivists, information scientists, and anyone invested in the future of information organization and retrieval.'
Nina Servizzi, Associate Dean, Knowledge Access and Resource Management Services, New York University Libraries, USA

Entity Modelling

Entity Modelling
The Third Generation of Cataloguing

Prologue by Philip E. Schreur
Forewords by Carlo Bianchini and Maurizio Vivarelli
Introduction by Mauro Guerrini
Translation by Jonnel Licari

Tiziana Possemato

facet publishing

Published by Facet Publishing
www.facetpublishing.co.uk

Facet Publishing is wholly owned by CILIP:
the Library and Information Association.

British Library Cataloguing in Publication Data
A catalogue record for this book is available from the British Library.

ISBN 978-1-78330-727-2 (paperback)
ISBN 978-1-78330-728-9 (hardback)
ISBN 978-1-78330-729-6 (PDF)
ISBN 978-1-78330-730-2 (EPUB)

First published 2026

Originally published in Italian as *Entity Modeling: la Terza Generazione della Catalogazione*

MIX
Paper | Supporting responsible forestry
FSC® C013604
FSC www.fsc.org

The manufacturer's authorised representative in the EU for product safety is Logos Europe, 9 rue Nicolas Poussin, 17000 La Rochelle, France (contact@logoseurope.eu, www.logoseurope.eu).

Typeset from author's files by Flagholme Publishing Services in 10/13 pt Palatino Linotype and Open Sans.
Printed and made in Great Britain by CPI Group (UK) Ltd, Croydon, CR0 4YY.

To Alberto,
who has defined the *before* and *after* of my existence.

LAUDISI: Don't listen to him! – Are you sure you can touch me as you see me? You cannot doubt yourself. – But for heaven's sake, don't tell your husband, nor my sister, nor my niece, nor the lady here . . . how you see me, because all four of them will otherwise tell you that you are mistaken, while you are not mistaken at all! Because I am indeed as you see me. – But this does not mean, my dear lady, that I am not also as your husband, my sister, my niece, and the lady here see me . . . and they are not mistaken either.
SIGNORA SIRELLI: And how is it, then, that you change from one to the other?
LAUDISI: Of course, I change, my dear lady! And you, don't you change too?
Luigi Pirandello, *Right You Are (If You Think So)*

Contents

Figures and Tables

Figures

Tables

About the Author

Tiziana Possemato holds a degree in Philosophy (La Sapienza Rome), diplomas in Archival Science and Library Sciences (Vatican Schools) and a Master's degree in Archival Science, Librarianship and Codicology (University of Florence). She earned her PhD in Library Sciences at the University of Florence.

Tiziana is a metadata specialist and she has led numerous national and international projects for library automation, analysis, mapping and conversion of catalogue data and the design of information retrieval systems, with a specific interest in Linked Open Data and the Semantic Web, and is involved in numerous working groups of IFLA and other organisations.

The author of publications and contributions in the field of library and information science, she is the Chief Information Officer of Casalini Libri, and founding partner and director of @Cult.

ORCID: https://orcid.org/0000–0002–7184–4070
ISNI: 0000 0004 4808 5795

About the Author

Prologue by Philip E. Schreur

All humans effortlessly thrive in a complex web of intersubjectivity, a web of shared, yet unspoken, beliefs and assumptions. What allows us to exchange a colourful piece of paper, called a euro, for a croissant and an espresso? How can the logo for Volkswagen be instantly understood across the globe? What imbues meaning into the classification systems and cataloguing rules that libraries create? What makes the International Federation of Library Associations' Library Reference Model (IFLA LRM) authoritative? It is the acceptance of an implied reality that common beliefs create. Whether it is a shared delusion, or a *folie à deux,* these mutual beliefs allow humans from vastly different cultural backgrounds to communicate and be understood; they breathe meaning into our world. But more than that, humans delight in the ambiguity that intersubjectivity creates, the play of light and shadow. The extraordinary flexibility of intersubjectivity, that is, the ability to create a shared reality between individuals or groups, is arguably one of the few elements that is unique to humans. But as Dr Possemato points out, 'the goal [of the *semantic* web] has been to build a mechanism that can describe, *in a machine-understandable way,* everything in our world.' How can we imbue the flexibility that intersubjectivity creates into a world that has been built on 0s and 1s?

Cataloguers have one of the most challenging professions in the modern information ecosystem. They are charged with describing any resource that may exist in today's ever-evolving world, whether it be tangible or intangible. Not only must they describe the resource as a unique object, they must embed it semantically in a web that potentially encompasses all possible objects. Each resource must be described uniquely so that it is discoverable, but in such a way that its location is navigable in an endless web of data. But even as intersubjectivity allows us to create mutually accepted entities, whether they be concepts or real-world objects, the perception of these entities shifts with time: corporate names evolve, gender may alter, even physical characteristics may change. And the intersubjective reality unconsciously assigned by one group of people may be perceived differently by another. How can all these complex entities be uniquely described in such a way that a machine can unambiguously identify them?

As the world turns to artificial intelligence and machine learning to springboard us into a brave new world, this is perhaps the most critical question to answer. The modelling of these entities to allow for both the varying intersubjective realities required by humans and the unequivocable identification required by the machine must be resolved. In such a world, a world of *chiaroscuro*, human and machine can partner to create a world of unlimited potential. But this potential can be achieved only if human and machine can communicate their realities in a single web of meaning.

Philip E. Schreur PhD
Deputy University Librarian
Stanford University

Foreword by Carlo Bianchini

Tiziana Possemato's work, *Entity Modelling: the Third Generation of Cataloguing* addresses the topic of entity modelling, which concerns the ways in which entities – increasingly less distinct in nominal and semantic terms as traditionally understood – are identified and described with absolute certainty regardless of the form of the names by which they appear in sources. The focus of entity modelling, in particular, is on recognising the identity of entities that may appear in different contexts through different informational profiles, especially by using different names as a result of changes in various contexts: cultural, linguistic, graphic, historical, social, etc. The real-world entity presents itself as an object of observation – a real-world object – with numerous possible facets in the context of the identification process essential for any indexing tool. The varying observation points of the same entity make it a different object each time, based on the diverse purposes of the indexing processes, which lead to the use of specific names and the definition of properties peculiar to that same entity.

The problematic aspect highlighted in Tiziana Possemato's investigation – namely the starting question of the doctoral research of which this work is the result – is whether one can explain the meaning of an entity such as Expression (envisioned by international conceptual models like Functional Requirements for Bibliographic Records (FRBRer) or Functional Requirements for Bibliographic Records (FRBRoo), etc.) without first clarifying what is meant by entity, as well as whether one can link different phenomena like the names of an entity without first clarifying what is meant by identity. The answer to these questions is then placed within a clearly defined framework, that of cataloguing; and the approach is correct and the only possible one, as these questions have not yet found a general solution in the philosophical field.

With this approach, the precedence between ontology and metaphysics is pragmatically resolved, also noting that this is what 'cataloguing and classification science has done for years: it has compiled inventories of entities that best represent the bibliographic universe, and then defined their nature and relationships' (p. 8).

In Chapter 1 ('I Contain Multitudes'), the author offers a careful and detailed reflection on the entity/identity pair. Starting mainly from a philosophical perspective within the realms of ontology and metaphysics, these fundamental concepts of international theoretical cataloguing are explored and outlined. The analysis develops through the perspective of the synchronic and diachronic identities assumed by the entities present in the bibliographic universe, leading to the conclusion that it is a

> community that establishes what is essential and what is incidental in the definition of an entity and its relationships; it is a community that, based on its own needs, determines, in a relative and not absolute way, what is change and what is permanence. This relativist position allows us to look at many of the data models and the many ontologies created for the bibliographic world (and beyond) with a different approach, one that starts from the organisational and informational needs these models seek to address.
>
> (p. 39)

In Chapter 2 ('The World is my Representation'), the focus is on the reflection of the ways that objects are represented within indexing tools: specifically, on how objects in the bibliographic universe are traditionally represented and described through records and how these should increasingly orient toward the representation of real-world objects. The approach from the previous chapter, which distinguished between entity and identity, finds confirmation in the field of computer science, especially in object-oriented programming (OOP) and the distinction it applies between real-world object and real-world entity. This perspective suggests that the focus of the identification process (and entity resolution) should not be an absolute object, represented holistically with all its characteristics from every point of view, but rather entities identified and represented based on the purposes of the specific universe being described.

The investigation shifts in Chapter 3 ('Panta Rei, or the Fluidity of the Universe') to analysing the boundaries that can be established between the identities of the same entity. These boundaries develop and change with great fluidity, but it becomes essential to determine them precisely to make them interoperable for machines. The central problem is, therefore, identifying with exactitude the boundaries that differentiate the identities of the same entity, even through the reworked concept of a Cambridge change, which refers to shifts that are not decisive from a metaphysical perspective, such as the change in the height ratio – measured at different times – between a mother and a growing daughter (at one time, the mother 'is taller'; at a later time, the mother 'is the same height').

The focus in Chapter 4 ('O Romeo, Romeo, Wherefore Art Thou Romeo?') is on analysing the entity agent, which has traditionally received much attention in cataloguing rules and theoretical models (starting with FRBR, continuing with Bibliographic Framework (BIBFRAME) and, more recently, IFLA LRM). This entity is particularly significant as a cross-domain entity, which can help find points of convergence in metadata production and data reuse from both a LAM (libraries, archives and museums) modelling perspective and a semantic web perspective. In this key chapter, the author, through two specific cases – the modelling of the names of popes, with the examples of John Paul II and Benedict XVI, and of continuing resources – along with an extensive and accurate analysis of how these objects in the bibliographic universe are treated according to the current cataloguing tradition, arrives at original and well-founded reflections and a concrete application proposal (clearly summarised, particularly through Figure 4.6, on page 225) currently proposed for practical application in Share Virtual Discovery Environment (Share-VDE or SVDE).

The volume concludes with an appendix focused on the ontology of Share-VDE, understood as an extension of the BIBFRAME ontology, and by a rich, up-to-date definitive bibliography.

The study makes careful use of the most important reference sources for analysis, based on research conducted at national and international levels on projects applying the linked data paradigm in the LAM field. It also extensively utilises unpublished sources and data, resulting from the fulfilment of some ongoing projects and the direct study of data. Even in the first three chapters, which develop a broad survey of interdisciplinary studies and literature (philosophy, computer science and cataloguing), the author demonstrates excellent command of the relevant bibliography for the discussed topic.

This work as a whole – conducted through original reflection on the contrast between entity and identity, between real-world object and real-world entity, between synchronic identity and diachronic identity, and through the application of the concept of individuation of emerging properties and the reference context – constitutes an innovative reading of great interest to specialists in the field. The commitment of Firenze University Press in publishing it to ensure it reaches the widest possible circulation within the relevant scientific community, is absolutely commendable.

Carlo Bianchini
Associate Professor in Library and Information Science
University of Pavia

Foreword by Maurizio Vivarelli

This book by Tiziana Possemato puts forth many well-informed points, both regarding the specifics of the subject matter – entity modelling – and the manner in which the topic is presented, argued, and discussed.

Entity modelling, the current evolutionary phase of traditional bibliographic cataloguing, is a fundamental and crucial activity in the perspective of the semantic web. It aims to ensure the automatic processing of data by machines, following and building on Tim Berners-Lee's original insight directed at the semanticisation, through specific ontologies, of the relational value of the hypertextual link between two entities present in the digital environment (Berners-Lee, 2001). In this way, the linguistic representation models of bibliographic resources find themselves in a sort of metaphorical frontier territory, which on one side looks towards human cognitive structures and on the other is directly situated at the heart of the infosphere, populated by gargantuan quantities of data that can now only be estimated by resorting to the dizzying measure of zettabytes, produced by interactions between humans and machines and manageable and relatable only by resorting to the computational power of the machines themselves.

Each of us is therefore immersed in this authentic information Babel, in which many of the 'interrupted paths' that Heidegger had anticipated in the last century (Heidegger, 1968)[1] are outlined, disturbingly and dystopically. However, the possibility remains to define, on the web and for the web, representative models of reality that are utopically concrete. That is, they are endowed with meaning, useful for attempting to guarantee access to knowledge even in the posthuman and Anthropocene landscape, and thus find the theoretical and methodological way to access the 'clearings of the forest' – evoking María Zambrano – of the bibliographic universe and recorded knowledge (Zambrano, 1977). In this phase, therefore, the archaic and original *nómos* of libraries, in whatever form manifested and which for millennia has lingered within our cultural traditions with the mission of ordering the indistinct, must rediscover and necessarily renew its *hodós*, its path, and for data and the representations of data, give rise to and render hospitable what Maurizio Ferraris has very effectively defined as Abel's library, thus carrying on the incremental and never definitive construction of *homo sapiens* (Ferraris, 2022).

Possemato's book fits into this context with consistency and rigour, demonstrating, first and foremost, a great command of the scientific literature related to the field of library and information science. At the same time, it manages to contribute additional and valuable qualities, both theoretical and stylistic as well as expressive, to an already broad and up-to-date base of techno-methodological knowledge. In this sense, the paratextual structure of the book, starting from the title ('Entity Modelling: The Third Generation of Cataloguing'), configures in the text, the interesting figure of an Ideal Reader far from being a mere mechanical applicator of standardised cataloguing rules, but rather outlines, in filigree, the physiognomy of an expert and knowledgeable intellectual operator, aware of their role in the construction of 'bridges', that is, models of representation of objects in the real world destined to fulfil their function within the web of data.

The book is an elaboration of the doctoral thesis entitled 'Another Brick in the Wall: Building Bridges of Knowledge in the Digital Age' and therefore maintains within it the symbolic and metaphorical value of the famous Pink Floyd song from the album The Wall, released in 1979, when the internet was beginning to take its first steps. The metaphorical wall evoked by the thesis title, quite different from the one imagined by the protagonist of the Pink Floyd song, seems to indicate everything that hinders the construction of a unitary and integrated environment for access to knowledge, through the constitution of the mediating functions of the bibliographic universe and recorded knowledge. Each of the book's four chapters is also characterised by the profile (and aura) of an intellectual personality that performs, still paratextually, the guiding function attributed to the epigraph. The four profiles are those of Fernando Pessoa, Arthur Schopenhauer, Heraclitus and William Shakespeare. Pessoa introduces the contents of the first chapter (I Contain Multitudes), dedicated to dealing with the concepts of entity and identity, from a synchronic, diachronic perspective, and according to the whole–part relations. Schopenhauer initiates the reflection of the second chapter (The World is my Representation), centred on the distinction between real-world object, real-world entity and the presentation of the fundamental concepts of entity modelling with specific in-depth analysis dedicated to the BIBFRAME ontology and the modelling of the Opus entity in the activities of the Share community. Heraclitus establishes the starting point of the third chapter (Panta Rei, or The Fluidity of the Universe), in which the problem of modelling entities immersed in the becoming of change flows is posed.

Finally, Shakespeare represents the viaticum for the fourth chapter (O Romeo, Romeo, Wherefore Art Thou Romeo?), which deals with the concept of agent in the cataloguing tradition, in the MARC format, and in the semantic web with a thorough review of modelling practices that passes through IFLA LRM, BIBFRAME, Wikidata, Resource Description and Access (RDA), CIDOC Conceptual Reference Model (CIDOC CRM), Schema.org, Dublin Core (DC) and Records in Context Ontology (RiC-O).

The task as configured is quite clearly not simple, and in order to proceed, it is necessary for traditional cataloguing to take a sort of quantum leap, or metanoia, allowing it to achieve results, following the convincingly proposed trajectory by Mauro Guerrini. Within this fascinating and well-structured organisation, verbatim and narrative, lies the central conceptual dilemma of the book that identifies entity modelling as the new frontier of cataloguing, according to an interdisciplinary perspective that intertwines philosophy, computer science, and library science. The proposed elaboration develops from original reflections that illustrate the relationships, as well as differences – according to Possemato's lexicon – between ontology (reflection on what there is) and metaphysics (reflection on what is). In light of these basic and foundational concepts, the tasks of ontology (which identifies entities) and metaphysics (which defines the profiles of the identities of entities) are identified.

This division of tasks corresponds to the functions and objectives of representations of cataloguing data, which therefore acquire ontological characteristics, related to the inventory of what there is, and metaphysical characteristics, which concern the description of the identities of what is, first in the territories of metadata (Guerrini, 2020), and then in those of entity modelling. As they continue to suggest the metaphorical elements of the title, it is necessary to understand the nature, function, and position of the bricks destined to give origin, consistency, shapes and structure to the bridges that must be built; and for this reason, the author is obliged to inquire about what are the fundamental elements of the conceptual, methodological and applicative perspective of entity modelling, thanks to which the bricks that become the cornerstones of the symbolic building of the bibliographic universe can be realised. A comparable operation was attempted, some years ago, by Elaine Svenonius, trying to identify the *ubi consistam* of bibliographic systems and their languages. In this book, Possemato also tackles the task of ensuring entity modelling an autonomous and consistent conceptual and reflective basis (Svenonius, 2008).

Particularly relevant in this sense is the careful analysis of the nature of the entities that must be identified and modelled within the framework of entity modelling, the real-world objects, and their problematic relationship with the real-world entities. Do the two expressions mean the same thing?

Possemato's conceptual and terminological choice is clear and convincing, consisting of using the term 'real-world entity' to refer to entities of the real world (which ontology deals with), and 'real-world objects' to refer to identity, that is, the qualities of objects (which metaphysics deals with). Within the lexicon and perspective of object-oriented programming (OOP), the activity of modelling coincides with the creation of the representation of a real-world object, which is constituted by a state (the differential variations that make the thing what it is), to which behaviours are connected, i.e. the possibility that that modelled representation has of doing something. This representation (the software object) therefore concerns the real-world object, that is, the object from the perspective of its perceived qualities, and not the real-world entity, which remains hidden, concealed and withdrawn and can be represented only by starting from the adoption of a specific point of view that, of the real-world entities, sees some things and not others.

Real-world entities, with this subtle terminological attention, are modelled into objects manageable by machines, characterised by states and behaviours achieved through the adoption of specific representations and programming languages. The object itself, the 'thing-in-itself' of the Kantian tradition, is therefore not entirely knowable. The knowability of the object constructively goes from potentiality to actuality when that object is observed from a particular point of view, based on which, pragmatically, those qualities of the object that are considered useful in that particular context are selected. However, even if they are conceived with this conceptual and terminological precision, neither the objects nor their representations are static – as confirmed by the famous paradox of the ship of Theseus, mentioned several times in the text – but change incessantly, acquiring new identities of which machines must be informed. It is not easy to pinpoint the theoretical result of the change, which is why the concept of a Cambridge change – associated with Bertrand Russell's philosophy – is invoked. It accounts for the stage that certifies an object's identity change through the acknowledgement of a break (both *ontological* and *identifying*). Therefore, a thing changes, according to Russell and Cambridge change, when it is associated with a property that can be either true or false, as in the case of the position of a city relative to a subject – north or south, for example – a position that changes depending on the subject's position relative to the city. In terms of representing change in the languages of the cataloguing tradition, this problem is aptly illustrated by the variant linguistic forms of the denomination of the Supreme Pontiff. The same graceful oscillation between philosophical reflection and cataloguing application is also evident in the section dedicated to the treatment of the agent in the semantic web, particularly regarding the treatment of popes in the cataloguing tradition.

As a whole, Tiziana Possemato's book places itself authoritatively in a national and international movement of theoretical reflection on the prospects for the development of traditional cataloguing. For Italy, it explicitly references initiatives promoted by Mauro Guerrini, which highlight points of contact with the disciplinary traditions of archival science and museology[2]. The book, in its current structure and configuration, represents the culmination of an informed, aware, and mature theoretical and practical perspective. This allows for the identification of a foundation for entity modelling that is updated to the level of the current debate, even on the most specifically philosophical issues, which are absorbed and integrated within a viewpoint that can certainly be defined as solid. In any case, it positions itself with adequate awareness in the current theoretical and methodological debate on data representation in a digital environment.

But the quest for foundational principles does not conclude here. One needs only to consider the works of authors such as Graham Harman (2018) and Timothy Morton (2018) to see the continued developments of contemporary reflection on ontology.

The former, with his object-oriented ontology (OOO), has delved into issues related to the possibility of knowing objects only indirectly. Such objects ('real objects' in Harman's lexicon) are described as 'withdrawn' and 'withheld' and, therefore, can be known only through their properties ('sensual objects' according to Harman's lexicon). It seems to me that, in this case, a precise and meticulous conceptual and terminological correspondence between Possemato's definitions and those of Harman can be identified: real objects correspond to real-world entities, and sensual objects to real-world objects (the models with which some of the properties of entities are represented). As compared to Possemato's perspective, Harman's point of view is even more complex. In the American philosopher's thought process, the issue is not only how to communicate the value of the qualities of things to machines, but also to question the constitutive limits of human cognitive activities. Humans must acknowledge that they live in a reality in which real objects have their own life, which cannot be understood with the anthropic ways in which they are recognised.

Timothy Morton, for his part, adds to the many pieces of the puzzle, the uncertain and opaque physiognomy of hyperobjects, which are, so to speak, a consequence of adopting an ontology and an epistemology situated at the limits of the human, between words and things. The hyperobjects to which Morton refers (meteors, tornadoes, tsunamis, earthquakes, climate change as a whole) are not simple mental representations (or representations to be communicated to machines) but real entities whose knowledge is entirely precluded to humans. Morton's hyperobjects, in their most evident certainty, actually correspond to all the real objects in Harman's lexicon and to some types of real-world objects in Possemato's.

These very brief summaries only partially describe the great complexity of these areas of reflection, and yet they suggest further scenarios for the development of a future entity modelling that continues to meet the challenge of giving form to what is invisible, shapeless and depicted by the object, such as the formalised and standardised representation of emotions, and their effects on information seeking, a topic that is of significant interest in the extended dimension of LIS[3] as well.

The entity-modelling phase therefore constitutes the arrival point of a trajectory of elaboration and development that is still ongoing, one which can only be followed by further phases and which we hope will continue to be fostered by the trust conjured as the final and synthesis element of the values highlighted by Michael Gorman (Gorman, 2015).

In this way, we sense and catch sight of the uncertain and opaque contours of a multitude of other Pillars of Hercules, waiting to be identified, imagined, conceived and ultimately, once again, represented and experienced.

Maurizio Vivarelli
Full Professor in Library and Information Science
University of Turin

Introduction by Mauro Guerrini: Entity Modelling or Rather, the Next Generation of Cataloguing

The research that led to this book was cultivated during the preparation of Tiziana Possemato's doctoral thesis defining a cataloguing language typical of the digital age, which I had the honour of supervising. The expertise of Share-VDE, part of the broader Share Family initiative, of which the author is one of the main protagonists, was crucial. This project involving major American and Northern European libraries aimed at defining a new bibliographic model both conceptually and in practical actions related to resource description and the publication and use of their metadata, when possible, as linked open data (LOD). An international observatory that is highly stimulating and collaborative on both theoretical and practical levels. The cataloguing paradigm in the digital era involves various web domains, starting with those closest to the library world, such as archives and museums. It is no coincidence that 'Entity Modelling: The Third Generation of Cataloguing' has an emblematic title that alludes to an evolutionary transition. This development requires, first and foremost, the awareness of undergoing radical transformations and, consequently, the acquisition of language typical of the semantic web to facilitate increasingly transversal communication between the bibliographic universe and the reader.

The investigation into entity modelling, the central theme of the author's work, introduces a reflection that aims to surpass both the methodologies that have characterised the 'Great Tradition' of cataloguing mentioned by Michael Gorman in *Our Enduring Values Revisited* (Gorman, 2015) – a tradition which, according to the author, begins with Antonio Panizzi and ends with Seymour Lubetzky – and the transition from cataloguing to metadata creation that occurred at the turn of the 21st century. Entity modelling, in other words, goes beyond metadata creation and represents the third generation of cataloguing. It is undeniable that the cataloguing dimension has now entirely shifted to the web, and it is necessary to determine what still holds from the traditional framework and what needs to be newly conceived. Will the result of this innovative process still be called a catalogue, an ordered list of bibliographic records compiled according to conventions or standards?

Cataloguing has always meant creating metadata, that is, recording structured data according to a defined method, a format that functions to offer a representation of the distinctive and characteristic aspects of the described resource, regardless of the type of resource – a person, a work, an art object – or the metadata necessary for its identification and retrieval.

What, then, has changed? Tiziana seeks to answer this question.

The rise of digital technology has led to the proliferation of metadata families, significantly expanding the boundaries of traditional cataloguing. In a time of profound bibliographic transformation, the analysis of the elements that characterise descriptions is considered inadequate, and at the centre of her original reflection are two concepts: entity, understood as every real-world object, and identity. The reader will find the articulated answer by reading this volume. They will encounter innovative concepts and terms in a challenging text, much like any book that critically reflects on behaviours considered acquired and instead requires verification regarding their correspondence to the changes in today's cultural, editorial, and technological context. The book introduces an unprecedented scenario in the long theoretical and practical tradition of cataloguing, sensitive to the opportunities offered by conceptual models developed both in the library field, especially those issued by IFLA, and in the computer field as contemporary technology. The author demonstrates the validity of the new scenario, in progress, matured and experimented with internationally, in the aforementioned Share Family initiative.

Entity modelling thus appears as the third generational transition in bibliographic data management. It is an evolution that necessitates a change in the methods of data processing and formalisation; it implies a language that uses the semantic and syntactic parameters specific to the digital context. The perspective proposed by the author creates a virtuous circle in which the theoretical and applicative dimensions enrich each other to generate a new structure, functional to the mediation between the bibliographic universe and the reader. This results in the transcending of the catalogue conceived for the conventional era, now with the proposition of something that is still being defined but is perceived as a significant qualitative leap from the past. In the new model, data is defined singularly and is as interoperable as possible. In metadata creation (unlike traditional cataloguing) the descriptive overview of the resource includes a series of data necessary for its identification, retrieval and use, in an increasingly rich, broad, and heterogeneous information context. Another important perquisite of metadata creation compared to traditional cataloguing is the openness it allows in the structure of data presentation and access to descriptions: These can be defined subsequently without the predefined constructions provided by ISBD. This standard, which has had such meaning and value internationally in structuring metadata for sharing in different databases, with the predetermined sequence of areas, elements and conventional punctuation, loses significance in an era in which each individual metadata becomes self-significant – that is, acquires meaning and is created to be understandable to machines. With the creation of metadata, therefore, there is no longer a linear sequence of descriptive metadata, and the search extends from only the access points (before the 2009 ICP they were called headings) to a huge amount of metadata related to the searched resource and deriving from various sources, two significant peculiarities. It can thus be said that metadata creation is the cataloguing of the digital age in which everything is connected. The cataloguing tradition is affirmed in its essence precisely at the moment when its techniques are updated and strengthened. This allows the catalogue not only to be on the web but to become part of the web, that is, to use the language of modernity as it has always done in its long history. The focus is now on the characterisation of entities and their relationships, from which the creation of descriptive metadata and access to bibliographic resources derive. The catalogue thus becomes (though it has always been) the enabling tool for services because a library that does not provide services is a repository and not a library.

The proposal of entity modelling as the new generation of cataloguing aims to find a common process to identify and describe resources across all knowledge domains, regardless of overly restrictive and rigid standardisation rules in any specific context. The idea derives from, and is based on, the Entity-Relationship model conceived in the field of computer science in the second half of the 20th century. It emerged as a methodology for data analysis and modelling for database design and related applications and was embraced in the cataloguing field in 1998 with FRBR. A model whose importance has shaped descriptive standards and, at least ideally, cataloguing practices.

Conceptual models and cataloguing standards today are increasingly focusing their attention on entities and the relationships between them rather than simply characterising entities through attributes. This is evident in the transition from FRBR to IFLA LRM, as well as in the transformations undergone by the RDA standard following the RDA Toolkit Restructure and Redesign Project and the emerging BIBFRAME standard, with its growing implementations, starting with the Library of Congress. This leads to a change in the structure of catalogues, which are now organised as simple relational databases, becoming semantic databases capable of sharing metadata with the outside world, thus promoting interoperability between domains and moving away from the logic of siloed catalogues, closed within themselves. Some libraries have already begun experiments in this direction, such as the Bibliothèque Nationale de France with data.bnf.fr (since 2012!), which has redesigned its catalogue based on FRBR, the famous 'FRBR-isation' of the catalogue. Data.bnf.fr is a significantly enhanced search tool compared to a traditional catalogue, capable of simultaneously querying multiple databases and offering countless search paths. Its acquisition is now consolidated thanks to discovery tools. What matters most is the quality of the data, i.e., the bibliographic and research dimension of the catalogue, not only as a discovery tool but above all as a device for embodied knowledge consistent with the developments of historical-bibliographic and editorial research present since Antonio Panizzi (but even as early as Audiffredi) onwards, culminating with Àkos Domanovszky.

The aforementioned shift in the cataloguing paradigm progresses through the theoretical elaborations that the book extensively and convincingly presents to provide the basis for a variety of applications that allow, for identifying entities by benefiting from data enrichment techniques without losing the specific characteristics of representations or identities. The outcomes contribute to building the foundations of a new bibliographic ecosystem associated with the third generation of cataloguing. The benefits extend to users (scholars and students) and to the machines that use the data, which can now be provided with an extremely functional search tool for accessing information, transparently with respect to the complexity of metadata structuring and their interconnection between databases. The benefits also extend to the maintenance of metadata – whose quantity will continue to grow rapidly – through new forms of international collaboration.

Is this kind of restructuring truly useful for the user, or more precisely, for all types of users? Are the new tools offered by the market easy and intuitive to use, or does data searching become *more* complicated?

In this phase of bibliographic transition, it is necessary to pause and reflect on the consequences this could entail. Today's priorities seem to be maximum sharing and visibility on the web, the ability to navigate through resources and discover new ones, and the ability to reuse data to optimise cataloguing processes and make them faster and more sustainable.

Do users want all of this? Are we aware of what it means to structure a mediation tool between collection and reader in a way that allows this degree of integration on the web?

As an example, let's consider describing a book referencing the second edition of the RDA standard. The description tends towards atomisation, and many metadata that were previously considered attributes of a resource have become relationships between entities, each of which is further characterised.

The first element we record for a book is the title, which is a type of *nomen*, i.e., an entity associated with a dataset that is associated with a set of attributes or metadata specifying properties such as language, type of writing, the string of *nomen*, etc. Many other metadata are treated in the same way, such as the place of publication, the publisher's name or the publication date, each of which is appropriately characterised. This is crucial when operating in an environment based on metadata reuse and exchange, where each piece of data must be adequately accompanied by a series of metadata specifying its semantic context to be used correctly. However, such detailed information might not interest a library user, who often asks catalogue-specific questions about the presence of a particular resource.

When we talk about entity modelling, web technologies, and enrichment tools from different sources, we are talking about a series of strategies that are designed to serve different user groups, from machines to humans. The identification of entities and, therefore, the shift of attention to the object itself (whether it is an author, a book, a geographic location, a concept, or anything else that is part of our horizon) proposes a model of information creation in which everyone can maintain their own point of view in both the description phase and the fruition phase. Entity modelling, whose linked open data paradigm is just a technological facilitator for its implementation, proposes to look at the world and its things from a position that is the most comfortable (in relation to the context from which that thing is viewed) and useful for an individual purpose (each, that is, according to their informational needs).

In the evolution of cataloguing, an age-old and still unresolved question is how to construct languages that transcend individual knowledge domains to facilitate the exchange, reuse and understanding of information across different domains. For years, in compliance with cataloguing rules that standardised the language of communication between collection and reader, valuable information assets have been created. But they have been closed off in silos and, in certain respects, understandable only to librarians and experts. There is now a prevailing desire to allow dialogue between different domains – pursued through mapping activities between different languages or pursued in the future with a radical change to information – where it will no longer be the mapping from format to format that ensures communication, but the structuring of a transversal language (as proposed by entity modelling) in which each domain can offer its own vision of what is collaboratively described.

The refusal to recognise and adopt internationally shared web standards fossilises one's own domain, one's disciplinary language, and places it outside the contemporary context.

Tiziana's book is a sign of hope that cataloguing, metadata creation, or whatever it may be called in the future, remains at the centre of scientific interests so that the new tool of mediation between the portion of the bibliographic universe in possession of libraries and the user is increasingly functional for the purposes and needs of today's and tomorrow's readers.

Mauro Guerrini
Professor Emeritus
University of Florence

Acknowledgements

I would like to express my deepest gratitude to Mauro Guerrini, who strongly supported this work, the result of an important journey we have taken together. Thank you for encouraging me always to do more and for believing in me despite the organisational challenges.

Many thanks to Carlo Bianchini for reading this work so carefully, for writing a Foreword and for suggesting a wider dissemination.

Thank you to Maurizio Vivarelli for his insightful analysis of the text and for his valuable reflection on this work, which enriched the final result.

And to Gianfranco Crupi, who, during my doctoral studies, from which this work derives, generously shared his time, experience and enthusiasm for transferring knowledge to others, and who encouraged me in difficult times.

Heartfelt thanks to Barbara, Ulla and Michele Casalini: the research that produced this work was supported by their foresight, cultural sensitivity and generosity, in memory of Gerda and Mario Casalini. Thank you for entrusting me with such a special role. And thanks especially to Michele, for supporting and helping me in this endeavour. His incredible availability and unlimited support facilitated the entire work and ensured its path to publication.

Thanks to Mennato Tedino, Andrea Gazzarini and Alessandra Moi, who guided certain aspects of my reflection and helped me in particular moments of my investigation. Thanks to Annalisa Di Sabato for having the strength and patience to reread the entire text, sacrificing many of her evening hours of rest.

I am sincerely thankful to Philip Schreur, for inspiring many of the reflections recorded in this work. His worldview, his clarity and his deep understanding of phenomena concerning our bibliographic universe, accompanied by a special modesty, have been an essential stimulus for addressing certain issues. Thanks to him for always taking the time to discuss everything and for sharing his thoughts with me.

Finally, special thanks to my sisters, who are always there when I need them, and to Luigi and Alberto, who have continued to endure my irritability and have had the patience to wait for my return.

This work is dedicated to Alberto and my family, who made my childhood happy, despite everything.

List of Acronyms

3R	RDA Toolkit Restructure and Redesign Project
AACR	Anglo-American Cataloguing Rules
AACR2	Anglo-American Cataloguing Rules 2nd edition
AACR3	Anglo-American Cataloguing Rules 3rd edition
ACE	Automatic Content Extraction project
ACNP	Catalogo italiano dei periodici
AI	Artificial intelligence
AIB	Associazione italiana biblioteche
ALA	American Library Association
ALCTS	Association for Library Collections and Technical Services
BIBFRAME	Bibliographic Framework Initiative
BIG	BIBFRAME Interoperability Group
BiRO	Bibliographic Reference Ontology
BNB	British National Bibliography
BNCR	Biblioteca Nazionale Centrale di Roma
BnF	Bibliothèque nationale de France
CAT	Catalogo delle risorse archivistiche
CFLA-FCAB	Canadian Federation of Library Association/Fédération canadienne des associations de bibliothèques
CIDOC CRM	CIDOC Conceptual Reference Model
CKB	Cluster Knowledge Base
CILIP	Chartered Institute of Library and Information Professionals
CLA	Canadian Library Association
CONSER	Cooperative Online Serials Program
CRCC	Continuing Resources Cataloging Committee
DC	Dublin Core
DCMI	Dublin Core Metadata Initiative
DEI	PCC Advisory Committee on Diversity, Equity and Inclusion
DNB	Deutsche Nationalbibliothek
DTD	Document Type Definition

EAC-CPF	Encoded Archival Context for Corporate Bodies, Persons, and Families
EAD	Encoded Archival Description
EDIBA	PCC Advisory Committee on Equity, Diversity, Inclusion, Belonging and Accessibility
EDT	Entity Detection and Tracking
EGAD	Expert Group on Archival Description
ER	Entity Resolution
EURIG	European RDA Interest Group
FaBiO	FRBR-aligned Bibliographic Ontology
FOAF	Friend of a friend
FRAD	Functional Requirements for Authority Data
FRBR	Functional Requirements for Bibliographic Records
FRSAD	Functional Requirements for Subject Authority Data
FRSAR	Functional Requirements for Subject Authority Records
GLAM	Galleries, Libraries, Archives and Museums
GND	Gemeinsame Normdatei
IBC	Istituto per i beni artistici, culturali e naturali della Regione Emilia-Romagna
ICA	International Council on Archives
ICAR	Istituto centrale per gli archivi
ICCU	Istituto centrale per il catalogo unico delle biblioteche italiane e per le informazioni bibliografiche
ICP	International Cataloguing Principles
IFLA	International Federation of Library Associations and Institutions
IFLA LRM	IFLA Library Reference Model
IIA	Istituto italo-africano
IIPC	International Internet Preservation Consortium
ILS	Integrated Library System
IMS	Identity Management System
ISAAR	International Standard Archival Authority Record for Corporate Bodies, Persons and Families
ISAD(G)	General International Standard Archival Description
ISBD	International Standard Bibliographic Description
ISDF	International Standard for Describing Functions
ISDIAH	International Standard for Describing Institutions with Archival Holdings
ISI	Information Sciences Institute
IsIAO	Istituto italiano per l'Africa e l'Oriente

ISMEO	Associazione internazionale di studi sul Mediterraneo e l'Oriente
IsMEO	Istituto italiano per il Medio ed Estremo Oriente
ISNI	International Standard Name Identifier
ISNI IA	ISNI International Agency
ISSN	International Standard Serial Number
ISSN-L	Linking ISSN
ISWC	International Semantic Web Conference
JCricket	JCricket Entity Editor
JSC AACR	Joint Steering Committee for the Revision of the Anglo-American Cataloguing Rules
JSC RDA	Joint Steering Committee for Development of RDA
JSON-LD	JavaScript Object Notation for Linked Data
LAM	Libraries, Archives, Museums
LCDGT	Library of Congress Demographic Group Terms
LCNAF	Library of Congress Name Authority File
LD4P	Linked Data for Production
LOD	Linked Open Data
MADS	Metadata Authority Description Schema
MARC	Machine-Readable Cataloguing
MLA	Medical Library Association
NACO	Name Authority Cooperative Program
NAR	Name Authority Record
NIST	National Institute of Standards and Technology
NLP	Natural Language Processing
NRC	National Research Council (US)
NV	Norme per il catalogo degli stampati della Biblioteca Apostolica Vaticana (Norme Vaticane)
OAD	Ontology for Archival Description
OOO	Object-Oriented Ontology
OOP	Object-Oriented Programming
OWL	Web Ontology Language
PCC	Program for Cooperative Cataloging
PCC PoCo	PCC Policy Committee
PE-IMS	Privacy-Enhancing Identity Management System
PREMIS	Preservation Metadata Implementation Strategies
PROV-O	Provenance Ontology
PTPL	Potomac Technical Processing Librarians
PUC	Permanent UNIMARC Committee
RDA	Resource Description and Access
RDF	Resource Description Framework

REICAT	Regole italiane di catalogazione
RiC-CM	Records in Contexts–Conceptual Model
RiC-O	Records in Context Ontology
RICA	Regole Italiane di catalogazione autori
RSC	RDA Steering Committee
RWO	Real World Object
SAN	Sistema archivistico nazionale
SBN	Sistema bibliotecario nazionale
SEI WG	Sapientia Entity Identification Working Group
SGML	Standard Generalized Markup Language
Share-VDE	Share Virtual Discovery Environment
SKOS	Simple Knowledge Organisation System
SPARQL	SPARQL Protocol and RDF Query Language
SVDE	Share Virtual Discovery Environment
UBC	Universal Bibliographic Control
UNIMARC	Universal Machine Readable Cataloguing
URBE	Unione Romana biblioteche ecclesiastiche
URI	Uniform Resource Identifier
VIAF	Virtual International Authority File
VRA	Visual Resource Association
W3C	World Wide Web Consortium
WEM	Work Expression Manifestation
WEMI	Work-Expression-Manifestation-Item
WiGeDi	Wikidata Gender Diversity project
XML	eXtensible Markup Language

The Context

The reflections gathered here stem from the desire to trace the theoretical foundation of several years of work as an expert in cataloguing and metadata. Over the years of my professional life dedicated to this area, many opportunities for analysing certain bibliographic themes and for comparison of different strands related to cataloguing practice in the archival and library fields have presented themselves. The national and international 'observatory' that my professional path afforded me has provoked an increasingly urgent desire to dedicate time to reflection, to construct a theoretical vision that arises from and is rooted in daily practice.

Examining the concepts of entity and identity in the cataloguing field constitutes the starting point of this work. The deeper meaning of these two concepts and their application to cataloguing have been little explored and investigated. And they have never been analysed specifically in relation to the activity of modelling entities in the bibliographic field.

The investigation conducted has its roots in the history of cataloguing, with particular regard to the formulation of entity definitions used within the framework of different cataloguing rules. The analysis of specific case studies concerning some bibliographic entities serves to highlight the ontological foundation of many choices matured or under discussion within the Share Family initiative, which involves numerous North American and European libraries on various courses of action related to the publication and use of linked open data.

The entity is understood as a real-world object and this formulation is investigated in its relation to the concept of real-world entity, drawing on computer science and particularly object-oriented programming (OOP), which introduces the concept of modelling and managing an 'object' through the definition of attributes and relationships. The in-depth study of entity resolution mechanisms applied to the bibliographic field leads us to hypothesise another way of looking at cataloguing: entity modelling emerges as the third generational step in bibliographic data management, imposing or requiring a change in perspective in information treatment as well as in the language used to formalise it.

Entity modelling demands a particular attention to identifying entities through the various profiles in which the entity itself can present itself. The multiplicity of profiles or identities makes the entity a multifaceted object, with boundaries that are not always clear and defined. Things in the world change their properties over time, but we cannot forgo identifying their boundaries, despite this element of fluidity. Particular reflection is dedicated to those changes in the properties of entities that can prove decisive in terms of their identifiability or their own metaphysical nature. The concept of Cambridge change and its partial redefinition help us to specify a certain type of semantic relationship, important to recognise in entity identification processes. The agent, in the various declinations that the cataloguing tradition has proposed for this entity, is certainly one of the most fascinating entities to investigate in terms of entity modelling. Despite its apparent concreteness, which should guarantee a more easily profiled entity, there are several ontological or identity situations that complicate its definition. The concepts of ontological break and identity break are defined and studied, starting with certain complex entities and applied to cataloguing cases debated in different cataloguing traditions. The result of this experimentation is the awareness that the agent entity can demonstrate how the approach to the entity instead of the record opens up bridges of collaboration between different domains. There is no archival document, work of art, book, administrative act, post, film, musical work, video or any product of human activity (and not only) that is not referable to an agent. Hence the certainty that defining identity boundaries can facilitate the breaking down of barriers between different domains. The change in approach, which in the bibliographic field is seeing the progressive transition from name strings to entity identification, influences the ability to transmit knowledge even in historical terms. The perspective of clusters and the possibility of identifying an entity and its possible multiple identities offers a new scenario even in the cataloguing field. The study concludes with a proposal for the concrete realisation of this new scenario.

The theme

The theoretical reflection starts with the analysis of the *transitional crisis* that memory and culture institutions are experiencing, squeezed between an imposing tradition of cataloguing rules and principles – widely discussed, shared and applied standards and formats that have produced what is recognised by the term 'information silos' – and a whole new trend towards the atomisation of information according to a logic of precise identification of each *entity* and its relationships with other entities beyond geographical, cultural, linguistic and disciplinary barriers. One of the most relevant results of this complex transition is the concept of *entity modelling* as the next generation of cataloguing. The activity of cataloguing is increasingly becoming one of identifying and describing entities, with their many facets, or even through the different points of view from which that entity can be observed. In this sense, identifying the boundary of an entity and the different profiles it presents to the world, with an abundance of characteristics and relationships linking it to other entities, really becomes one of the most complex and also significant moments in this new way of cataloguing resources. In this study, I have used the term *ontological break* to identify the boundary crossed beyond which it is possible to speak of a new entity compared to the previous one; and I have used the term *identity break* to identify that boundary which, once crossed, yes, the entity retains its being but expresses itself under another identity. It was telling, for this investigation, to find in the Official RDA Toolkit the term *entity boundary* to indicate precisely this dividing line, this before and after, that in the flow of things in continuous change, generates something new – an entity related to the one of origin but different from it.

The starting point for this analysis was inspired by a reference Philip Schreur made in his presentation at the European RDA Interest Group 2017[4] to a study by Todd Rose, entitled *The End of Average* (Rose, 2015). Rose documented the development of the concept of the *average* as *ideal*, beginning with Quetelet's writings from the early 19th century[5]. Quetelet used, in the field of social sciences, the scientific method of data collection to define, from an anthropomorphic point of view, the ideal average measurements of the Western male. This concept of 'average as ideal' was applied in the 20th century to various fields of knowledge, strongly influencing the definition of some standards (intelligence tests, measurement of the physical and mental development of children, ideal description of archival or museum book resources). In his study, Rose demonstrated the inapplicability of an ideal model for complex objects or systems, hardly reducible to standard averages, deeming it impossible to define an average intelligence, an ideal method of learning, an ideal body shape or a standard archival or museum book resource (Schreur, 2018). The last assertion is all the more valid when one considers the extent of formats, types of resources, means of transmission, and use of information, which are difficult to contain in rigid and universal models. The assortment of information resources in which cultural heritage manifests itself in ways that are not always predictable and able to be standardised therefore invites new thinking, starting from established tradition, to uncover new forms of expression and transmission of the information message.

The historical context

In the 15 October 2002 issue of *Library Journal*, Roy Tennant prophesied the end of the historic MARC (Machine-Readable Cataloguing) format, created in the 1960s for sharing catalogue data, in an article titled 'MARC Must Die'[6] (Tennant, 2002). In it, Tennant interpreted the true nature of the MARC record as an anachronism developed at a time when memory, storage capacity and data processing were rare and expensive commodities. This view challenged for the first time a data format used by most libraries around the world and which, originally created as an exchange format, had then shaped generations of cataloguing software. The premonition of the necessary death of MARC did not seem imminent, so much so that even today many cataloguing systems rely on MARC formats. But that article was planted in a highly fertile ground of change that generated a real revolution in thinking.

In 2009, Christian Bizer, Tom Heath and Tim Berners-Lee published an article titled 'Linked Data – The Story So Far' (Bizer, Heath and Berners-Lee, 2009), where they drew the first conclusions about a new way of publishing and connecting data on the web, which had already spread widely across many information fields within a few years[7]. Additionally, they referred to a previous study by Berners-Lee himself in 2006 which defined the meaning of the semantic web and its relationship with linked data and listed some rules for publishing data on the web, which became the basis for thousands of institutions (Berners-Lee, 2006).

This new web model begat a new perspective on data sharing and reuse that spread to all domains of knowledge and, meeting with the provocation launched a few years earlier by Roy Tennant, resulted in an epochal shake-up of the tradition of structuring data into bibliographic and authority records. So much so, that embracing these stimuli and urgings, the Library of Congress (LC) as early as 2008 formalised the new trend with the report *On the Record*, which urged libraries to reflect deeply on future models of bibliographic control. What the future of bibliographic control would be is a question that the LC had periodically investigated, accelerated by the dramatic transformation of the field of library science brought about by digital technologies.

All of this is, therefore, the official declaration of a profound change of direction that, like a real storm, has progressively involved all institutions of memory, culture and information.

The state of the art

The number of linked data projects involving central and national academic, public, and private institutions (without any preclusion as to their nature, type, and size) in the GLAM (galleries, libraries, archives, and museums) sector is revealing. Equally significant is the type of data, the variety of which has not constituted any limit in the adoption of this new bibliographic and cataloguing perspective, including repertory tools, indices, ontologies, subject headings, thesauri, etc.

The most interesting aspect of this is the blending of very different frameworks in terms of origin, mutually enriching and promising a model of co-operation open to positive influences, investing in the institutional and professional role, and being called upon to develop and share new approaches and work practices.

In this same context are the projects of the Share Family[8], promoted by various types of libraries in diverse cultural and geographic contexts to establish procedures for identifying and reconciling entities, converting data into linked data, and creating an environment of discovery for personal use. Important initiatives fall under this umbrella, such as the Share Catalogue, part of a larger project to share data and services among university libraries in Campania, Lucania and Salento; Share-VDE (Share Virtual Discovery Environment), a collaborative effort of some 20 North American and European university libraries; Parsifal, the URBE network's project to create an integrated unified catalogue and shared authority file; as well as projects dedicated to specialised subject areas that are currently being implemented or analysed.

Among the new and very recent challenges is the complex one of raising the level of use of linked data from the publication stage to the data creation stage: LD4P (Linked Data for Production) is perhaps the most important in this respect.

Research sources and articulation of the work

The primary sources for this work were studies conducted at the national and international levels on projects applying the linked data paradigm in the GLAM setting. Particular emphasis was given to material, in numerous cases unpublished, resulting from the implementation of these projects, many still ongoing, and to the direct study of the data.

As this is an innovative field of research, with pockets of issues still completely unexplored and unpublished, this work was carried out in collaboration with a broad community of Italian, European, and North American libraries, participating in various capacities in the mentioned projects. Some history of cataloguing tradition is cited, but a historical reconstruction has been deliberately left out as it has been extensively documented in Italian and foreign studies. Rather, this study takes these historical foundations as established and attempts to explore areas still being formed, hoping to create a possible starting point for reflections on the new generation of cataloguing practices.

This study is also meant to be a tribute to the disciplines that have accompanied my educational and professional journey:

- Philosophy, on which rests the inquiry into how to interpret entities and identities in the bibliographic field advanced in the first of the four chapters. Philosophy has accompanied my university studies and has come to the aid of this investigation, identifying and following the thread that leads us to view the world, including the bibliographical one, as a multitude of things that rarely express themselves in a single and unique identity.
- Computer science, which has been a part of my professional world for years and which underpins the second chapter devoted primarily to entity resolution processes. The logic of analysing and using data for the purpose of identifying and modelling an entity adapts and conforms to the logic of object-oriented programming and the declaration of the impossibility of representing an entity in its complexity and richness, accepting that it is always represented from a specific and contextual point of view.
- Library science and, in particular, cataloguing, which has absorbed my energies and time throughout my academic and professional journey. Chapters 3 and 4 synthesise the theoretical study and much practical experience gained over many years of working first in a library and then for libraries.

The body of work does not claim to be definitive concerning the topics discussed, which are still too immature or in the making to be declared conclusive. Instead, it aims to be a snapshot of the current state of a complex and far from exhausted course: one that goes from traditional bibliographic cataloguing, centred on the bibliographic record and its construction, to looking at the real world in its complexity, formed by thousands of multifaceted entities, many of which are also part of the bibliographic universe.

CHAPTER 1

I Contain Multitudes

Do I contradict myself?
Very well then I contradict myself,
(I am large, I contain multitudes).

(Walt Whitman, *Song of Myself*, 51)

Introduction

The central theme of this chapter is the result of an investigation into how the concepts of *entity* and *identity* have been instrumental in shaping much of the theory and practice of cataloguing, particularly in terms of the selection and structuring of access points to resources and the definition of bibliographic models. These two concepts, widely used, have never really been explored and investigated in their most profound meaning and in their application to cataloguing, especially regarding e.g. entities in an ontological context.

The investigation conducted is rooted in the history of cataloguing, with particular regard to the formulation of entity definitions used in various cataloguing rules, and extends into Chapter 2, dedicated to the semantic web and the shift in focus to the real-world object[9] which, borrowing from the domain of artificial intelligence (AI), is defined as *a real object of the world*, whether concrete or abstract. As Karen Coyle clearly explains on her website Coyle's InFormation,[10] with specific reference to the world of information, the need to identify everything that makes up the world in which we live and move – whether concrete objects, people, abstract concepts, etc. – stems from the need to make our world comprehensible to machines, and thus to artificial intelligences. Even what we take for granted, in terms of meaning, because it is learned progressively in our cognitive journey, must instead be uniquely identified and explained to a machine so that it can use reasoning. Hence, the emergence of ontologies, which schematise and define the different domains of knowledge with the still-distant but possible goal of identifying and explaining in a manner understandable to machines every single 'thing' (understood in the Latin sense of *res*) that constitutes the world in which we live.

This introductory part of the paper narrates the inquiry around the metaphysical and ontological foundation of many choices that have matured or are currently under discussion and investigation within the Share Virtual Discovery Environment (Share-VDE) project[11] through the analysis of some specific case studies on the treatment of entities. Each of these cases will be examined in light of some philosophical currents that have questioned what the inventory of objects that are part of the real world is (ontology) and what these objects are (metaphysical aspect), in order to define or identify tools that are also useful for reinterpreting current and past cataloguing rules and models.

Questions to resolve

Identifying and defining the things, whether concrete or abstract, is one of the most frequently recurring problems in life and one that we often face and solve without even realising it. Identifying a street or a store, finding useful information on the package insert of a drug we need to take, identifying the part of the washing machine that needs to be replaced or even just following the instructions to assemble a toy are recurring situations we deal with in interacting with the world. Not all contexts, not all domains, nor all situations, however, offer clear definitions and unambiguously defined objects. In some cases, a 'common understanding' about specific terms and concepts must be discussed and reached for communication to be understandable and relationships possible.

The cataloguing domain is one that has traditionally used concept and object definitions, investing a great deal of study and reflection in this definitional activity. To classify a source; to define concisely but clearly the subject matter of a book; to catalogue a DVD, an e-book, or a site; to draft a cataloguing norm or standard: these are all critical operations of cataloguing that have required enormous intellectual and practical investments. The development of taxonomies, controlled vocabularies, subject catalogues and ontologies are the most tangible result and product of this aptitude and necessity. Apparently, therefore, nothing in this field should still require investigation and exploration, since the national or international sharing of cataloguing standards and tools has required and, in some cases, imposed a common vocabulary composed first and foremost of the definitions.

Yet, not everything is as simple as it may seem, even in a domain so well defined and traditionally controlled by standards and rules. Agreeing on certain terms, on the meaning of certain seemingly unambiguous concepts, has always been a challenge, a reason for discussion and confrontation within the library community. Consider, as an example, the terminological revolution introduced by Original RDA (Resource Description and Access)[12] including:

- *Elements* rather than *Areas*
- *Authorised access point* rather than *Heading*
- *Variant access point* rather than *See reference*
- *Access points* rather than *Added entries*
- *Carrier description* rather than *Physical description*.

An example of complexity that we will not cease to present is that related to the entity-relationship data model Functional Requirements for Bibliographic Records (FRBR)[13]: the use of the original model to generate an ontology produced several of them:

- Essential FRBR in OWL3 DL ontology [14]
- FRBRoo [15]
- FRBRer [16]
- FRBRcore [17]
- FRBR FaBiO (Aligned Bibliographic Ontology)[18]
- BiRO[19] (Bibliographic Reference Ontology)

The entity *Expression* is one of the main classes in the FRBR model proposed by IFLA and is defined as follows: 'The second entity defined in the model is expression: the intellectual or artistic realisation of a work in the form of alpha-numeric, musical, or choreographic notation, sound, image, object, movement, etc., or any combination of such forms.'[20]

The ontological transposition of this data model should hold no surprises, certainly not in the definition of an entity (Expression) so central to, and defined in, the original model. Again, we are not surprised to find that the definition of expression in the different ontologies derived from the same model is not perfectly identical, or not identical in all ontological structures. Even slight distinctions seem incomprehensible to an entity born within that model and which we all expect to be unambiguously identified. Let us look at a few examples:

- *FRBRcore: Expression*[21] – A realisation of a single work, usually in a physical form. This class corresponds to the FRBR group one entity 'Expression'.
- *FRBRer: Expression*[22] – The intellectual or artistic realisation of a work in the form of alpha-numeric, musical, or choreographic notation, sound, image, object, movement, etc., or any combination of such forms.

- *FRBRoo: Expression*[23] – This class comprises the intellectual or artistic realisations of works in the form of identifiable immaterial objects, such as texts, poems, jokes, musical or choreographic notations, movement patterns, sound patterns, images, multimedia objects or any combination of such forms that have objectively recognisable structures. The substance of F2 Expression is signs.
- *FaBiO: Expression*[24] – A subclass of FRBR expression, restricted to expressions of FaBiO: Works. For your latest research paper, the preprint submitted to the publisher and the final published version to which the publisher assigned a unique digital object identifier are both expressions of the same work.

These definitions of the same entity in FRBR should be equivalent in the ontologies mentioned, as they are derived from a single original definition; in reality, as we have seen, there is not a perfect equivalence, albeit within a standard semantics (speaking of one of the leading entities of FRBR).

Yet another formulation of the definition of the entity *Expression* is the one provided by IFLA LRM (Library Reference Model), the model created as a harmonisation of the three models of the FR family (FRBR, Functional Requirements for Authority Data (FRAD), Functional Requirements for Subject Authority Records (FRSAR))[25]: 'A distinct combination of signs conveying intellectual or artistic content' (IFLA LRM, 2017, 23). One explanation for these differences in definition can undoubtedly be found in the abstract nature of this entity, which is primarily functional for the purpose of grouping and does not express a concrete object that the senses can easily verify. However, this reasoning is clearly weak, as the same happens with much more 'tangible' and seemingly unambiguous entities.

The degree of complexity increases as the boundaries open to other domains: what is the *title* of a publication, and what is the *title* of a photograph? Who is the *author of* a musical work, and who is the *author* of a correspondence? What is the *substance of* a periodical, and what is the *substance of* an archival file? The inception of the web, especially the semantic web, has further exacerbated the problem of identifying things because it has blurred the boundaries that have been drawn between different domains and, at the same time, forces us to reorganise the common language and redraft a shared alphabet, starting from a language that machines can understand. As mentioned earlier, any concept, any term we want to use to express even very simple assertions, must be explained to a machine by providing a definition and offering a network of relationships that place this concept, this object, in a known context within which the machine can orient itself. It is like saying that, in the context of the web, we must not only present the character in a play but also the scene within which the character is acting and which makes them a character. Ontologies are made for this, to explain the world to machines. But like humans (seeing that they are created by them), they have different ways of 'explaining' the same *thing*, using different words and often even expressing different concepts with seemingly identical terms.

So many points need to be resolved when we try to give definitions to things, starting with the terms we use to express a definition. Can we explain FRBR's entity Expression without first clarifying, if not to ourselves (which is equally necessary) then at least to machines, what we mean by an *entity*? Can we try to resolve the issue of the same entity being expressed through one or more identities if we do not first clarify, if not to ourselves then at least to machines, what we mean by an entity *identity*?

It is precisely from these basic questions that we will try to navigate our way through an information quagmire that, needing to formalise everything in a new language, is forced to provide definitions and define relationships, even for seemingly well-defined and clear concepts.

Starting precisely from the first of these questions – 'What do we mean when we refer to *entities*, and how do we relate this concept to that of *identity?*' – we will try to identify the theoretical foundation that best meets the cataloguing and modelling needs of the bibliographic universe. To do this, we will rely on some reflections that have developed in the philosophical realm, which are perhaps not fully resolved as they continue to be widely discussed.

The application to cataloguing theory and practice is not forced. What do we mean when discussing the entity Work? Are we sure that a journal that changes its title over time remains the same entity, or should we consider it a different entity? And how do we consider the subject of entity and identity when authors use pseudonyms or create heteronyms? On closer inspection, the subject matter that we deal with as cataloguing theorists is not at all distant from the same questions posed in the philosophical or psychological field. It is precisely from the philosophical sphere that we start to identify some key concepts and establish definitions in a way that is functional for their use in bibliographic cataloguing.

Entities and identities

The first and most pressing question to answer is, as already mentioned, that of defining the terms *entity* and *identity*, as applied to the context of cataloguing above all, because these terms are widely used (or implied, in some cases) in the clustering processes, which we will discuss extensively later. The primary purpose of cataloguing is to identify as unambiguously as possible the different entities that populate the bibliographic universe (*entity identification*[26]) and their relationships to other entities, regardless of what name has been assigned to them. When we mention *Shakespeare*, we are quite confident that we are referring to the famous English playwright and poet who lived in the 16th century. And the citation by surname seems sufficient to assure us of the identity. In reality, behind the term Shakespeare lie several entities[27] (including even a programming language!). The problem might seem to be resolved by adding a given name to the surname, thus citing the English playwright as William Shakespeare. But even this is not enough. Quoting this combination of given name and family name gives us several corresponding entities.[28] At this point, the only thing to do is add distinctive attributes that apply exclusively to the English playwright William Shakespeare, such as place of birth, date of birth, and date of death. To identify our William Shakespeare, the one we can describe as an English playwright and poet, we need to feed the machine a string such as:

William Shakespeare, Stratford-upon-Avon, 1564–1616.

Perhaps, to avoid repeating the identification process each time, we could add a unique identifier using only a sequence of letters and/or numbers to the William Shakespeare entity. There, that seems to solve the problem. And if someone were to mention The Bard of Avon? Can we then say with certainty that this is simply a different name for the same entity? Can we infer from this that William Shakespeare had an identity different from his baptismal name, by which he is better known?[29] Can we, in a cataloguing context, assign the name The Bard of Avon the same weight in the cataloguing field that we would assign to an actual pseudonym used by the same entity to sign, for example, different works? Can we define a pseudonym as a different identity of the same entity?

We must, therefore, return to the initial question, focusing on what we mean by entity and what we mean by identity, trying to identify the dividing line that determines the 'identity gap' that marks the passage from one entity to another or the passage from one identity to another. Within the bibliographical universe we need to consider, then, those cases in which there is a greater need to reflect on the nature of certain entities, their horizontal and vertical relationships with other entities, and the relationships between the possible different identities of the same entity.

Definitions of entities and identities

In arriving at a definition of the concepts of *entity* and *identity* which is functional for the bibliographic universe, it is appropriate to begin with the definitions, greatly simplified, of *ontology* and *metaphysics*, because it is between ontology and metaphysics that we will try to position these concepts and use them for our purposes:

- Ontology is the philosophical activity that deals with 'that which is there'; hence, it attempts to answer the question 'what is there?'
- Metaphysics deals instead with 'that which is' and deals, therefore, with answering the question 'what is it?'

> According to today's common usage, ontology is concerned with establishing what there is, i.e. drawing up a kind of inventory of all that exists, while metaphysics is concerned with settling what is that that is there, i.e. specifying the nature of the items included in the inventory.[30]
>
> (Varzi, 2007 [translated])

Everything that can be said to exist is a being; the being is, in fact, *that which is*. The essence of a being is *being a thing that is*; this essence is *the entity of the being*. In other words, the entity of the being is the *property* of the being itself such that it is *a being* – that is, a thing that is. *That which is,* therefore, is first and foremost, but it is *also* something more. By the very fact of *being*, it is one and *the same*. The *identity* of the being is the *property* that makes the being *itself*, by which every being is necessarily itself. Therefore, the being *is there* insofar as *it is,* and it is there in the form of *identity*.

Therefore, trying to formulate a definition, we can say:

- *Entity* is the essence of the being, that which makes it a being, that which makes it a thing *that is*.
- *Identity* is the form that the being assumes and that which makes it *itself*; we could say that identity is the *selfness* of the being.

Willard Van Orman Quine's assertion 'no entity without identity,' which is much debated in the field of analytical philosophy and has generated quite a few currents of thought, seems to be the only possible one in a dimension where any entity that exists does so only through an expression of itself that we call identity. We can, therefore, define identity as anything that makes an entity definable and recognisable, conveying a set of qualities or characteristics that distinguishes that entity from other entities: identity is either what makes two things the same thing or what makes them different.

Let's take the definitions of ontology and metaphysics previously given as valid or sufficient. We can also affirm that ontology concerns itself with identifying entities (what exists in the universe in which we live). Metaphysics concerns itself with defining the profile and thus the identity of what is (what is that which is).

Whether ontology should precede metaphysics or vice versa, ancient and contemporary philosophy has debated extensively without arriving at any definite conclusion (so much so that the debate is still widely open and discussed, and we assume it as such, without attempting to resolve it). But in the cataloguing field, we can follow Varzi in arguing that 'ontology must somehow come before metaphysics: one begins by establishing what exists, after which one can study its nature and speculate on the characteristics that make each thing the thing that it is' (Varzi, 2007, 2). This is what cataloguing and classification science has done for years: it has compiled inventories of entities that best represent the bibliographic universe and then defined their nature and relationships. In doing so, it has encountered many thorny, ambiguous cases where that differentiation that we have called the 'identity break' is not clearly identifiable, and in which even the definition of the core attributes of each entity is not sufficient to uniquely identify its being, to grasp its *selfness*. This issue is most evident in complex entities: those that, by choice or nature, present themselves as a multitude of identities in cases of pseudonymity and the more complex cases of heteronymity. The same happens in changes of category, such as when events undergo profound changes over time (are the 2020 Tokyo Olympics the same event when they actually happened in 2021?). Upon closer inspection, the issue runs even deeper. It is rooted in the philosophy of language and also becomes a 'definitional' problem: are 'the victor of Austerlitz' and 'the loser of Waterloo' the same person? Are the morning star and the evening star the same thing?[31] The language traditionally used in bibliographic control seeks to be highly standardised (classification systems, ontologies and controlled vocabularies have precisely the purpose of defining and applying standardisation criteria), although from time to time they have then had to deal with and resolve issues related to multilingualism, multiple alphabets, etc. Quoting Elaine Svenonius: 'In a perfectly ordered language, everything has a unique name, and a name is used to refer to a unique thing' (Svenonius, 2008, 18). But this kind of artificial language is quite different from the richness of natural language, in which each concept can be defined in a multitude of ways and in which multiple meanings can be hidden behind a term. This unresolvable ambiguity of natural language has been and remains a constant challenge for those involved in organising information, especially considering that the criticality in identifying entities increases in processes of clustering, which require machines, through automated comparison of an incredible amount of data, to identify an entity even when it presents itself in different ways or when several entities ostensibly present themselves under the same identity.

> It seems that the most colossal effort of all concerning the organisation of information is to create an unambiguous language of description, a language that confers a systematic approach and method to natural language and, at the same time, allows users to find what they want using the names they know.
>
> (Svenonius, 2008, 19)

Diachronic and synchronic identities in the bibliographic universe

By vocation, cataloguing is a defining discipline, having always expressed an attempt or striving to identify, classify and define entities that play a role in the context of the bibliographic universe, generating and fuelling discussions and disputes over different rules and codes for centuries. Elaine Svenonius helps us trace the history of a discipline, that of information organisation, which dates as far back as 2000 BC but matures as a fully-fledged descriptive and semantic cataloguing discipline from the mid-19th century, when Sir Anthony Panizzi was commissioned to organise the library holdings of the British Museum Library and, following that, with the conception of the great classification systems that have formed the foundations of the major bibliographic systems (Svenonius, 2008, 4 ff.). The electronic revolution, which destroyed the physical boundaries of the paper tradition that maintained documentary resources, 'changed the nature of the entities to be organised and the means of organising them' (Svenonius, 2008, 18).

In the processes of identifying entities, the relationships between them play a fundamental role. In a certain sense, identifying things in the universe requires placing them in relation to each other. When we meet someone on the street with a familiar face but in a decontextualised setting (outside, therefore, of the network of relationships in which we usually place them), we often fail to recognise them at all, or rather, we fail to identify them: 'I know that I know that person, but I cannot attribute an identity to them that allows me to recognise them precisely because they are evidently distanced from the context of relationships in which I am used to placing them.' When we say that the identification of an author is by means of the recognition of their work and that, conversely, identifying a work is by means of the identification of its author, we are stating exactly that: namely, that it is not possible to identify an entity without placing it in relation to other entities (or by placing it in relation to the attributes that determine its identity).

The categories of relationships between cataloguing entities were masterfully outlined by Barbara Tillett in her work *Bibliographic Relationships: Toward a Conceptual Structure of Bibliographic Information Used in Cataloging* (Tillett, 1987),[32] and widely used in all subsequent bibliographic entity-relationship models, especially to realise the *navigation* function in the catalogue. Tillett identifies seven types of bibliographic relationships through analysis of cataloguing rules rooted primarily in the Anglo-American tradition, analysing 24 different cataloguing codes from the 91 Rules of Panizzi (Panizzi, 1841, v–ix) to the second edition of the *Anglo-American Cataloguing Rules* (AACR2). These types of relations have as their basis the bibliographic entities which, using a historical anachronism (the IFLA FRBR model was published about ten years after Tillett's work was written), can be referred to the FRBR model – Work, Expression, Manifestation and Item. Also recognised is a type of relation that links works to the different agents that have contributed in various ways to that resource (relationships of responsibility), as well as subject relations, namely that an entity (of whatever type) is used as the subject of a work. But let us stay within the scope of the relationships defined as *primary* in the FRBR model, thus the relationships between the bibliographic entities Work, Expression, Manifestation, and Item, and see what categories have been identified:

1 *Equivalence relations* express an identity between entities. In terms of bibliographic resources, this can refer, for example, to an original and its photocopy or its facsimile reproduction.
2 *Derivative relationships* (also called horizontal relationships): the relationship between an entity and something derived from it. Regarding bibliographic resources, we immediately think of translations, revisions, different editions of the same work, adaptations and changes in literary genre (e.g. a dramatisation of a text). The first and immediate thought that comes to mind with this type of relationship is that of *dependence*: the second entity of a derivative relationship would not exist without the first (we could not have a translation of a work into another language without the original work).
3 *Descriptive relationships*: these express a relationship between an entity and something that comments on, describes or illustrates that entity. In this case as well, the relationship is one of strong dependence, since it is not possible to produce an annotated edition of a work, for example, without the original work.
4 *Whole–part relationships* (also called vertical or hierarchical relationships): these are relationships that connect a whole with its component parts, such as a volume in a series, a work by an author contained in a larger anthology[33] or an archival file within a series or an individual document within a file.
5 *Accompanying relationships*: these are relationships between a resource and anything that can be considered as accompanying material, such as

the supplement to a magazine issue, a DVD that comes with a manual, etc.

6 *Sequential (chronological) relationships*: these are relationships between bibliographic entities that are in chronological succession to one another, such as a serial publication that changes name over time or a subsequent volume of a monographic series.
7 *Shared characteristic relationships*: these are relationships established between bibliographic entities that have something in common, such as a publication date, language or country of publication.

Tillett's relationships, as mentioned, involve bibliographic entities that can be likened, for our convenience, to those in Group 1 of FRBR. This is the first limitation we face when using them for our purposes: namely, to establish more general identification criteria applicable to the different entities that populate the bibliographic universe. Tillett's approach to reading cataloguing rules from Panizzi to AACR2 and analysing the practice of using relationships within the Library of Congress is perfectly in line with the time in which this work was conceived – that is, prior to the profound change in perspective proposed by the linked data paradigm. The shift from record to entity – about which so much has been written recently and which we will have the opportunity to revisit later in this work – had not yet taken place. Tillett's investigation, profound and decisive for a whole strand of thinking about the importance of relationships in defining bibliographic models, takes place within the domain of the record as a description of a resource and extends to the analysis of access points as indicators of records. We are still a long way from entities and that real-world object which we will discuss later. This classificatory scheme of relationships, which is still so relevant and helpful in framing and defining relationships between entities, becomes insufficient if the aim is to extend one's view to that more general inventory of the bibliographic universe understood as entities (ontological aspect) and to the metaphysics of these objects.

Another limiting factor in using these categories of relationships is that they do not sufficiently convey nor dwell on that identity break we were talking about, assuming that the relationship between two fundamentals is always a relationship between entities. We are left with doubts. Can an Italian-language work, for example Collodi's *Pinocchio*, and its English-language translation be considered the same entity presenting with different identities, or should they be considered different entities? The various bibliographical models – FRBR, Bibliographic Framework (BIBFRAME), IFLA LRM – resolve the issue in different and perhaps simplistic ways.[34] Thinking, for example, about the equivalence relationship is simple or complex depending on the type of entity.

An equivalence between an original and a copy of a publication (the original and its photocopy) is an intuitive relationship. The discussion is complicated, and not just a little, when we try to view this relationship, for example, in the context of an entity such as agent – can we call two individuals or two institutions equivalent? Under what conditions?[35]

In this first part of this book we will focus on cases of entities traditionally more critical, namely those whose identities are debated within cataloguing and whose ambiguity has grown at a time when, with the massive increase of data from different sources being compared, the identification processes have been delegated to machines:

1 Complex entities with multiple identities: In this category, we can include pseudonyms and heteronyms, but also the original work and its translations, as well as different representations (performances) of the same musical work or two recordings from two different perspectives of the same theatrical work.
2 Entities in whole–part identity relationships: the subseries versus the series, the volume versus a piece of work in a multi-volume work, the article versus the issue and the issue versus the periodical, the sub-entity versus the main entity, the single photograph versus a photo exhibition, etc.
3 Entities in transitional relationships (chronological variations): gender transitions, entities that change their name or corporate body due to merger/division of operations, continuing resources (websites, serials/periodicals, etc.).

For now, let us set aside these categories and try to look at things from a viewpoint other than Barbara Tillett's. Let us observe these different entities with respect to a space–time element,[36] categorise the three types of entities listed above, and identify common points of interpretation. Complex entities, as well as entities of whole–part relationships, seem to be strongly dependent on the spatial dimension alone. A pseudonym, in comparison to a name from the official register, is not affected by the temporal dimension, or rather, it is not affected by the passage *of* time. (It may be, to the extent that an individual decides, at some point in time, to give birth to a pseudonym or to reject it, but it is not time that helps us identify the entity that we seek.) The same can be said of entities in whole–part relationships: it is not the element of time that helps us decide whether Dante's *Inferno* can be considered an entity of the Work type, autonomous from the *Divine Comedy*, or strongly dependent on it.

On the other hand, the third type of entity (connected by transitional relationships) seems to be strongly influenced by the element of time. In the case of a gender transition, there is a time in which the change takes place. There exists, therefore, a before and an after, as is the case for continuing works or entities that change their name, a change that almost always also reflects a legal-administrative or organisational change of the entity itself.

> Documents with uncertain boundaries, continual and constantly growing, or that substitute parts of themselves, have identity issues. One cannot maintain identity in a flow. (One cannot enter the same river twice.) A single frame is not representative of a film. A snapshot cannot accurately describe information that is dynamic. These are not simply theoretical problems, for what is difficult to identify is difficult to describe and therefore difficult to organise.
>
> (Svenonius, 2008, 18)

Suppose *space* and *time* are two possible criteria for interpreting these entities. In that case, we would then try to reinterpret them through the application of two principles: that of *synchronic identity*, understood as the identity of entities that are in the same place at the same time, and that of *diachronic identity*, understood as the identity of an entity in a single place or in different places, at different times. This categorisation should provide us with co-ordinates, precisely space–time ones, useful for looking at the complex world of bibliographic information through a new vantage point with respect to tradition, with the aim of finding a broader and more shared agreement as to how to interpret, and thus identify and represent, these entities and the relationships between them that from time to time we define.

Synchronic identities

Synchronic identity refers to entities that are in the same place at the same time: for example, this identity could be useful for framing situations of pseudonymity or all those cases in which the temporal factor (the passage of time) is not the triggering factor for an identity break, seeing as the entities are observed in the same place 'at the same time'. One of the best examples that illustrates synchronic identity is the planet Venus, identified both as the morning star or Lucifer and as the evening star or Vesper, remaining, in each case, itself, the same entity, the same planet. Another important example of synchronic identity is a marble sculpture, which can be seen as a marble block of a particular shape or as a statue made of marble material. Possible synchronic identity relationships are *reflexive* (we are dealing with the same entity), *symmetric* (if x is identical to y, then y is also identical to x), and *transitive* (if x is identical to y and y is identical to z then x is identical to z). There is no dispute about these possible relationships. But to address this dimension of existence, we cannot limit ourselves merely to identifying possible relationships, we must also discuss Leibniz's well-known principle of the (a) identity of the indiscernibles and (b) the indiscernibility of identicals, that is, 'x will be identical to y if and only if x coincides with y in all its properties' (Runggaldier and Kanzian, 2002). The *identical* is such only if a condition of indiscernibility persists, and reciprocally, where this condition persists, there is *identity*.

This assertion seems to be the first piece needed to identify the identity or metaphysical break we were talking about earlier, defining the criteria or conditions necessary and sufficient for a statement of synchronic identity to be true: if and only if x and y have coinciding attributes, then we can assert that x and y are identical[37]; and as identical, x and y are indistinguishable. But what attributes can or should we consider to define x and y as identical? If I use the Latin form 'Aphrodite' or the ancient Greek Αφροδίτη to name the Greek goddess of beauty, love, and fertility, I can be certain that the entity I am referring to is exactly the same (the goddess who was born to Uranus and foam of the sea, or the daughter of Zeus and Dione). From this, it can be inferred that the name attribute is indeed important (otherwise, I would not have had a way to talk about this goddess). Still, the form in which it appears (in Latin or ancient Greek) is entirely secondary, not affecting the entity at all nor the identity of Aphrodite. When, in cataloguing, we identify and record, in an authority record, *variant forms* of a name, we know that they are variations of a label (in this case, of the label 'name'), but the *substance* behind that name is exactly the same. As we can see, IFLA LRM redesigns the name by transforming it from a label or string to an entity (*Nomen*): the entity Nomen derives from the blending of the entity *Name* of FRAD and *Nomen* of FRSAD. It is defined as the 'association between an entity and a designation that refers to it. A *nomen* associates any designation (i.e. combination of signs) used to refer to an instance of any entity in the bibliographic universe with that entity. Every entity referred to in the discourse universe is denominated through at least one *nomen*' (IFLA LRM, 2017, 31). The issue becomes more complex when we think of Venus as *the equivalent of* Aphrodite in Roman mythology: what does it mean for two entities to be equivalent, and what are the attributes that, identified as the same, would make Venus and Aphrodite identical and therefore indiscernible? Looking at the bibliographic universe, is it possible to consider pseudonyms, alter egos[38] and heteronyms[39] as synchronic identities? Let us try to analyse some known cases of pseudonyms, alter egos and heteronyms to formulate a possible answer to the question.

Pseudonyms, alter egos and heteronyms

The Treccani dictionary defines a *pseudonym* as 'a name different from the real name used by a writer, poet, journalist, artist, etc., who is unwilling or unable to sign their works with their real name . . . From a legal perspective, a pseudonym is protected by law when it has acquired the same importance as the name, afforded with the same processes that protect the rights of a name.'[40]

In literature, we have a great many instances of pseudonyms, behind which individuals or collective agents are concealed. The example of Lewis Carroll is interesting because of the characteristic, common to a great many other authors, of having used his real name and his pseudonym to write different works (writing or otherwise producing works of different genres), thus expressing a clear intention to distinguish separate identities. The importance given to this type of pseudonym is not different from that of those created, for example, by shortening very long names, but it certainly helps us understand the significance of the voluntariness in creating an identity alternative to that of one's birth or registry. Lewis Carroll is the pseudonym used by the Reverend Charles Lutwidge Dodgson (1832–1898), adopted in 1856 for the publication of a romantic poem entitled *Solitude*. The same pseudonym was used nine years later, in 1865, in Carroll's best-known work, *Alice's Adventures in Wonderland*. It is interesting how Wikipedia recounts the choice of the pseudonym and the importance it gained in terms of identity: 'The book was an immediate and overwhelming success, and "Lewis Carroll" soon became a beloved and very famous public figure, almost an alter ego leading a life of its own, parallel to Dodgson's.'[41] Defining a pseudonym as a kind of alter ego leading a life of its own means recognising the importance of an identity created for the purpose of associating an expressive activity (in this case, writing poetry or fiction) by establishing a distinction from the author *person* identifiable by the registered name, a name nonetheless used in Dodgson's extensive and seminal photographic work as well as in his treatises on logic. Therefore, in the case of pseudonymy, we can think of encountering two synchronic identities, Charles Lutwidge Dodgson and Lewis Carroll, linked to the same person entity. The 'name' attributes as well as the relations to the works produced by each identity are clearly important components for the identification of each, but less relevant to identify the entity behind them: Charles Lutwidge Dodgson will be identical to Lewis Carroll if and only if Charles Lutwidge Dodgson coincides with Lewis Carroll in all his properties. Regardless of what the person is called, we should identify other elements that, when compared, can give us the certainty that we are dealing with the same entity.

The alter ego almost entirely overlaps the pseudonym; in this case, however, the aspect of a different *personality* or, better, a different person, with a different outward presentation and different stylistic and expressive choices than the person whose *alter* it is. There are countless cases of alter egos in literature and art, the best-known of which is certainly in the 1886 Gothic novel *The Strange Case of Dr Jekyll and Mr Hyde*, by Robert Louis Stevenson. Through the use of a particular potion, Dr Jekyll – tall, polite and of sound moral principles – brings forth and gives life to a second personality, a second nature, that of Mr Hyde – short, stocky, prone to evil and the worst atrocities. The two personalities are closely related, with one entirely dependent, in terms of existence, on the other. In cataloguing terms, the case of Dr Jekyll and Mr Hyde leaves us with few doubts, perhaps only in the structuring of subject headings (but is certainly not a convincing case to discuss). But other alter egos propose, in the cataloguing scenario, the same complexity of treatment already encountered with pseudonyms and other complex entities.

Some examples: Stephen Dedalus, the alter ego of James Joyce, whose autobiography is immortalised in the work *A Portrait of the Artist as a Young Man*, or Slim Shady, the more comedic part of the artist Eminem: 'When the rapper dyes his hair blond, no doubt about it . . . he is playing Slim Shady, one of the most famous alter egos in music history!'[42] Ziggy Stardust was David Bowie's bisexual alter ego for five years. And so many other instances. An alter ego is often reserved for performances and particular works, expressing a personality that the creators (of the alter ego and the related work) feel is different and separate from the better-known personality.

Perhaps the most extreme case of a complex entity, in the sense of the term as used in our discourse, is that of *heteronomy*, which Wikipedia defines more effectively than, for example, the Treccani dictionary:

> The term heteronym takes on a particular meaning in the field of literary writing, denoting a fictitious author (or pseudo-author) who, despite being imaginary, possesses a personality of his own. The author behind the heteronym is called an orthonym. Heteronyms differ from pseudonyms because the latter replace the name of a real author, who thus remains unknown. Heteronyms, on the other hand, coexist with the author and form a kind of extension of the author's character; they are entirely different characters who seem to live a life of their own, often writing in a style different from that of the orthonym.[43]

The heteronym, therefore, is more of an alter ego than a pseudonym, having an authentic life of its own compared to the orthonym.[44] The literary case that generated this meaning of the term *heteronym* is that of the Portuguese writer Fernando Pessoa, who applies a proper literary translation to this term, whose original grammatical meaning indicates the use of substantially different words to expound similar concepts that express the polarity of genders but are etymologically independent: brother/sister, son/daughter, father/mother, and so on, both in the human and animal worlds (cow/bull, sheep/ram). Fernando Pessoa revisits this substantive by extending its semantic field and creating living heteronyms, other writers who seem to have lives of their own, with dates of birth and death, with different languages and poetics, who live within him or, rather, outside him. The difference between heteronomy and pseudonymy is very clear: we are not faced with an identity kept secret by adopting a false name. Here, we are faced with real parallel existences, interacting and influencing the author's life and that of his contemporaries, like a multitude of people in one. Pessoa doesn't write much under his real name: newspaper articles, a couple of poetry collections, a small booklet called *Mensagem*, a collection of letters to his fiancée Ofélia Queiroz published posthumously, and little else. What he himself calls his 'hysteria' produces innumerable other personalities. These other authors co-exist with the one identified as the orthonym, as 'self', and in this co-existence, they take on body and form and assume characteristics and attributes.

> My heteronyms have their origin in a deep-seated form of hysteria . . . The mental origin of my heteronyms lies in my organic and constant tendency toward depersonalisation and simulation . . . Ever since I have known myself as the one I call 'I', I remember mentally drawing, in appearance, movements, character, and history, various unreal figures that were as visible and mine to me as the things of what we call, perhaps abusively, real life. [45]

For the most part, four of his heteronyms are the best known: Bernardo Soares, Alberto Caeiro, Alvaro de Campos and Ricardo Reis, though, by recent counts, there seem to be at least 136 different heteronyms, including both male and female. A number so significant (though the four best-known ones cited already constitute a considerable number on their own!) that it forced Pessoa to define himself as the orthonym, meaning 'that which is really him', that Fernando, the author of not many works but the generator of every other heteronym (the matrix of every other heteronym) – *Una sola moltitudine* (Pessoa, 2021). That multitude which, from a literary point of view, constitutes an almost unique case of absolute autonomy and complete dependence on what is painstakingly recognised as the matrix of everything[46]. Each heteronym has its own biography and is the author of works of different genres, perfectly consistent with its author. We can only imagine from a cataloguing point of view how these many-in-one may have been treated and managed or how they will be treated in an age when the description of something, that is, the bibliographic or authority record as an authoritative description of an author or work, has been almost completely undermined by a completely different conception of identifying real things in the world.

We will discuss all this further, using a few significant examples to follow how these literary (and legendary) cases have been solved in the cataloguing field and how they could be resolved in a completely different context, that of linked open data. At the end of this examination of some examples of complex entities, we need to go back to where we started to see if there are conditions to define these cases as synchronic identities: identities that differ from each other but co-exist and refer to a single entity that is perhaps recognisable precisely because of its rich expressiveness. Synchronic identity helps us here to elaborate a sort of metaphysical classification of these literary cases. We can interpret them as entities whose selfness is so little containable within a single and limited profile that they need to go beyond to express themselves with identities that can hardly be reduced to a before and an after, but that, in a time span marked by the entity's existence, burst forth in seemingly different forms, all referring back to the same substance. Can Fernando Pessoa be considered the same entity as Bernardo Soares or Alberto Caeiro, even in the face of a number of different characteristics (real, such as the literary output of each of them, or imaginary, such as the different dates of birth and death) that would seem to refer to entirely different people? The question that perhaps helps us to define a position on this point is: would Alberto Caeiro exist without Fernando Pessoa? And would Fernando Pessoa be Fernando Pessoa without Bernardo Soares, Alberto Caeiro, Alvaro de Campos, Ricardo Reis and all his other heteronyms? A synchronic entity dropped into the bibliographical universe that we are discussing is an entity that contains within itself others, or rather, is an entity that expresses itself and is itself through a multitude of different identities. What then is the boundary between the central self (or orthonym, in the case of Pessoa's heteronyms) and the other identities created to meet a need to express a complex entity or many identities, is not something easily definable with unambiguous and objective criteria. Whether Alvaro de Campos is exactly or is more or less Fernando Pessoa, or whether Lewis Carroll is exactly or is more or less Charles Lutwidge Dodgson, is extremely difficult to determine and perhaps not even that useful to determine. What we need to understand is who and how to identify. To reference the work *The Game of Logic* (1887), we must of course refer to Charles Lutwidge Dodgson but when thinking of the more famous *Alice's Adventures in Wonderland,* we cannot but associate it with Lewis Carroll. More complex is the work *Livro do Desassossego,* often referred to as one of Fernando Pessoa's greatest works. But it is signed by the heteronymous Bernardo Soares, so how can this work be identified, and to whom can it be attributed? And if we assume that Bernardo Soares is a different identity from Fernando Pessoa, what are the attributes of each identity that allow us to identify one and the other? We will verify, in the remainder of this discussion, that this is one of the critical points to be discussed and resolved, even in the face of a unanimous consensus in considering the cases of pseudonymy, alter ego, and heteronymy as instances of complex entities, of units containing multitudes.

Translations, performances and other synchronic identities

Pseudonyms and alter egos, and even more so heteronyms, have helped us to frame a certain type of complex entity (referable in this case to agents, such as people and collective agents) to which different identities contribute – in a time frame indifferent to a *before* and *after* – to constitute the *one,* and in which it sometimes becomes complicated to trace back to a main self, which generates other forms of self. This concept of synchronic identity, in which, indeed, the entity's identification cannot disregard the multiplicity of expressions through which that entity appears, applies to other types of entities that make the bibliographic universe rich and complex. The outline of Family of Works by Barbara B. Tillett shown in Figure 1.1 on the next page clearly and schematically exemplifies a good number of entities. Those represented in the diagram as 'Same work' (in the 'Derivative' area, starting from the left, before the dotted line indicated as 'Cataloguing Rules cut-off point') we would try to define as synchronic identities and expressing, precisely in this case, the identity shift we have been talking about, and therefore the transition to another entity (a new work).

To define what is included in the section of this figure labelled 'Same work', Tillett says 'Next we come to works/expressions/manifestations that are related through a 'derivative' relationship. These comprise a range of new expressions, such as translations, different performances, slight modifications, and editions that move along the continuum across a magic line . . .'[47] In this case, too, it is almost intuitive to see the extent to which a work can be considered a complex entity that cannot be separated from the expressions that can be produced from it, if it is to be entirely comprehended. The discussion of synchronicity here is more subtle, and perhaps at times even seemingly forced because, referring, for example, to a translation into another language of a work originally conceived and written in Italian, we are reminded of a before and an after (thus, an a-synchronicity). But the complexity of treating translated works (as well as different performances of the same work, different editions, etc.) is precisely in the synchronicity of the various translations being understood as different identities of the same entity

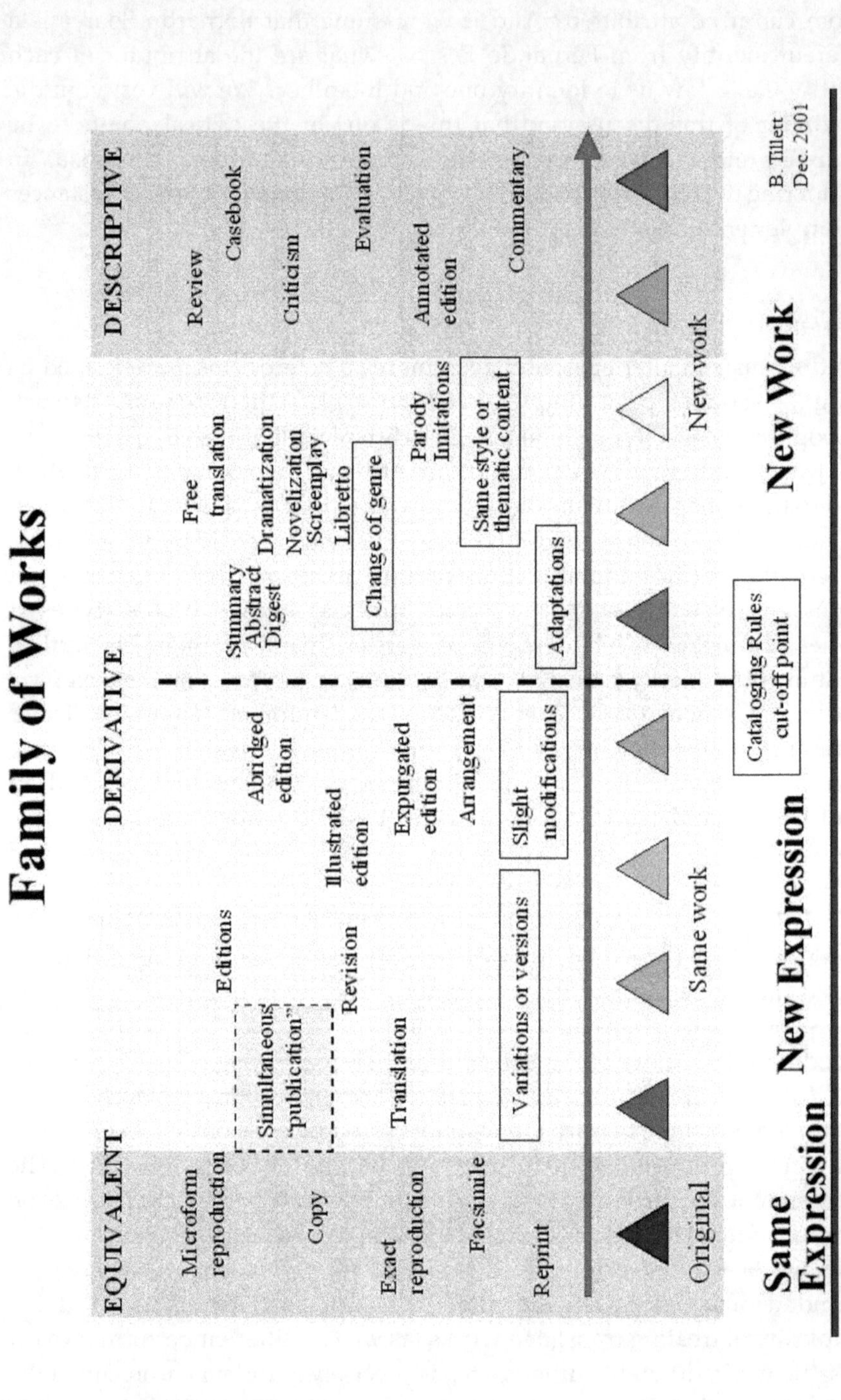

Figure 1.1 *Family of Works scheme by Barbara B. Tillett* (Tillett, 2001. Permission conveyed through Copyright Clearance Center)

that is the original self, the work conceived and produced by its author, in its original form. The determining element is the content of the work (a single content expressing the entity, the message conveyed, the work as conceived), which manifests itself in multiple forms (thus under multiple identities) but which persists as a foundational entity beyond the many, varied expressions which, over time (understood only as a temporal sequence, with no bearing on the identification of the entity work) enrich the original with a multitude of versions.[48] Staying with the content of the work, the dotted line of demarcation that Tillett refers to as the 'cut-off point' marks a real break in identity. It is a line that, once crossed, forms content different from the original work, albeit within derivative relations, signifying a new entity, a new work.

Beyond that line, we find adaptations, parodies, imitations, abstracts, and free translations. These are all works that we can certainly consider as inspired by the original one, but which take on an identity all their own, becoming another entity. The cases of the kind of synchronic identity we are focusing on in the realm of creative works are so numerous in the bibliographic universe that we can provide only a few examples. Consider for a moment the currently most translated book in the world, *Le Petit Prince*, by Antoine de Saint-Exupéry, with 253 translations, or *The Adventures of Pinocchio*, by Carlo Collodi, which follows in second place with 240 translations[49]. Further reflection is needed for more complex situations, such as different performances of the same work (encore performances of a concert) or – to cite an even more extreme case – two video recordings of the same performance of, for example, a theatrical production. Consider two cinematographers filming the same scene from two different angles. The resulting videos will have captured the same content but offer different perspectives of that same performance. Each of these shots will express the point of view of the cinematographer, and so they will certainly be different from one another. And in each of the two shots, the eye of each cinematographer or, at any rate, the particular view given the framing, can be recognised. But what is the existential autonomy of each shot with respect to the performance itself? Returning to the discussion of our inventory of existing things, and thus to the ontological discourse from which we started, we can include, among the objects that populate our ontology:

- the performance
- recording 1
- recording 2

or should we think that the object is the performance and recording 1 and recording 2 are *different expressions* of the same performance? If, in order to simplify the ontological discourse (what entities that can be identified in the performance and the recordings of that performance) and a metaphysical one (what is the performance itself without a point of view to frame it?), we would start from the idea of a complex entity that expresses itself in multiple identities. We could argue that the performance itself is the entity, and recording 1 and recording 2 are different, and synchronic, identities of that entity. This assumption, seemingly the most straightforward – just as the assumption of the entity Pessoa, with his many identities, the heteronyms, seemed to be the most straightforward – is not so widely shared. We shall then see, in the course of this study, that for most issues concerning the existence of complex objects, an even more drastic yet practical solution has been chosen, that of identifying, in the example we are giving, recording 1 and recording 2 as different entities, expressions of a different entity (the recorded work). The complexity of identification that cases such as these inherently present shifts from the entity (they are all, equally, entities) to the relationships between them (the performance is the entity as well as the recording, and they are in a relationship of expression, thus one is the expression of the other). In both cases (one entity/multiple identities and many different entities), we come to accept a solution out of practicality. In order to draw up an inventory of existing things and then be able to model them, we must provide a practical, albeit reductive, answer to existential questions that are complex and controversial.

Diachronic identities

The problem we face from the start in trying to define diachronic identities is that relating to the identity of an object or event *over time*. Wanting to apply the temporal dimension to the process of entity identification, we must address significant questions related to the *persistence of the entity over time*, its change, and its ability, or lack thereof, to remain itself over time despite change. Statements of identity in the diachronic sense assert that x in this instant t_1, is identical to y at another instant t_2. For example: I (x) now (t_1) am identical to that little girl (y) pictured in the school photo from 40 years ago (t_2).

Looking in the mirror and recognising oneself as the same 10-year-old seen in an old photo is to acknowledge an identity over time, to think of oneself as a single entity regardless of how it changes. If this sense of selfness is hard to find over time, certain that we are always different, many different selves connected only by a relationship of continuity, then the perspective of viewing and interpreting reality changes, and so does the ontology of reference necessarily transform. Asking ourselves whether things remain the same despite changing over time, or asking ourselves 'on the basis of what elements can we say that something is no longer the same?', is a matter of metaphysics (questioning the nature of things), but it is also, and above all, a question of ontology, because we need to understand what to include in our inventory of existing things. The concept of *time passing*, associated with the objects of our daily living and even to people, immediately brings to mind the idea of *change*, to the point of regarding the two concepts, that of time and that of change, as closely connected. Change is often even the yardstick by which we measure or simply perceive, time. We do this on a daily basis as part of our human cultural heritage. Think, for example, of time-measuring systems based on observing the alternation of day and night or the change of seasons; of measuring the age of trees by observing the circles that have been added to enlarge the trunk over time; but think of instinctively measuring time by merely looking at old family photos, calculating the time passed with the change recorded in objects and people. The ability to continue to identify things over time, despite the changes that occur, responds to a very practical need: that is, to recognise the world around us without having to start from scratch each time, even though we would hardly be able to identify and list those elements that make the changed object the same item it was some time ago. We recognise that object as the same, but we do not question what element is essential for that object to no longer be the same but instead something different. These issues, far from common sense, are instead the basis of much philosophical reflection as well as the basis of the observation and classification of the bibliographic universe in which we operate. When an institution changes its name, when a website changes its content daily, when a person changes gender identity, what criteria should we adopt to identify them as the same entities or as different entities?

The paradoxes of identity over time

Philosophy addresses the question of identity over time through the inquiry into the *persistence* of things over time, a concept closely related to what is known as the *growing argument*.[50] According to this argument, just as if we add one number to another number, that first number is no longer the same, in the same way, if we add or remove a part of an object, it no longer remains the same. This topic has been the subject of reflection and debate throughout the history of Western thought, generating different and opposing positions and currents of thought without ever reaching a unanimous consensus. Sceptics in Plato's Academy held that even the smallest change in matter causes the destruction of the entity and the generation of a different entity: when even a small part of matter is taken from or added to a thing, that thing ceases to exist, and a new entity is generated.[51] This view is opposed to that of the Stoics, according to whom an individual's identity is given by that intangible substratum constituted by the properties or qualities that make it so.[52] Following Aristotle, the Stoics distinguished between the physical substratum (ὑποκείμενον), which is transformed when a change of matter occurs, and the 'peculiar or precise qualifications' of the individual (specialised entity) (ἰδίος ποιὸν) that persist beyond the change and enable the entity to remain what it is over time.[53]

The Stoic response to the Academics' positions regarding the growing argument comes from the construction of a singular philosophical paradox, the puzzle of Dion and Theon, presented by the Stoic Chrysippus of Soli in the lost work, *On the Growing Argument.* We are left with an account in Philo of Alexandria's *On the Eternity of the World* in defence of the principle of the preservation of individual identity. The puzzle of Dion and Theon goes something like this: Let's assume the existence of two individuals, Dion, with an intact body, and Theon, who is composed of every single part of Dion except for one foot. The two are distinct people because they occupy two different parts of space at the same time. Suppose now that Dion, initially intact, has one foot amputated. Common sense would no doubt assert that Dion remains the same despite this amputation. But now that the two perfectly coincide, the question arises, 'Which one disappears?'[54] The question arising in ancient philosophy, at least from Aristotle onward, is what constitutes a thing or a person in its individuality and thus in its existence as an entity. What distinguishes one thing from all others, and what guarantees the permanence of that thing beyond changes? Still, in answer to this fundamental question is the paradox of Theseus' ship, recounted in Plutarch's *Life of Theseus:*

> Up to the time of Demetrius Phalerus, the Athenians preserved the trireme on which Theseus sailed with the young hostages and then returned safely. The old timbers were removed and replaced with sturdy ones, firmly connected together. As such, it served as a model, even to philosophers when they discussed the issue of growth, some claiming that it was the same ship, others contending that it was not.
>
> (Plutarco, 1996, 117)

And in revisiting the paradox in the modern age, Thomas Hobbes adds:

> and, if someone had kept those same planks in the order in which they were taken off, and having kept them then put them back together in the same order, rebuilding the ship, there is no doubt that this would have been, numerically, the same as the one in the beginning; numerically, we would have had two identical ships, which is utterly absurd.
>
> (Hobbes, 1972, 184–5)

Can we consider the ship of Theseus, from which the original planks were removed over time and replaced with new ones, still that of Theseus? Or is Theseus' ship the one that, over time, has been rebuilt with the same planks and thus the same material, as the original one? Also interesting in this sense is the famous example used by Ferdinand de Saussure in Chapter III of his work, *Course in General Linguistics*, to explain the difference between *language* and *words* with particular reference to the identity of the symbol, which is not given by the materiality of the elements but by the relations between them and other elements in the system and thus by the *function* they play in a given context:

> In this same manner, we can talk about identity in regard to two 'Geneva–Paris 8:45 p.m.' trains, which depart at twenty-four-hour intervals. In our eyes, it is the same train, and yet probably the locomotive, cars, personnel, everything is different. Or, if a road is demolished and then rebuilt, we say that it is the same road, although perhaps nothing of the old road remains materially. Why is it possible to rebuild a road from top to bottom without it ceasing to remain the same? Because the entity it constitutes is not purely material; that entity is based on certain conditions to which its incidental matter is foreign, such as, for example, its position in relation to others. Similarly, what constitutes the train is the time of its departure, its route, and generally all the circumstances that distinguish it from other trains. Every time the same conditions are realised, the same entities are obtained. And yet these are not abstract, since a road or a train cannot be conceived outside of a material realisation.
>
> (Saussure, 2013, 107–8)

The solutions to the puzzles exemplified by these paradoxes have moulded and conditioned philosophical reflection for more than two millennia, generating various currents of thought and different positions on how to read and interpret the world around us. We will not attempt to summarise this complex debate here, but two currents of thought – *three-dimensionalism* and *four-dimensionalism* – which have tried to answer the controversy over the principle of individuation of entities in time can help us to frame our discussion of modelling and therefore, in ontology and metaphysics, of diachronic entities in the bibliographical domain.

Both positions under discussion here respond to the question of the persistence of entities over time, taking into consideration the temporal dimension as either irrelevant to the identifiability of the thing or, on the contrary, strongly conditioning the thing itself. Both start from the position most acceptable to those who need to classify and thus give definitions of the world: the idea that an object can be recognised even in change, whatever that may be. The definition of persistence as *perdurantism* or *endurantism* is by David Lewis, who introduces the debate on the two philosophical positions in this way:

> Let us say that something *persists* if, somehow or other, it exists at various times; this is the neutral word. Something *perdures* if it persists by having different temporal parts, or stages, at different times, though no one part of it is wholly present at more than one time; whereas it *endures* if it persists by being wholly present at more than one time. Perdurance corresponds to the way a road persists through space; part of it is here, and part of it is there, and no part is wholly present at two different places. Endurance corresponds to the way a universal, if there are such things, would be wholly present wherever and whenever it is instantiated. Endurance involves overlap: the content of two different times has the enduring thing as a common part. Perdurance does not.
>
> (Lewis, 1986, 202)

Three-dimensionalism or *endurantism*[55] originates from Aristotle's thought and holds that things resolve their existence in the three spatial dimensions, regardless, therefore, of the temporal dimension: they *persist* over time, remaining the same thing beyond possible changes. An object is the same object at different times, and it remains so in its identity, even in the face of changes that illustrate its evolution, its mutation. Even if it does not remain exactly the same when observed over time, that object has its own identity that, indeed, persists. Therefore, each thing has an identity with itself, *identical to itself* in whatever fraction of time it is observed.

Four-dimensionalism or *perdurantism*[56] adds to the three spatial dimensions a fourth, the temporal dimension: objects persist over time because *they extend* through time. The same object in two different times contains different information – for example, different space–time co-ordinates. From an ontological and metaphysical point of view, it should be regarded as two objects that are not absolutely identical. And indeed, as Lewis himself goes so far as to argue, every object ceases to exist at every moment in time to be replaced by a similar entity. Yet, our ability to have a global, therefore summarising, view of the world pushes us to look for some sort of common thread, a unit of identity beyond these multiple differences. It is a bit like watching a film, which is, in fact, composed of a series of successive frames, each different from the other, but which together (and in our ability to look at the many as a whole) gives us back the dimension of the film as one. The solution we offer for the problem of entities becoming elusive over time is nonetheless a functional imposition of our need for things to persist over time by preserving an identity of their own (Wittgenstein, 2009).

Reflections on diachronic entities are complex and, like many philosophical doubts, unresolved. But what interests us here is how they can help us understand how, in the history of cataloguing and the definition of bibliographic ontologies, these entities have been interpreted, which we could simplify into those mentioned earlier as *entities in transitional relationships*: gender transition, entities that change structure or name, continuing resources (websites, serials or periodicals, etc.). These cataloguing cases have in common an observable change over a certain time, a change that raises doubts about who to identify and how to do it. Doubt that once again can be exemplified by the research into understanding where that break in identity occurs that, in a specific time frame, defines different entities or that, in its absence, assures us of the consistency of the entity beyond the change. The cases that we present as diachronic identities are among the most complex in the cataloguing field, and the Aristotelian-scholastic position is perhaps the one that comes closest to the common understanding of the reality around us, as a set of things each composed of a substratum that, in the absence of change (where change pertains only to what we define as accidental, and therefore not relative to the substance of things) we can identify as 'the thing' that selfness we are continuously seeking in this analysis.

Gender transition

The first case to test what theoretical foundation guides us in the identification of diachronic entities is perhaps one of the most complex, as it requires careful attention in the application of cataloguing rules given the impact, whichever way it is applied, on personal matters: the case is that of gender transition and therefore of individuals who, at some point in their lives, make a change in gender and therefore a change of identity. It is easy to imagine that the cataloguing choices in handling such cases are complex: the application of a cataloguing norm must take into account an important individual choice, concerning whether or not to maintain a continuity with one's past or to revise it according to the transition made. The element of volition, that is, the extent to which an author has a desire or not to disclose their identity or to form a connection with another identity, is also a widely discussed theme in dealing with pseudonyms. Often, the choice of a pseudonym expresses a clear desire to conceal an identity, making it complicated to avoid cataloguing choices that might contravene the author's desire for anonymity. The same thing can happen in gender transitions, where the decision to create a relationship between the old and the new identity should be left entirely to the author. But, of course, this isn't always the case, especially in an open forum such as the web, where information spreads beyond the wishes of authors and where it is almost impossible, due to the volume of data and information, to adopt unique cataloguing solutions corresponding to the will of each individual.

Let us look at some well-known cases, especially in cinematography, of gender transitions involving individuals who have artistic output associated with both a previous and a new identity. Wikipedia defines the term *transgender* as follows:

> The term *transgender* (often shortened as 'trans') is an umbrella term for people whose gender identity does not match the gender and/or sex they were assigned at birth. Some transgender people who wish to access medical treatment to align their physique with their gender identity call themselves transsexual.[57]

Elliot Page is a Canadian actor and producer; she was born in 1987 as Ellen Grace Philpotts-Page. On 1 December 2020 she announced on her Twitter profile that she was transitioning her gender by declaring a new name and asking to be identified by male or neutral pronouns. As Ellen Page, the actor had appeared in several cinema and television films and was nominated for or won several awards. The online encyclopaedia Wikipedia, consulted in summer of 2021, speaks of Elliot Page[58] in masculine terms and reconstructs the actor's biography but alternates between references to both the male and female identities of the actor through the strategy of mentioning only the surname in a discreet and sometimes equivocal alternation. Elliot Page's entry recounts the story, biography and career of a diachronic identity that publicly establishes the 'before' (1987–30 November 2020) and 'after' (1 December 2020–present) in a narrative that follows the entity in its changes but also in its permanence over time.

Wikidata also assigns Ellen and Elliot Page to a single identifier[59] (or rather, the identifier has the male version Elliot as the entity label, with redirection from Ellen), identifying, therefore, the entity 'Ellen/Elliot' and preferring (also in deference to the actor's request) the Elliot identity as the main one, while the Ellen identity is registered under the label 'also known as'. The name Ellen Grace Philpotts-Page is also recorded as the 'birth name' and this name is assigned the gender transition declaration date, 1 December 2020, as the 'end date' of the name. Meanwhile, the name Elliot is recorded as the 'given name', with the same date, 1 December 2020, declared as the start of the use of that name. The main difficulty in identifying Elliot or Ellen Page, which to some extent is avoided by Wikidata, lies in how to associate with Ellen/Elliot the works interpreted or created before the transition and how to associate with the works interpreted or created thereafter, if the identifier is only for the entity and not also for the different identities? Does the gender transition bring about the change, referring to the philosophical perspective mentioned earlier, a change of substance or accident? Or should the change be understood as irrelevant to the 'function' category (artist, performer) which we assign to Elliot and Ellen Page? The Virtual International Authority File (VIAF) renders even less clearly the different identities of Elliot/Ellen Page:[60] both the feminine and masculine names are listed as preferred forms at the same level, with no indication of the reasons for this dual nomenclature. In the wake of the other projects is the International Standard Name Identifier (ISNI),[61] with the only difference that it gives more prominence to the female identity than to the male, thus demonstrating, in other cases, a flaw in the ability to update the data. The WorldCat Identities project, which works more than VIAF on the identification of works associated with an artist, is also interesting in its treatment of this entity.[62] The reference to Page is always in the masculine form, but all the artist's performances prior to gender transition, and thus expressed in his female identity, are also associated with the male identity. These choices could reflect the specific will of the author, that is, to identify himself using the identity felt and chosen as 'his own'.

From a cataloguing point of view, this desire for 'retro-identification' presents a few doubts, if only when considering the many resources (movie posters, DVDs, interviews, film and series credits) with which the old identity has been associated: how to reflect an individual's identity choices without thinking of generating a glaring discordance between what can be detected on the catalogued resource and the subject's new identity?

An extremely interesting and perhaps even more complex case is that of the collective identity recognised as The Wachowskis, also known as The Wachowski Brothers, later to become The Wachowski Sisters. Wikipedia describes this duo as follows, under the heading Lana and Lilly Wachowski: [63]

> *Lana Wachowski*, born as Larry (Chicago, June 21, 1965), and *Lilly Wachowski*, born as Andy (Chicago, December 29, 1967), are two U.S. film directors, screenwriters, and producers who have worked in artistic partnership for most of their careers. They are both transgender women, formerly known as the *Wachowski brothers*, later as the *Wachowski sisters*.[64]

This case is especially complex and we try to analyse it starting from the treatment in Wikidata, pointing out some particularities. The identity in Wikidata is defined as the Wachowskis[65] and the Wachowski Brothers and Wachowski Sisters are referred to as 'also known as' along with single formulations of the names assigned at birth (Larry Wachowski and Andy Wachowski) and individual names acquired after gender transition (Lana Wachowski and Lilly Wachowski). The Wachowskis are defined as an 'instance of sibling duo', a category used by Wikidata to denote a subclass of a 'duo' or group of people working together. The entity the Wachowskis is linked to the entities Lana Wachowski and Lilly Wachowski through the property 'has part', which indicates that something belongs to the same described subject. This points us to a relevant aspect of the definition given by Wikidata: the consideration of the Wachowskis duo as a separate entity composed of two other individual entities. Should this be considered a specific ontological choice? Can we consider the duo as an entity to be included in our inventory of existing things? Certainly, yes, if we take this categorisation as valid, we will prefer it to the hypothesis of a collective pseudonym understood as another identity of one (or more) entities. And if we consider the Wachowskis as an entity, how do we interpret the Wachowski Brothers later becoming the Wachowski Sisters? Can we consider them as two identities of the same diachronic identity? Two moments of a single, continuous timeline? We will say nothing about VIAF and how this authority file considers the Wachowski Sisters, as it provides no useful informative note concerning the ontological approach chosen for the duo,[66] nor does the description in the Library of Congress Name Authority File.[67] Instead, it is interesting to explore how the entity the Wachowskis was treated in ISNI. Although the description does not clarify the ontological choice, it engenders a fair amount of confusion. 'The Wachowskis' does not have its identifier in ISNI but instead redirects to two entries (hits), which are:

Wachowski, Andrew Paul 'Andy' (Polish-American film director)[68]
Wachowski, Lana (1965–)[69]

each with its identifier. On each of the two pages devoted to each of these entities, in the section dedicated to the name attribute, we find both the name of the male entity, the name of the female entity, and the collective name as well as, at the exact same level, several variant forms of these appellations:

For Wachowski, Andrew Paul 'Andy'

Andy Wachowski (amerikai filmrendező)
Andy Wachowski (Polish-American director)
Lilly Wachowski (Amerikaans schrijver)
Lilly Wachowski (amerikanische Regisseurin)
Lilly Wachowski (filmaozerez amerikan)
Lilly Wachowski (Polish-American film director)
Lilly Wachowski (réalisatrice américaine)
The Wachowski Brothers
Wachowski, Andrew Paul

Wachowski, Andrew Paul 'Andy'
Wachowski, Andrew Paul (Frueherer Name)
Wachowski, Andy
Wachowski, Andy (Frueherer Name).
Wachowski Brothers (Frueherer Name)
Wachowski-Brüder (Frueherer Name)
Wachowski-Geschwister
Wachowski, Lilly
Лили Вачовски (кинорежиссёр США)
ウォシャウスキー, アンディー

And for Wachowski, Lana:

The Wachowski Brothers
Wachowski Brothers
Wachowski Brothers (Frueherer Name)
Wachowski-Brüder (Frueherer Name)
Wachowski-Geschwister
Wachowski, Lana
Wachowski, Larry
Wachowski, Larry (Frueherer Name).
Wachowski, Laurence (Frueherer Name).
Wachowski, Laurence 'Larry'
Wachowskis The

As is evident, each entry presents the many possible forms (birth names, names acquired after the gender transition, the collective name referring to male entities, while entirely absent is the feminine version, such as Wachowski Sisters). Still, without any real 'categorisation' and definition in ontological terms of these different forms, each is similarly considered a variant form of a name.

What jumps out at us from these analysed sources – with one exception, perhaps, insofar as it is seen only in Wikidata – is that we see little if any activity of modelling entities that undergo a change of identity over time, what we have called diachronic entities. The treatment of the different cases does not express an ontological or metaphysical reflection, which investigates and defines a common mode of identification for these complex personalities. In the section of this research work that is devoted to the transition from the bibliographic record to the real-world object, we will see how, in some sources, this transition from a 'flat' description to a view of the entity in all its reality is stated, but without any analysis and entity modelling. And we will see if it is possible to bridge this lack of ontological insight and with what practical elements it is possible to express it.

Name changes in corporate bodies

A common instance of diachronic identity in the bibliographic universe is that of corporate bodies, defined in Official RDA Toolkit as 'A collective agent that is composed of persons who are organised for a common purpose or activity.'[70] The history of an entity may be long and last as long as necessary to fulfil the purpose for which that entity was created but over time the entity may change its name for a variety of reasons, such as through a merger with other entities or division into separate entities. Cataloguing rules therefore give attention to name changes when handling these cases, using all the rules for constructing an access point. But again, in cataloguing rules as well as in international authority data projects, encyclopaedic sources and bibliographic datasets, it is very difficult to understand how an entity that changes its identity over time is modelled from an ontological point of view. As a case study, we will look at the Istituto Italiano per l'Africa e l'Oriente (IsIAO), which Wikipedia describes as:

> Formed in 1995 from the merger of the Istituto italiano per il Medio ed Estremo Oriente (IsMEO), founded in 1933 by Giovanni Gentile and Giuseppe Tucci, with the Istituto italo-africano (IIA), founded in 1906.[71]

We have, then, an institution that arose from the merger of two other institutions. How do we address this? Can we argue that the new institution represents not a different identity of the same entity but an actual entity with its own identity? Let us see how the sources we've used for our analysis so far treat the three different institutes, evidently identified as three different entities.

1. *Istituto Italo-Africano (IIA), founded in 1906*

The online encyclopaedia Wikipedia does not offer a page for this institute,[72] which is, however, present in VIAF,[73] with variant forms of the name (the traditional 'see all' reference) produced by different institutions that contributed to the construction of the entry and that evidently reflect different historical phases of the institute:

- Istituto coloniale fascista
- Istituto coloniale italiano

- Istituto fascista dell'Africa italiana
- Istituto italiano per l'Africa (1947–1971)

However, for entities related to the Institute with the traditional 'See also' reference, which directs to authorised access points and therefore to entities with their own institutional autonomy and which are not considered simply variant forms of a name, it lists some of the names already presented as variant forms, plus other forms, including:

- Istituto fascista per l'Africa italiana (1937–1946)
- Istituto italiano per l'Africa e l'Oriente

in a bewildering confusion between variant forms of the name of the same entity and different entities (or rather, variant forms presented as different entities) that denotes an almost total lack of entity modelling work. In the case of VIAF, however, this approach is justifiable, because of the still traditional view of cataloguing treatment, very much focused on record management and not entity management.

In the ISNI,[74] the treatment of this entity is quite similar to VIAF. In addition to presenting several variant forms of the name (including several acronyms), it presents the same categorisation, with the same confusion between variant forms of the name of the same entity (presented as variant forms) and variant forms presented as related entities. The sources and data used to create the form in VIAF are exactly the same as those used in ISNI, with also the same processing logic.

Even in the WorldCat Identities project,[75] the same confusion arises, which in this case turns out to be more blameworthy, given that the project presents itself specifically as a database of 'identities' and not as a traditional authority file understood as a set of Machine Readable Cataloguing (MARC) records. In this case, forms of the name such as Istituto italiano per l'Africa or Istituto italiano per l'Africa e l'Oriente are reported with exactly the same identifiers both in the Alternative Names section (thus, as variant forms of the name that is used as the preferred form) and as Related identities (in theory, as other identities or entities, relating to the one described, but autonomous). In WorldCat, as in the other projects, the dependency relationship between the entity Istituto italo-africano and the entity Istituto italiano per l'Africa e l'Oriente (to which the former flowed) is never clearly expressed.

2. *Istituto italiano per il Medio ed Estremo Oriente (IsMEO) founded in 1933*
Both Wikipedia[76] and Wikidata[77] devote a page to this Institute, registering only some variant forms of the name under 'also known as'.

The VIAF[78] and ISNI,[79] in this case, are more detailed and clear in their categorisation, recording several variant forms of the name (in the traditional 'see all' reference), including the Istituto italiano per il Medio ed Estremo Oriente e Asiatica (1936–1943)[80] and proposing, as a related entity (thus autonomous as 'see also/see also all' references) the Istituto italiano per l'Africa e l'Oriente, generated precisely by the merger of IsMEO and the Istituto italo-africano.

WorldCat Identities[81] records as *aliases* for the Istituto italiano per il Medio ed Estremo Oriente the various formulations of the acronym IsMEO, without any reference to the institutes that generated the entity.

More straightforward, then, for this institution is the categorisation between variant forms and autonomous yet related organisations.

3. *Istituto italiano per l'Africa e l'Oriente (IsIAO, founded in 1995)*
Wikidata[82] offers a straightforward description of this Institute, with only a reference to the acronym and no link to the entities that gave rise to it by merging. In some places the data are incorrect or outdated, such as in the indication of the link to the official site.

VIAF,[83] ISNI[84] and WorldCat Identities[85] offer the same indications, with some variant forms of the name and links to the two institutes from which the entity in question is derived. VIAF adds a relationship (such as 'see also/see also all') to the International Association for Mediterranean and Oriental Studies (ISMEO).[86]

The analysis of these three entities, closely related to each other to the extent that one arises from the merger of the other two, conducted using some of the most authoritative sources in the international bibliographical landscape, once again suggests the lack of in-depth modelling for the identification and profiling of entities and their respective identities. These entities, with their changes of name, which often express deeper changes, as a result of the mutations produced by mergers and divisions, are certainly identifiable as diachronic identities and would certainly allow, in modelling, a dual exercise: that of characterising the identity break that produces a new entity (indeed the birth of an institute from the merger of two other existing institutes clearly defines that identity break) and that of verifying and tracking the *persistence of an entity over time,* despite all the changes.

Continuing resources

Continuing resources are publications whose editorial plans do not have predetermined conclusions but are developed continuously over time, as long as the project of which they are an expression lasts. This type of resource includes *serials* (including series and e-journals) and *supplementary resources* (updateable loose sheets, databases, websites). Continuing resources are different from multivolume monographs, with one of the main elements being the publisher's project intention. For the monograph, it is generally known how many volumes will make up the set when the resource is published, whereas this is not the case for supplementary resources, whose term is undefined (ALCTS, 2012).

Continuing resources represent, therefore, a very common type of diachronic identity and one that is very complicated to model, especially in cases where the resource changes name or editorial responsibility over time. Determining the point of separation between one piece of work and another that is completely autonomous from the first – or between a different version of the same work, which we might consider, therefore, a different identity of the same entity – is in some cases extremely complicated. In certain resources, the complexity increases – for example, in supplementary resources where change is a part of the resource itself, which we know we have to examine from the beginning. Let us consider a website or a database and try to imagine whether this resource can be considered the same even in the face of major changes such as content, graphic design or access address, or whether we have to make an effort here to pinpoint a possible identity break.

To facilitate thinking about this kind of diachronic identity we can use the example of a periodical with a long but straightforward publishing life, an organ of the Italian Library Association (Associazione Italiana Biblioteche – AIB). For this type of resource it is not easy to compare treatment across different sources, because we have to keep in mind that projects of international authority are attentive to the treatment of agents while they are still somewhat behind in the treatment of pieces of work.

The official bulletin of the AIB originated in 1955 under the name *Notizie AIB* (AIB News) and was published under this title until the year 1960. Through the 'followed by' property in Wikidata,[87] it is linked to the title *Bollettino d'informazioni. Associazione Italiana Biblioteche,*[88] which has a publication start date of 1961 and a publication end date of 1991. This periodical is linked to the previous title through the 'follows' property and to the periodical *Bollettino AIB* (AIB Bulletin) through the 'followed by' property. The AIB Bulletin[89] covers the years 1992 to 2011 and is linked to the subsequent title *AIB Studi* (AIB Studies),[90] through two properties, 'followed by' and 'replaced by'.[91] *AIB Studi* began publication in 2012 and is still in print. Obviously, it is linked to the previous title with inverse properties, that is, with the 'follows and 'replaces' properties. All of these titles, which Wikidata defines as individual entities, retain the same publisher and thus most likely represent the same editorial project. Are they to be considered different entities, or are they 'different moments' of the same story and the same entity, as we have imagined the sequence of images that together constitute a film?

Bollettino AIB as well as *AIB Studi* are published in both print and online versions, and Wikidata proposes linking to both versions for each title through reference to the ACNP Italian Periodicals Catalogue:[92] The print and online versions are certainly different identities of the same entity, and as such, they are not surveyed separately by Wikidata, which seeks to work precisely on the entities and not on the bibliographic descriptions of the resource, as the pre-RDA cataloguing tradition envisioned. This will be discussed extensively when we address the previously mentioned topic of the momentous shift from record to real-world object.

The last case study we will analyse as an example of diachronic identity is that of a supplementary website-type resource, the *Sacred Space* site[93], a prayer site of the Irish Province of the Society of Jesus. A website is an evolving object by definition, an expression of a specific entity or project. Among existing bibliographic resources, there is nothing more fluid and changeable, and at the same time uniquely identifiable, than a website. When sites lose this characteristic of continuous and progressive updating, they also often lose their very nature and reason for their existence. The site we are discussing is not highly complex in its identification, because it is not one that has undergone major revisions and rewrites over time. However, let us start here to frame the case history and reflect on the nature of this type of entity.

The *Sacred Space* site is described in both VIAF[94] and on the Library of Congress Linked Data Service project pages[95]. As a variant form of the name *Sacred Space* (understood here really only as a variant form identifying the exact same resource) both sources record the address of the site www.sacredspace.ie as well as the form of the name associated with the order.[96] Perhaps the other relevant datum is the chronological indication of the project's birth, 1999, expressed in the Library of Congress data with the Metadata Authority Description Schema (MADS) <creationDateStart> property.

This example of a website is very simple because we are unaware of different editions of the same publication with significant differences between the before and after. However, significant change of this kind is widespread in websites, where revisions may result from technological upgrades or project evolution, as well as substantial changes in the corporate structure that the site represents. These important differences are of the sort Aristotelian philosophy would consider substantial and not by chance. Precisely because of the indescribable fluidity of the web, a need arose over time to create a kind of collective memory of this heritage and its evolutions. One of the most important projects in this regard is the Internet Archive,[97] a project defined by Wikipedia as follows:

> *Internet Archive* is a nonprofit digital library with the stated mission of providing 'universal access to all knowledge.' It offers a permanent digital space for access to various types of resources such as websites, audio, moving images (video), and books. Internet Archive was founded by Brewster Kahle in 1996 and is part of the International Internet Preservation Consortium (IIPC). In addition to its primary archiving function, Internet Archive is an organisation that advocates for a free and open Internet and is an officially recognised nonprofit foundation in the United States of America.[98]

The most interesting purpose of this project is described, again on Wikipedia, in these few lines:

> The largest digital collection of the library is the web archive, a sort of collection of 'snapshots' of the World Wide Web catalogued by date of acquisition.

This immediately brings us back to that idea of diachronic identity, here represented by the entire world wide web playing like a film made up of many 'snapshots', many frames each with its own value and character – each with its own selfness that is worth collecting and not to be lost within a broader and unspecified all-encompassing unit.

Entities in whole–part relationships

We have indicated the entities in the identity relationship, whole–part[99] (or part–whole) as being among the most complicated entities to deal with when modelling the bibliographic universe: the subseries compared to the series, the monographic volume compared to the series, the single volume compared to the multi-volume, the article compared to the issue and the issue versus the periodical, sub-entity versus main entity, single photograph versus a photographic exhibition, and so on. In terms of modelling, we are referring primarily to that subcategory of whole–part relationships, the relationships defined by Barbara Tillett as 'abstract' and thus 'pertaining to an abstract unit, referring to the relationships between an intellectual unit and its intellectual components, that is, works that are not merely contained in a physical unit but are parts of an intellectual body of work' (Ghiringhelli and Guerrini, 2018 [translated]). We have left for the end of this discussion this particular type of resource, which is not singular but includes different types, because of its peculiarity in expressing, at the same time, both a type of synchronic entity (e.g. the *Divine Comedy*, which is composed of the three canticles *Inferno*, *Purgatorio*, and *Paradiso*) and a type of diachronic entity (e.g. monographic series, such as the famous *Biblioteca de Autores Cristianos* published, starting in 1943, by Editorial Católica and consisting of different subseries).

But to conclude the discussion we started on diachronic and synchronic entities, perhaps one of the most significant case studies is precisely that of Dante Alighieri's *Divine Comedy*, which, like many other works of this kind, raises doubts regarding ontological modelling and cataloguing activities.

Wikidata offers a very rich data set for this work[100] so that it can be appropriately identified. Among the various properties associated with this entity, there is the 'has part' (P527) type, which links it to the three canticles, Inferno,[101] Purgatorio[102], and Paradiso,[103] also identified as separate entities connected to the primary one with the inverse property, that is with the 'part of' property (P361).

Now, in ontological terms, this example poses another important question regarding the nature of the whole with respect to the part and vice versa: would the *Divine Comedy* exist as a work, and thus as an entity, without its component parts? Another philosophical paradox that could address this doubt is the *sorites* paradox, also known as the paradox of the heap, attributed to Eubulides of Miletus, a philosopher from the 4th century BC. The paradox states:

> Given a heap of sand, if we remove one grain from the pile, we still have a pile. Remove another grain: It is still a pile. Remove another grain, and then another: the heap will become smaller and smaller until only one grain of sand remains. At what point is that initial heap no longer a heap?[104]

This paradox has been used over the years and in the philosophical tradition to argue various positions of thought – for example, the comparison between qualitative elements (the heap) and quantitative elements (the number of grains it takes to constitute it) – but it has also been used to reason around diachronic identities and how they persist over time. This is precisely why it is useful to us: to stimulate reflection on how much 'ontological autonomy' the parts possess with respect to a whole and how much the whole itself can have its own ontological autonomy apart from the parts that constitute it. Resources in whole–part relationships are complex precisely because they are diachronic identities (a work consisting of a series, just as a journal or an e-journal has its own life by persisting over time), and at the same time, they can be made up of parts that each, in turn, have their own existence and ontological dignity.

The modelling of bibliographic entities, which has now taken over much of the theorising activity of cataloguing, must take into account these many doubts and resolve them as they arise. And this is precisely the right time to do so, as we are faced for the first time with practical, concrete issues of implementing models that, until a few years ago, we could discuss and delegate to theoretical reflection alone. The introduction of RDA as a cataloguing guide and the implementation of the first real projects for the application of linked open data – with all the issues of defining and choosing ontologies that structuring data according to this paradigm requires – has made it urgent to address and resolve problems of identifying and modelling entities and their relationships, as we could no longer delegate anything to theoretical reflection alone.

Conclusions on the concepts of entity and identity

Managing the conceivability of change and the complexity of a reality that is by no means simple and linear has always been a complicated, often unresolved challenge. The Aristotelian and Stoic answer, which, among the many possibilities, we have preferred here in order to create the conditions for categorisation in the approach to entity analysis, is the one that seems not only most akin to common sense but, in some cases simplifies the process of identifying and thus shaping reality. But of course, no road or solution can claim to answer fully and resolve the case histories that lie behind the varied reality. Having constructed a reference horizon, the only possibility we would have of overcoming the reappearance of cases not contained therein would be constituted by a radical change which 'instead of suffering the entity as ontologically independent of the subject, approaches it as ontologically instituted by the subject itself. In this sense, a community of subjects is constituted around an agreement that establishes, in that specific ontological region or even in that particular ontology, the rules of mutation and permanence, accepting Aristotelian praxis.'[105] It is, therefore, a community that establishes what is essential and what is incidental in the definition of an entity and its relationships; it is a community that, based on its own needs, determines, in a relative and not absolute way, what is change and what is permanence. This relativist position allows us to look at many of the data models and the many ontologies created for the bibliographic world (and beyond) with a different approach, one that starts from the organisational and informational needs these models seek to address. And from this perspective, even certain seemingly questionable modelling choices, such as that of the BIBFRAME model that merges the two entities Work and Expression of FRBR, become sharable if they are functional in meeting a specific need. In the case of BIBFRAME, this is to arrive at a concrete dataset in linked open data, starting from existing data (those in MARC 21) that very rarely allow a real distinction between the two entities.

But even other seemingly irreproachable and effective choices, such as distinguishing the abstract entity of Work in Work and Expression, which has influenced the most popular and well-known bibliographic models – including FRBR and IFLA LRM – can be criticised if viewed outside of certain knowledge, closely tied to the bibliographic record and to respond to the concrete research needs of the end-user. The hypothesis that what the FRBR model defines as Expression may be a different identity of the Work entity, and not an ontologically autonomous entity, becomes a likely hypothesis and, more importantly, open to forms of conversation and comparison.

And it is all this that we will try to keep in mind throughout this study, addressing the many practical applications of theoretical models in a very concrete way.

CHAPTER 2

The World is my Representation

> It is Maya, the veil of deception, which blinds the eyes of mortals, and makes them behold a world of which they cannot say either that it is or that it is not: for it is like a dream; it is like the sunshine on the sand which the traveller takes from afar for water, or the stray piece of rope he mistakes for a snake.
>
> Arthur Schopenhauer, The World as Will and Representation

Introduction

In this section we will discuss the subject of *entities* interpreted as *real-world objects*.[106] We will verify how this formulation has been introduced in the cataloguing field and how much it coincides with, or differs from, the concept of *real-world entity*. While, in Chapter 1, we looked for a philosophical foundation for the increasingly widespread practice of identifying entities in the bibliographic universe, in this chapter we will rely on information technology and in particular object-oriented programming (OOP), which introduces the concept of modelling and managing an object through the definition of attributes and relationships. From there, the research has shifted to the practice of *entity resolution*, already widely used in data management and machine learning, which is the set of methods by which entities are generated and modelled from descriptive profiles included in one or more data sources. The adoption of these methods in the bibliographic field shifts the focal point from the act of cataloguing, which had already expanded toward more general metadatation with the advent of digital data, towards the data web that dictates a new understanding of objects and how to treat them. Entity modelling introduces itself as the third-wave shift in the management of bibliographic data, imposing or requiring a change of perspective not only in the management of information but also in the language we use.

On the Record: the declaration of a new approach to adapting the language of the web

In November 2006, Deanna Marcum, Associate Librarian for Library Services at the Library of Congress, formed a working group to consider the future of bibliographic control in the 21st century. The charge to the Working Group on the Future of Bibliographic Control is summed up in few but crucial points:

- Analyse new perspectives of bibliographic control and other descriptive practices to support effectively library resource management and access in the new era of web technologies.
- Identify and recommend ways through which the library community could collaboratively achieve the goals set to address challenges posed by the new theoretical and practical environments.
- Support the Library of Congress in redefining its role and priorities in this new scenario.

On 9 January 2008 the Library of Congress Working Group on the Future of Bibliographic Control published the report *On the Record* (Library of Congress, 2008),[107] which proposed a number of guiding themes explicitly aimed at libraries, including the transformation of textual description into a usable data set for automatic processing by machines, the need to make data identifiable within the information context of the web, the urgency for data to conform to web technologies and standards and the importance of using a language that is transversal and interoperable within the broader reality of the web:

> Recent data modeling exercises in library and other arenas . . . have provided sophisticated models that highlight important areas for attention. At the same time, the emergence of resource-oriented architectures in the Web environment has made the bibliographic community alert to the benefits of providing access to data resources using simple Web-based protocols and schemas. The combination of these two strands suggests an important future direction for the Library of Congress and for Web-based, network-level bibliographic control. The Working Group envisions a bibliographic infrastructure wherein data about entities of interest (e.g. works, places, people, concepts, chronological periods) are encoded in agreed-upon ways and made available through agreed-upon Web protocols for ready and efficient use by other applications and services. LC and the library community need to find ways of 'releasing the value' of their rich historical investment in semantic data onto the Web.
>
> (Library of Congress, 2008, 32–3)

This was 2008, just two years after Tim Berners-Lee defined in Linked Data his well-known 4-point best practices for publishing and linking structured data on the web, known as the Linked Data principles (Berners-Lee, 2006).[108]

However, deliberations on the need for a new approach to categorising bibliographic information had already begun a few years earlier, with thoughts on using Extendable Markup Language (XML) as a possible replacement for MARC. David Fiander, in an article published in 2001 in *Cataloging & Classification Quarterly*, pointedly titled 'Applying XML to the Bibliographic Description', reflects on how it may be appropriate to extend the choices about metadata languages already used for describing resources on the web (Dublin Core above all) to the cataloguing of traditional material as well, not in the least demonising MARC but identifying elements of its obsolescence and rigidity with respect to more recent descriptive needs (Fiander, 2002). In this article, Fiander proposes some scenarios for the application of XML to bibliographic descriptions, not ignoring the limitations of XML – first and foremost, the fact that it is a metalanguage that provides criteria for describing the format of information and not criteria for structuring the information itself.[109]

Roy Tennant, in the famous and much-cited 2002 article 'MARC Must Die', resumes these critical analyses of MARC to encourage a change of course in the formatting of bibliographic information, pointing out the technological marginalisation that MARC has produced over the years and the hypothesis that the adoption of XML might be a viable alternative (Tennant, 2002). But we have yet to reach the point we wish to emphasise. This process, which evidently began as early as the 1990s, still did not focus on what would later become the turning point in bibliographic data modelling. A mention of the FRBR model, made by Tennant himself in the article cited above, anticipates an alternative to the monolithic character of MARC[110] without fully grasping the opportunity presented by a change not only in technological language (adherence to web languages) but also in a theoretical perspective that is the logical approach to entities and relationships rather than to the record.

Reflections on the topic continue to advance and mature,[111] but it is only with the report *On the Record* that the need to adopt, in the definition of standards and rules, the new web technologies and related languages is officially declared in order to evolve from the rigid, monolithic and domain-limited language of MARC in all its formulations, towards an open and globally understandable language (the wider web). This is an important and highly influential consideration for a significant re-foundation of Universal Bibliographic Control (UBC), which, bumping up against new web technologies and the more general paradigm of linked open data, must change in order to continue to make sense in a network of information that goes far beyond any single national or international domain of knowledge (Library of Congress, 2008).

The section of the report entitled 'The Future of Bibliographic Control' recounts what prompted the Library of Congress to turn serious attention to the future of bibliographic control in a speculative and technological age so very different from the one in which MARC was born. This examination ranges from the 2000 report on the National Research Council's digital strategies[112] to 2004, when the Joint Steering Committee for the Revision of the Anglo-American Cataloguing Rules (JSC AACR) began work on a new code to replace the AACR.[113]

The implementation of RDA is supported and facilitated by two key IFLA works on new bibliographic models – *Functional Requirements for Bibliographic Records* (IFLA FRBR Study Group, 1998 and 2009) and the early studies, dated 2003, for the new IFLA Cataloguing Principles (Tillett, Gömpel and Oehlschläger, 2004).

But let us return to the excerpt from the report *On the Record* and focus on the expression 'resource-oriented architectures in the Web environment'. My reflection has focused precisely on this watershed moment. In the report, as in many other works in the cataloguing field developed in the same era, the term real-world object (RWO), which would later come into widespread use in specialised literature, starting from the second decade of the 21st century, is not yet used. Instead, the resource-oriented concept that is assimilated to RWO seems to be very clear. The report expresses the full realisation that the MARC record, which for 50 years was left unquestioned, cannot simply be replaced by another metadata language – Standard General Markup Language (SGML), XML or similar – but must be rethought and re-established at its roots, introducing also, in the bibliographic context, that approach to the analysis, identification description of a resource or *object* that has already become the protagonist of the semantic web and, before that, of the computer programming language.

The terminology for understanding things in the real world – those of which something can be said and which can be concrete or concepts – is not unambiguous in its formulation but nevertheless clear in its expressive intentions. From the earliest writings in which Tim Berners-Lee outlines the idea of a semantic web, the goal has been to build a mechanism that can describe, in a machine-understandable way, everything in our world: indeed, everything about which something can or should be said.

> In the next step, the Semantic Web will break out of the virtual realm and extend into our physical world. Uniform Resource Identifiers (URI) can point to anything, including physical entities, which means we can use the Resource Description Framework (RDF) language to describe devices such as cell phones and TVs.
>
> (Berners-Lee, Hendler and Lassila, 2001)

The pages of the World Wide Web Consortium (W3C), where the principles and technological components of the semantic web are documented, are significant in showing the terminological evolution of the concept of *real-world thing*; although the terms entity, resource, real-world object and thing have been used interchangeably over time. Below, for illustration purposes only, are some formulations extracted from the W3C pages:

- Resource Description Framework (RDF) Model and Syntax Specification (W3C Working Draft 20 July 1998):[114] 'to facilitate the definition of metadata, RDF will have a class system, not unlike many object-oriented programming and modelling systems. A collection of classes (typically authored for a specific purpose or domain) is called a *schema*. Classes are organised in a hierarchy and offer extensibility through subclass refinement. This way, in order to create a schema slightly different from an existing one, it is not necessary to reinvent the wheel, but one can just provide incremental modifications to the base schema. Through the shareability of schemas RDF will support the reusability of metadata definitions . . . In object-oriented design terminology, resources correspond to objects and properties correspond to instance variables.'
- RDF Primer (10 February 2004):[115] 'The Resource Description Framework (RDF) is a language for representing information about resources in the World Wide Web. It is particularly intended for representing metadata about Web resources, such as the title, author and modification date of a Web page, copyright and licensing information about a Web document or the availability schedule for some shared resource.'
- Resource Description Framework (RDF): 'Concepts and Abstract Syntax (10 February, 2004):[116] The Resource Description Framework (RDF) is a framework for representing information in the Web.'
- OWL Web Ontology Language Guide (10 February 2004):[117] 'The OWL Web Ontology Language is a language for defining and instantiating *Web ontologies*. *Ontology* is a term borrowed from philosophy that refers to the science of describing the kinds of entities in the world and how they are related. An *OWL ontology* may include descriptions of *classes, properties* and their instances.'
- OWL Web Ontology Language Reference (10 February 2004):[118] 'Two OWL class identifiers are predefined, namely the classes owl:Thing and owl:Nothing. The class extension of owl:Thing is the set of all individuals. The class extension of owl:Nothing is the empty set.'
- A Semantic Web Primer for Object-Oriented Software Developers (9 March 2006):[119] 'This note therefore introduces Semantic Web languages

such as RDF Schema and OWL and shows how they can be used in tandem with mainstream object-oriented languages.'

- Cool URIs for the Semantic Web (3 December 2008):[120] 'The *Resource Description Framework* RDF allows users to describe both Web documents and concepts from the real world – people, organisations, topics, things – in a computer-processable way.'
- Paragraph 3 cites the term real-world object right in the title and refers to the objects we talk about on the Web, perhaps for the first time so clearly, as *real-world objects*: 'On the Semantic Web, URIs identify not just Web documents, but also real-world objects like people and cars and even abstract ideas and non-existing things like a mythical unicorn. We call these *real-world objects* or *things*.'
- RDF 1.1 Concepts and abstract Syntax (25 February 2014):[121] 'Any IRI or literal denotes something in the world (the 'universe of discourse'). These things are called resources. Anything can be a resource, including physical things, documents, abstract concepts, numbers and strings; the term is synonymous with 'entity' as it is used in the RDF Semantics specification.'

In these brief references to terminology usage, with the chronological sequence in parentheses, it is interesting to note that in the year 2008, the term *real-world object* is presented in the W3C framework as equivalent to the term *thing*. And it is no coincidence that this follows the 2006 document entitled *A Semantic Web Primer for Object-Oriented Software Developers* (W3C, 2006). This document establishes a kind of collaboration and mutual assistance between object-oriented programming and the semantic web to achieve the goals of software reusability and interoperability. Object-oriented software or object-oriented programming (OOP) refers specifically to programming oriented toward objects. It is a programming paradigm that emerged in the late 1960s that allows software 'objects' to be defined and linked together through the exchange of messages. This approach to programming represents an evolution, both conceptually and chronologically, with respect to sequential or unstructured programming,[122] procedural programming,[123] and modular programming.[124]

From this type of procedural/modular programming, OOP facilitates further interaction by creating and managing simpler objects whose data, usable through specific procedures, are encapsulated in a core not visible to the user. The OOP paradigm is based on the fact that *objects* are modelled and developed to interact with each other reciprocally, exchanging messages but each maintaining its own state and data (HTML.it s.d.) (Meyer, 1997). The Wikipedia page for object-oriented programming enumerates the primary advantages of this programming paradigm as follows:

- the ability to provide natural support for software modelling of real-world or abstract concepts to be reproduced
- easier management and maintenance of large projects
- the feature of organising code in the form of classes to promote modularity and code reuse (Wikipedia, 2022).

W3C (2006) describes points of convergence and divergence between OOP and some components and technological languages of the semantic web in order to construct a hypothesis for co-operation and mutual benefits. This may have been the occasion that also fostered an inevitable hybridisation of terminology, or it may have been the common mechanisms underlying the two paradigms[125] that fostered this sort of osmosis. Indeed, in the Resource Description and Framework Model and Syntax document, this strong derivation between RDF and OOP is stated and it would be the same later for OWL, another essential component of the semantic web. The fact remains that the term *object,* or rather, *real-world object,* which is the cornerstone of OOP, becomes very common in the vocabulary of the semantic web and, subsequently, in bibliographic jargon. In the W3C Library Linked Data Incubator Group Final Report (W3C, 2011), which aims to bring together experts and practitioners of the semantic web to support libraries in making their data interoperable through the linked data paradigm,[126] the expression *real-world* object is used in quotation marks to emphasise perhaps its novelty in the bibliographic field:

> In the Linked Data paradigm, it is generally expected that HTTP URIs will also be used to identify 'real-world objects'.
>
> (W3C, 2011)

In the same year, Tom Heath and Christian Bizer, speaking about the principles of linked data, make a clear and overt use of the term, writing explicitly:

> The first Linked Data principle advocates using URI references to identify, not just Web documents and digital content, but also real-world objects and abstract concepts. These may include tangible things such as people, places and cars, or those that are more abstract, such as the relationship type of knowing somebody, the set of all green cars in the world, or the colour green itself. This principle can be seen as extending the scope of the Web from online resource to encompass any object or concept in the world.
>
> (Heath and Bizer, 2011, 7–8)

This analysis, which takes its inspiration from the *On the Record* report – identified as the declaration of a new orientation toward the language and standards of the web – introduced us to the term and concept of *real-world object.* We will reflect on this in order to understand how its use in cataloguing expresses a substantial change in perspective and methodological approach to metadata, leading us toward modelling usable and reusable objects or entities (entity modelling).

What is a real-world object?

In response to a question received about the meaning and importance of the concept of real-world objects, Karen Coyle published, in her blog Coyle's InFormation on 16 February 2015, a post entitled Real-World Objects. In the comment section on BIBFRAME, Coyle references the post about RWO, calling it 'this mysterious RWO thing' (Coyle, 2015b) and attempts to explain it, or rather, open up a dialogue on the topic. The origin of the term and concept is established in the field of AI and is explained quite clearly. Imagine having to produce robots for our world with which we can communicate about anything that is part of our world, whether a physical object or an abstract concept. Imagine, further, that we must make a list of things in the world, and it must be done in such a way that it is shareable with and understood by the machines. This is the ambition of AI and the semantic web – to create and exploit collections (ontologies) in which anything existing in the world is described in order to converse with machines. Every RWO can be described in an ontology. To capture the meaning of the term real-world object in the context of AI, Coyle uses an example related to the bibliographic world. If we analyse any bibliographic record, we find that the fields of the record can describe the publication object but also the record object itself (as well as many other things, for example the publisher). The publication is an RWO (the object I would like to have in my hands and read), but the record is also an RWO (that textual description that I might request from another library to include in my catalogue). The record has an identifier that in some way allows us to recognise it, while generally speaking (and at the time of the post, in very few cases), other objects do not have their own identifier. Let us verify this by identifying descriptive elements attributable to the different *objects* using a bibliographic record in MARC 21, referencing an English translation of the work *Pinocchio* (*The Adventures of Pinocchio*) by Carlo Collodi. For the sake of simplicity, I will not refer to the bibliographic data models and related *entities* but simply follow Coyle's example and distinguish the object 'record' from the object 'book':

```
=LDR 00725cam a2200217u 4500
=001 8344172
=005 20061211162228.0
=008 810213s1946\\\\nyu\\\\j\\\\\\000\0\eng\\.
=906 \$a0$bc$cpremunv$du$encip$f19$gy-gencatlg
=035 \$9(DLC) 46022697
=010 \\$a 46022697
=040 \$aDLC$cCarP$dDLC
=050 00$aPZ8.L887$bAd 25
=100 1\$aCollodi, Carlo,$d1826–1890.
=240 13$aLe avventure di Pinocchio. English [from old catalogue]
=245 14$aThe adventures of Pinocchio,
=260 \aNew York,$bGrosset & Dunlap$c[1946]
=300 \$ap. cm.
=700 1\$aKredel, Fritz,$d1900–1973,$eillus.
=700 1\$aMurray, Mary Alice, [from old catalogue]$etr.
=991 \$bc-GenColl$hPZ8.L887$iAd 25$p00003427754$tCopy 1$wPREM
```

- Object **Record**: information around the record is recorded in fields 001 (record identifier), 005 (date and time of last update), 035, 010 (control numbers), 040 (information about the agency that created, transcribed into MARC, or modified the record).
- Object **Book**: a description of the book *Pinocchio* recorded in fields 245 (title of publication), 260 (publisher and year of publication information), 300 (physical description of publication), fields 100 and 700 author, illustrators and translators. We also know that the book in our hands is not in the original language of the work but is a translation of it.

Now, if we merely skim the surface of this analysis, we can identify several real-world objects, the characteristics of which we then imagine could be communicated to a machine, blending different descriptive elements of objects into the same discourse. If we delve a little deeper into identifying the objects about which the whole record conveys information, we find that there are at least four more:

- a **person** named Carlo Collodi, born in 1826 and died in 1890, author of the book *Pinocchio*
- a **person** named Fritz Kredel, born in 1900 and died in 1973, illustrator of the book *Pinocchio*
- a **person** named Mary Alice Murray, who was responsible for the English translation of the work *Pinocchio*

- a **publishing house** by the name of Grosset & Dunlap located in New York and which published, presumably in 1946, the book *Pinocchio.*

Looking through that simple bibliographic record, we might find other information, other objects to communicate to our robot, for example, the cataloguing agency, identified through an acronym, along with information about the language used to describe the object book.

These would be the real-world objects that I need to talk to my robot about so that we could, to some extent, understand each other. One of the main problems with the MARC record in terms of its ability to convey an understandable set of messages to a machine is precisely that it fails to distinguish, clearly and unambiguously, 'our metadata and the thing it describes' (Coyle, 2015a), which is precisely what we need to be able to identify and describe in a machine-understandable language.

Why, then, does Karen Coyle examine real-world objects? Wasn't it a term already employed in the field of bibliography?

Real-world objects in cataloguing

The use of the term real-world object in cataloguing is peculiar because it exists and co-exists in a dual sense. The one analysed so far – inherited from the world of AI, the semantic web and object-oriented programming – and the one more traditionally rooted in cataloguing, which utilises the term real-world object as a synonym for *non-bibliographic material, realia* or *non-book* material. The use of the term in the sense of realia or non-book material is widespread and refers to three-dimensional objects such as coins, tools and textiles, which are owned by libraries but do not fall into the traditional categories of book material. The extension of cataloguing rules to all types of information materials and the overlap with other Galleries, Libraries, Archives and Museums (GLAM) domains (consider the heterogeneity of resources managed in an archive or museum) have amplified this need to define methods of managing and cataloguing three-dimensional objects or those otherwise different from traditional objects and to introduce new terminology to identify them. AACR2 devotes chapter 10 to rules for describing three-dimensional artifacts and natural objects. In the glossary, the term realia is defined as 'artifacts or objects found in nature', as opposed to 'copies' and is cross-referenced to the term *object* (Joint Steering Committee for Revision of AACR, 2004). After specifying how the term is to be understood in the context of library classification systems,[127] the Wikipedia entry 'Realia (library science)' adds: 'Recently, the usage of this term has been criticised by librarians based on the usage of the term realia to refer to artistic and historical artifacts and objects, and suggesting the use of the phrase "real-world object" to describe the broader categories of three-dimensional objects in libraries', referring precisely to the real-world object entry in the same online encyclopaedia and proposing here a bit of intermingling with the world of information technology and a still-tentative reference to BIBFRAME.[128]

In 2019 the use of the term real-world object in specialised literature is still ambiguous: one of the most apparent cases of this ambiguity is Jessica Simpson's article, notably entitled 'Real-World Objects: Conceptual Framework and University Library Consortium Study' (Simpson, 2019). The study starts precisely from a reflection on the terminological gap regarding three-dimensional objects in library collections (and here again, the reference is to terms such as non-bibliographic material, realia, non-book materials and non-library materials) and proposes the adoption of the term real-world object for this material, a term (and here the conceptual confusion) already used in object-oriented programming for AI, absorbed by the MARC Standard and into the BIBFRAME vocabulary as an attribute of a three-dimensional object. Despite this initial reference to the meaning expressed in the AI and OOP domains, the rest of the article continues to associate the term with realia, thus with what is simply different from the more traditional book material.

In the same years, however, the term real-world object was officially and definitively absorbed into library jargon. In 2015, the Program for Cooperative Cataloging (PCC) Task Group on URIs in MARC (URI TG) was formed to identify and direct choices for enriching the MARC record with identifiers (URIs). The group's work lays the groundwork for facilitating the transition of MARC data to linked data. Among the various proposals and solutions is one to include a new subfield $1 for the RWO's URI record[129] in the fields related to names, titles, subjects, classifications, etc.[130]

In 2017, MARC Proposal No. 2017–08 entitled Use of Subfield $0 and $1 to Capture Uniform Resource Identifiers (URIs) in the MARC 21 format, was published. The purpose of the proposal is to outline a criterion for enriching bibliographic and authority records with URI identifiers in a way that is clearly distinguishable:

- URIs identifying a record or authority describing an object (URI as a pointer to a description)
- URIs identifying the object itself (sometimes referred to as real-world object or RWO, whether real or conceptual).

To this end, the document proposes limiting the use of subfield $0[131] to URIs and control numbers that refer to *the record describing a thing* and to define a new subfield, $1, for URIs that refer directly to the *real-world object*. The proposal becomes operational and Appendix A, 'Control Subfields of MARC 21 Bibliographic Format' officially introduces this important distinction between identifiers for descriptions and identifiers for RWOs:

> *$0 – Authority record control number or standard number*
> Subfield $0 contains the system control number of the related authority or classification *record*, or a standard identifier. These identifiers may be in the form of text or a Uniform Resource Identifier (URI). If the identifier is text, the control number or identifier is preceded by the appropriate MARC Organisation code (for a related authority record) or the Standard Identifier source code (for a standard identifier scheme), enclosed in parentheses. When the identifier is given in the form of a Web retrieval protocol, e.g. HTTP URI, no preceding parenthetical is used.
>
> Subfield $0 may contain a URI that identifies a name or label for an entity. When dereferenced, the URI points to information describing that name. A URI that directly identifies the entity itself is contained in subfield $1.
>
> *$1 – Real-world object URI*
> Subfield $1 contains a URI that identifies an entity, sometimes referred to as a thing, a real-the RWO, whether actual or conceptual. When dereferenced, the URI points to a description of that entity. A URI that identifies a name or label for an entity is contained in $0.

This distinction, in a way, completes the circle by responding to the perplexity expressed by Karen Coyle, common among many experts in metadata and data modelling, with respect to the lack of distinction in the bibliographic and authority record between 'our metadata and the thing it describes'. I will return to this, along with some examples of the use of the two different types of URIs, later in this chapter. It is also important to emphasise here that the work of the PCC Task Group on URIs in MARC, initiated at the behest of the PCC Policy Committee (PoCo),[132] has involved a broad library community, with official or supporting participation from important and influential institutions in the field of metadata standards definition, including Library of Congress, OCLC, PCC, British Library, National Library of Medicine, University of Alberta, Cornell University, Stanford University, German National Library, George Washington University, University of Washington and several other institutions and expert groups. Many of the libraries participating in the group are also members of the Share-VDE community and have actively participated by sharing experiences, proposals and concrete examples of data from Share.

Real-world objects and real-world entities

Complicating the whole terminological picture is the use of the term real-world entity,[133] often as an alternative to or in conjunction with the term real-world object. Real-world entity is defined on some sites as an entity with a physical location within the universe,[134] thus with a definition that, in itself, does not suggest anything different from real-world object: *object* and *entity* are used interchangeably. As an example, consider the use of the two terms within a page of each other in 'Linked Data; Evolving the Web into a Global Data Space' (Heath and Bizer, 2011):

- The first Linked Data principle advocates using URI references to identify, not just Web documents and digital content, but also real-world objects and abstract concepts. These may include tangible things such as people, places and cars, or those that are more abstract, such as the relationship type of knowing somebody, the set of all green cars in the world, or the colour green itself. This principle can be seen as extending the scope of the Web from online resources to encompass any object or concept in the world. [p. 7].
- To publish data on the Web, the items in a domain of interest must first be identified. These are the things whose properties and relationships will be described in the data and may include Web documents as well as real-world entities and abstract concepts. As Linked Data builds directly on Web architecture, the Web architecture term *resource* is used to refer to these *things of interest*, which are, in turn, identified by HTTP URIs. [p. 9][135]

And the same is true of much of the literature that addresses these topics. The terms real-world object and real-world entity often appear to refer to the same concept. Finding a precise definition of the two terms is complex, so the exploration continued by analysing the individual terms *entity* and *object*, especially in an ontological context. Consulting the University of Southern California (USC) Information Sciences Institute website[136] aided the investigation of these concepts, though it did not offer a clear and unequivocal definition of whether they represent semantically coincidental or wholly different concepts. However, it did allow for hypothesising a definition, which I will attempt to elucidate. One assertion made in the many resources explored on this website refers to a practice used in some 'top-level' ontologies that distinguishes 'physical objects' from 'abstract entities'. This practice stems from an idea of metaphysical diversity between an object with its own physicality and an abstract concept and in this sense, might lead one to think that real-world object means the physical objects of the real-world and real-world entity means the abstract entities of the same world. But looking back at all the sources where the two terms are used, often with the specification that, in either case, we are always talking about concrete objects or abstract concepts, I had to abandon this path.

A study entitled 'Unsupervised Entity Resolution on Multi-type Graphs' presented at the 15th International Semantic Web Conference (ISWC) and published in the proceedings of the same conference,[137] provided some progress in resolving the doubt about the sameness of the two terms. The abstract of this study states: 'Entity resolution is the task of identifying all mentions that represent the same real-world entity within a knowledge base or across multiple knowledge bases' (Zhu et al., 2016). This assertion is not a definition but in some ways recalls ideas and concepts discussed thus far, where 'mentions' refer to all the representations that the same entity, denoted by the term real-world entity, can take. But again, in literature, especially regarding the semantic web and in particular machine learning, this terminology is often inverted, going so far as to define the *entity* as a sort of representation of the *real-world object*. This is the impression left by the following assertion, which refers to the methods of entity resolution processes (which we will discuss later). 'They [the ER methods] focus on transforming the input profiles into an accurate set of entities that is as close as possible to the corresponding real-world objects' (Papadakis et al., 2021).

Here, it seems evident that what is intended by 'profiles' is the descriptions of entities; by 'entities', the representations (collected in a database of entities) of something real; and by 'real-world objects', that 'reality' which we seek to represent.

However, despite the shuffling of cards over the use of this terminology, a way to make sense of the very subtle semantic distinction between these terms appears to have been identified, albeit it is still not entirely clear. We know that we live in a world made up of entities of various kinds (physical and conceptual 'things'), we know that these entities are often highly complex, and we know that no system[138] that aims to represent them can seek to do so entirely. Indeed, there will always be an aspect of an entity that is not easy to grasp or that the context for which that 'thing' is described does not require representation. What if there is the same semantic relationship between the expressions *real-world entity* and *real-world object* that we identified in Chapter 1 of this study between *entity* and *identity*? From this hypothesis, my research begins again, returning to the concept of real-world object as modelled in the OOP language.

Real-world objects in object-oriented programming

We have already discussed what OOP is. Here, we try to better understand the mechanism and logic of this programming methodology by providing some useful elements to understand why this programming is so relevant to the topics discussed in this chapter.[139]

Object-oriented programming, or more simply object programming, is based on defining *classes* that contain the declaration of data structures and the procedures that operate on them. The class forms a blueprint for what will later be the *objects* derived from it, a kind of template that defines the shape of the object, a mould from which to form individual objects later. A class defines something in terms of:

- *State*: the variables that constitute that kind of thing.
- *Behaviour*: the behaviours (methods, procedures) that such a thing has.

This model, defined by the class, is then applied to the objects created from the same class.

We will use the class 'Dog' to exemplify some of these mechanisms and hint at some of the pillars of OOP, which are also common in the criteria and principles of ontology modelling.

To construct a class *Dog*, I will define a state (of attributes) such as:

- breed
- height
- life span
- colour
- hair type
- coat.

And behaviours such as:

- runs
- barks
- bites
- wags tail.

Thus, the class provides a form for describing the objects that are part of it. The class here does not say anything about the specific breed; it specifies colour, but only that the object (the instance) I will create using that model (that class) will have attributes such as breed, height, average age, etc. So, the class indicates the profile of the objects it will contain.

From this class 'Dog,' then, I want to create the individual instances, so I use the template that the class provides for me, to create the individual objects, the instances. If I wanted to create the object 'Bobby, John's dog' I will take that form which is the class Dog and make the mould that will contain this information:

- breed
- height
- life span
- colour
- hair type
- coat.

And behaviours of the type:

- runs
- barks
- bites
- wags tail.

that define a specific dog, assigning values that establish properties (I will define variables for the real-world object 'Bobby, John's dog'):

- breed: beagle
- height: 36 cm
- average age: not defined
- colour: red
- hair type: short
- coat: two-tone.

and behaviours of the type:

- runs: slowly
- barks: in a cavernous tone
- bites
- wags tail.

These features are the variables and methods of the instance.

Now, to this instance, I could add a variable or method that is not in the Dog class, for example:

- name: Bobby
- owner: John
- ear: cropped.

These, too, are instance variables (as is the height of 36 cm), handled at the single instance level because they are not necessarily present in the model offered by the Dog class.

But the Dog class could itself have class variables and methods, that is, attributable to the whole class and not to the individual, so, for example:

- species: mammals
- diet: carnivorous
- family: canids
- trainable: yes (and this distinguishes the dog class from the wolf class, which are still canids but not trainable).

These are class variables and methods because they refer to the entire class of dogs. Obviously, each dog instance will inherit these features without them being specified for individuals each time.

To simplify entity modelling through object creation, the programmer can also define subclasses and then a model for all those exemplars that have common characteristics but may have something more than or different from the class.

Connected to the class Dog, three subclasses are created, for example:

1 Small dogs: weight between 5 and 10 kg; height between 25 and 35 cm
2 Medium-sized dogs: weight between 10 and 25 kg; height between 35 and 50 cm
3 Large dogs: weight between 25 and 45 kg; height between 50 and 70 cm.

To model the entity 'Bobby, John's dog,' and knowing that he is 36 cm and weighs 12 kg, I could define him as an instance of the subclass medium-sized dogs: in this case, I could not include the weight and height variables at all, assuming that, in general, these can be derived from the variables of the weight and height subclass (thus, Bobby will certainly be between 10 and 25 kg, and between 35 and 50 cm). This mechanism of *inheritance* is one of the pillars of OOP.

Why are we, in this context, interested in talking about classes and instances of classes, hence objects? Because in the OOP context, an item of software is created from (and as a representation of) something real in the world, a real-world object. The programmer is called upon to reproduce in a different dimension (that of software, precisely) the real world, with its many objects (whether physical or conceptual). And just as objects in the real world, so too real-world objects, all have a *state* (attributes that identify them) and a *behaviour* (the ability to do something).[140] Likewise, software objects must be able to be modelled with a state and a behaviour. Thus, an object is a software package of data and related methods representing a real-world object. Why does it represent a real-world object and not a real-world entity? Can we imagine that it is not just a coincidence that most of the time (but unfortunately not always) in OOP, AI and the semantic web, we talk about real-world object and not real-world entity? It is precisely OOP that helps us understand the reasons for this choice of terminology, thus leading us back to what was already discussed in Chapter 1, namely, the complexity of the entity in its various identities.

Object-oriented programming declares, quite explicitly, the difficulty or even impossibility of representing in a software object the complexity of an entity. The software object is the representation of a real-world object and not of a real-world entity because the entity, in its richness, can never be represented exhaustively. OOP constructs objects that represent a particular 'face' of the entity, and only that one is suitable and functional for the specific context in which it is used. The definition of a class for 'library user' will have attributes that are functional for creating instances that represent a person in his being a library user: whether the instance 'John Smith' has blood type O RH+ and weighs 60 kg or 120 kg, for the purpose for which I am creating that instance, is not needed. It will serve biographical attributes related to user type and behaviours (has fines to pay/does not have fines to pay; is admitted to the manuscript room/is not admitted to the manuscript room), but not physical or weight characteristics. If I am modelling, on the other hand, a 'hospital patient' object, I will have to include in the attributes of the 'John Smith' instance his physical characteristics, including weight, height, blood type. This is another pillar of OOP, called *abstraction*, and it helps us focus attention on our topic and on the only seemingly subtle difference between real-world object (John Smith in his being a library user or in his being a hospital patient) and real-world entity, (John Smith in his complex and multifaceted entity).

Computer science, object-oriented programming, does not have the unrealisable ambition of representing all at once the thousand characteristics of an entity but *selects* those suitable for the context in which that object is to be dropped (hiding or ignoring altogether the many other characteristics of state and behaviour attributable to that same entity).[141] Simply thinking about everyday life, one can imagine how many hundreds of times each of us is presented with a different 'interface'. I can be an employee of a company and be modelled as such in my software system. At the same time, I can be a university student, or I might be a member of a gym and be part of a band performing in clubs; I can be the parent of a child attending school and at the same time the library user, bookstore customer, post office user; I might be present on an insurance company's database and as a bank customer. Each of these 'interfaces' belongs to the same entity, but no software application would ever have the ambition to represent all of them, merely constructing objects, each of which could represent a particularity of that entity, its way of posing, its different identity. Here again, we have touched on another of the pillars of OOP, namely *polymorphism*, defined as the ability to use the same name to do different things or, more clearly, the ability to represent 'many forms of the single entity'.[142] And how much all this brings us back to the issues addressed in Chapter 1, where the different cases of the same entity expressing many identities are analysed? Doesn't what was said bring us back to how to deal, in the cataloguing field, with cases of pseudonymy, heteronymy, alter egos, or even just variations in titles or names due, simply, to the use of different alphabets?

Entity resolution and entity modelling[143]

Object-oriented programming has thus helped us to find a possible distinction between the entity and the object, between real-world entities and real-world objects. The mechanism of 'creating' an object,[144] relating it to something else, so typical of this programming paradigm, is not at all different from the new way of understanding the cataloguer's activity in the bibliographic universe, increasingly oriented toward identifying the entities that participate in this universe and their modelling. Modelling an object means, therefore, identifying those salient features that make it what it is and that enable it to be or do something in the world, at least in a given context (Possemato, 2018; Schreur and Possemato, 2019; Possemato, 2022).[145] If we agree with the image of a complex entity that, by its own volition – as in the cited cases of pseudonymity, for example, or simply due to cultural, linguistic, or even qualitative diversity (with reference to the data describing it) – is present in different forms from the same information source or in different sources, we can imagine how complex the mechanism of entity (or real-world entity) identification is. But forgoing the attempt to describe fully the complexity of the entity does not mean giving up the necessity to *identify* it in its many expressions. Computer science accepts that there are limits to representing the complex personality of Lewis Carroll in a single object, and it will probably take two or more objects (as Charles Lutwidge Dodgson of *The Game of Logic* and as Lewis Carroll of *Alice's Adventures in Wonderland*) to do so. But in a more complex reality, such as that of the semantic web and AI, can we renounce the idea of recognising the same entity behind these two profiles? This is exactly the task of entity resolution (ER), that of identifying all mentions that represent the same entity within the same knowledge base or in multiple knowledge bases (Zhu et al., 2016).

Entity resolution (ER)

At the heart of all data integration, cleansing and search processes lies the complex mechanism of entity resolution, which is the ability to identify the same and unique entity among a thousand different expressions, representations, profiles and identities.

One of the pages on the IBM website presents definitions of some of the key concepts necessary to understand what ER is. We will look at how much all of this concerns and pertains to the area of modelling the bibliographic universe. I believe it is useful to summarise these basic concepts here, not least because they seem almost to confirm the line explored and proposed in the first chapter of this discussion:

- **entity:** an entity is a collection of one or more identities that represent the same person, organisation, place or item. Entities are stored in the entity database.
- **identity**: identity is a collection of attributes from a data source that represent a person, organisation, place or item.
- **attributes**: attributes are characteristics or traits that describe a person, organisation, place or item. Common attributes include information such as names, addresses, phone numbers, credit card numbers, tax identification numbers and licence numbers.

This definition of some key ER terms has been freely translated and revised from the IBM[146] website, but is obviously extendable to everything we have so far defined as real-world objects, referring to any type of entity. The same website helps summarise the most significant macro-phases of an ER process, which obviously can be much more complex than as outlined here.

Entity resolution is the process that establishes entities and detects useful relationships to identify them. ER processes execute entity resolution while processing data related to the different identities, in different stages, which are only briefly summarised here. The process as a whole generates a database of entities in which data identifying an entity is recorded for use (searches, statistics, etc.) or even to iterate the 'entity-fication' processes and make them increasingly effective. To make these steps more familiar, we can imagine that the input data used for entity resolution are bibliographic records or authority records from a cataloguing database, and that the entity database is, for example in the Share-VDE project, what is defined as a Cluster Knowledge Base (CKB).[147]

1 **Recognition**: In this initial stage of the process, data from the various entity descriptions (think of bibliographic and authority data) are validated, optimised and reclaimed/standardised where possible. The

criteria and frameworks for these procedures are those of the domain or otherwise fine-tuned before the recognition process starts. In the case of bibliographic databases, for example, 'quality rules' are primarily defined based on the cataloguing rules and standards in use by the entity that produced the data.

2. **Resolution**: This is the stage where identities are broken down into entities. After the data values in the identity records have been cleaned out, standardised, or qualitatively improved, sophisticated search and data analysis algorithms are applied. The purpose is to compare (matching) the input data values (attributes and relationships) with existing entities in the database to determine whether it is the same entity or a different one. As mentioned, this step in the process is often reiterative, because each new description, each new identity, is checked to activate matching procedures with the existing database.
3. **Relationship**: During entity resolution, the detection of relationships, which are an indispensable element for entity identification, also usually takes place. At this stage those relationships that are of interest for this identification are also detected and highlighted, as opposed to weaker and less relevant relationships.[148]
4. **Score:** During entity resolution, the system calculates how well the attributes of an incoming identity match the attributes of an existing entity. The results of this computational analysis are expressed in scores that the system uses to resolve identities into entities and detect relationships between entities.

The starting point, therefore, for the processes of entity resolution consists of a set, a collection of information that expresses the identity of a particular real-world entity. This unit of information, in the context of ER, is often referred to as a *profile* and is reminiscent of the result of that abstraction we found as a pillar of OOP. In the work *The Four Generations of Entity Resolution* (Papadakis et al., 2021), the authors define a profile as a subset of a data source that provides information about a real-world object. They define an entity as a set of profiles related to the same real-world object.

> **Definition 2.1** A profile p_i is a subset of a data source DS, i.e. p_i ADS, providing information about a real-world object. An entity e_k is a set of profiles, i.e. $e_k = \{ p_i, \ldots, p_n \}$, where all $p_i, \ldots, p_n$ pertain to the same real-world object.[149]
>
> (Papadakis et al., 2021, 5)

Profiles are used to organise data of very different types: structured data (such as those in relational databases), semi-structured data (such as knowledge bases) or unstructured data (for example, full text). In an ever-widening information context, such as the one that the semantic web proposes, where databases are heterogeneous and not necessarily authoritative, profiles (which we might identify, for example, with bibliographic records or even with the authority records of a library) are often dirty, incomplete, incorrect or redundant. The success of ER is being able to identify and integrate very different profiles that actually refer to the same entity. The success of these processes depends very much on the quality of the data source, which in the same work, cited above, is classified as follows:

- a data source containing at most one profile per entity is termed *clean (Clean DS,* where DS stands for *data source).* An example of a clean data source in the bibliographic context is one in which only one authority record exists for the same entity: the Library of Congress Name Authority File (LCNAF) proposes only one profile for the author Aeschylus, identified by the URI http://id.loc.gov/authorities/names/n79055702
- a data source containing multiple profiles for the same entity is defined as *dirty (Dirty DS).* An example of a dirty data source in the bibliographic context is one in which several authority records exist for the same entity. The VIAF source proposes more than four profiles for *Aeschylus,* including:

  http://viaf.org/viaf/268526195
  http://viaf.org/viaf/78769732
  http://viaf.org/viaf/104143945
  http://viaf.org/viaf/267617710
  http://viaf.org/viaf/750154380930930290321
  http://viaf.org/viaf/261472932
  and several other profiles.

Therefore, if we define as duplicates two profiles related to the same entity found in the same data source, then we can say that a clean data source is one in which no duplicates exist; meanwhile, a data source is dirty when duplicate profiles exist. In reality, the classification of a source is far more complex than this exemplification. In the same data source we can find instances of very well-modelled entities and others with multiple profiles. The 'veracity'[150] of a source is a complex parameter that relies on numerous algorithms and whose success relies on a rather high percentage on the quality of the source data.

The goal of processes focusing on data accuracy is to link profiles or descriptions of different entities *(record linkage)* and deduplication, i.e. to identify duplicates and resolve them. Following the steps of the schema of Papadakis et al., through which the entity resolution flow is accomplished, we can outline the process in the following way.

Entity resolution flow: 1. Schema alignment

Records from different sources may adhere to different metadata schemas, or even just be expressed in different formats following different cataloguing rules, or inexact beings. Consider Parsifal[151], the discovery portal of integration and publication in linked open data of the bibliographic catalogues of the Union of Roman Ecclesiastical Libraries[152] (URBE) where entity identification processes had to deal with very complex cases of cataloguing dissimilarity. An example is the block of bibliographic and authority records (of which only the personal name type access point is reported here) used in the stages of identification of the entity *Egidio d'Assisi.*

100 0 $aAegidius Assisias,$cb.,$dm.1262
100 0 $aGiles of Assisi,$cO.F.M., b.,$dcirca 1190–1262
100 1 $aAegidius Assisiensis,$cO.F.M
100 0 $aAegidius Assisiensis,$cb., $dm. 1262
100 0 $aAegidius Assisiensis,$cbeato,$dcirca 1190–1262
100 0 $aAegidius Assisiensis,$cO.F.M., b.,$dcirca 1190–
100 0 $aEgidio d'Assisi,$cb.,$dm.1262
100 0 $aAegidius Assisiensis,$cfrancescano, b.,$dcirca 1190–
100 0 $aEgidio d'Assisi,$cbeato.,$dmorto 1262
100 0 $aEgidio d'Assisi,$cb..,$dmorto 1262
100 0 $aAegidius Assisiensis,$cb., $dmorto 1262
100 0 $aAegidius Assisiensis,$cbeato,$dm. 1262

Schema alignment, in this case, can mean standardising all title formulas associated with the name (reported here in the $c of the MARC record) or dating formulas (ca., circa; m., morto) through a mapping process with existing vocabularies or through the creation of a controlled list of terms designed for the purpose, as, for example, in Table 2.1 on the next page.

This alignment reduces the amount of data to be compared, and thus simplifies the process:

(1) Aegidius Assisias, beato, morto 1262
(2) Giles of Assisi, francescano, beato, circa 1190–1262
(3) Aegidius Assisiensis, francescano
(4) Aegidius Assisiensis, beato, morto 1262

(5) Aegidius Assisiensis, beato, circa 1190–1262
(6) Aegidius Assisiensis, francescano, beato, circa 1190–
(7) Egidio d'Assisi, beato, morto 1262

Table 2.1 *Standardisation of title formulas associated with the name*

Access points from the original records	Access point after alignment
100 0 $aAegidius Assisias,$cb.,$dm.1262.	Aegidius Assisias, beato, morto 1262 (1)
100 0 $aGiles of Assisi,$cO.F.M., b.,$dcirca 1190–1262	Giles of Assisi, francescano, beato, circa 1190–1262 (2)
100 1 $aAegidius Assisiensis,$cO.F.M.	Aegidius Assisiensis, francescano (3)
100 0 $aAegidius Assisiensis,$cb., $dm. 1262	Aegidius Assisiensis, beato, morto 1262 (4)
100 0 $aAegidius Assisiensis,$cbeato,$dcirca 1190–1262	Aegidius Assisiensis, beato, circa 1190–1262 (5)
100 0 $aAegidius Assisiensis,$cO.F.M., b.,$dcirca 1190–.	Aegidius Assisiensis, francescano, beato, circa 1190– (6)
100 0 $aEgidio d'Assisi,$cb.,$dm.1262	Egidio d'Assisi, beato, morto 1262 (7)
100 0 $aAegidius Assisiensis,$cfrancescano, b.,$d circa 1190–.	Aegidius Assisiensis, francescano, beato, circa 1190– (6)
100 0 $aEgidio d'Assisi,$cbeato.,$dmorto 1262	Egidio d'Assisi, beato, morto 1262 (7)
100 0 $aEgidio d'Assisi,$cb..,$dmorto 1262	Egidio d'Assisi, beato, morto 1262 (7)
100 0 $aAegidius Assisiensis,$cb., $dmorto 1262	Aegidius Assisiensis, beato, morto 1262 (4)
100 0 $aAegidius Assisiensis,$cbeato,$dm. 1262	Aegidius Assisiensis, beato, morto 1262 (4)

Entity resolution flow: 2. Blocking

Blocking is intended to reduce the time and cost of comparing each new profile with those already existing in the entity database. Let us imagine that those below represent a very limited part of an entity database: in order for entity identification and grouping of the various expressions representing each new profile to occur, one would have to go through an entire list and do comparative (matching) operations on each existing profile:

Aefsky, Fern
Aegean Foundation. Scientific Symposium
Aegean Foundation. Scientific Symposium (4. :, 1987 : London).
Aegean Foundation. Scientific Symposium (5. :, 1988 : Istanbul).
Aegean Foundation. Scientific Symposium (6. :, 1988 : Columbus, Ohio).
Aeger, Carl
Aegerter, Emmanuel, 1883–1945
Aegidius in Bocholtz
Aegidius in Cesaro, O.F.M.Conv.
Aegidius Assisias, beato, m.1262

Aegidius Assisiensis, beato, circa 1190-1262
Aegidius Assisiensis, beato, m. 1262
Aegidius Assisiensis, beato, morto 1262
Aegidius Assisiensis, O.F.M.
Aegidius Assisiensis, francescano, beato, circa 1190-
Aegidius Aureaevallensis, m.1251
Aegidius Bononiensis, sec. XIII.
Aegidius Corbeiensis, 1140-1224
Aegidius de Aurelianus, 12-
Aegidius de Fuscarariis, -1289
Aegidius de Lessines, O.P., 1230-1304
Aegidius de Lessines, O.P., 1230-c.1304
Aegidius de Lessines, O.P., f. 1278
Aegidius de Lessinia, 1230-1304
Aegidius de Lessinis, O.P., 1230-ca.1304
Aegidius de Lessinis, O.P., 1230-circa 1304
Aegidius de Moncourt, O.M.
Aegidius Denique, attivo 1684-1728
Aegidius Gotthardus, O.E.S.A., secolo XVII
Aegidius Gutbier, attivo 1663-1667
Aegidius, magister
Aegidius, Magister, secolo XIV
Aegidius Maria a Sancto Iosepho, s., 1729-1812
Aegidius Maria a Sancto Ioseph, santo, 1729-1812
Aegidius, Parisiensis, 1162-circa 1220
Aegidius Romanus, 1243-1316
Aegidius Romanus, arcivescovo di Bourges, circa 1243-1316
Aegidius Romanus, c. 1243-1316
Aegidius Romanus, O.E.S.A., 1243?-1316
Aegidius Romanus, O.E.S.A., 1244-1316
Aegidius Romanus, vescovo di Bourgesdca, 1243-1316
Aegidius Viterbiensis, cardinale, 1469-1532

The process limits candidate matches to only similar profiles, considered as such according to certain criteria. In the example above, possible matching candidates include all profiles containing *Aegidius - Assisiensis,* those containing *Aegidius – beato – morto 1262,* and hence, the possible *Egidio – beato – morto 1262*. As a result, it increases the overall efficiency of data processing time. Creating blocks of candidate profiles compresses data, reduces duplicates, focuses attention on similar profiles and then allows for more efficient matching operations.

Entity resolution flow: 3. Matching

At this stage each new profile is compared with existing ones, grouped into blocks and classified as possible candidates to determine through different matching logics (e.g. that of *similarity score*) which profiles truly belong to the same entity. In this phase, each profile subjected to comparison processes is classified with different levels of alignment, such as 'match,' 'non-match,' 'uncertain,' or 'full-match,' 'non-match,' 'near-match'.

Entity resolution flow: 4. Clustering

Clustering is the stage in which the entity becomes a 'cluster'. Identification of the entity concludes by analysing, with the previously mentioned mechanisms, the various forms, hence the various profiles with which the same entity presents itself. The cluster thus produced is usually used to repeat the same operations on external databases, employing other data and therefore enriching the profile created for the entity through the reuse of global and collective information. The *Egidio d'Assisi* example above acquires descriptive data not initially present in the local database (below are some possible forms captured from the data.bnf.fr source):[153]

Aegidius Assisiensis (1190?–1262) (latin)
Egidius de Assisio (1190?–1262) (latin)
Aegidius Assisias (1190?–1262) (latin)
Egidio d'Assisi (1190?–1262) (italien)
Frère Égide (1190?–1262) (français)
Egidius d'Assise (1190?–1262)
Egidius von Assisi (1190?–1262)

As mentioned, entity resolution processes are much more complex than described here, but this form of simplification helps us understand the power of these mechanisms and their effectiveness, especially with respect to multiple profiles coming from heterogeneous and numerically relevant sources.

Entity modelling

Entity resolution allows us to identify entities, real things in the world, from descriptions contained in one or more sources through processes of data comparison. Among millions of information sources, millions of profiles that could refer to the same entity, we look for those useful in defining the object, in identifying it. These processes rarely rely on single data, or on profiles with little information: the more feature-rich the profile used, the more attributes are expressed in defining a particular object described, the more chance of identifying it. But for a machine to identify an object, it must first know its contours; it must know what to look for and how it expects to find that object. It must know, then, how that thing is *formed*. This is not true just for machines, but for humans as well.

When we search for an object on the web, on a commercial site, for example, we try to construct a query string that contains keywords referring to possible attributes of the object sought. Searching for a backpack for a 15-inch laptop, size 45 × 30 cm, made of waterproof fabric, colour blue, I have an object in mind and I translate that image into attributes (size, type of fabric, colour) and relationships (relating to the PC, as a PC-carrier). I build a profile that will be used by the search engine to compare the given attributes with its own metadata, identify the object of likely interest and elect it as a candidate. The construction of the object – the definition of the profile in a way that is, above all, responsive to the needs of identification – is an activity of the utmost importance, especially in an open and almost boundless context such as the web. And to understand what entity modelling is, let us start again from that object which OOP creates by attributing a state and a behaviour, and that the semantic web reformulates, enriches so as to make it both usable and understandable to machines. The mechanism of object creation in OOP starts with the definition of a model, what we have defined as a kind of matrix or template and which is used to create many instances that take precisely the form from that model. These matrices or classes, with their state and behaviour characteristics, can be built specifically for the individual object, within the context of a specific project making those objects little 'usable' outside the original context, or they can be defined globally, as a result of an agreement that a community decides to share. Ontologies and data models, in all the contexts in which they are used, are exactly that – a matrix that defines the form that representations of a real-world object will take in the manner that is as faithful as possible to the entity being represented, in accordance with what is defined by a community.

Models and ontologies of the bibliographic universe

Aware of the complexities of entities, we set aside any aspiration to represent them in their entirety, choosing instead a criterion of *utility* to filter or select useful characters for a given purpose. For what purposes do I represent this entity? In the context of the cataloguing discipline, the definition of cataloguing principles and rules, the choice of headings (which later become access points) and the definition of the entities to be represented, are all factors closely related to the objectives and functions of the catalogue, which, starting with Cutter as early as the end of the 19th century, have been strongly influenced by the needs of the user (user's tasks). In his work *Rules for a Printed Dictionary Catalogue,* Cutter defines the objectives of the catalogue precisely in terms of its usefulness to users (Cutter, 1876):

1. Enable a person to find a book of which they already know
   a. Author
   b. Title
   c. Subject
2. Show what the library possesses
   d. By a certain author
   e. On a specific subject
   f. In a particular literary genre
3. Facilitate the choice of a book
   g. through an edition (in a bibliographical sense)
   h. by means of characterisation (in a literary or topical sense).

This criterion of user needs has guided all subsequent revisions of cataloguing models and rules as well as the definition of the entities needed to support those needs. In her doctoral thesis *Study of Library Data Models in the Semantic Web Environment* Sofia Zapounidou outlines, in Table 2.2 opposite, the relationship between user needs and the definition of objects useful to satisfy those needs (Zapounidou, 2020, 38). This in the lead up to the 2016 revision of the Statement of International Cataloguing Principles (ICP).

To expand the overview of bibliographic models related to user needs, we could add Table 2.3, which refers to IFLA LRM[154] and BIBFRAME:[155]

The input to define principles, rules, models and ultimately ontologies comes, first of all from what users expect to experience from using the catalogue. There is extensive literature on this topic, which I would like to summarise with what Mauro Guerrini calls to mind in the introduction to the Italian version of *The Intellectual Foundation of Information Organisation*, where, tracing the work of Elaine Svenonius and the theoretical and methodological approach especially in the author's in-depth examination of the goals of information retrieval systems: 'Svenonius poses an important premise: bibliographic *axiology* (the goals of cataloguing) precedes, not follows, bibliographic *ontology* (the set of entities, attributes and relationships)' (Svenonius, 2008).

At least in the bibliographic field, those who are tasked with defining cataloguing models, modelling knowledge, do so with a clear understanding of the purpose of each element that becomes part of that model. I think it is interesting to cite two examples of evolutionary proposals of an existing model: one, that of Rahmatollah Fattahi, which never materialised in the terms suggested by the author[156] but was already in line with what, just a couple of years later, would become the FRBR model; the other, that of the Library of Congress, with the inclusion of the Hub in the BIBFRAME model, as recently as June 2021.

Table 2.2 *Sofia Zapounidou's outline of user needs, their definitions and the entities identified to address each*

Definition in	Objectives/User tasks	Entities acknowledged
Cutter, 1876	Finding Collocating Selecting	Book Edition Author Subject
Lubetzky, 1960	Find Collocate	Work Edition Publication Author
Paris Principles, 1961	Find Collocate	Work Edition Book Personal Author Corporate Body
FRBR, 1998, 2008	Find Identify Select Acquire/Obtain	**Group 1** (Work, Expression, Manifestation, Item) **Group 2 (**Person, Corporate Body) **Group 3** (Concept, Object, Event, Place)
ICP, 2009	Find Identify Select Acquire/Obtain Navigate	**Group 1** (Work, Expression, Manifestation, Item) **Group 2** (Person, Family, Corporate Body) **Group 3** (Concept, Object, Event, Place)
ICP, 2016	Find Identify Select Acquire/Obtain Navigate and Explore	**Group 1** (Work, Expression, Manifestation, Item) **Group 2** (Person, Family, Corporate Body) **Group 3** (Thema, Nomen)

Table 2.3 *Table extension on user needs, their definitions and the entities identified to address each in IFLA LRM and BIBFRAME*

IFLA LRM	Find Identify Select Acquire/Obtain Navigate and Explore	LRM – E1 Res LRM-E2 Work LRM-E3 Expression LRM-E4 Manifestation LRM-E5 Item LRM-E6 Agent LRM-E7 Person LRM-E8 Collective Agent LRM-E9 Nomen LRM-E10 Place LRM-E11 Time-span
BIBFRAME	Find Identify Select Acquire/Obtain Navigate and Explore	bf:Work bf:Instance bf:Item bf:Agent bf:Hub

The search for a grouping element for collocations

In his article 'Super Records: An approach toward the description of works appearing in various manifestations', Rahmatollah Fattahi anticipates a theme (Fattahi, 1996) that is a notable part of his research and would later be an integral part of his doctoral dissertation (Fattahi, 1997). Fattahi conceives the introduction of super records into the catalogue to serve primarily the function of catalogue *collocation*, which allows the grouping of the works of a certain author and the editions and indexes of a particular work, owned by the library. Although the main purpose of a researcher using the online catalogue is to find something known (what he or she is looking for) one should not forget other uses. For example, that of displaying different editions of a work, in a precise order and grouping, so as to facilitate choice. Both in the article cited above and later, more structured, in his doctoral dissertation, Fattahi theorises and prototypes this aggregation mechanism. In paragraph 2.1 of Chapter 7 of his doctoral dissertation, Fattahi explains the concept of the super record as follows:

> While it is assumed here that the basic unit of description is the item in hand and that records describing items would fulfil the finding, selecting and locating functions, two kinds of 'super records' can be constructed for the effective discharge of the collocating function: one for voluminous authors containing the author heading and titles of the works by that author…; and one for voluminous titles that appear in different editions and manifestations.. . . The super record for authors can have a simple arrangement of works by the author (e.g. alphabetical, chronological, by type of style, i.e. genre, or by type of contribution of the author, e.g. principal author, joint author, editor, compiler or translator). It may also display different forms of the author's name under the established heading; this has not been displayed in the examples that follow.
>
> (Fattahi, 1997)

The concept of the *super record* in an online context is intended to meet the needs of those libraries that consider the functions of finding and collocating equally important, thus echoing what Seymour Lubetzky had already said in this regard, when he proposed the two functions as complementary but both essential to ensure the effectiveness of the catalogue (Lubetzky, 1960). Super records are, therefore, advised for:

- prolific authors, containing the author's headings and the titles of the works associated with them
- substantial titles, which have different editions and manifestations.

In both his article[157] and doctoral dissertation[158] Fattahi refers also to another concept, that of 'super work' – 'The set of all manifestations of an original work and all manifestations derived from it' – which had already been proposed by Elaine Svenonius in the proceedings of the Seminar on Bibliographic Records, held in Stockholm, 15–16 August 1990, and then published in 1992 in the article 'Bibliographic Entities and their Uses' (Svenonius, 2018).

This was in a time still focused on the 'record', even though we were on the verge of the entity-relationship model (later formalised in FRBR), which officially arrived just a couple of years after Fattahi's super-record proposal.

Another significant example of the extent to which the theoretical model must follow, and not precede, practical needs, is demonstrated by the introduction in BIBFRAME of the *Hub* as an element capable of realising the collocation function, understood as grouping, which had already been realised in MARC with authority records for name and title and through the use of tags 130 and 240 for recording uniform titles in bibliographic records. The experimentation of the Hub, modelled as a type (rdf:type) of BIBFRAME Work,[159] begins in Phase 2 of testing related to the concrete application of the BIBFRAME model to Library of Congress data (the phase called *Pilot 2*). This experimentation was introduced following the experience gained in the first phase of the project (*Pilot 1*), where the need arose to create grouping elements for the set of Work created during the conversion from MARC 21 to RDF according to the BIBFRAME model. The Library of Congress decided to start from MARC 21 to identify all possible 'aggregating' elements present in authority and bibliographic descriptions.[160] We will return to this experience, formalised in 2021 with the official introduction of the Hub in the BIBFRAME model, later in this chapter. But it is interesting to mention here this experience – which is in fact ongoing and is presented as in progress (McCallum, 2022) – to recount an empirical approach to entity modelling starting from a practical need that is summarised in the usability, by users (first and foremost) and machines, of the data in a catalogue. Figure 2.1 on the next page shows an example of a hub created to group under a single real-world object the many works present for different expressions of this work in the Library of Congress catalogue. Figure 2.2 shows the representation of one of the Works connected to the Hub above, with the link to the Hub and Instance.

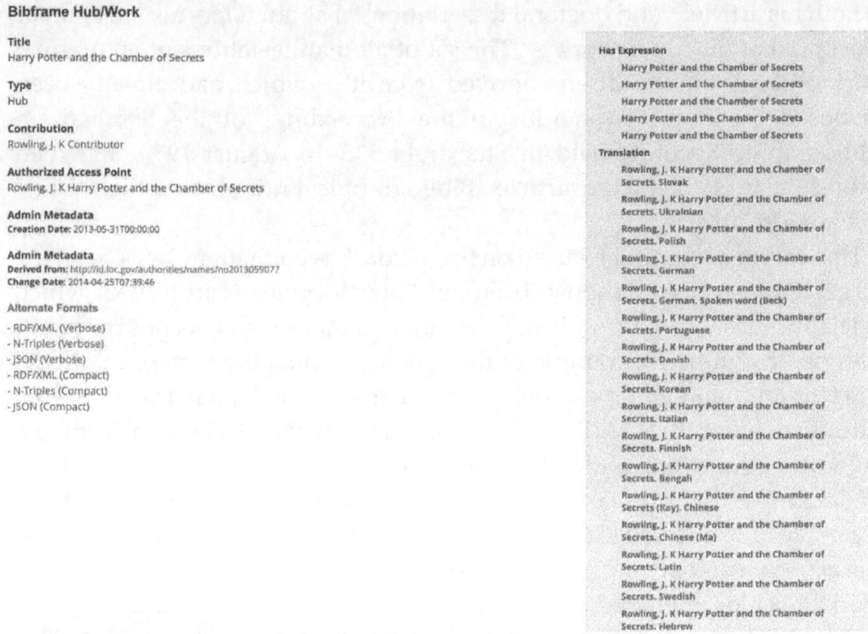

Bibframe Hub/Work

Title
Harry Potter and the Chamber of Secrets

Type
Hub

Contribution
Rowling, J. K Contributor

Authorized Access Point
Rowling, J. K Harry Potter and the Chamber of Secrets

Admin Metadata
Creation Date: 2013-05-31T00:00:00

Admin Metadata
Derived from: http://id.loc.gov/authorities/names/no2013059077
Change Date: 2014-04-25T07:39:46

Alternate Formats
- RDF/XML (Verbose)
- N-Triples (Verbose)
- JSON (Verbose)
- RDF/XML (Compact)
- N-Triples (Compact)
- JSON (Compact)

Has Expression
Harry Potter and the Chamber of Secrets
Harry Potter and the Chamber of Secrets
Harry Potter and the Chamber of Secrets
Harry Potter and the Chamber of Secrets
Harry Potter and the Chamber of Secrets

Translation
Rowling, J. K Harry Potter and the Chamber of Secrets. Slovak
Rowling, J. K Harry Potter and the Chamber of Secrets. Ukrainian
Rowling, J. K Harry Potter and the Chamber of Secrets. Polish
Rowling, J. K Harry Potter and the Chamber of Secrets. German
Rowling, J. K Harry Potter and the Chamber of Secrets. German. Spoken word (Beck)
Rowling, J. K Harry Potter and the Chamber of Secrets. Portuguese
Rowling, J. K Harry Potter and the Chamber of Secrets. Danish
Rowling, J. K Harry Potter and the Chamber of Secrets. Korean
Rowling, J. K Harry Potter and the Chamber of Secrets. Italian
Rowling, J. K Harry Potter and the Chamber of Secrets. Finnish
Rowling, J. K Harry Potter and the Chamber of Secrets. Bengali
Rowling, J. K Harry Potter and the Chamber of Secrets (Kay). Chinese
Rowling, J. K Harry Potter and the Chamber of Secrets. Chinese (Ma)
Rowling, J. K Harry Potter and the Chamber of Secrets. Latin
Rowling, J. K Harry Potter and the Chamber of Secrets. Swedish
Rowling, J. K Harry Potter and the Chamber of Secrets. Hebrew

Figure 2.1 *The proposed Hub for the work* Harry Potter and the Chamber of Secrets *with, in the section on the right, the Work related to it (such as expressions and Hub translations).* Courtesy of the Library of Congress

The Library of Congress > Linked Data Service > **BIBFRAME Works**

Bibframe Work

Title
Harry Potter and the Chamber of Secrets

Type
Text

Contribution
- Rowling, J. K. Contributor
- Kay, Jim (Illustrator) Contributor

Subject
- Wizards--Fiction.
- Magic--Fiction.
- Schools--Fiction.
- England--Fiction.
- JUVENILE FICTION / Fantasy & Magic.
- JUVENILE FICTION / Action & Adventure / General.
- JUVENILE FICTION / Social Issues / Friendship.

Genre Form
fiction

Language
English

Illustrative Content
illustrations

Classification
- LCC: PZ7.R79835 Haj 2016 (Assigner: dlc)
- DDC: [Fic] full (Assigner: dlc)
- JUV037000
- JUV001000
- JUV039060

Content
text (Source: rdacontent)

Expression Of
Rowling, J. K. Harry Potter and the Chamber of Secrets

Has Instance
New York, NY : Arthur A. Levine Books, an imprint of Scholastic Inc., 2016.

Figure 2.2 *One of the Works created for the work* Harry Potter and the Chamber of Secrets, *with, in the section on the right, the link to the Hub and Instance.* Courtesy of the Library of Congress

An example of entity modelling: the Opus in Share-VDE

The Share-VDE (SVDE) initiative[161] brings together, enriches and integrates the bibliographic and authority catalogues of a large community of libraries in a shared environment based on the linked data paradigm. The SVDE initiative represents a single, massive challenge to integrate data from different contexts into a single catalogue presented according to the philosophy and technologies of the semantic web, with the aim of facilitating the co-existence of sometimes seemingly irreconcilable cataloguing cultures and traditions.

The SVDE project was born at a time when various theorisations and studies had already been elaborated around the momentous shift of cultural institutions from a more traditional sphere – identifiable by the online catalogue, structured in MARC format (in one of the different possible variations) – to the more extensive web, with data structured in linked open data.

Originating in the 1960s, the MARC format immediately transcended the initial purpose for which it was intended, namely the possibility of exchanging data in a machine-readable format. It became a cataloguing standard of expressing most bibliographic, authority and management information. Over the course of more than 60 years, a whole range of services provided by libraries have been built on the MARC format, from online catalogues to new resource acquisition services, periodical management and loans. MARC has become a sort of communication system that has primarily involved libraries and to a lesser extent archives (with little or no involvement from museums), facilitating the emergence of integrated management systems (IMS), often referred to as integrated library systems (ILS). Nearly all cataloguing databases in the world have been structured in MARC formats, creating a virtual collective that is often self-referential (given the general complexity of the MARC format) and not very open to other domains. The advent of the web and related technologies, with an ever-expanding and heterogeneous community, has highlighted perhaps the most negative aspect of this adoption of the MARC format, namely a certain isolation of libraries with their hyper-structured catalogues but in a language that is not easily understandable and far removed from the *lingua franca* of the web. We have already discussed this, starting with Roy Tennant's aforementioned 'MARC Must Die' article, which led to the emergence of BIBFRAME as a possible successor to MARC. This is exactly the context that saw the birth of the SVDE project at the end of 2016, articulated in different phases to allow for a gradual transition from a prototypical and experimental form to a consolidated production phase.[162]

The Share community has several working groups within it, which address certain areas that are more complex or those requiring further specialised analysis. These study and working groups are made up of librarians and technicians, not necessarily part of the Share initiative but often present to share their expertise and experience or out of special scholarly interest. They deal with issues ranging from entity modelling to the study of issues related to the presentation of data to make it as close as possible to users' needs (the working group on the Share portal interface). The groups are co-ordinated by an *Advisory Council* that charts the course of the initiative and co-ordinates the various components involved, as well as relationships with related initiatives and groups.[163]

The Sapientia Entity Identification Working Group (SEI WG)[164] deals with all issues related to data modelling from conversion from MARC 21 to BIBFRAME to managing semantic compatibilities with other ontologies and communities. It is also working on revising Share's data model to bring it closer to the needs of resource searchability and identification, especially in such an extensive and rich context as the one produced by the SVDE initiative. Below I outline the path followed by the working group to identify a new entity, *Opus*, not present in the BIBFRAME model that the Share community adopts as the main ontology for rendering its catalogues in linked open data. The processes of analysis and recommendations, as well as that of solution hypotheses, are quite long and in summer 2024 were still ongoing; they have involved many American and European libraries in the discussion around the possible extension of the BIBFRAME model.

The starting point: BIBFRAME ontology

When discussing data models in cataloguing, thoughts turn immediately to the Functional Requirements for Bibliographic Records (FRBR), the conceptual model developed by IFLA with the aim of developing an entity-relationship model that identifies the minimum requirements that bibliographic descriptions used in a catalogue or bibliography require to meet the different needs of users. The report prepared by IFLA and published in 1998 identifies four essential requirements of a cataloguing record that are useful in enabling the user to:

1 use the data available to *find* material that matches the criteria established in the search
2 use the data obtained to *identify* an entity
3 use the data to *select* a resource that matches one's needs
4 use the data to *obtain* access to the described resource.

FRBR establishes four entities, structured hierarchically from the most abstract to the most concrete:

WORK – an artistic or intellectual creation; an abstract entity, devoid of material object. The work is realised in the

EXPRESSION – the intellectual and artistic realisation of a work. The work exists only in the commonality of content that subsists among the various expressions of the work. The expression materialises in the

MANIFESTATION – the physical realisation of the expression of the work. It is represented by

ITEM – a single specimen of a manifestation.

The limitation of FRBR has always been, however, that it expresses an abstract model, distant from the reality of the daily practice of cataloguing that has been carried out for centuries through the analysis of publications, thus expressing the Manifestation and Item entities of the model. The bibliographic records expressed in MARC in compliance with different cataloguing standards – Italian Rules for Cataloguing Authors (RICA), Italian Cataloguing Rules (REICAT), AACR and ISBD – have always been aimed at describing the publication understood as Manifestation, with the addition of Item data to facilitate its circulation, and with rare references to attributes referable to the Work and Expression entities. Adapting the FRBR model to such a bibliographic reality was yet another challenge to the library community and it was accomplished with the definition of RDA[165] as a content standard, which replaced AACR2. RDA, in its first version identified as Original RDA, was born as a standard designed for the digital environment and is fully aligned with FRBR and FRAD.[166]

The Library of Congress closed the RDA testing and analysis process on 31 March 2013, after a period of testing and training of its cataloguers and all external cataloguing agencies (including, in Italy, Casalini Libri). From 2 April of the same year, all international bibliographic agencies traditionally providing bibliographic and authority records to the Library of Congress were invited to produce their data in RDA, albeit still in a traditional manner, namely according to the MARC 21 format. Thus 2013 marks the watershed between a merely formal and theoretical adoption of the FRBR model and its practical and concrete application.

RDA is understood and applied by almost the entire North American library community as a guideline and content standard. The situation is different in Europe, where the nature of RDA as a conceptual entity-relationship model is also valued and emphasised in practical application, through conversion into linked data that highlight its nature as a data model as well as a content standard.[167]

The presence of so many US libraries within the Share community, starting with the Library of Congress, strongly guided the decision to adopt BIBFRAME.[168]

Until June 2021 (the date of the official introduction of the Hub entity into BIBFRAME by the Library of Congress), the BIBFRAME model in version 2.0 organised the information useful for modelling the bibliographic universe, into three main levels of abstraction (Figure 2.3).

- **Work** – The entity that identifies the intellectual content of a resource. The Work entity is the highest level of abstraction in the BIBFRAME context and reflects the conceptual content of a catalogued resource: authors, language and content (subjects).
- **Instance** – The entity that identifies a single material manifestation of a Work. A Work may have one or more material manifestations: for example, one or more particular publication formats. These represent Instances of a Work. An Instance reflects information such as publisher, place and date of publication, format.
- **Item** – The single example of an Instance. An Item is an actual copy (physical or electronic) of an Instance. It reflects information such as location (physical or virtual), shelf indication and barcode.

These main entities are supplemented by a substantial set of related entities including, of course, Agents.

Let us see how BIBFRAME has been applied in modelling SVDE data.

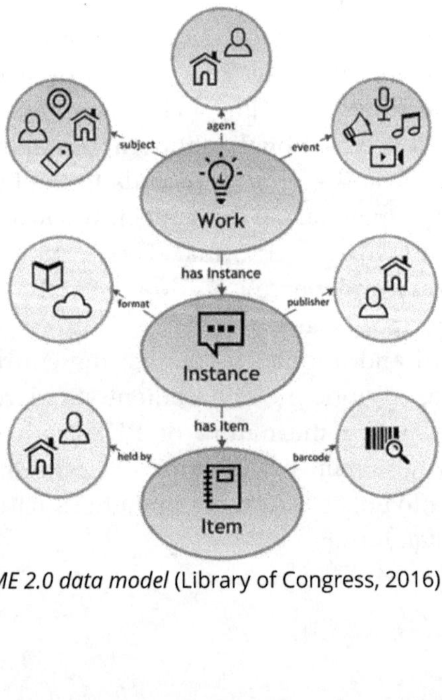

Figure 2.3 *The BIBFRAME 2.0 data model* (Library of Congress, 2016)

Applications of the BIBFRAME model

During the first phase of the SVDE project, from October 2016 to January 2017, two samples of bibliographic and authority records taken from each of the participating libraries were analysed and converted into BIBFRAME. The two samples were selected based on the period of creation – prior to the introduction of RDA (the 1985 set) and after the introduction of the standard (the 2015 set) – totalling 2,249,387 bibliographic records and 3,601,327 authority records. This sample of records was modelled according to the then-current 1.0 version of BIBFRAME and the data were made available in RDF for subsequent analysis.

In the subsequent phase of the project, from March 2017 to May 2018, the entire catalogues of the participating libraries were analysed and converted, without any selection of significant samples, but rather testing the systems and conversion mechanisms developed, especially in terms of the amount of data and variety of resource types. At the end of the second project phase, there were 94,378,728 bibliographic records converted to RDF triples, and there were 24,150,238 authority records used mainly for entity identification processes.

By the end of May 2018, therefore, a huge amount of linked data was made available to the entire library and web community to see first-hand and in a practical way the results of applying BIBFRAME to the data conversion processes originally in MARC 21. It is interesting to note that at that time, no European libraries had yet joined the initiative, which was entirely North American in origin and orientation.

Analysis of conversion results and a proposal for an extension of the BIBFRAME model

In addition to the conversion into BIBFRAME, the second phase of the project involved publishing the data on a portal for end users (students, researchers, etc.). The presentation of the data in graphs was intended to provide an overview of the results of the entity identification process and the creation of relationships between them, which the detailed analysis of RDF triples could certainly not offer (even more so, considering the huge amount of data, amounting to about 24 trillion triples).

Following the BIBFRAME model, the presentation of the data on the SVDE portal immediately highlighted an initial difficulty in terms of usability: all works (whether original or translations) were presented at the same level, without any hierarchical organisation to identify the original creative work in relation to its different expressions. The lack of an available attribute in the data model, as well as BIBFRAME's merging of the Work and Expression classes into the single class Work, generates a series of works without the possibility of identifying the actual origin of this chain. To better illustrate this limitation of BIBFRAME and its difference from the RDA model, which instead proposes separate Work and Expression entities, Figure 2.4 shows a mapping between the main classes and relationships of the two models, extracted from the article 'Mapping Derivative Relationships from RDA to BIBFRAME 2' (Zapounidou, Sfakakis and Papatheodorou, 2019).

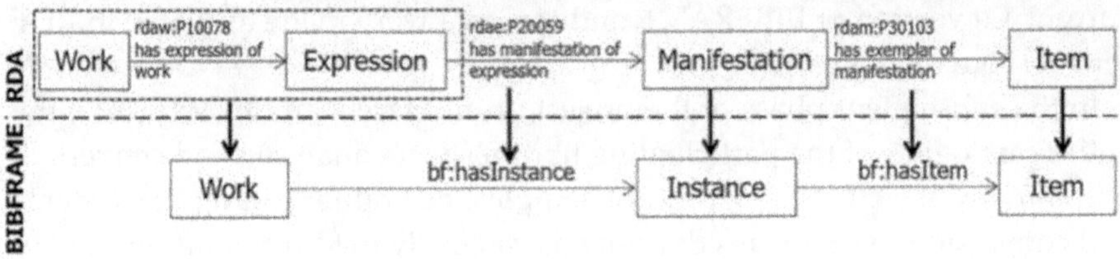

Figure 2.4 *Mapping of the main classes and relationships in the RDA and BIBFRAME models* (Zapounidou, Sfakakis and Papatheodorou, 2019). Permission conveyed through Copyright Clearance Center

Using the BIBFRAME property *hasExpression*[169] and its inverse *expressionOf*[170] would not have resolved the need to navigate between works by perfectly identifying the origin of a chain or sequence of expressions: in the case of a *Pinocchio* work translated into Chinese (Work A) derived from a German version (Work B), the relationship between the two works would be this:

Work A *hasExpression* Work B (or: Work B *expressionOf* Work A)

without any ability to trace it back to the Italian version, which should be understood as the original creative work and which should group all other existing expressions under it.

The lack of a top-level element in BIBFRAME that directs the user to an original work, the creative work that was in the mind of its author and then expressed in many different ways, is not resolved even with the 'translation of' property of BIBFRAME. This property, in fact, can only indistinctly relate an original work and its translation[171] as well as a translation into one language from another non-original expression and thus from another translation.[172] This places all BIBFRAME Works on the same horizontal line, without any indication of an original work. Taking another example, that of Maurizio De Giovanni's *Buio per i bastardi di Pizzofalcone* (in Italian) and its English translation, the result of converting the data (especially authority data) in BIBFRAME would have generated two Works placed exactly at the same level:

a bf:Work for De Giovanni, Maurizio, 1958- Buio per i bastardi di Pizzofalcone;
a bf:Work for De Giovanni, Maurizio, 1958- Darkness for the bastards of Pizzofalcone;

Based on this and considering the enormous amount of data produced as a result of the conversion of the catalogues of the participating libraries, with a very high number of works, the SEI WG proposed in September 2018 the experimental introduction of a new entity, the *SuperWork,* with the specific function of grouping different expressions under a single semantic unit. The original BIBFRAME model, therefore, becomes insufficient to address the need expressed above: thus, a first proposal for the extension of the BIBFRAME model was formulated, as illustrated in Figure 2.5.

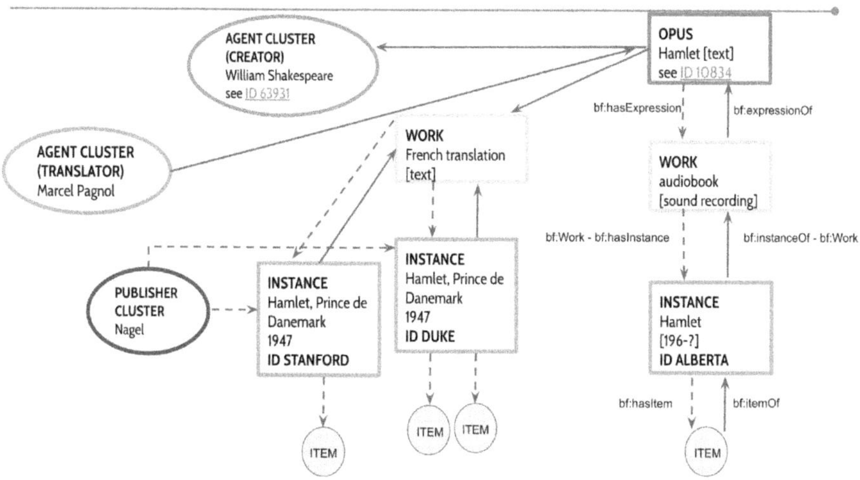

Figure 2.5 *A simplification of the SVDE data model as conceived and designed in September 2018 (updated diagram, with Opus replacing SuperWork)*

Introduction of the Hub entity in the BIBFRAME ontology

The suggestion of this new entity was well supported in numerous meetings with librarians and observers, buoyed by the Library of Congress, which, during the ALA Annual Conference in Washington, DC in June 2019, introduced for the first time the concept of a *Hub.* In the presentation by Sally McCallum, Chief Network Development/MARC Standards Office of the Library of Congress, at the LC BIBFRAME Update Forum,[173] explicit reference was made to this new class used for the purpose of grouping different Works linked by a common denominator: 'BIBFRAME Works are linked via BIBFRAME Hubs'. Although a clear definition of the nature of the Hub was still lacking, some clarifying elements were provided in the various meetings between representatives of the Library of Congress and the SEI WG, as well as on public occasions. In particular, during the European BIBFRAME

Workshop held at the Kungliga Biblioteket in Stockholm on 17–18 September 2019,[174] Kevin Ford, linked data specialist at the Library of Congress, offered an overview of the rationale behind the introduction of the Hub (although still in the study and testing phase) into the Library of Congress catalogue modelling process, explaining, in part, also its birth:

> – Pursued because we realised we were trying to do too much with bf:Work
> – Pursued because we realised we had no good solution for Title/NameTitle access point
> – Pursued because aforementioned Title/NameTitle access points were all blank nodes
> – Pursued because of engagement with SVDE and Casalini and the concept of SuperWork
>
> (Ford, 2019)

Analysis of the MARC 21 fields that were used to write the algorithms for the creation of the Hubs[175] also expresses quite clearly the possible nature of this new entity, which can be identified with a kind of *aggregator*, providing an element for grouping similar or related things[176] and which, by its nature and composition, serves three functions:

- subject of a work
- related work
- the work in the sense given to this concept in RDA.[177]

From a semantic point of view, the Hub represents a group or collection of works, a resource that serves as an aggregation and connection point for other resources, which may be the Hubs themselves or the Works as defined in BIBFRAME. Figure 2.6 opposite shows a scheme of possible relationships between the Hub entity and other BIBFRAME entities presented by Kevin Ford at the European BIBFRAME Workshop event in Stockholm.

Figure 2.7, taken from the Library of Congress website in the section devoted to publishing catalogue and vocabulary data in linked data, shows an example of the Hub and its use primarily for correlating information and relationships with other Works.

The definition of the Hub entity in the BIBFRAME ontology was, after much consideration, articulated as 'An abstract resource that functions as a bridge between two Works.'[178] The Hub was initially modelled as a subclass of the Work entity of BIBFRAME.[179] Between October and November 2023, the Hub was remodelled as a separate class and no longer as a subclass of bf:Work.[180]

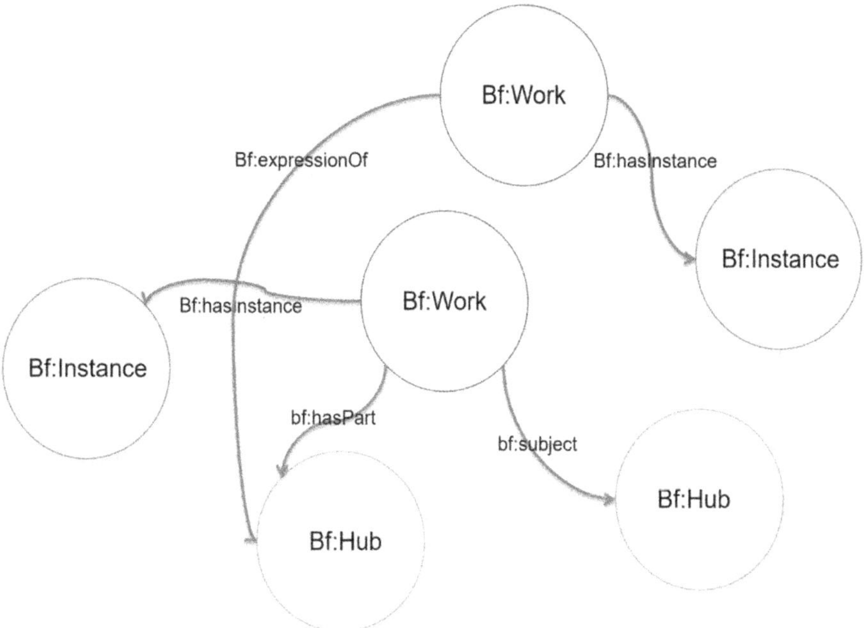

Figure 2.6 *Representation of relationships between Hubs and other entities in the BIBFRAME model* (Courtesy of Kevin Ford, Library of Congress)

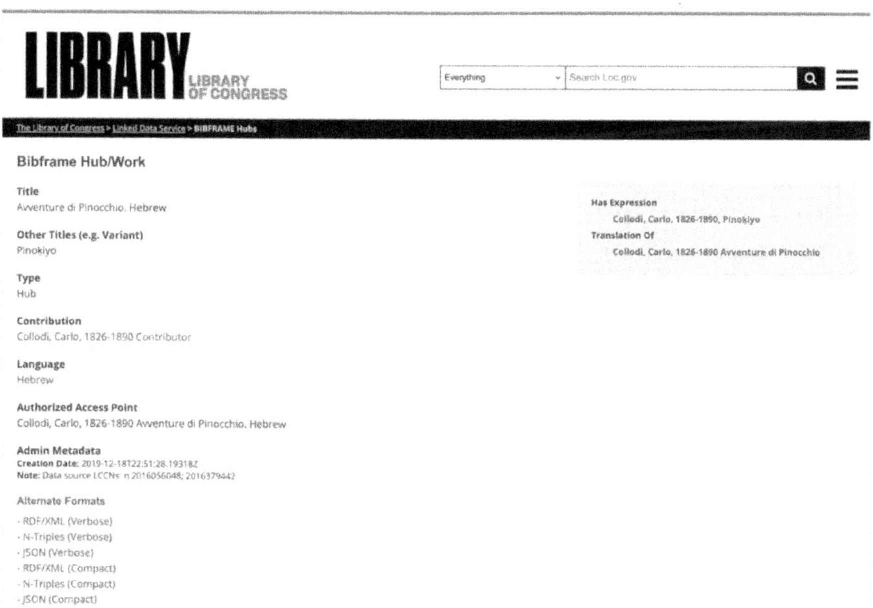

Figure 2.7 *Presentation of the Hub that refers to the* Adventures of Pinocchio *in Hebrew on the Library of Congress website* (Courtesy of the Library of Congress)

Opening Share community to the European context

This significant openness of the Library of Congress to a concept or entity not previously envisioned by the BIBFRAME data model, and this declaration of a more manifest and open willingness to reconcile with another world – that of the four separate entities of FRBR and RDA and that of SVDE – opens up new scenarios for participation in the Share initiative to that cultural area, especially northern Europe, most closely linked to FRBR and its IFLA LRM evolution. The entry into the SVDE community, between June and October 2019, of the National Library of Norway, the National Library of Finland and the British Library, all libraries with deep ties to the European cultural context and to IFLA raises an important question about the compatibility of the BIBFRAME model with that defined by IFLA as the harmonisation of the FR family, and thus with the IFLA Library Reference Model.

With the entry of these new libraries from the European area, the SEI WG changes in nature, becoming more transversal and less BIBFRAME-centric, opening up to the prospect of extending its reference horizon to the IFLA LRM model. This model inherits the levels of the various manifestations of the FR family and develops a much more complex conceptual model, which nonetheless reintroduces as its main entities those of FRBR:

- **Work** – the intellectual or artistic content of a given creation
- **Expression** – a certain combination of markings that conveys intellectual or artistic content
- **Manifestation** – a set of everything that is presumed to share the same characteristics with regard to intellectual or artistic content and aspects of physical form. The set is defined by both the overall content and the production plan of the medium(s)
- **Item** – an object or objects bearing markings intended to convey intellectual or artistic content.

Figure 2.8 opposite shows a representation of the IFLA LRM data model.

In BIBFRAME, when concretely modelled, Work – which incorporates the semantic entities of Work and Expression from FRBR – expresses more Expression than Work, especially when compared with the Hub, which, in its modelling, does not precisely coincide with the Work of RDA or IFLA LRM.[181] This difficulty in defining the contours of Hub and Work may be due to the objective limitation of clearly identifying, in bibliographic and authority records, the attributes of a Work compared to those of an Expression. With the caveat, however, that the librarian community perceives it as a problem when the starting point within a work with a very rich editorial history is lost as the expression lattice takes shape. It is no coincidence that IFLA LRM

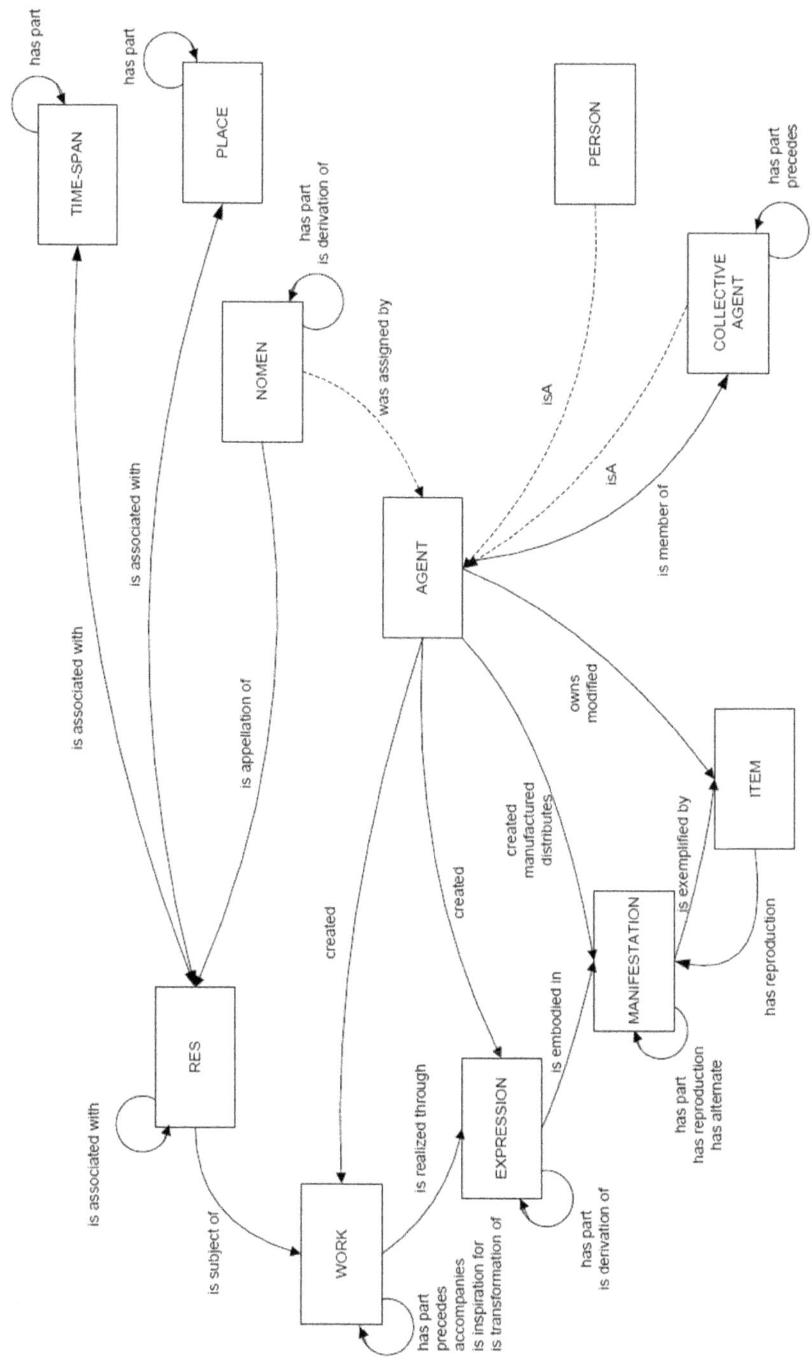

Figure 2.8 *The IFLA LRM data model* (IFLA LRM, 2017)

introduces the concept of *Representative Expression,* which should be, if identifiable, the first expression of a work, the one that best expresses the original work, the one closest to what was ideally conceived by its creator: 'In many respects, end users specifically seek expressions that exhibit the "original" characteristics and are particularly interested in the manifestations of these expressions' (IFLA LRM, 2017).[182]

The result of the SEI WG's first reflections on this issue and the many comparisons with domain experts led, in January 2019, to a first official formulation of that apex entity, defined a few months earlier as *SuperWork,* which could encompass all the related expressions; something, therefore, very close to the concept of Work in FRBR/RDA and IFLA LRM. Figure 2.9 is a representation of the comparison between the IFLA LRM, BIBFRAME and SVDE models after the introduction of the Hub (in BIBFRAME) and SuperWork (in SVDE).

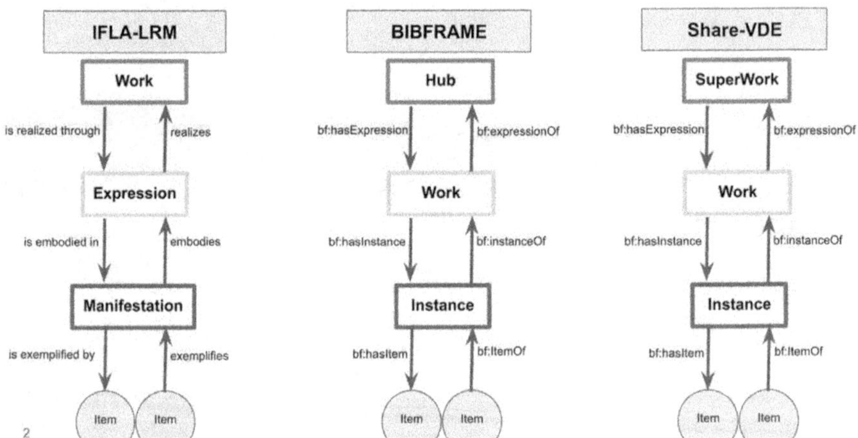

Figure 2.9 *Comparison of the main entities of the IFLA LRM, BIBFRAME and Share-VDE conceptual models*

Obviously, by rethinking Work in BIBFRAME (bf:Work) in terms of identifying a more purely abstract part (svde:SuperWork) and a part more related to Expression and thus with an already lower level of abstraction, the very semantics of bf:Work in SVDE became inapplicable as a representation of the Work of BIBFRAME, generating the need, therefore, to model a different type of Work (closer to the Expression of IFLA LRM), called the *svde:Work.* However, the introduction of a new entity as an extension, whether local or official, of a model (BIBFRAME) recognised by a community could generate, first of all, an interoperability problem. This is a problem strongly felt by all libraries interested in modelling their data according to the BIBFRAME ontology but unwilling to lose the possibility of a fluid dialogue and exchange of data and services with the community adhering to the IFLA LRM model.[183]

At this point, the elements for a timely comparison between the three ontological models – that of SVDE with the proposed changes to the original model, that of BIBFRAME and that of IFLA LRM – were mature, thus opening the way to a careful comparative evaluation aimed at ensuring a more effective response to the user's information need but also full compatibility with the major and most popular bibliographic models. In January 2020, partly to establish the semantic function assigned to the top-level SuperWork class and to avoid confusion with other past definitions of 'superwork', the SEI WG, with the endorsement of the Advisory Council, renamed this new class as SVDE Opus (svde:Opus).

With the aim of staying focused on the concrete and practical aspect of applying a model to the reality of existing catalogues, the study group developed an example of applying the concepts of Hub and Opus to a specific case of Work with its expressions and publications: the work *The Plague* by Albert Camus was represented in the BIBFRAME context (as Hub) and in the SVDE context (as Opus). The representation of the same work in the two models can be seen in Figures 2.10 and 2.11 and immediately demonstrates the greater aggregative capacity of Opus compared to the Hub, closer as a concept to FRBR's Expression than that of Work.

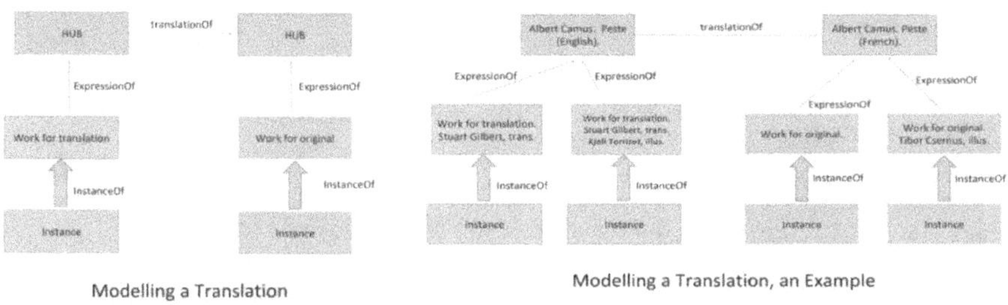

Figure 2.10 *Example of Albert Camus' Work* The Plague *and related expressions and instances in the LC BIBFRAME context, proposed by Kevin Ford* (Library of Congress)

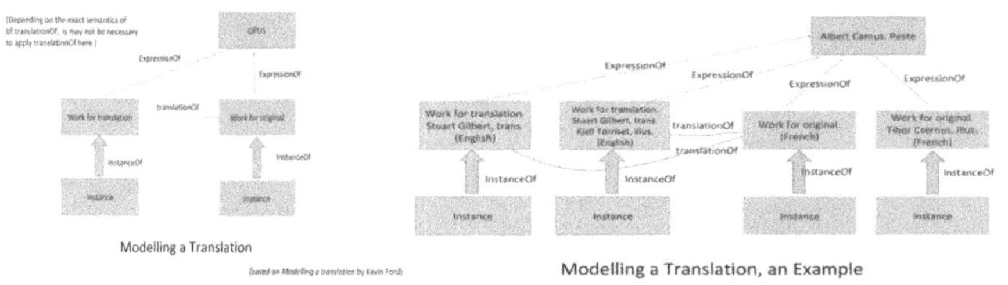

Figure 2.11 *Example of Albert Camus' Work* The Plague *and related expressions and instances in the SVDE context, proposed by Oddrun Pauline Ohren* (Nasjonalbiblioteket)

The definition of the svde:Opus class and its modelling

Having defined the svde:Opus class at the theoretical level, we needed to make it operational, that is, capable of being modelled with properties and relationships and usable by other communities. Modelling an entity means defining a class that produces 'objects' identifiable in terms of variables (properties) and behaviour (the ability to do things), according to that OOP model that has come to our aid many times. Thus, the SEI WG hypothesised three possible Opus modelling scenarios, to which a fourth was later added as a variant of the third scenario. The modelling exercise allowed the group to evaluate all the pros and cons of each scenario, starting with a few key elements understood as 'desired' and never losing sight of the principle of interoperability in the broader web community. In the representation diagrams of the three starting scenarios, which are the original ones produced and discussed within the SEI WG, the formulation of the new entity still carries the nomenclature SuperWork instead of Opus.

Option 1 (Figure 2.12) of the data model is constructed as follows:

- The SuperWork is understood as a class defined independently of BIBFRAME.
- The properties linking the SuperWork to other entities will have to be defined within the SVDE model (semantically equivalent properties in BIBFRAME are restricted to domains containing only BIBFRAME entities).
- The proposed relationships between different SuperWork are partitive relationships, derivative relationships, accompanying relationships and sequence relationships.

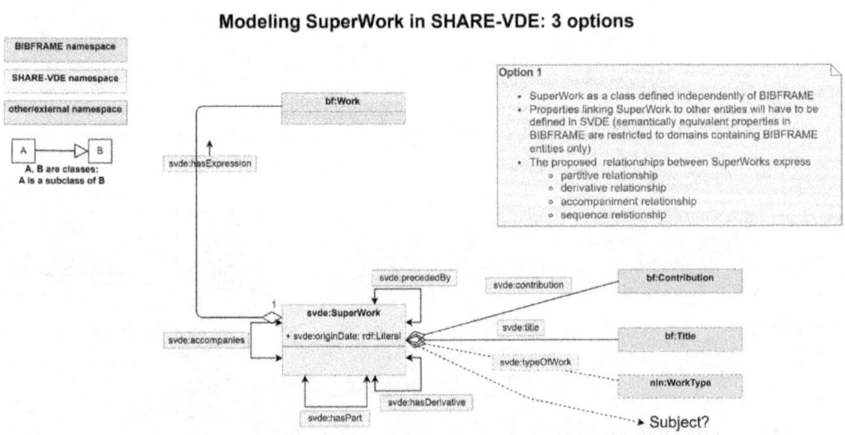

Figure 2.12 *Opus entity modelling option 1, at the time of this prospectus still called SuperWork*

Option 2 (Figure 2.13) of the data model consists of these essential points:

- SuperWork is understood as a subclass of bf:Work (remaining, therefore, completely within the BIBFRAME domain).
- SuperWork should also be defined as *disjoint* from each of the other subclasses of bf:Work.
- Properties that link the SuperWork to other entities can be selected from those defined in the BIBFRAME domain for the bf:Work.
- It will be possible to propose additional properties in the SVDE domain, where useful or necessary to better define the SuperWork and its relationships.

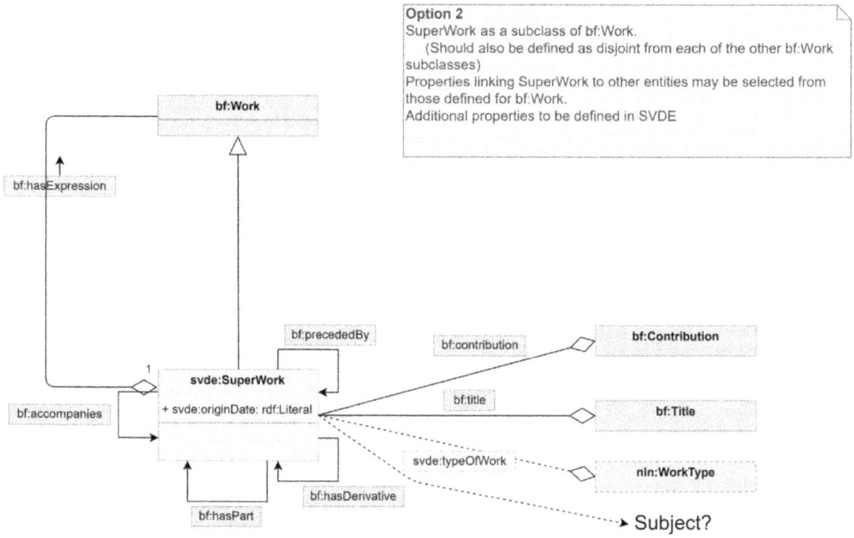

Figure 2.13 *Opus entity modelling option 2, at the time of this prospectus still called SuperWork*

Option 3 (Figure 2.14 on the next page) consists of these essential points:

- SuperWork is defined as a subclass of bf:Work.
- SuperWork should also be defined as *disjoint* from each of the other subclasses of bf:Work.
- The Work in the context of the SVDE model (svde:Work) is defined as another subclass of the bf:Work, and is semantically more comparable to the Expression of FRBR.
- The bf:Work could be defined as the *DisjointUnion* of the svde:SuperWork and the svde:Work: in this way the svde:SuperWork

and the svde:Work, although internally disjoint, semantically cover the entire bf:Work class.

- Properties linking svde:SuperWork and svde:Work to other entities can be selected from those defined in the BIBFRAME domain for bf:Work.
- New properties in the SVDE domain could be added if useful or necessary.

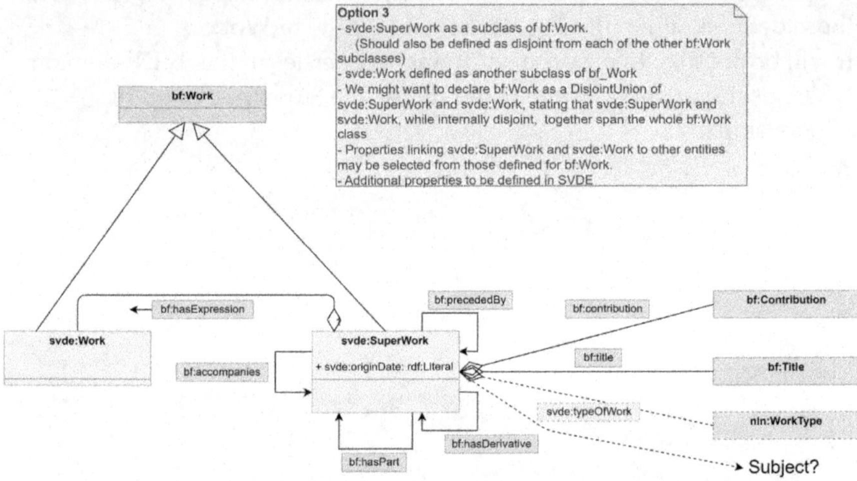

Figure 2.14 *Opus entity modelling option 3, at the time of this prospectus still called SuperWork*

A slight remodelling of Option 3, the one the SEI WG was increasingly moving towards, was proposed and formalised in Option 4 (Figure 2.15), in which, by the way, the final formulation of *Opus* officially appears: the new

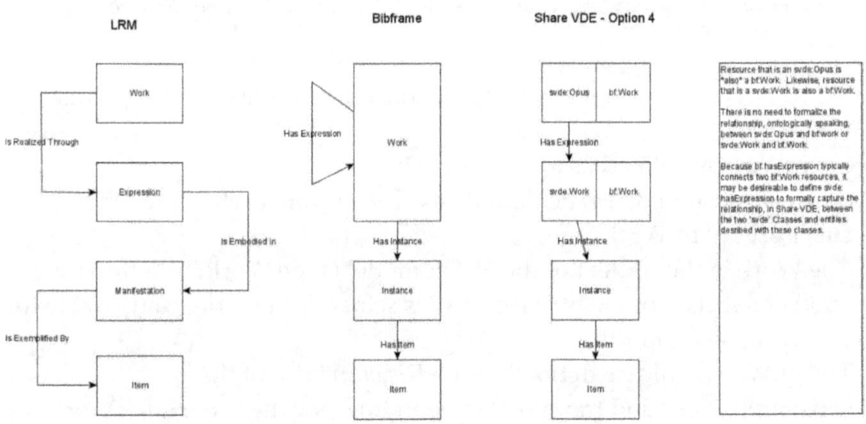

Figure 2.15 *Opus entity modelling option 4*

entity takes the name *Opus* to better express the concept of 'work, labour' as the creative action that produces a distinct content; and the reference is to the concept of *Work* as expressed in IFLA LRM, that is, as the intellectual or artistic content of a distinct creation.[184]

This option envisions that a svde:Opus (the Opus in the SVDE domain) is also a bf:Work (the Work in the BIBFRAME domain). Similarly, a svde:Work (the Work in the SVDE domain) is also a bf:Work. The svde:Opus can be defined as a type of bf:Work, and similarly a svde:Work can in turn be defined as a type of bf:Work. This makes it unnecessary to formalise, from an ontological point of view, the relationships between svde:Opus and bf:Work and between svde:Work and bf:Work. Since the hasExpression property of BIBFRAME connects two bf:Work, the suggestion is to define a domain-specific hasExpression property in SVDE (svde:hasExpression). The aggregative power of an Opus, meaning its ability to group all expressions and publications of an abstract work, is rendered by the svde:hasExpression and svde:hasInstance relationships and not by hierarchical constraints of classes and subclasses. It is these relationships, together with the hasItem relationship, that express the different degrees of abstractness among Work-Expression-Manifestation-Item (WEMI) classes.

The working group's discussion thus focused on the comparative analysis of Model 3 and its version 4, with the specific mandate of the Advisory Council to study and formalise the scenario that would best suit the purpose of identifying, describing, converting and maintaining library data, while also taking into account interoperability issues with other models.

To arrive at a joint decision, therefore, the SEI WG formulated a list of 'desired' for entity modelling, with the respective formalisations achievable in the two options selected as possible. Table 2.4 (below and on the next page) is a schematic presentation of the analysis carried out.

Table 2.4 *List of 'desiderata' for entity modelling formulated by the SEI WG*

Feature of the desired model	**Representation in Option 3**	**Representation in Option 4**
An entity representing the abstraction of the work corresponding to the class bf:Work is needed: such an entity is svde:Opus Each svde:Opus should be considered as a bf:Work	Through subclasses: svde:Opus is defined as a subclass of bf:Work	Through instantiation algorithms: svde:Opus is defined as a separate class, not as a subclass of bf:Work. All instances of svde:Opus are also explicitly declared instances of bf:Work
An entity representing the 'expression type' entities corresponding to the bf:Work class is needed: such an entity is svde:Work. Each svde:Work should be considered as a bf:Work	Through subclasses: svde:Work is defined as a subclass of bf:Work	Through instantiation algorithms: svde:Work is defined as a separate class, not as a subclass of bf:Work. All instances of svde:Work are also explicitly declared instances of bf:Work

Table 2.4 *Continued*

Feature of the desired model	Representation in Option 3	Representation in Option 4
Each svde:Work can also be considered as one of the subtypes of bf:Work	Through instantiation algorithms: each instance of svde:Work can be declared as an instance of bf:Text, bf:Audio, etc.	Through instantiation algorithms: each instance of svde:Work can be declared as an instance of bf:Text, bf:Audio, etc.
No entity can be both an abstract work (svde:Opus) and an 'expression type' entity (svde:Work) at the same time	Through class constraints: svde:Opus is declared as disjoint from svde:Work	Through class constraints: svde:Opus is declared as disjoint from svde:Work
No single entity can be both an abstract work (svde:Opus) and one of the subtypes of bf:Work represented by various types of media	Through class constraints: svde:Opus is declared as disjointed from each bf:Text, bf:Audio, etc.	Through class constraints: svde:Opus is declared as disjointed from each bf:Text, bf:Audio, etc.
It must be formally possible to reuse any property defined for bf:Work in any svde:Opus entity and in any svde:Work entity	Through subclasses: svde:Opus and svde:Work are both defined as subclasses of bf:Work	Through instantiation algorithms: all instances of svde:Opus and all instances of svde:Work are also explicitly declared instances of bf:Work
In the svde:Opus and svde:Work entities, it must be possible to define other properties in addition to those in BIBFRAME	Through the definition of svde:Opus and svde:Work within the SVDE domain	Through the definition of svde:Opus and svde:Work within the SVDE domain

At the conclusion of the comparative study, a summary table was drawn up (Table 2.5 opposite) to consider the pros and cons of the two modelling scenarios, which will lead to the decision (still under discussion) to adopt the scenario in version 4.

The verdict on the choice of option 4 was made by the SEI WG and shared with the Share community and all those who contributed to the deliberation of such a delicate modelling intervention. It is reported first here, as it is not yet published in official sources but found only in internal working documents:

> Option 3 is connected to BIBFRAME at *model level/class level*, whereas option 4 is connected to BIBFRAME only at *application level*, i.e. when the model is used.
>
> This means that option 3 is more tightly and statically connected to BIBFRAME than is option 4. As such, option 3 is more susceptible to future changes in BIBFRAME. For example, substantial changes to the bf:Work class made in some future BIBFRAME version will most likely affect its subclasses as well.

Table 2.5 *Summary table for the evaluation of pros and cons of the modelling scenarios assumed for Opus by the SEI WG*

Model options	Pro	Against
Option 4	1 Fulfils the desired model feature flexibly. 2 Allows time for best practices to develop further and provide improvements to instantiation algorithms. 3 Although the entity cluster mappings and instantiation algorithms are different, the approach is similar to that of the Library of Congress with respect to the bf:Hub.	1 Without a formal definition of subclasses, documentation of entity and property cluster mappings becomes unavoidable 2 (Perhaps not a con.) As best practices and standards develop, application of the features of the model presented here may be desirable at the BIBFRAME ontology level.
Option 3	1 Meets the desired model feature (some concerns are noted in the Against column) 2 Provides a formal definition of svde:Opus and svde:Work as subclasses	1 The use of subclasses raises the question of how to preserve the equivalence between svde:Work as a subclass of bf:Work and bf:Work in SVDE. This reveals interoperability issues about input and output to/from external sources. 2 Several questions could benefit from further analysis and development of best practices.

According to our current insight, option 4 seems a more flexible solution, using an instantiation pattern by which it is easy to attach or detach svde:Opus and svde:Work instances to or from other classes. With its relative independence of BIBFRAME (compared to option 3), it is also perhaps easier to perceive its potential for equal interoperability with other models, e.g. LRM and RDA.

This modelling solution is exemplified in Figure 2.16 on the next page, with the four-entity model of SVDE and with the instantiation of Mark Twain's novel *The Adventures of Tom Sawyer*. In it, the central decision, the one that really makes this ontological extension compatible with BIBFRAME and with IFLA LRM (and RDA), is as follows: the resource type svde:Opus is not defined as a subclass of bf:Work but is still instantiated as a bf:Work (thus it is *a type of* bf:Work) just as the resource svde:Work is also a bf:Work. The two entities modelled for SVDE become BIBFRAME Work *types*, thus being perfectly compatible with both BIBFRAME and the Work and Expression entities of IFLA LRM. The 'aggregation power' of an Opus, that is, its ability to group together all variants and publications of an abstract work, is provided by the *hasExpression* and *hasInstance* relationships, not by a hierarchy of classes/subclasses. It is those relations (along with *hasItem*) that express the different 'degrees of abstractness' among WEMI classes.

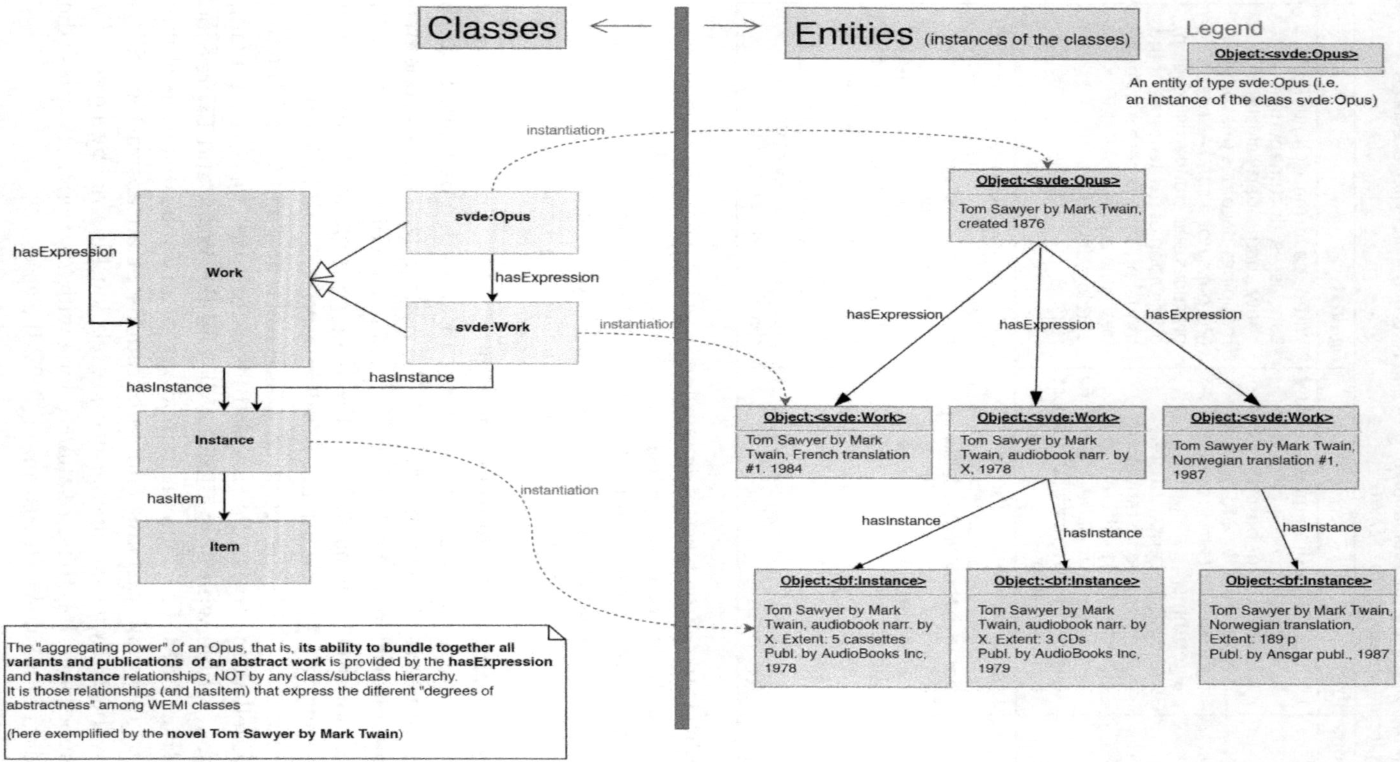

Figure 2.16 *The four entities under discussion within the SEI WG (Opus – Work – Instance – Item) exemplified in the instantiation of Mark Twain's novel* Tom Sawyer

The modelling of svde:Opus as 'a type of' bf:Work was however extensively discussed within the SEI WG, to the extent that the proposed schema in Figure 2.17 represents this entity as a separate class, contrary to earlier scenarios that had it modelled as a subclass of bf:Work. The working group completed the analysis of the attributes associated in the BIBFRAME ontology with the bf:Work entity, redistributing them in the Share model to svde:Opus and svde:Work, defining their profile.[185] In the Appendix, it is possible to verify the work of associating the properties, referable in the BIBFRAME model to bf:Work, to the two entities svde:Opus and svde:Work. To facilitate comparison between the svde:Opus entity and the bf:Hub entity, a list of properties referable to the Hub has also been added.

The current state of research activity around the svde:Opus and svde:Work entities

In the second quarter of 2023, the SEI WG has begun a more technical phase of generating the SVDE ontology in OWL. For this purpose, the working group agreed to use the open-source software Protégé,[186] importing the BIBFRAME ontology and analysing possible extensions needed to more effectively express the SVDE data model. In particular, the SEI WG modelled the svde:Opus and svde:Work classes and defined properties that cannot be derived from the BIBFRAME ontology. A topic that required more in-depth analysis, and remains unresolved, is the definition of svde:Opus as a subclass of bf:Work or as a separate and autonomous class. This issue, already discussed in the definition of the aforementioned scenarios 3 and 4, required a revisit for broader consideration. The diagram of relationships between bf:Work on the one hand and svde:Opus and svde:Work on the other in its current version and subject to ongoing discussion, is shown in Figure 2.17 on the next page.

The result of this further phase of analysis and modelling of the main classes of the Share ontology is summarised in an article published in open access on Zenodo (Hahn and Possemato, 2023). It is interesting to report the definitions of the classes Opus and Work, which have helped the working group to better focus on the form and function of these classes, together with the OpusType class, which is created to better specialise the Opus:

- svde:Opus: The class svde:Opus is the distinct conceptual result of an artistic or intellectual activity. The Opus, representing the highest level of abstraction in SVDE, is an entity that allows grouping works that are considered functional or nearly equivalent. The Opus is defined by a constellation of elements that form the shared content of works, and groups the entities svde:Work. The Opus is not equivalent to bf:Hub. The

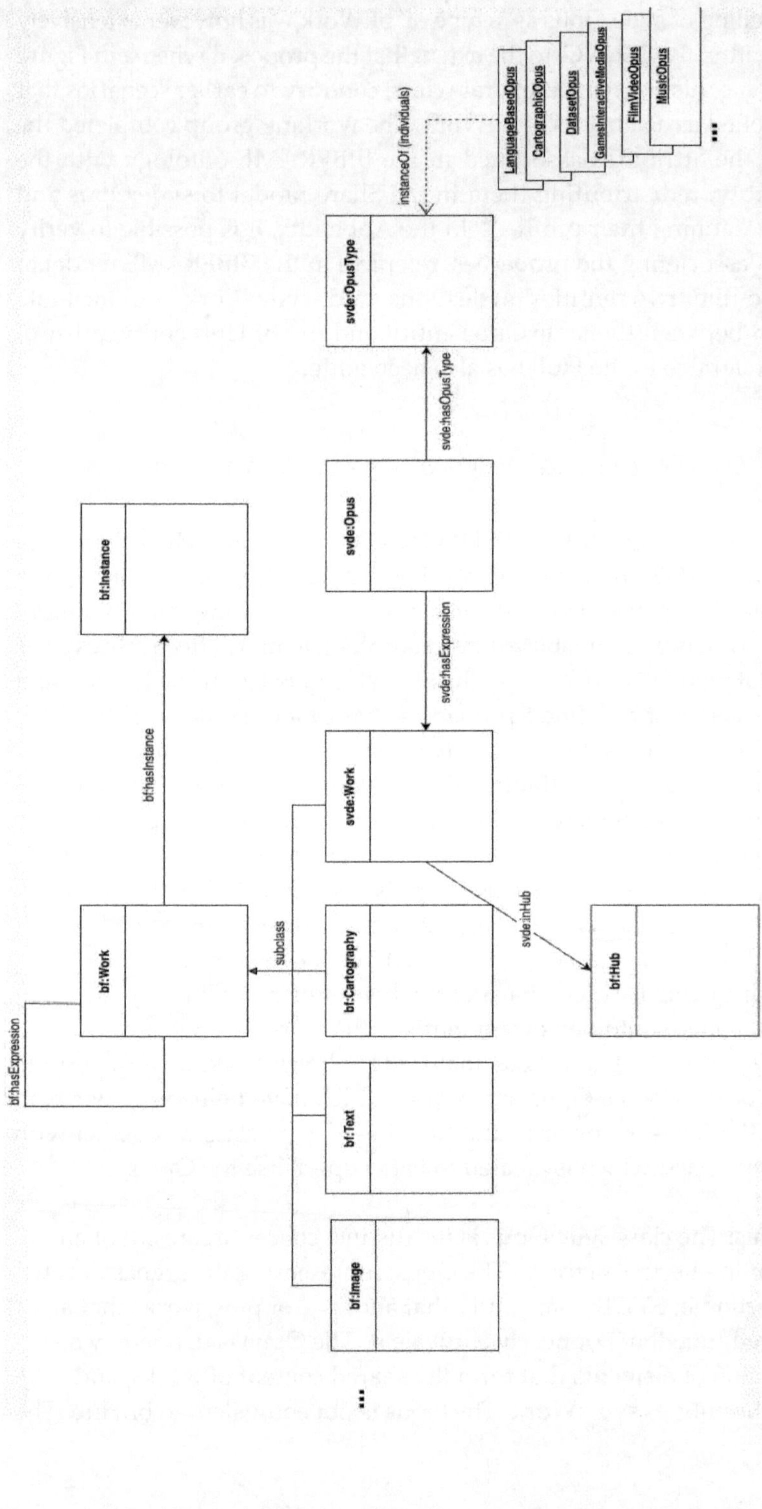

Figure 2.17 *The most recent version (March 2024) of the representation of the relationships between bf:Work, svde:Opus and svde:Work developed within the SEI WG and still under discussion*

Opus can be an artistic, literary or musical work, a scientific result or a creation within some other artistic or intellectual domain. The class svde:Opus is parallel to the Work of IFLA LRM and the Work of RDA. The set of attributes that comprise the svde:Opus is analogous to the set of attributes of the Work of IFLA LRM and the Work of RDA.

- svde:Work: The class svde:Work is defined by a constellation of elements that represent the distinct intellectual or artistic form that an Opus assumes whenever it is realised. The individuals of the class svde:Work express an identity of the Opus entity. The svde:Work is a subclass of BIBFRAME Work. The set of attributes that comprise the svde:Work is analogous to the set of attributes of the Expression entity of IFLA LRM and RDA.
- svde:OpusType: The individuals of the OpusType class support the identification of Opus categories.

It is worth noting in these definitions the formalisation of svde:Work as an expression of an identity of the svde:Opus entity. Although correctly modelled as distinct classes, each svde:Work represents a possible identity of the svde:Opus entity.

The work of the SEI WG is now focused on a clearer and more defined typing of Opus, useful especially for the searchability of these entities on the Share bibliographic portal by end users. Here, too, the debate among members of the working group has intensified and is still ongoing, focusing on the selection of categories of works capable of representing the multiplicity of forms in which human (and not only human) creativity can be expressed. What are the types of Opus that an institute of recorded memory may find itself managing, how to model them, how to define them, how to identify the boundary between types of works and types of expressions? Among the themes that has fuelled the working group's discussion is one that guided the decision on modelling the elements to include in the list of values associated with a type of Opus. The possible options were between types of Opus and individuals of the OpusType class: by types, we mean categories or subclasses that bring together instances that share general characteristics, repeatable across multiple individuals. Individuals (or tokens), in turn, are not general things, they are not repeatable; instead, they are particular entities, such as Paul McCartney and John Lennon (instances of 'person') or Jupiter and Mars (instances of 'planet').

Although we seem to be able to grasp this distinction intuitively, the boundaries between types and individuals are not always definitively drawn in everyday discourse (Dadalto et al., 2024).[187] Within the SEI WG, this discussion was translated into an option between the definition of subclasses of the Opus and the definition of a controlled value vocabulary, understood as individuals of the class OpusType. The choice to define individuals of the class OpusType was mainly guided by considerations of simplifying identification and clustering processes: Subclasses are static objects and carry with them the concept of inheritance from the main class, with the aim of specialising what is not declared in the class (or declared generically).

Defining a cartographic resource as belonging to a subclass of Opus means having a clear idea of the type of resource during the metadata analysis phase. This is not always possible when starting from traditional metadata. The static nature of the subclass imposes a sort of upfront choice. I am building an object belonging to the subclass of cartographic resources and I know from the start that it is a cartographic resource, so I will model my cluster with the properties of this subclass. An attribute associated with the Opus through the relationship with an OpusType, which indicates, even after modelling the object, that the resource is a cartographic resource type, is much easier to manage during the identification phase of an entity. Moreover, it is a type of data that can be modified without needing to remodel the Opus object. The association of a resource with a subclass therefore requires a more complex process of identifying the resource itself using metadata that is not always sufficient to achieve the goal. Defining a resource as an 'individual' of the OpusType class through the association of a value taken from a controlled vocabulary is a much simpler operation and, above all, more easily modifiable.

Once the decision to define various individuals of the OpusType class was made, work focused on selecting these individuals. The greatest difficulty in this case was identifying types that could be associated with the Opus and not the Work, with the original work as conceived by the author and not its expression. To select the values to include in the set of possible individuals of OpusType, lists of values and vocabularies from various ontologies, data models and cataloguing standards were analysed.[188] The Additional Resource - Share-VDE Ontology (available from www.facetpublishing.co.uk/page/detail/entity-modelling/?k=9781783307272) presents the SVDE ontology as defined in April 2024.

The analysis of the Opus entity and the review of the Work entity within the Share initiative reached an advanced stage of development in the first quarter of 2024, though it is still ongoing and, at the time of writing, the ontological modelling work has not yet been fully completed. For this reason, I can report a part of the work done thus far on the Share data model without being able to share the final and definitive results of the research and implementation activities surrounding this operation.

Entity modelling as the third generation of cataloguing practice

What has been said so far about entity resolution and entity modelling is mainly concerned with massive data processing, therefore machine processes carried out in projects converting from one format to another (e.g. MARC to RDF) or in the context of machine learning. However this assumption was valid until very recently. Now *entity-oriented* logic is maturing and involving manual cataloguing practices and therefore the processes of original cataloguing. It remains an open question how ILS and data management platforms will position themselves with respect to librarianship's ever-closer approach to web languages and techniques. Some practical answers come from the applicable context of conversions (crosswalks, which serve as *from–to* frameworks for mapping different metadata schemas, are now widely adopted in conversion projects) and that of discovery systems[189] – always, so far, with massive conversion and indexing processes of their own data. But the change of perspective offered by the semantic web, the library world's approach to it and the increasingly widespread and thorough training in new web technologies,[190] surpass the traditional context of conversions and discovery. Projects focused on the new operational scenarios proposed by the semantic web are being launched which define use cases focused on the local creation of data in RDF, analysis of the impact on production processes, development of cataloguing modules in linked data and editors for their local management. Some examples include:

1 The project to develop an RDF cataloguing module, Libris (XL), initiated as early as 2018 by the National Library of Sweden to manage the new version of the national Union Catalogue (Wennerlund and Berggren, 2019).
2 The Linked Data for Production (LD4P) initiative, a long-term collaborative project aimed at identifying new solutions to support, through analysis and action, the transition from traditional MARC-based cataloguing to systems capable of handling mixed cataloguing or already natively linked data (mainly through the BIBFRAME ontology). Among its goals, LD4P aims to make library resources more accessible in environments outside the catalogue and improve the discovery mechanism. The project is currently in Phase 3, continuing the programme of Phase 2, focused on developing a cataloguing environment based on BIBFRAME and called Sinopia (Schreur, 2019).
3 The Library of Congress' BIBFRAME editor,[191] a tool designed to allow bibliographic descriptions to be modelled according to the BIBFRAME ontology.

4 JCricket, the entity editor designed and developed within the Share Family initiative, which allows for the curation of data produced by automatic RDF conversion processes through functions of updating, creating, deleting, merging and splitting entities.[192]

By looking at these editors and their focus on the entity instead of on a record, one can fully grasp the change in perspective and outlook that is developing in libraries as well. When a cataloguer begins to think about how to *model an object* (e.g. a book, or a person, or an event), what attributes and which relationships should be added to better represent the object being described, to make it as identifiable as possible even outside the library, then they have already stopped cataloguing – they are *modelling the entity.* The cataloguer starts with a class (or a profile or template) expressed in a globally recognised reference ontology in order for the result to be as broadly understandable as possible. This theme reconnects with and extends the path of cataloguing toward metadata, which is a process that has been well established for quite some time (Gorman, 2018, 121) and which has recently sparked a lively theoretical debate in Italy. This is perhaps related to the desire to enshrine formally something that from a practical perspective has already occurred but which also brings with it an inevitable revision of the language and terminology (Guerrini, 2020; 2022a; 2022b).

Thinking about what entity modelling means and how much it embodies that hoped-for shift from the record to the real-world object that I have been discussing in this volume, I would like to try to point to another way of looking at this evolution, as a sort of change in perspective, observing and describing the same object but from a different point of view. Let us summarise the key elements of each of these three generations of the same activities – cataloguing, metadata and entity modelling – to try to define the boundaries of each:

1 **Cataloguing:** This term best expresses the more traditional dimension of bibliographic activity, namely, representing with a catalogue (which has evolved over time) a library's holdings or other bibliographic information, through the application of rules and standards that have the user's interest as the driving force. Cataloguing means, therefore, adopting methods with rules and standards, as well as tools to create, maintain and share a catalogue. The spatial dimension sufficient to guarantee this dynamic relationship between the library's activity and its users is that defined by the library itself and in some way delimited by it. The catalogue reflects, for the most part, what is owned by a library or what is conveyed by the library. The user base is that of the library itself.

2 **Metadata:** The simplest definition of this term is 'data about data' or 'information about information' (Riley, 2004). In various contexts, the term has been used to refer to information about *anything* – books, museum objects, finding aids for archival material, images. 'Broadly speaking, metadata encapsulate the information that describes any information-bearing entity.'[193] The ALA Committee on Cataloguing: Description and Access defines metadata as structured, encoded data that describe the characteristics of information-bearing entities and, as such, enable functions to identify, discover, evaluate and manage entities (Zeng and Qin, 2016, 11). As Zeng and Qin recall in their seminal work *Metadata*, from the early days of handwritten and printed catalogues and indexes to the present day of web services and apps, the nature and purpose of describing information-bearing entities have remained more or less unchanged. However, methods and technologies have changed significantly. As the world around us becomes increasingly complex and we continue to experience information overload, the organisation and management of that information becomes a critical task for both institutions and individuals (Zeng and Qin, 2016, 3). The extension of the library and cultural institutions' frame of reference from a local dimension to an increasingly broader one, the enrichment of materials that have become part of collections or simply referenced in them, and the expansion of services offered by the exponential increase in digital resources, are all factors that have led to a real explosion of metadata,[194] to the point that the term 'metadating' is supplanting the term cataloguing.

3 **Entity modelling:** We have been talking about entity modelling, how it accomplishes that change of mindset before the technological one that puts the entity, or the real-world object, at the centre of one's attention, as an object to be constructed and modelled. The reference landscape is no longer even that of the traditional web but that of the semantic web, the data web, in which objects are constructed following the linked data paradigm and adding semantics to information so that it can be shared with machines. The technology, standards and protocols seem to become more complicated. To some extent that is indeed the case. But first and foremost it is a change of perspective, a new step toward a broader universe – the global universe of the web – where even the terminology must overcome its own limitation of referring to single domains. I think of the entity Pier Paolo Pasolini, no longer limited to his being 'author of . . .' (author of books in my library), no longer only 'director of . . .' (films in a film library), and not even to his being a sender or receiver of a message (thus, subject producer of an archive) but I think of Pier Paolo

> Pasolini in his complexity as a man and as an artist. I will certainly have to choose what to represent of him, of his discrete aspects, but I will try to do so by re-establishing something that is as close as possible to the entity itself, transcending the boundary of the single domain and making the pieces of information needed for determining the profile and aspects of this entity usable and reusable by anyone, in any domain, geographical location, or cultural and linguistic context.[195]

If we tried to analyse the concrete result of the three operations listed above – cataloguing, metadata and entity modelling – we would find that there is no difference in the practical result: a bibliographic record, a metadata set, an RDF dataset (Table 2.6 opposite). Metadata, of different types and levels of depth, but still metadata.

If instead, we tried to analyse those three activities in a different way, changing our perspective, we would realise how different they are and how legitimate even a radical change of terminology is. Figure 2.18 on pages 103 and 104 represents an object (an apartment) viewed through three different spatial dimensions.

1 The local dimension with a *floor plan* that has no reference outside itself and meets the need to represent the object without any important references to the external context. The metadata associated with the floor plan is typical for identifying a building in a given location, an address with its fields. This dimension represents cataloguing and its function of representing a more local reality.
2 The dimension extended to the municipality, with a *cadastral map* in which that same apartment is no longer represented in isolation. The same object, the same apartment, is identified with respect to a broader horizon and the descriptive elements needed to identify it are different and, above all, they are in relation to other objects and for other purposes: urban area, page, parcel, sub-parcel. Its dimension represents that of metadata, and its function of representing richer data spanning different functions: descriptive metadata, administrative metadata (technical, preservation and rights metadata), structural metadata and markup languages.
3 The geospatial dimension, with yet the same object[196] viewed from an even wider dimension. Here latitude and longitude become the reference points for identification, thus relating to the wider globe. This dimension represents entity modelling, whose fulfilment background is the much broader one of the semantic web.

Table 2.6 *Representation of a bibliographic record, metadata set, RDF dataset*

Example of a bibliographic record in MARC 21	Example of metadata in VRA Core	Example of entities in BIBFRAME
=LDR 00790nam a2200241 to 4500 **=001** 1553692 **=005** 19920128072618.6 **=008** 911107s1991\\\\ie\\\\\\\\\\\\000 \0\eng\\. =035 **\$9**(DLC) 91214554 =906 \$a7bccorignew$d3$encip$f19$gy-gencatlg =955 **\$arc09** 11-7-91; ep51 12-23-91; ea41 to SCD 01-03-91; fd11 01-07-91 (PR6057.O... U...); fp23 01-28-92 =010 **\\$a** 91214554 =020 **\$a0948339675** :**$c£8**.50 =020 **\$a0948339683** (pbk.) :**$c£4**.95 =040 \$aDLC$cDLC =050 **00$aPR6057.O735$bU6** 1991 =082 **00$a821/**.914$220 =100 **1\$aGorman**, Michael,$d1952- =245 **10$aUp** she flew **/$cMichael** Gorman. =260 **\aGalway**, Ireland **:$bSalmon** Pub.,**$c1991**. =300 **\$a90** p.;**$c22** cm. =922 \$aap =991 **\$bc-GenColl$hPR6057.O735$iU6 1991$tCopy** 1$wBOOKS\	<?xml version="1.0" encoding="utf-8"?> <vra xmlns="http://www.vraweb.org/vracore4.htm" xmlns:xsi="http://www.w3.org/2001/XMLSchema-instance" xsi:schemaLocation="http://www.vraweb.org/vracore4.htm http://www.loc.gov/standards/vracore/vra-strict.xsd"> <work id="w_1" source="Core 4 Sample Database (VCat)" refid="1"> <agentSet> <display>unknown (French architect)</display> <notes/> <agent> <name vocab="ULAN" refid="500125274" type="personal">unknown</name> <role>architect</role> </agent> </agentSet> <dateSet> <display>begun 1194 (creation); consecrated 1260 (other)</display> <notes/> <date type="creation"> <earliestDate>1194</earliestDate> <latestDate>1194</latestDate> </date> <date type="other"> <earliestDate>1260</earliestDate> <latestDate>1260</latestDate> </date> </dateSet> <locationSet> <display>Chartres, Centre, France</display> <notes/> <location type="site"> <name type="geographic" vocab="TGN" refid="7008267" extent="inhabited place">Chartres</name> <name type="geographic" vocab="TGN" refid="7002877" extent="region">Centre</name> <name type="geographic" vocab="TGN" refid="1000070" extent="nation">France</name> <name type="geographic"	@prefix ns2: <http://id.loc.gov/datatypes/>. <http://bibframe.example.org/1553692#Work> at <http://id.loc.gov/ontologies/bibframe/Work>, <http://id.loc.gov/ontologies/bibframe/Text>; ns0:contribution [a ns0:Contribution, ns1:PrimaryContribution; ns0:agent <http://id.loc.gov/authorities/names/n92000435>; ns0:role <http://id.loc.gov/vocabulary/relators/ctb>]; ns0:title [at ns0:Title; ns0:mainTitle "Up she flew"]; ns0:hasInstance <http://bibframe.example.org/1553692#Instance>. <http://id.loc.gov/authorities/names/n92000435> to ns0:Agent, ns0:Person; ns1:name00MatchKey "Gorman, Michael, 1952-"; ns1:primaryContributorName00MatchKey "Gorman, Michael, 1952-"; ns1:name00MarcKey "1001 $aGorman, Michael,$d1952-"; rdfs:label "Gorman, Michael, 1952-". <http://id.loc.gov/vocabulary/relators/ctb> to ns0:Role. <http://bibframe.example.org/1553692#Instance> to ns0:Instance, ns0:Print; ns0:carrier <http://id.loc.gov/vocabulary/carriers/nc>; ns0:media <http://id.loc.gov/vocabulary/mediaTypes/n>; ns0:identifiedBy [at ns0:Isbn; rdf:value "0948339675"];

Continued

Table 2.6 *Continued*

Example of a bibliographic record in MARC 21	**Example of metadata in VRA Core**	**Example of entities in BIBFRAME**
	vocab=”TGN” refid=”1000003” extent=”continent”>Europe</na me> </location> </locationSet> <titleSet> <display>Chartres Cathedral</display> <title type=”cited” pref=”true” xml:lang=”en”>Chartres Cathedral</title> <title type=”cited” pref=”false” xml:lang=”fr”>Notre-Dame de Chartres </title> <title type=”cited” pref=”false” xml:lang=”fr”>Cathédrale Notre-Dame de Chartres</title> </titleSet> <worktypeSet> <display>buildings; basilicas; buildings; religious buildings; churches; cathedrals</display> <worktype vocab=”AAT” refid=”300007501”>cathedral</w orktype> <worktype vocab=”AAT” refid=”300170443”>basilica</wor ktype> </worktypeSet> </work> <image id=”i_100” href=”http://core.vraweb.org/exa mples/html/example001_full.ht ml” refid=”100” source=”VRA Core Oversight Committee, Core 4 Sample Records”> <relationSet> <relation type=”imageOf” refid=”1” source=”Core 4 Sample Database (VCat)”/> </relationSet> <titleSet> <display>Total view of West facade</display> <title type=”generalView”>Total view of West facade</title> </titleSet> <worktypeSet> <display>digital image</display> <notes/> <worktype/> </worktypeSet> </image> </vra>	ns0:responsibilityStatement “Michael Gorman”; ns0:title [at ns0:Title; ns0:mainTitle “Up she flew”]; ns0:extent [to ns0:Extent; rdfs:label “90 p.”]; ns0:dimensions “22 cm.”; ns0:instanceOf <http://bibframe.example.org/15 53692#Work>; ns0:hasItem <http://bibframe.example.org/15 53692#Item050–12>. ns0:itemOf <http://bibframe.example.org/15 53692#Instance>.

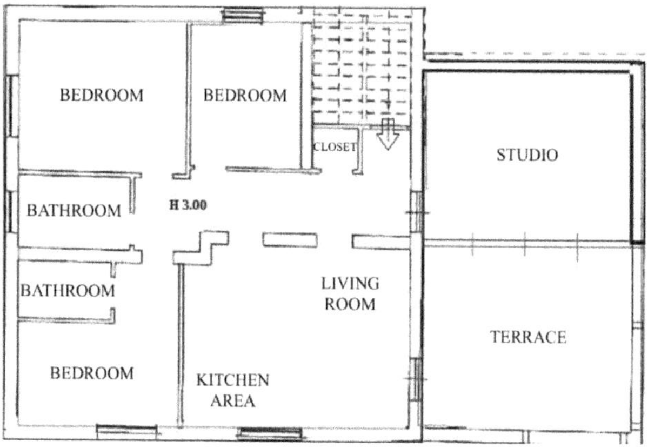

Floor plan:
Address expressed with:
Street/Square
House no.
Postal code
Municipality
Province

Example:
Street/Square: Via Casale Giuliani
House no.: 15
Postal code: 00141
Municipality: Roma
Province: RM

Urban Cadastre:
Urban area
Page
Parcel
Sub parcel

Example:
Urban area: -
Page: 9
Parcel: 570
Sub parcel: 3

Figure 2.18 *Representation of the same object from three different visual and functional perspectives: a floor plan, an urban cadastre map, a geolocation map*

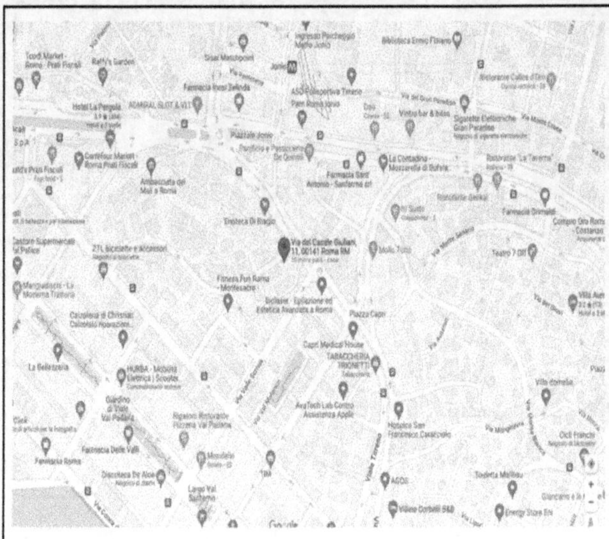	Coordinates of geolocation: *Latitude* *Longitude* Example: Latitude: 41.94465077744865, Longitudine: 12.527141436237137

Figure 2.18 *Continued*

It is important to emphasise that the change in perspective is not an end in itself, nor is it a philosophical choice or a trend; it has a functional necessity, to identify, describe and communicate the same data for different purposes. This might seem, for a library, to be a departure from its primary or traditional goal, that of its catalogue and its users. In reality it is an expression of a positive, and I would say, inevitable broadening of the horizon. It is as if things are being looked at from an increasingly broader perspective, in an ever-expanding horizon. Starting with the local dimension of one's own catalogue, it moves to include new material, new services, new types of users, as well as unavoidable influences from related worlds (cross-domain and interoperability). For now, this journey leads to the web, where every local 'thing' becomes tremendously small and limited when compared with the vastness that the web represents. And it is inevitable that a change in perspective also generates a change of language. If previously it was sufficient to speak of *document*, despite all the uncertainties about what a document really is (Buckland, 1997),[197] now we must adopt more globally recognisable terms, such as that of *resource*,[198] which in its generality and neutrality best expresses the totality of things describable on the web.[199]

Conclusions on the transition from record to entity modelling

The reflections proposed in this chapter start from a concept overused when talking about linked data applied to the bibliographic field, namely the shift from record to real-world object, in order to try to better define what is meant by real-world object and how this term has entered bibliographic jargon and is used. The investigation carried out here is closely related to the analysis proposed in Chapter 1, in which the entity/identity pair is investigated from a predominantly philosophical perspective to identify a criterion for applying this terminology within the cataloguing discipline. The distinction between real-world entity and real-world object, or more simply between entity and real-world object, implies the conjecture of a complex entity that expresses itself through different identities. Computer science, especially in its capacity for object-oriented programming, helps us to better focus on this hypothesis of shaping the bibliographic universe, which had long since relied on entity-relationship models but struggles to focus and build consensus on the concept of the real-world object as a new protagonist on the cataloguing scene. In the remainder of this study, using the case of agent modelling, we will see how entities are modelled as real-world objects in different cultural contexts and how it may be possible to hypothesise that an identifier is assigned not only to the real-world object as an expression of an entity's identity, but for the entity itself to address, in terms of modelling, the challenges that especially diachronic and synchronic entities pose to current metadata activities.

CHAPTER 3
Panta Rei, or the Fluidity of the Universe

> One cannot descend twice into the same river and touch a mortal substance twice in the same state, but because of the impetuosity and speed of change it disperses and gathers, comes and goes.
>
> (Heraclitus, *On Nature*)

> The bud disappears when the blossom breaks through, and we might say that the former is refuted by the latter; in the same way when the fruit comes, the blossom may be explained to be a false form of the plant's existence, for the fruit appears as its true nature in place of the blossom. These stages are not merely differentiated; they supplant one another as being incompatible with one another. But the ceaseless activity of their own inherent nature makes them at the same time moments of an organic unity, where they not merely do not contradict one another, but where one is as necessary as the other; and this equal necessity of all moments constitutes alone and thereby the life of the whole.
>
> (G. W.F. Hegel, *Phenomenology of Spirit*)

Introduction

Entity modelling requires special attention to the identification of entities through the different profiles in which the entity itself can be presented. The multiplicity of profiles, which could correspond to different identities or even simply to different descriptions of the same identity, makes the entity a multifaceted object, with boundaries that are not always clear and often fluid. It is this element of fluidity that is investigated in this part of the study, beginning with the assumption that things change their properties over time, despite which we cannot forgo identifying their boundaries. In this context, special consideration is therefore necessary for those changes of properties in entities that may prove decisive to their identifiability or their very metaphysical nature. The concept of *Cambridge change*, used to denote metaphysically non-decisive changes, and a partial redefinition of it help to point to a certain kind of semantic relationship that cannot, perhaps, be ignored in the logic of entity identification. The challenge for those who must identify and classify things in the world is to grasp their traits from their fluidity, and to define them in some way so that they are then transmissible to machines.

The entity as a prism

In the previous chapters, we have discussed the complex entities that populate our world and become specific objects of study when they are part of the bibliographic universe being investigated. Each entity is complex in its own way, even those that seem simplest to us. Certainly, some entities are particularly complex or become so when richly expressed or shared in different information contexts. Profiling a monographic work published just once, in a single language, is far less challenging than defining the contours of a work published across several editions, in many different languages and formats. Identifying this kind of entity, in entity modelling processes, is indeed complex.

The prism and its faces in synchronic and diachronic identities

The complexity of entities can be expressed with a prism, a solid figure in which each face represents a unique identity or a different way of expressing the same identity. Focusing on this image, we now revisit some examples of complex entities referred to in the first chapter to try to represent them with a prism.

In the case of synchronic identities – such as pseudonyms, alter egos, heteronyms – we imagine that the entity is the prism in its entirety and that each face is a different identity. Thus, the cases we used as a study of this type of entity can be schematised, simplistically, in this way:

entity a: person Charles Lutwidge Dodgson and his pseudonym;

> *identity 1*: Charles Lutwidge Dodgson, Daresbury 1832 – Guildford 1898, (registry or birth identity), Victorian-era British writer, mathematician, photographer, logician and Anglican priest
>
> *identity 2*: Lewis Carroll, author of the poem *Solitude*, published in 1856 and author of famous novels such as *Alice's Adventures in Wonderland* and *Through the Looking Glass and What Alice Found There*

entity b: person Marshall Mathers, his alter ego and pseudonym;

> *identity 1*: Marshall Bruce Mathers III, American rapper, record producer and actor
>
> *identity 2*: Slim Shady, musical alter ego of Marshall Mathers
>
> *identity 3*: Eminem, pseudonym of Marshall Mathers, U.S. rapper active since 1992, author of numerous albums, including *The Slim Shady LP, The Marshall Mathers LP, Encore, Revival*
>
> *identity 4*[200] : Bad Meets Evil, a rap duo formed by Eminem and the rapper *Royce da 5′9″*

entity c: person Fernando Pessoa, with his heteronyms;

identity 1: Fernando António Nogueira Pessoa (orthonym, 'that-he-is-him'), Lisbon, 13 June 1888 – Lisbon, 30 November 1935, was a Portuguese poet, writer and aphorist

identity 2: Bernardo Soares, a humble employee in an office in Lisbon's Baixa, semi-heteronym[201] of Fernando Pessoa, author of *Livro do Desassossego*

identity 3: Alberto Caeiro, born in Lisbon in 1879, bucolic poet, author of such works of poetry as *O Guardador de Rebanhos, O Pastor Amoroso and Poemas Inconjuntos,* heteronym of Fernando Pessoa

identity 4: Álvaro de Campos, born in Tavira, Portugal, on 15 October 1890, author of such poems as *Opiário, Ode Triunfal, Tabacaria* and *Ode Marítima,* heteronym of Fernando Pessoa

identity 5: Ricardo Reis, Latinist physician and monarchist, born in Oporto in 1887, author of the *Odes,* heteronym of Fernando Pessoa

In the case of synchronic identities, we can imagine that a prism is a live concert, and the different faces of the prism are the recordings of that performance from different points of view[202]:

entity a: live concert of Negramaro on 31 May 2008, at San Siro;

identity 1: Negramaro live concert on 31 May 31 2008, held by the band from Salento at the Giuseppe Meazza Stadium in Milan (San Siro 2008)

identity 2: *San Siro* Live, a live album by Negramaro released on 21 November 2008, in a boxed set, CD+DVD, documenting the 31 May 2008 concert, directed by Cristian Biondani. The box set contains not only the concert footage (109 minutes of music) but also 20 minutes of extra material

identity 3: unofficial amateur recording of the single *Parlami d'amore,*[203] by a live concert attendee (Emanuele Cisotti) and posted on YouTube

Again, the prism could represent the original work, and each face could represent the translation into a different language of said work:

entity b: *L'Étranger* by Albert Camus;

identity 1: *L'Étranger*, a novel by French writer and philosopher Albert Camus, published in 1942

identity 2: *Lo straniero,* Italian translation by Alberto Zevi of the novel *L'Étranger*

identity 3: *Lo straniero,* Italian translation by Sergio Claudio Perroni with introduction by Roberto Saviano of the novel *L'Étranger identity 4*: Der Fremde, German translation by Uli Aumüller of the novel *L'Étranger*

Or, as noted in Chapter 2, in the context of object-oriented programming, which observes and describes things from a certain point of view, each face of the prism could represent that particular point of view. The entity Charles Lutwidge Dodgson could be profiled with the identity of a writer, with the identity of a mathematician, photographer, logician, or Victorian British Anglican priest, depending on the context against which that entity is presented or observed.

Finally, a prism could also express an entity with each facet representing a *different interpretation of* the same identity. This is the case with bibliographic databases that are derived from the aggregation or integration of various sources, where the same entity and often the same identity is just represented differently for cultural, geographic, or linguistic reasons or due to the cataloguing rules adopted. Having different descriptive profiles of an author, of a work, of any object in the world, are the most common situations managed by data aggregation and, of course, in entity resolution processes.

A representation of one of the entities described here, the one regarding the rapper Eminem, is shown in Figure 3.1.

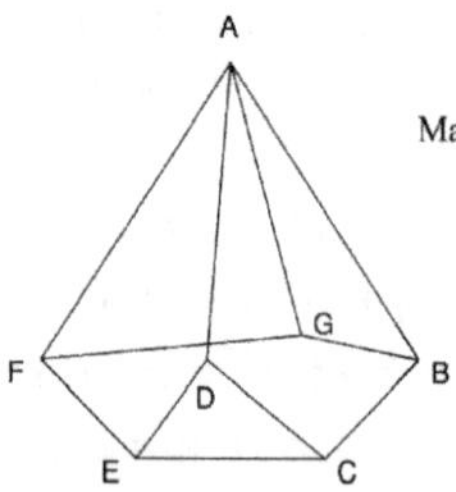

Marshall Mathers, his alter ego and pseudonyms;

- ABCD - *Identity 1*: Marshall Bruce Mathers III, American rapper, record producer, actor (registry name)
- CDE - *Identity 2*: Slim Shady, musical alter ego of Marshall Mathers
- ADEF - *Identity 3*: Eminem, pseudonym of Marshall Mathers, U.S. rapper active since 1992, author of numerous albums, including *The Slim Shady LP*, *The Marshall Mathers LP*, *Encore*, *Revival*

Figure 3.1 *The Marshall Mathers entity with some of its possible identities*

In these examples we have deliberately referenced the entity with as few terms as possible, just what is essential, highlighting the practical rather than theoretical difficulty of defining a specific entity without referring to one of its possible identities: how to define the *entity* Marshall Mathers without taking into account what is known to us about this person, namely his being a rapper, better known as Eminem, but also an actor, record producer and part of a musical duo? How to refer to the entity without mentioning at least one of the possible identities, even if only the demographic one? And how can one think that an entity could be better expressed by the birth identity (birth name, date of birth) in the context of the bibliographic universe within which these reflections are born and nurtured? There is one example of literary entity/identity that should, by itself, convince us otherwise: the writer Elena Ferrante,[204] whom we know as a woman, officially recognised as being born in Naples in 1943. We know, then, her work. This is her literary identity, useful for delineating her profiles and making them understandable to a machine. Around the author and her *real identity* there is extensive literature, beginning with her work *Frantumaglia: a Writer's Journey*, in which the writer tries to explain to the reader the importance of leaving her birth identity unknown for her vision of life and the relationship between author and writer:

> To explain all the reasons for my decision, is, as you know, hard for me. I will only tell you that it's a small wager with myself, with my convictions. I believe that books, once they are written, have no need of their authors. If they have something to say, they will sooner or later find readers; if not, they won't. There are plenty of examples.
>
> (Ferrante, 2016, 15)

Assuming that Elena Ferrante is a pseudonym and therefore an identity different from her birth identity, likely unknown to date, is irrelevant for our bibliographical universe. To identify this author as author of novels such as *Troubling Love* and *The Days of Abandonment*, defining the profile of the entity *per se*, understood metaphysically, or even just the birth identity, is of little significance. In the context of our universe and the entity modelling we are discussing, what we need is for the pseudonym or *nom de plume* identity to be recognisable, profilable and understandable to machines. In other contexts (imagine, for example, medical or fiscal ones), that identity might not be recognised and or considered valid, but that is not of interest to us here.

Even the case of Eminem, to which we earlier applied the prism representation exercise and the reference to the *Bad Meets Evil* duo[205] formed by Eminem and the rapper Royce da 5′9″ as another possible identity, draws attention to that boundary between entity and identity that is not easy to resolve definitively. We can only decide to simplify the thinking by accepting the more practical position of object-oriented programming, which forgoes describing and sometimes identifying the entity in its richness and focuses on what is *functional to the context*: how can I identify an entity if not by outlining its possible profile and thus possible identity? Whether *Bad Meets Evil* is a way for Eminem and Royce da 5′9″ to perform or whether it constitutes, in itself, a different entity with its own autonomous identity is, however, a question to be resolved, lest we confuse the message fed to the machines in the entity resolution process, where the final stage of identification involves the association of a unique and resolvable identifier.

In the case of *diachronic* identities, the prism representation becomes complicated for all the reasons already mentioned.[206] We imagined how complicated it might be to identify the boundaries of entities or identities that, over time, appear different or changed. We then reasoned about the need, functional to the definition of our bibliographic universe, to embrace the Aristotelian–scholastic position that helps us interpret things as constituted by a substratum; a substratum that, *in the absence of substantial mutation*, can be read as that selfness necessary to identify the thing itself. But it is precisely the assertion 'in the absence of substantial mutation' that, yet unresolved, confronts us with the need to delve deeper into what we mean, in defining the entities that make up the bibliographic universe or the broader informational universe, when we speak of mutations or changes. When well-defined boundaries represented by the individual faces of a solid figure are instead fluid, ceasing to have the sharpness necessary for identification processes, how can we continue to create profiles that are as sharable and communicable as possible to machines? In the first chapter of this study, we referred to some particular cases of diachronic identities, including:

- cases of gender transition in people
- cases of entities changing their names
- continuing resources.

In all these cases, analysed through specific examples, the question posed was whether and how the change resulted in an ontological mutation (thus the transition to a different entity) or whether and how the change resulted in a different identity, attributable to the same entity. Each time, in the analyses aimed at entity modelling, we focused on the *depth* of the change, on how much it affected or affects the generation of a different entity or simply a different identity. In this sense, entity modelling inquiries can be classified as the identification of *ontological break* or *identity break* of the things that constitute the bibliographic universe in order to better identify the *object* and communicate its profile, with its qualifying attributes and relations, to machines. And therefore, we must focus on the change to assess whether there really is a depth to it and whether the depth is classifiable with respect to our inquiry. To borrow the words of Lawrence Brian Lombard, the question to ask is 'Under what circumstances is it true to say of any object that it has changed?' (Lombard, 1978, 63).

Capturing things in change

To argue his theory of change (which we are not interested in revisiting and analysing in detail here but use only to sketch a brief philosophical outline of this concept) Lombard starts with the definition of change to which ancient philosophy referred:

> An object, x, changes if and only if there are distinct times, t and t^1, and a property, P, such that x has P at time t and fails to have P at time t^1 (or vice versa).

This definition of change is attributable to Plato's *Theaetetus* and Aristotle's *Physics*,[207] and is what Lombard calls 'The Ancient Criterion of Change'. Many centuries later this criterion for defining change is taken up almost identically by philosophers such as John Ellis McTaggart[208] and Bertrand Russell,[209] colleagues at the University of Cambridge, and is formulated as:

> A change has occurred if and only if there are distinct times, t and t^1, and a proposition, S, such that S is true at time t and false at time t^1.

In the article 'Cambridge Changes Revisited: Why Certain Relational Changes are Indispensable' David Weberman analyses Peter Geach's critique of this criterion of change as defined by the Cambridge school and identified as *Cambridge change*: Peter Geach qualifies this change with the expression 'mere Cambridge Change' to emphasise its triviality with respect to a hypothesis of *real* change. Change as expressed by McTaggart and Russell is false change insofar as it is too broad as a concept, making no distinction about the *type of* change: a thing x changes not only when it changes internally but also whenever it changes something to which x is in some relation, so that x comes to have different relational properties (Weberman, 1999). This is the point of Geach's critique of Cambridge change from which I attempt to define how changes affecting objects in the real world – and the bibliographic universe in particular – affect the definition of the entities. What interests us in this analysis is what kinds of change should be taken into consideration in the entity identification process and how to account for them in entity modelling procedures.

The 'mere Cambridge change' and a re-evaluation of relational change

If relational properties had a bearing on the definition of an entity's change, Socrates would change even after his death whenever a young student began to admire him. This is the perspective of Peter Geach in his critique of the Cambridge change, which identifies as a major limitation in the definition, thus formulated, the inability to distinguish between 'genuine changes, like the butter's melting, and bogus changes, like the butter's rising in price' (Geach, 1969, 72, 66).

In his critique, Geach proposes a more stringent formulation of change as an alternative: a thing *x* truly changes if and only if it has certain *intrinsic* properties at some time but not at another. This means that if entity *x* changes its relational properties (thus its relationships with other things) without any modification to its intrinsic (non-relational) properties, no change would be attributable to it. In the study that helps us think about change within the bibliographic universe, or rather the broader web, David Weberman seeks to relativise this position by analysing certain relational changes that are far from inconsequential to the nature of things and their definition. Weberman's position, 'doing justice to the metaphysics of certain aspects of reality requires recognising the genuineness of relational properties and relational changes' (Weberman, 1999, 140), is interesting to explore because it helps us provide a new theoretical foundation for the belief, certainly derived from practice, in the importance of relational properties in entity modelling. Following Weberman's analysis, let us see in what terms we can speak of qualifying relational properties for the identification and, in some cases, the definition of certain entities.

Intrinsic properties and extrinsic (or relational) properties

In Geach's proposed definition of change, *intrinsic properties* are those that a thing possesses regardless of its relationship to anything else, while *extrinsic* or *relational properties* are those that are wholly or partially dependent on something that is other than the thing itself. Only changes involving intrinsic properties are real changes, while anything related to extrinsic properties cannot be defined as such: being an uncle, being a judge's neighbour, being loved by Joe, or having red-haired sisters (all examples from Weberman's article) are all relational properties that, by changing (e.g. by moving to another neighbourhood, away from the former neighbour) do not change the entity itself. Even where the property apparently has no relational term outside the thing itself – in expressions such as 'perceives', 'is faithful', 'is gregarious' (Ishiguro, 1990) – we cannot but recognise relational properties, acknowledging as implicit the related term:

> Thus, the property ascribed to the subject carries implicit reference to other entities. An animal will not perceive unless there is an object, a phenomenon it perceives. A person is not faithful without there being another person related to him in a certain way to whom he is faithful. A person is not gregarious unless there are other people whose company he seeks. In this sense, these properties depend on some relation of the thing to other things and are, therefore, relational.
>
> (Ishiguro, 1990, 105)[210]

This distinction between intrinsic and extrinsic properties expresses a certain way of intuitively understanding things in the world. Precisely because it is intuitively possible, it has made its way into many reflections, including ethical and philosophical ones. Perhaps the simplest definition of 'intrinsic property' is the one given by Stephen Yablo: 'You know what an intrinsic property is: it's a property that a thing has (or lacks) regardless of what may be going on outside of itself' (Yablo, 1999, 479) and could be complemented by the definition given by David Lewis:

> Some properties of things are entirely intrinsic, or internal, to the things that have them: shape, charge, internal structure. Other properties are not entirely intrinsic: being a brother, being in debt, being within three miles of Carfax, thinking of Vienna. These properties are at least partly extrinsic, or relational. Properties may be more or less extrinsic; being a brother has more of an admixture of intrinsic than being a sibling does, yet both are extrinsic.
>
> (Lewis, 1983, 197)

These theoretical definitions of intrinsic and extrinsic properties have many limitations. They may work well on paper but much less so when applying them to the real-life things. According to these classifications, being a father is certainly a relational, thus extrinsic, property; but the supposition that being a father has a *relational depth* quite different from being a clerk at the post office, is something on which, without too much sophistication, we can all agree. And if one becomes a father or mother only at the birth of a child, there remains a strong feeling that one does not stop being a father at the moment that child should die. In the practice of entity modelling, as well as in the classificatory exercises we do daily to orient ourselves in the world, we are instinctively inclined to recognise the 'in-itselfness' of objects by distinguishing intrinsic from extrinsic properties: I differentiate a medical syringe from a pastry syringe not by the fact that the one object tends to be in a medicine drawer and the other in a kitchen drawer (I might inadvertently put the pastry syringe in the medicine drawer, which would not make it a medical syringe), but by what we consider, perhaps, the intrinsic properties of each of these two objects (the material, the size, the ability to insert a needle or a pastry nozzle). And this classificatory exercise is certainly what entity modelling requires and what the traditional cataloguing rules already suggested. The definition of *core elements*[211] in RDA, while never referring to a possible distinction between intrinsic and extrinsic properties, tends to emphasise the *signature elements* of certain entities, regardless of their relationships to other entities, useful in identifying and defining the entity itself. The Librarianship Studies & Information Technology website defines

RDA core elements, with reference to chapter RDA 0.6: Core Element of the Original RDA Toolkit, as follows:

> *Core elements* in *RDA* are minimum elements required for describing resources. Core elements are a new feature of RDA which allowed for certain metadata elements to be identified as 'required' in the cataloguing process. The assignment of core status is based on attributes mandatory for a national level record, as documented in the FRBR/FRAD modules. At a minimum, a bibliographic description should include all the required core elements that are applicable. Core-ness is identified at the element level. Some elements are always core (if applicable and the information is available); some are core only in certain situations.[212]

As an example, take the elements considered essential by RDA for the entity *Person* (in Section 9, Identification of Persons, of the Original RDA Toolkit). We find that *essential elements* are considered only the person's preferred name, dates of birth and death, and identifier, while other elements – such as the person's title, form of full name, profession or occupation – are considered essential only under certain conditions: specifically, when it is necessary to add qualifying elements to distinguish that element from others. We shall then see how the importance given by the cataloguing rules to the two categories of elements identifying an entity (attributes and relationships) increasingly assigns a fundamental role to relationships and less importance to attributes in entity description practices.[213] But in entity modelling processes and for the investigation of changes that may or may not give rise to a new identity, it is not unimportant to give weight to the different properties of an entity by analysing their depth. Entity modelling is not only concerned with describing an entity once it has been identified (as cataloguing mostly does) but is concerned with identifying those elements that are useful for the very resolution of the entity, and thus for profiling the entity before its description. Therefore, it is appropriate to return to the consideration of change and how it may affect the nature of entities.

The reality of relational changes

We saw that in response to a definition of change that is overly generic, presented in the form of the Cambridge change, Geach introduces the element of the intrinsic nature of properties which, if subject to change, can define *real change*. Geach's critique of the idea that any change is pertinent to the definition of the nature of an entity is reinforced by presenting the possible effects of this position. If Socrates' death not only causes Xantippe's widowhood, but also Xantippe's sister to become a widow's sister, and so on, the risk is that a nearly endless chain of changes will be generated:

> Recognizing the genuineness of relational change would seem to entail that if anything changes (at time t), everything changes (at time t) since everything bears some relation to any particular changing thing.
>
> (Weberman, 1999, 141)

The risk of an endless series of changes, producing a change in me at the flap of a butterfly's wings a thousand miles away, is obvious, and this risk, as a natural consequence of a failure to distinguish between real and false changes, seems clearly to support Geach's restrictive position. The risk of downgrading relational properties to *false* or *unreal* is equally high, which is why Weberman insists on arguing the case for the reality of not all but certainly some relational changes:

> First, I make no claim about *all* but only about *some* relational changes. Second, I assert neither that genuine relational changes are necessarily changes in essential properties nor that the distinction between extrinsic and intrinsic is indefensible. I propose only that some relational changes are genuine insofar as they are indispensable for making sense of certain structures of reality.
>
> (Weberman, 1999, 142)

Having defined one's position and the importance of identifying relevant relational properties in the modelling of things, other problems will have to be solved, including that of distinguishing which relational properties to consider as relevant and which not. And the examples Weberman proposes before defining a possible classification criterion are particularly interesting, because, by analogy, some of them bring us back to the entity modelling cases in the bibliographic universe. The examples refer to particular contexts in which relational properties can take on specific importance – value, kinship, institutions, art, historical events:

1 **Value:** Imagine a $1 bill[214] is stored in a drawer, no longer used since it was declared out of circulation. According to Geach's definition of change, loss of value does not constitute a real change in the banknote, which has not undergone any intrinsic alteration. This position would entail asserting that the substance of the banknote is not in its value (its purchasing power) but only in its physicality.
2 **Kinship:** Becoming a father, wife, or widower is certainly a change that involves relational properties rather than properties that we might

consider intrinsic.[215] For parenthood to produce substantial change in a person also requires some degree of awareness. Therefore, if a person becomes a parent without knowing it, we can imagine that the change is less profound. Still, parental status, or the civil status of having entered into marriage, is not insignificant, at least in legal terms. That relational change, then, does not seem to be false or trivial.

3 **Institutions:** Becoming president of the Republic, winning a Nobel Prize, or becoming pope does not change the person *per se*, but it certainly changes a community's perception of that person, as well as the power and strength (decision-making, influence) that comes with the role. A community's recognition of a role is a relevant relational (not intrinsic) change that is difficult to dismiss as false.
4 **Art:** Works of art are objects that have a strong relationship with the context they are in, greatly influenced by their surroundings. A figure in a painting changes not physically but aesthetically by virtue of the fact that it takes on new relational properties. Being surrounded by one background or another significantly changes the image of the figure itself, although it itself has not changed substantially.
5 **Historical events:** The perspective with which we view a historical event takes into account the role of that event in the larger narrative framework. In a historical reconstruction of an event, what happened before and after that event greatly influences the perception of the event itself. A historical event may itself be changed by the occurrence of different events or circumstances which were not previously known. Relational changes, again, greatly affect the shaping of the event itself. In the case of human history, for example, a simple shooting becomes a murder and thus changes as a result of the victim's subsequent death. Or the Russian Revolution of 1918 changes as a historical event following the collapse of Soviet communism in 1989–1991. With subsequent events, the nature of these historical facts changes significantly as relationships shift, thus capable of changing the past.

The common denominator among these examples is that they express entities that are identifiable not in terms of their intrinsic properties (in their objective physicality), but in terms of their *emergent* relational properties.

> In each case, we identify or individuate the entity or phenomenon not in terms of its intrinsic physical properties, but in terms of its emergent relational properties resulting in the circumstance that such entities can sometimes be said to change genuinely when they change relationally.
>
> (Weberman, 1999, 145)

Weberman introduces, therefore, this concept of emergent *properties* and emergent *entities* (those entities in which emergent properties involve real change) and describes these as entities that have their own physical concreteness, but which, because of their complexity or originality, are not reducible or completely explicable through their physical properties. The concept of *emergent property* is not unambiguous, and it is therefore difficult to give a definition. In general, we consider *emergent* those phenomena occurring in complex systems, which can be considered new, different (even unexpected, but this is not the feature we are interested in) from the properties of any single component of the system itself. These properties *emerge* from the organisation of the system, through the interactions that occur among the various components of the system.[216] The contexts used by Weberman for the examples are significant but not exhaustive of the various ontological situations that might correspond to these emergent entities (or entities with emergent properties). To connect these reflections to our specific bibliographic context we can use an example that might apply to all, that of the person who becomes pope and who writes both as a private individual and as pope. This is one of the most controversial entities in cataloguing practice, and therefore in entity modelling, but which can perhaps be analysed in the light of what has been said so far.

Examples of emerging entities in cataloguing

Attention to entity relationships in cataloguing has a long tradition. Barbara Tillett's masterful work on this topic has already been cited here (Tillett, 1987).[217] The FRBR model, which is the first entity-relationship model officially proposed in cataloguing, is based on the need to ensure the identification of resources and thus 'meet the needs of users more effectively'[218] (Bianchini, 2005, 54). Even from a technological point of view, and as a solution for creating links between records, in the mid-1970s the MARC formats added specific blocks of relationship tags intended to create links between different bibliographic descriptions (not yet between entities, as was later defined in the work of Tillett and then FRBR).[219] We have also noted how in IFLA LRM the number of attributes associated with each entity is increasingly reduced in favour of modelling new entities, and thus new possible relationships between entities.

What we are analysing here is the type of relational property that, even if not clearly identifiable, underlies a certain kind of entity to the point of changing its profile. To revisit another definition of emergent property, let us recall what is meant by this expression:

> Emergent properties are properties that arise as a result of various system components working together, not as a property of a single component. In other words, it is a property that a complex system or a set of parts of a system possesses, but that the individual parts do not possess.
>
> (Nelson, 2018)

And it is interesting to see how this type of property manifests itself in different bibliographic entities, or rather, in different contexts in which certain entities are expressed, and how it influences entity modelling activities far beyond what some intrinsic properties can do. To this point, I propose two significant examples – that of the Supreme Pontiff and that of continuing resources – both multifaceted and complex cases in terms of cataloguing, which pass on this complexity to entity modelling processes. I will then conclude this chapter with a counterexample: an intrinsic property that, due to a number of historical and sociological factors, might completely lose its significance in entity modelling procedures.

The case of the Supreme Pontiff

Among the most complex situations to deal with in both cataloguing and entity modelling is that of people who hold official roles and are signatories to official acts. This category includes popes, presidents, monarchs and all those who hold an official role in an institution or community. Complicating the picture is the possibility that the same person produces their own work, not related to their institutional profile but to their private one.

A well-known example of this type of entity is the Pope, the Supreme Pontiff of the Roman Catholic Church and thus the signatory of official documentation, e.g, encyclicals. A peculiarity that complicates the analysis of and heading choice[220] for this type of person is that assuming the role also involves the choice of a name other than their birth name, the *pontifical name*.

This cataloguing scenario is intricate (it already was in the traditional standard), and it has produced a vast amount of metadata, rendered inconsistent precisely due to the complexity of applying the standard. Entity modelling activities, starting therefore with mixed cataloguing data, are strongly affected by this complexity, which I will try to address here by relying on the concept of *emergent entities* or *emergent properties*. A broader examination of some cataloguing rules referring to the treatment of this type of entry and then arriving at some modelling hypotheses will be addressed in Chapter 4, concerning the Agent. Let's take a look at why the case of the Pope is significant and in what terms it corresponds to the idea of an emergent entity.

The Roman Pontiff as the Supreme Authority of the Roman Catholic Church

The Code of Canon Law, in canon 330,[221] establishes the close union between the Roman Pontiff and the bishops by the will of the Lord:

> Just as by the Lord's decision Saint Peter and the other Apostles constitute one college, so in a like manner the Roman Pontiff, the successor of Peter, and the bishops, the successors of the Apostles, are united among themselves.
>
> (Codice di Diritto canonico, n.d.)

The same concept is reiterated in canon 333, §2 where it states that the Roman Pontiff, in the fulfilment of his ministry as supreme pastor of the Church, is always united in communion with the other bishops and indeed with the whole Church:

> In fulfilling the office of supreme pastor of the Church, the Roman Pontiff is always joined in communion with the other bishops and with the universal Church. He nevertheless has the right, according to the needs of the Church, to determine the manner, whether personal or collegial, of exercising this office.
>
> (Codice di Diritto canonico, n.d.)

In this unique entity of the Roman Catholic Church with its bishops and Supreme Pontiff, we can see a complex organism within which an emergent property is expressed, namely, a property that is not found, in isolation, in each individual component of the organism but that is expressed, precisely within this complexity, as a specific property.

The ministry of Pastor of the Church, by which the Roman Pontiff exercises supreme authority over the Roman Catholic Church, is the *munus petrinum* (the spiritual office) which, together with the ministerium (the *ministerial office,* that is the concrete exercise of that power), makes the Pope that complex entity both in sacramental, juridical and then, cataloguing terms. The *munus* is exercised for the good of the whole Church to safeguard the unity of ecclesial communion (Ghirlanda, 2013). 'From the moment of valid election and acceptance, the person elected to the papal throne abandons ipso facto the college of cardinals and its status, to assume a new rank that confers to him, in a new and very special way, primatial authority' (Vitale, 2021). The insight into the power of this investiture, which makes an individual the Pastor of the whole Church, is evident in the cataloguing tradition, especially the Anglo-American one, which, as we shall see in Chapter 4, seeks to distinguish the sacramental investiture from the legally relevant figure that this investiture entails. This distinguishes official acts of the Roman Catholic Church, signed by the Pope by virtue of his primatial office, from works written under the pontifical name but as an individual and, therefore, outside that ministry. The change in status that occurs with the acceptance of the election as Roman Pontiff is a relational change, certainly, but one so profound that it generates a new identity and, according to a certain cataloguing interpretation, which we will explore later, even a new entity. Hence the use of an access point to the entity Roman Catholic Church, with reference then to the specific pope, for documentation issued as an official expression of this body. The Code of Canon Law, at canon 331, expresses rather clearly what, specifically, the emergent property we are identifying is and what, therefore, is the relative emergent entity:[222]

> The bishop of the Roman Church, in whom continues the office given by the Lord uniquely to Peter, the first of the Apostles, and to be transmitted to his successors, is the head of the college of bishops, the Vicar of Christ, and the pastor of the universal Church on earth. By virtue of his office he possesses supreme, full, immediate, and universal ordinary power in the Church, which he is always able to exercise freely.
>
> (Codice di Diritto canonico, n.d.)

Here again, it seems useful to recall the definition, cited earlier in the endnotes, that the Stanford Encyclopedia of Philosophy offers of 'emergent property': 'The general notion of emergence is meant to conjoin these twin characteristics of dependence and autonomy.' The Pope is totally dependent on the existence of a community and a universal Church but at the same time he freely exercises the power conferred on him by his election to the papal throne and by the acceptance of this investiture. Important from the perspective of cataloguing practice and especially entity modelling is that the first public act of the newly elected Pope – the presentation to the community of the Church and to the whole world – takes place via the announcement by the senior cardinal deacon of the *name of* the new pontiff who, in his new status, bestows the *Urbi et Orbi* blessing. The name assumed by the new Pope is one of the strongest qualifying attributes for the recognition of the new identity. However, it is also widely misunderstood, as we shall later see.

What is certain is that through this investiture, in its free acceptance and official presentation of a new name, we pinpoint the first of those identity breaks we have been talking about. Let us try to establish it before proceeding in our analysis (Table 3.1).

The relational property of having accepted the ministry of pastor of the Church has no bearing on the physicality *of* the entity, yet it produces a change in status that is far more influential than any physical change.

Table 3.1 *Identification of one of the possible identity breaks for the pope type entity*

Identity type	Event	Ontological/identity break[223]	Evidence of identity break
Pope	Acceptance of election to the papal throne	yes (I)	Pontifical name assumption

The Pope Emeritus and his renunciation of the office of Roman Pontiff

'Well aware of the seriousness of this act, with full freedom I declare that I renounce the ministry of Bishop of Rome, Successor of Saint Peter, entrusted to me by the Cardinals on 19 April 2005.'[224] These are the words of Benedict XVI on 11 February 2013, before the cardinals gathered in Consistory to declare his renunciation of the Petrine ministry. This act, not unique in the history of the Church but innovative with respect to its formulation,[225] introduced a topic of discussion that would later be widely discussed in the ecclesial community, in juridical, theological, and spiritual terms. The opinions on the significance of this renunciation are numerous and range from the most extreme, 'ridden by the most agitated and sedevacantist faction of Francis' opponents', (Tornielli, 2016) to the more moderate, willing to analyse its novel elements while excluding any hypothesis of a 'shared papacy' (Ghirlanda, 2013; Vitale, 2021).[226] Reviewing this issue briefly helps us focus on another nebulous element in the identification of the *pope* entity within the cataloguing tradition first and entity modelling later.[227]

Benedict XVI's renunciation of the Petrine ministry re-proposes a subtle yet complex element, namely the distinction between *munus* (the spiritual element) and *ministerium* (the administrative exercise). For some, Benedict XVI would have voluntarily renounced the *ministerium* and not the *munus*, which could go so far as to mean, in an extreme view, that Benedict XVI 'would have renounced acting as the pope but not being the pope' (Vitale 2021), paving the way for a hypothesis of an *enlarged papacy* and thus the presence of two popes simultaneously (Benedict XVI, Pope Emeritus, and Pope Francis). Supporting this hypothesis, part of the scholarly community refers to the same concept expressed in the constitution *Lumen gentium*[228] but here explicitly referring to the episcopal office, which is based on the double nature of the transmission of power: 'sacramental, regarding holy orders and the episcopal consecration upon which it is founded (*munus*); and juridical, regarding the conferral of the canonical mission and the consequent freedom in its exercise (*ministerium – potestas)*' (Vitale, 2021, 2–3).

The distinction between *potestas ordinis* and *potestas iurisdictionis* explains the admissibility of the term emeritus attributed to a bishop who, when having lost the *potestas iurisdictionis* (e.g. when, upon reaching the age of 75, he renounces pastoral governance), retains the *potestas ordinis* (thus the episcopal *munus*) that had been transmitted with consecration. To explain this mechanism, Vitale offers the example of the parental figure, a father who, having reached the age of 80, no longer has the strength to act as a father (practically, in taking care of his children) but does not cease to be a father. And it is precisely from this attribution of the term *emeritus* (considered by many, including Vitale, as 'affective or paternalistic') that Benedict XVI assigns himself the title of Pope Emeritus, evidently linked to the new status assumed upon his renunciation. As Ratzinger himself explained in the two missives sent to Cardinal Walter Brandmüller in November 2017 and published by the popular German newspaper *Bild*, the intent is simply to protect himself from potential excessive media exposure: 'With the Pope Emeritus I tried to create a situation in which I was absolutely inaccessible to the media and in which it was fully clear that there is only one pope.'[229]

The choice of the title of Pope Emeritus did not convince a large part of the canonist community, not only because of the novelty of the expression in the history of the Church, but also because of the risk of leaving an opening for those who believe a 'papacy of two' is possible. Perhaps this is why the Jesuit canonist Gianfranco Ghirlanda insists on proposing the adoption of another title for one who renounces the mandate: 'It is evident that a pope who has resigned is no longer the Pope, therefore he no longer has any power in the Church and cannot interfere in any governance matters. One may wonder what title Benedict XVI will retain. We think that he should be given the title of Bishop Emeritus of Rome, like any other diocesan bishop who steps down' (Ghirlanda, 2013).

Several canon law scholars argue against the applicability of the distinction between *munus* and *ministerium* to the figure of the pope including Rosario Vitale, from whom I have drawn some useful passages to frame the discussion, the aforementioned Gianfranco Ghirlanda (Ghirlanda, 2013), as well as Bishop Giuseppe Sciacca, secretary of the Apostolic Signatura and auditor general of the Apostolic Chamber.[230] The canonist Stefano Violi, however, seems to position himself in favour of the distinction. In his historical and juridical reconstruction of the pope's renunciation, Violi presents his interpretation through a precise analysis of Benedict XVI's February 2013 *Declaratio* and the text articulated during Pope Benedict XVI's last general audience of 27 February 2013[231] (Violi, 2013). Some points of this speech are particularly significant, not for settling the theological or legal question of the Pope's renunciation, but to understand the spirit and sentiment behind this historic gesture. Benedict XVI's words help us return to that identity shift that we have observed with his election to the papal throne:

> Here allow me to return once again to April 19, 2005. The gravity of the decision was precisely in the fact that from that moment on I was committed always and forever by the Lord. Always – he, who assumes the Petrine ministry no longer has any privacy. He belongs always and totally to everyone, to the whole Church. His life is, so to speak, totally deprived of the private sphere.

Here is the clear confirmation of that shift from the private dimension (expressed by the baptismal name of the one who will be Pope) to the spiritual and juridical dimension, which the acceptance of the election assigns. And Benedict XVI continues:

> The 'always' is also a 'forever' – there is no returning to private life. My decision to forgo the exercise of active ministry, does not revoke this. I do not return to private life, to a life of travel, meetings, receptions, conferences and so on. I do not abandon the cross, but remain in a new way near to the Crucified Lord. I no longer wield the power of the office for the government of the Church, but in the service of prayer I remain, so to speak, within St Peter's bounds. St Benedict, whose name I bear as Pope, shall be a great example in this for me. He showed us the way to a life which, active or passive, belongs wholly to the work of God.

Addressing the question between renunciation of the *ministerium* and permanence of the *munus* is a daunting challenge for anyone not an expert in canon law. And this is not the place to attempt it. What matters here, instead, is to verify whether the resignation of the ministry can be understood as a new identity shift in the figure of the Pope, which helps to explain some of the choices made in cataloguing and which recur with the same importance in entity modelling activities. From what has been reconstructed, with a partial selection of the many reflections and positions that Benedict XVI's historic decision has solicited, it seems to confirm the desire of the resigned Pope himself to confer the title Pope Emeritus with a different weight from that of any other title. Beyond the spiritual *munus*, which the individual may or may not retain following a declaration of resignation, certainly juridically, the Pope *no longer serves as pope* and therefore loses that power of administration of the ministry. As Pope Emeritus, we cannot expect the name to be associated with official acts of the corpus of the Catholic Church. Yet on the other hand, the return to the cardinal name (or to the name that expressed the priestly but private dimension) is also inadequate, since the element of spirituality granted by *munus petrinum* evidently remains. Here the identity shift arises from an absence, not by the assumption, of something. It is the renunciation of the Petrine ministry, of the governance of the universal Church, which removes that emergent property that makes the Supreme

Pontiff what he is. On the other hand, a return to the status of bishop or cardinal no longer seems possible, perhaps (but here I suspend judgment, deferring to Benedict XVI's private decision) because of that *munus*, that spiritual investiture that appears to remain. The identity break by subtraction is, however, juridically certifiable. The second identity break is defined in Table 3.2.

Table 3.2 *Identification of another of the possible identity breaks for the entity type 'pope'*

Identity type	Event	Ontological/identity break	Evidence of identity break
Pope Emeritus	Renunciation of the Petrine ministry	yes (I)	Assumption of the title 'Pope Emeritus'

Sanctity as a non-significant attribute

I would like to address at once possible questions as to why I used the example of Pope Emeritus and not other titles, such as *Blessed* or *Saint*, for the discussion of significant changes in entity modelling. In truth, in formulating the possible objection, I have already provided a partial answer: we are not concerned here with what attributes are useful to identify an entity, to disambiguate a case of homonymy or other ambiguous cases, where it is necessary to add qualifiers for a correct identification. This is indeed the domain of entity modelling, but at another operational level – when, for example, data present on bibliographic and authority records are mapped to improve entity resolution processes. To understand the context of this reasoning, we must return to Lawrence Brian Lombard's question: 'Under what circumstances is it true to say of any object that it has changed?' (Lombard, 1978, 63). The attribution of the title Blessed or Saint occurs through a process, respectively of beatification[232] or canonisation,[233] by which the Roman Catholic Church recognises merits or earthly virtues of a deceased person, and grants authorisation for public veneration. In both cases the Supreme Pontiff, in his authority as head of the Roman Catholic Church, grants that a faithful Catholic, whose particular merits have been recognised, may be publicly venerated. Specifically, canonisation is sanctioned in the 'final judgment by which the pope, by an act involving his infallibility, determines that a blessed person be inscribed in the catalogue of saints and that his memory may be celebrated in the universal Church.'[234]

The title of Blessed or Saint, which cataloguing rules in some circumstances recognise as a qualifying element for the identification of the described entity,[235] in no way expresses a substantial change or relational property relevant to the entity itself. Cataloguing rules have always devoted a few lines on how to record particular terms and qualifications in access points, focusing, for the most part, on the structuring of access and usage in relation to the description of individual resources. The primary aim has always been to disambiguate any potentially identical access strings. That power granted to the individual upon election to the papal throne, whose effects are visible in the governance of an autonomous state as well as in the indisputable power to grant the canonisation of a deceased person, does not concern the recognition of beatitude or sainthood. This recognition is limited to a community (that of the Roman Catholic Church) and therefore has no concrete effect in the bibliographic domain. And it is perhaps by resorting to a mechanism that is typical of cataloguing that I will attempt to better define the difference between a relational property like that of becoming pope and an honorific property like that of becoming a saint. If we consider possible cross-references between different access points related to the same entity, cataloguing rules offer various types of cross-references, among them these two:

- the *see* reference
- the *see also* reference.

The *see* reference is defined as a reference between strings (access points or headings) from a discarded (or variant) form to a chosen or authorised or preferred form. On the other hand, the *see also* reference (which the REICATs call *referral,* to distinguish it from the *see* reference) links two forms both accepted as preferred (or uniform or authorised, depending on the time of the rule). Without going into the details of the definitions of reference, cross-reference or refer to, in various cataloguing rules, I will focus on the mechanism that these types of references produce in cataloguing software.

The *see* reference obviously does not allow bibliographic records (thus, resource descriptions) to be associated with both the preferred or variant form. The cataloguer must make a choice among forms (of name, title, etc.) that, in different ways, refer back to the same entity or identity, expressed in different manners. Some examples:[236]

Guillaume d'Auvergne, *Bishop of Paris*
see **Guilelmus Arvernus**, *Bishop of Paris*
Aquinas, Thomas d'
see **Thomas, d'Aquinas**, *Saint;*
British Iron and Steel Research Association
see also **Iron and Steel Institute**

See also would establish the connection instead between *Joseph Aloisius Ratzinger, 1927–2022* and *Benedict XVI, pope* – therefore in this case between two identities of the same entity. Each form could be associated with one or more characterisations of bibliographic resources, that is, one or more bibliographic records in reference to the traditional context in which these forms of references originate and are implemented.

On the one hand, there is the 'surface' of a different form of a name, less known as a form but semantically equivalent to the preferred one, and still referring to the same identity. On the other hand, the greater depth of *see also* reference, where two different identities have evidently been identified, each autonomous for the purposes of bibliographic production.

In the same relationship, we can place the election as *pope*, which engages the entity on a different level compared to that of the private individual, and the recognition of titles such as *blessed* or *saint* that enrich the elements of description of the entity without expressing substantial changes, and therefore, without creating any ontological or identity break. Comparing this to the recognition of the status of blessed or saint, in ontological terms, we could define it as analogous to being awarded the honour of a knighthood, or receiving a Nobel Prize, a Pulitzer Prize or an Oscar. These are important recognitions that can even change an individual's life but cannot be thought of as determining the definition of one's identity.

Continuing or diachronic works

So far we have focused on agent entities to reflect on change and the criteria for identifying significant moments in terms of profiling the entity itself. The concept of emergent properties has supported this analysis and provided a framework for understanding a certain type of relational property, which becomes significant precisely because of the complexity of the system from which it derives. Entity modelling must study and establish criteria for identifying the entity in its many facets, and it is obvious that the degree of complexity of this operation increases the more the entity is subject to change. We can, therefore, only imagine how complicated all this is in the case of objects that, by their very nature, change. The term *continuing resource* perfectly expresses the sense of a constant and progressive change, of something that can hardly be captured with a single image but requires an entire film to be recorded. A continuing resource is a publication in physical or electronic format for which no end is planned: thus, it is published without a predetermined conclusion. It generally contains elements to assist in its use, such as numbering or dates or both. Serials (published continuously but in separate parts) and supplementary resources (published continuously but without reference to the separate individual parts) belong to this category of resources. The most relevant criterion for distinguishing continuing works from monographic works is the publisher's intention[237] – thus the editorial plan, which is generally clear and defined when the work is planned.[238] Now, if our inquiry must always relate to the question 'Under what circumstances is it true to say of any object that it has changed?' – a question we seek to answer not out of a pure metaphysical need but out of a practical urgency to understand the boundaries of each entity (in this case of the Work type) – we can imagine the complexity of the process of identifying a work that, by its very nature, is subject to continuous change. By what criterion can we determine that at some point in this continuous movement that resource ceases to exist in order to generate (or become) another? Or by what criterion do we identify a change as intended by the work plan, therefore within the work itself, compared to a significant change in terms of ontological or identity break?

To give a sense of the complexity of the topic, I will briefly summarise the types and characteristics related to the genre 'continuing resources', with reference to traditional national and international regulations, particularly of REICAT, AACR2, and RDA, which signify an important change with respect to the terminology used to classify these resources.

Modelling continuing resources

The guideline used to distinguish the class of monograph resource from that of continuing resource is the type of publication. Conceptual categories within which traditional bibliographic resources are included could be defined, based on this parameter, as:

1. *Finite resources*: originate with a completed editorial plan, regardless of the parts (one or many) that will make up the whole. They fall into this category:
   - *monographs*: works that are either complete in one part or that the publisher intends to complete in a defined, clearly stated number of parts
   - *finite integrative* resources: resources consisting of a set of integrated components designed not to receive updates. An example would be of a website created for a particular event.
2. *Continuing resources*: resources published over time without a predetermined plan for completion. These are resources for which continuous change or updating (replacing or accumulating) is planned.[239] They can be summarily divided into:
   - *serial* – resources issued in a succession of distinct parts, usually numbered, that do not have a predetermined conclusion (they can be of a different nature, thus periodicals, journals, continuations, etc.). The

'distinct parts' are the key element of this definition: serial numbers are parts that remain accessible and are themselves unchanged, while the serial title as a whole has new parts (numbers) continuously added. The distinct parts of a periodical can be numbered (e.g. issues), but in online periodicals they can also be separate articles not organised into issues.[240]

- *integrative resources* – resources that are continuously updated with additions of various kinds. Original RDA defines these as follows: a resource that is added or changed by updates that do not remain distinct and are integrated into the whole (e.g. a loose-leaf manual that is updated by replacement pages, a website that is continuously updated with new sections or html pages).

National and international cataloguing policies devote considerable space to the treatment of these resources, which have become increasingly complicated in terms of management as format types, usage policies, etc. have expanded and diversified.[241] What is apparent is a certain uniformity of treatment across the different standards, from REICAT to the Original RDA, especially with regard to defining possible criteria for identifying, in a continuing resource, those elements useful for understanding what changes to consider significant in order to declare whether it is the same resource or a different resource. What is interesting in these regulations is the progressive change in language, denoting a gradual move towards the concept of entity modelling. Starting from more traditional terminology linked to the operation of creating records or bibliographic descriptions, it evolves toward the Official RDA which, reformulated on the basis of the data model proposed by IFLA LRM, speaks of *Diachronic works* and *Entity boundary*, understood as the entity's profile. Let's review some relevant passages from various cataloguing codes and regulations.

> REICAT: 1.7.3 Variations Between Successive Units of a Serial Publication. Periodical and serial publications or those with integrated updates are subject to a *single bibliographic description* in the case of minor variations or changes in the identifying elements that appear in individual units or parts. They are, however, the subject of *separate descriptions* in the case of a change in the title or, if the title consists of a generic expression, when the responsible authority changes, and in the case of significant changes in the indication of edition or type of material. A new description is also prepared if, as a result of a change in title (or in the other cases listed), the publication resumes a previously used title.
>
> (Commissione permanente per la revisione delle regole italiane di catalogazione and ICCU, 2009, 39)

> AACR2: 21.2C1. Serials. If the proper title of a serial changes, a separate master entry is made for each title.
> 21.3B1. Serials. A new entry is made for a serial when one of the following conditions occurs, even if the proper title remains the same:
> (a) if the header for the entity under which the serial is registered changes
> (b) if the main registration of the serial is made under a personal or collective header and the person or entity named therein is no longer responsible for the serial.
>
> (Joint Steering Committee for Revision of AACR, 2004)

Up to this point, in the traditional cataloguing era, generally two elements are identified as directing the decision whether or not to create a new description (hence a new bibliographic record): the significant change in the title and/or the significant change in the institution responsible for the publication, along with (for REICAT) a change in the edition statement or the type of material. The instructions guide the decision whether to make a new bibliographic record or to modify the existing bibliographic record on the basis of an inconsequential change (noting, for example, the title change if insignificant). It should be noted here that there is no reference to entities, thus no new bibliographic records referring to a new work or a different expression, and therefore no reference to the entity–relationship model of FRBR. And while this is obviously consistent for AACR2, with reference to its date of conception and publication (preceding FRBR, which was officially presented in 1998), it is less understandable with REICAT, officially published more than 10 years after FRBR (in 2009), so reference to the generation of a new work or a new expression of the same work in continuation could have been made more clearly. Nor does Chapter 8 of REICAT, concerning Work and Expression, help. Here definitions of these two entities and some particular cases of handling works or expressions are given, but no reference to the subject of continuing resources can be found to guide us in this regard. However, the time was becoming ripe, and the first step forward in terms of investigating significant changes for entity modelling is seen in the Original RDA, which in instruction 6.1.3, 'Changes Affecting the Identification of a Work', introduces the concept of a change that, impacting the authorised access point, evidently involves the Work. This represents a bridge between the traditional cataloguing approach, focused on resource description and access point analysis, and the new entity-centred vision, emphasising their definition and identifying those changes essential to their identification. Specifically, for continuing works, two instructions with different outcomes are indicated:

- for serial works: a change in responsibility or proper title generates a new work
- for supplementary works: a change in responsibility or proper title requires a return to the access point and a modification that incorporates and reflects the change, with linkage to the old access point as a variant form. There is no direction, therefore, to create a new work but to modify the existing one.

The transition to the Official RDA, published in December 2022[242] with an entirely new framework compared to the Original RDA and characterised by the absorption and reshaping of the guidance based on IFLA LRM, introduces novel elements regarding the treatment of continuing resources. It also includes the introduction of terminology that is truly significant in expressing a new approach to resource management explicitly oriented toward entity modelling. For the first time, the term *diachronic work*[243] is officially used to replace the term *continuing resource*: a diachronic work is a work designed to be unfolded over time, rather than in a single act of publication. As the plan unfolds, the content of the work changes over time as it is realised through one or more separate and distinct expressions, which are materialised in one or more manifestations. The essence of a diachronic work is a plan for content change. An *extension plan* describes the planned method of extending the content of a work over time.[244]

In the same section of the guidebook another expression is introduced that is very significant in terms of the evolution of language, as a reflection of a change in approach to the treatment of bibliographic resources: *transformation boundary*, meaning a perimeter and thus an *entity profile* for a diachronic work.[245] The term *entity boundary* that I have also rendered here with the expression *entity profile* I think can be equated semantically with that ontological or identity break I have been talking about. The definition of this term is really a significant expression of a new approach to cataloguing. It is the official ('official' here meaning *'authoritative'*, having been formulated in an authoritative tool, the Official RDA) statement of a new direction and the transition from cataloguing to entity modelling, which I have simplified in Chapter 2.[246] An RDA entity boundary (the profile of an RDA entity) is the set of criteria applied by an agent creating metadata to determine whether a description of a new RDA entity is needed. The criteria are specified as differences in the values of one or more elements associated with a single entity, and these criteria may indicate a new entity of the same type or of a different type. For example, the criteria applied to an expression may determine whether a new work or a new expression is described. In practice, the values of a set of existing metadata descriptions are compared with the values that characterise the entity being described to determine whether the existing metadata describe the same entity or a different entity. If it is determined that a different entity is involved, a new description is required. Differences in the values of an element are not considered significant when they result from the use of different recording methods, options within a recording method or the result of different levels of granularity in the descriptive metadata. For example, the difference in the values 'nineteen-sixty' and '1 January 1960' for a related time period is not sufficient to determine that the two items describe different entities.[247]

The mechanism is precisely that of entity resolution described in Chapter 2, in which the entities that make up the bibliographic universe and beyond are brought into focus through algorithms (therefore by automated processes) or through the manual activity of analysing, identifying and describing profiles. In order to define the boundary of an entity and thus where one entity ends and another begins (the same can be said for the identity profile), it is necessary to identify the 'break': that is, those elements which, introduced at a certain moment (or co-present, in the case of synchronic identities) define a new thing or a different way of presenting the same thing.

The definition of these elements in a work that arises as a work in continuity (and therefore never static) has already been identified as potentially complex. At this point, especially in this new dimension of entity modelling as opposed to the classical cataloguing tradition, it becomes easier to attempt to define those elements necessary to identify an ontological or identity break in a diachronic work. It is worthwhile here, even at the risk of being overly didactic, to quote faithfully from the text of the Official RDA to highlight those elements that here, perhaps for the first time so clearly, are emphasised as necessary for profiling a diachronic work:

> A *diachronic work* is planned to be realised by a set of one or more expressions over time. A difference in plan is necessary to determine a distinction between two diachronic works. A difference in plan is indicated by a change in any of these aims and objectives:
>
> - scope or editorial policy
> - genre or literary form
> - target audience
> - style[248]

A change in terminology, a change in perspective, and also in defining the elements useful in identifying a diachronic work and profiling it emerges here and is evident. Identifying the ontological break is not so straightforward, for it requires knowing the publisher's intention to generate a new work with respect to the one that existed previously. Here again, let's attempt to repeat the exercise of tracing this break, with reference to cataloguing practices before and after the Official RDA (Table 3.3).

Table 3.3 *Identification of ontological or identity break with reference to cataloguing practice before (b) and after (a) Official RDA*

Identity type	Event	Ontological (O)/identity (I) break	Evidence of ontological/identity break
serial works (b)	change in responsibility	yes (O)	new work
serial works (b)	change in proper title	yes (O)	new work
integrating resources (b)	change in responsibility	no	update of the existing work
integrating resources (b)	change in own title	no	update of the existing work
diachronic works (a)	change of scope or editorial policy	yes (O)	new work
diachronic works (a)	change of genre or literary form	yes (O)	new work
diachronic works (a)	change of target audience	yes (O)	new work
diachronic works (a)	change of style	yes (O)	new work

But the key point to emphasise, once again, is that for the first time in a practical cataloguing guide, terminology oriented toward entity modelling has been introduced, thus presenting a new way of understanding the management of bibliographic resources. We have used the example of continuing resources to examine how cataloguing practice, from the traditional to the contemporary, has attempted to model these resources by intercepting, in a flow of constant and programmed change, those elements that, when they occur, disrupt that flow to identify a new one. The topic is so widely felt that, as referenced in endnote 241, numerous presentations, seminars, and workshops can be found online regarding what has traditionally been defined as *continuing resources*.

Along this line of analysis and proposals is the International Standard Serial Number (ISSN) *linked data application profile* document published in its second version in September 2020 (ISSN International Centre, 2020). The ISSN[249] originated in 1975 as a system for assigning unique and persistent identifiers to continuing resources, covering not only periodicals, series and newspapers, but also publications such as academic databases, websites and blogs. The identifiers are managed by an intergovernmental organisation, the ISSN International Centre, consisting of a network of national centres working together for this purpose. The ISSN International Centre maintains a central database, the ISSN Register, and provides tools and services to enable access to and use of the data it contains.

The issue of identifying such complex resources, due to their specific 'dynamic and event-oriented' nature (ISSN International Centre, 2020, 4) which was already recognised in the late 1970s and gave rise to the initiative, has been greatly amplified with the advent of web technologies and linked data in particular. Identifiers should now simplify linking to different information sources and enriching metadata. This also means amplifying the risk of misinformation where monitoring is not rigorous and thorough. The encounter with linked data has also prompted a rethinking of the system in terms of ontologising information. The ISSN linked data application profile document presents a mapping between the bibliographic elements recorded in the ISSN register and the ontologies and vocabularies used for modelling in linked data. Special attention is paid to ontologies from the bibliographic universe, first and foremost IFLA LRM but also BIBFRAME and Marc21rdf.info.[250] The corollary to this is simpler, cross-cutting ontologies, including Schema.org and Dublin Core. The ISSN data model has the *ISSN Resource* at the centre of the graph, representing the continuous resource, with data useful for its identification.

Among the other entities that are part of the data model are the ISSN Record, which identifies the record that describes the resource (so again the distinction between the real-world object, which is the resource, and its description, the record) and the *Publication events*, which is an important entity because it traces the history of the resource. Each event identifies the publication of the resource by a given publisher, in a given place, at a given time. These are very important elements for identifying and modelling a continuing work, because they mark obviously significant transitions in the evolution of the resource. And it is modelling that I want to focus on, because this ISSN document, among many, offers particular clarity. The FRBR model, on which BIBFRAME was also based (albeit with numerous modifications, especially in terms of simplification), had already declared the need to revisit the modelling of continuing resources: 'In particular, the notion of "seriality" and the dynamic nature of entities recorded in digital formats merit further analysis' (IFLA FRBR Study Group, 1998 and 2009, 5). The IFLA LRM, which replaces the FRBR model, acknowledges the difficulty of reconciling its rigid hierarchal structure with the dynamic nature of continuing resources: 'The "thing" described may have changed dramatically in the past, and may do so even more dramatically in the future' (IFLA LRM, 2017, 95). Different manifestations of a continuing resource may evolve over time, diverging from the original work and generating a whole new one:

> One may consider a title corresponding to a 'different language edition' of a main title as a different 'expression' of a same work. However, this title may progressively diverge from the main title and present original content, hence becoming a separate work. Another example: the online equivalent of a print title (that may be initially considered a different 'manifestation') may also evolve over time and present content non-published in the print version, becoming again a new 'work'.
>
> (ISSN International Centre, 2020, 9)

Grouping different manifestations or different expressions under one work is, therefore, not possible with continuing resources. And indeed, IFLA LRM insists on the model that sees each manifestation (e.g. each entity identified by an ISSN) as corresponding to a new expression and a new work (IFLA LRM, 2017, 95). With reference to BIBFRAME, this would mean that each continuing resource would correspond to an Instance and a Work. This modelling (one instance, one expression, one work) is also what the Official RDA calls *WEM lock*: 'This means that a *diachronic work* is realised by one and only one expression and embodied by one and only one manifestation. This is known as a *WEM lock*.'[251] However, a form of grouping, for resources identified individually with respect to different formats and media (one ISSN for print, one for online version, etc.), can simplify searching and enable end users to navigate their way through even a very complex 'family' of resources. The ISSN Linking Resource (ISSN-L) provides an identifier for the title regardless of the medium, ensuring a link between the different ISSNs assigned to resources in different formats.

This brief overview of the treatment of continuing resources in traditional cataloguing has given us the opportunity to emphasise the complexity of these entities and entity modelling operations. It also reminds us of the parallelism from which we started, with emergent properties. *Continuing resources* express a complex organism, consisting of individual parts (the files, individual articles, html pages, etc.) that, in turn, have their own autonomous identity but are enriched by the characteristics of the continuing resource. IFLA LRM defines this articulated and complex nature well:

> Since the *work* entity is defined, in IFLA LRM, as one 'that permits the identification of the commonality of content between and among various *expressions*', a serial *work* can be modelled as a particular case of the *work* entity, although the notion of 'commonality of content' is not to be understood in the same sense as for monographs. Each issue of a serial aggregates distinct articles, and it is therefore not possible to claim that the same ideas are common to the various *expressions* embodied in the *manifestations* of all the issues that make up a

> serial, while it is possible to claim that the same ideas are common to the English text of *Romeo and Juliet* and an Italian translation of it. Rather, the 'commonality of content' that defines a serial *work* resides in both the publisher's and the editor's *intention* to convey the feeling to end-users that all individual issues do belong to an identifiable whole, and in the collection of editorial concepts (a title, an overall topic, a recognisable layout, a regular frequency, etc.) that will help to convey that feeling.
>
> (IFLA LRM, 2017, 95)

The publisher's intention determines that common thread, that commonality that underlies each individual content of every part that makes up the continuing resource. Each component part takes on, in addition to the properties associated with it, that context that is granted by being part of a more complex organism. Revisiting Weberman, in the example of works of art as emergent entities, one cannot help but think of continuing resources by analogy:

> Artworks are compositions that depend on the interrelation of their parts. A figure in a painting comes to have different aesthetic and representation properties as a result of the figures that surround it. So a figure in a painting changes not physically but aesthetically in virtue of its taking on new relational properties, i.e. its coming to be surrounded by these rather than those other figures.
>
> (Weberman, 1999, 144)

This passage makes us think of continuing resources but also of musical works, of the properties that arise from the relationship between the parts that make up that work – between a score and a libretto, for example: the way each part acquires value in its relationship to the other. It makes us think of works such as films and screenplays that, while readable as stand-alone works, are enriched by characteristics acquired through their relationships with other aspects of the work, through the direction, the soundtrack, the set design and the costumes. I preferred to use the example of continuing resources because of the complexity of their nature, *changeable* by definition, which becomes a significant challenge for those who want to take on the concept of entity modelling.[252]

All of this reiterates the importance of the context within which the entity exists and manifests itself, to the point that we can, perhaps, speak of a *context identity* – that is, a way of the entity presenting itself to the world that is strongly conditioned by, or relative to, the context in which this manifestation takes place. In Chapter 2, regarding the OOP approach to the object to be created, we emphasised the practical necessity of choosing a context for representing the entity, if only due to the impossibility of capturing the entity in its multifaceted richness. This refers to the practical choice of a programmer, yet the same can be applied to individual choices, to our being several things at the same time, often in relation to the context in which we move. Simplifying what was said earlier regarding the papal election, the individual chooses to express himself (or must express himself) in the official context of the institution of the Roman Catholic Church, as well as in a more private dimension when he decides to write about the beauty of snow-capped mountains. *Contextual identity* also applies to Gianluca Gori, who, in the context of his artistic, theatrical expression, appears as Drusilla Foer, and to all the diachronic and synchronic identities we have attempted to profile.

The transience of intrinsic properties, the persistence of relational properties

The scant evidence of the publisher's intention or will as criterion for continuing resources necessitates particular effort in defining the identity profile of such works by analysing a number of contextual elements that are not always immediately discernible from the source. In a continuing or diachronic work, on the other hand, the intrinsic properties are meagre and because of the characteristic of continuity over time, they are not easily captured in fixed elements.

The importance of relational properties in entity identification

Entity modelling bases a substantial part of the entity identification processes on relationships, making use of relational properties, instead of what one would call intrinsic properties of an object, to define its profile. In the case of agent identification, for example, the suggested, or perhaps in some cases obligatory, step in resolving the entity is the identification of works related to it:[253] Here are some examples:

1 Carlo Calcaterra

(a) cluster 1 =100 1\$aCalcaterra, Carlo,$d1884–1952
(b) cluster 2 =100 1\$aCalcaterra, Carlo,$csac.

The first clustering process did not reconcile name (a) and name (b) due to the lack of matching elements of birth and death dates – cluster 2 has a qualifying element but no dates.

There is, however, one common work between the two clusters, used for the new reconciliation of cluster 1 and cluster 2: Catechesi pasquale di Ambrogio di Milano.

The passage for the work allows the merger of cluster 1 with cluster 2: Calcaterra, Carlo, 1884–1952 (ID 56085).

2 (i) Gregorius Nazianzenus

(a) cluster 1 =100 0\$aGregorius Nazianzenus,$cs.,$dca. 330–390

(b) cluster 2 =100 0\$aGregorius Nazianzenus,$cs.,$d308–ca. 390

Again, the first clustering process did not reconcile name (a) and name (b) due to the lack of matching birth and death dates: the weight assigned to the pair as 'potentially reconcilable' is high, because of one of the corresponding birth dates; but still the clusters remain separate for the lack of a coinciding probable date of birth.

However, the two clusters have a common work used for the new reconciliation of cluster 1 and cluster 2: Cinque discorsi teologici.

The connection through this work allows for the merger of cluster 1 with cluster 2: Gregorius Nazianzenus, santo, circa 330–390 (ID 52412).

2 (ii) Gregorius Nazianzenus

cluster 3 =100 0\$aGregorius Nazianzenus,$cs., patr. di Costantinopoli,$dc. m. 389

In this cluster, the dates of birth and/or death did not match those of the clusters in case 2 (i), and no work with the same title associated with this cluster was found in both clusters in example 2 (i).

The lack of a coincident title resulted in the creation of a new cluster: Gregorius Nazianzenus, santo, patriarca di Costantinopoli, morto circa 389 (ID 100357).

In these examples, the use of the relationship to the works helped the process of identifying agents, refining the reconciliation processes of entities that were initially, and erroneously, considered different.

The intrinsic nature of an entity's properties is not something that necessarily guarantees its use for the purpose of entity modelling. In the MARC 21 Authority Format, some attributes were included as agent descriptions only from 2009. These included:

- field 374 – Occupation
- field 375 – Gender
- field 376 – Family information
- field 377 – Language associated with the agent

This means that in all records prior to this date the descriptive elements are not present. Therefore, clustering processes can certainly use them, where present, to enrich the cluster, but without the guarantee that they can be used for identification purposes. Using, for example, the *occupation* field (the profession of the entity described, with, where possible, the time period related to the exercise of the activity) to disambiguate homonyms is possible but not completely reliable, since we know that prior to a certain date (2009 in this case) this indication was not provided in authority records in MARC 21 format. Yet, this data is strongly disambiguous, so much so that even in more recent projects, it is used to give immediate evidence of different entities. In Wikidata, the entity *Carlo Conti* is listed as:[254]

- Italian television host, radio host, and television author (www.wikidata.org/entity/Q933508)
- Catholic priest (www.wikidata.org/entity/Q241447)
- composer (www.wikidata.org/entity/Q3659212)
- scientific illustrator (Austrian painter and engraver) (www.wikidata.org/entity/Q51360666)
- Italian politician (www.wikidata.org/entity/Q110817402)
- Swiss politician, jurist (www.wikidata.org/entity/Q119574)

The importance of relational properties in the various steps involved in entity identification can be perceived by examining, where publicly available, various entity resolution rules and procedures. Regulations for the creation of the metadata set useful for entity identification, at the registration stage, are defined in the ISNI project's database feeding rules,[255] shared with agencies that are part of the circuit of contributors, in the *Data Completeness & Assignment Rules* section.[256] ISNI distinguishes three macro-categories of data completeness: *Rich, Non-sparse,* and *Sparse*. Without delving into the technical criteria for defining the three levels, it is interesting to note that, among the rules defined for the highest level of completeness in structuring the entry is the indication of a related title (or an associated musical instrument or the name of a related person or entity, such as a co-author or an affiliating institution).

It is important to remember the two planes of entity analysis, the metaphysical one (the inquiry around *what* an object *is*) and the more practical and functional dimension of cataloguing (what do I need, in this domain, to identify the object?). The two planes intersect in entity modelling, but the practical dimension inevitably comes to terms with the intrinsic and/or relational properties that different descriptive traditions, in different contexts, have assigned to the entity.

Very interesting – regarding properties to associate with the description of an entity – is the wide discussion within the library community surrounding the *gender* property for agents, which I will briefly discuss in order to convey the dimension of certain sociocultural phenomena underlying the choices in cataloguing practices.

Recording gender in the entity 'person': an ongoing discussion

To avoid straying too far from our inquiry into how to grasp and capture change in entities, let us recall that in the processes of entity resolution discussed in Chapter 2, identifying the profile of an entity beyond the appearances or substance of change is essential and indispensable. However, speaking about intrinsic and extrinsic properties with respect to the set of entities that the real world and the web can propose is not an easy thing to do. What does it mean for an agent or, moreover, for a work, to have intrinsic properties understood as their own, which are independent of their relationship to any other object? The *gender* property[257] for a person entity has traditionally been considered an intrinsic property. Yet, the extensive discussion of the terminology to be used beyond the traditionally binary terminology of male/female is illustrative of how the intrinsic nature of a property and its use is not at all a matter of course. Especially where definitions are oversimplified and unresponsive to the complexity of reality.

Here I would like to summarise an interesting discussion on the appropriateness of recording gender information of a person, a discussion under way in several communities, including the library community.

Starting from the end of the story, in the spring of 2021 the PCC (Program for Cooperative Cataloging) Advisory Committee on Diversity, Equity and Inclusion (DEI) reconvened the Ad Hoc Task Group on Recording Gender in Name Authority Records to update a report that had been released in October 2016.[258] In 2022, the PCC Policy Committee (PoCo) approved the *Revised Report on Recording Gender in Personal Name Authority Records,*[259] sharing its findings with cataloguing agencies that were part of the PCC around the world. The recommendation approved by the PoCo is not to record the RDA element of *gender* (field 375 of MARC Authority[260]) in personal name authority records and, if records are changed for any reason, to delete existing fields 375. Thus, gender, as a possible identifying attribute of a person, should no longer be expressed in that field, which had been introduced in the MARC Authority in 2009.

Let us try to trace the origin of this decision which, set within the cataloguing context, actually touches upon several social, psychological and cultural realms.

The Report of the PCC Ad Hoc Task Group on Gender in Name Authority Records 2016 was created in response to concerns raised by some PCC members about best practices for recording gender information in name authority records (NARs). The purpose of the group was to draft instructions on recording gender information in MARC Authority field 375 for later publication in the Descriptive Cataloguing Manual, Section Z1 (DCM Z1), prepared by the Policy, Training, and Cooperative Programs Division of the Library of Congress. Members of the working group met and held discussions focusing particularly on assigning gender information in authority records for people who do not identify with the more traditional binary terms male and female.[261]

The recommendations seek to overcome the limitations of the Library of Congress's interpretation of Original RDA Rule 9.7 regarding gender records for persons. In an earlier article on the same topic (Billey, Drabinski and Roberto, 2014) some members of the PCC working group had criticised the LC's position with respect to the interpretation of that rule, which was considered regressive regarding the understanding of gender identity. The article is very critical of the Library of Congress's position, and particularly of the way librarians have been trained with respect to this sensitive issue. The general opinion is of an oversimplification in the cataloguing approach: 'For LC, gender is easy: to know about oneself, to determine on behalf of others, and to encode forever in a MARC Authority record.' The critique of the Original RDA standard and LC's simplistic interpretation of it is rooted in queer theory, a field of analysis that provides a useful theoretical framework for rethinking the static categories and naming systems that characterise library knowledge organisation schemes. Queer theory introduces and supports the understanding of new ways to conceptualise definitions of *sex* and *gender* by challenging the narrow LC and Names Authority Cooperative Program (NACO) articulation of these inherently complex identities. Queer literature discusses the rigid and static classification (with respect to the temporal element) that traditional definitions of gender and sex offer, forgetting how much social, political and historical context influences our understanding of what gender or sex is:

> Critical to queer theory is a resistance to social practices that freeze identities in time and universalise them, erasing the real differences that accompany same-sex sexuality on the scales of time and place . . . For queer theorists, gender and sex are always negotiated and socially constituted and fixing them as RDA asks cataloguers to do, denies the shifting and contextual nature of gender identities.
>
> (Billey, Drabinski and Roberto, 2014)

Pay attention to that last sentence: fixing gender and sex, as RDA asks cataloguers to do, denies the changing and contextual nature of gender identities. Again, the focus is on change and the difficulty of pigeonholing it into rigid, static categories, as classificatory systems often try to do. The rigidity of fixing a binary-only system excludes or even exerts passive hostility toward transgender individuals. The problems caused by this cursory classification outweigh the results one would like to achieve, namely a more precise identification of the person or the enhancement of searchability through the application of filters ('find all the women writers of the early 20th century who have written about a certain subject').

> The problems begin with the assumption that gender is a natural human characteristic that is easily identified and fits into a simplistic binary. While gender is certainly experienced as natural and binary by many people, it isn't by everyone.
>
> (Billey, Drabinski and Roberto 2014)

Even the ability to define through specific subfields the dates associated with a sex change seems to suggest a practice that ignores that gender changes do not necessarily follow a linear path and are, in some cases, closely linked to a specific context.

Building on these reflections, and through subsequent comparisons with other communities and other stakeholders, the 2016 Report of the PCC Ad Hoc Task Group on Gender in Authority Records sets out some rules or best practices for recording gender-related information. Such relevant points, functional mainly to respect the wishes of the person described, include assigning gender only where clearly requested by the person and as indicated by the person, basing gender assignment not on the analysis of photographs or name and not considering the gender assigned at birth, defining gender based on recognised biographies, websites and social media of the person, direct communications with the person described, and other similar criteria. In principle, however, the suggestion to cataloguers is to include the gender designation only in special cases, when the risk of harming the person is not higher and more serious than the results obtained from using that specific data.

One of the most tangible results of the work of this PCC group is the selection and expansion of the vocabulary from which to take terms to be included in Field 375, to overcome the strictly binary (male, female, unknown) dimension of MARC and RDA. The Library of Congress Demographic Group Terms (LCDGT) vocabulary is being enriched with new terms (cisgender people, two-spirit people, gender non-binary people, agender people and others, as reported in Appendix C of the Report), while existing terminology undergoes revision.

All this took place in 2016. As mentioned, in the spring of 2021 the same group, with the addition of a couple of new members, was reconvened: evidently what had been decided in the 2016 report regarding gender registration was still not satisfactory given the sensitivity and complexity of the issue. A new PCC Advisory Committee on Diversity, Equity and Inclusion (DEI)[262] had been formed in February 2021 as part of PCC's extended Strategic Direction. Among its tasks was to take up the points left open in the 2016 Report. Hence, the opportunity for the Ad Hoc Task Group to review and recall, especially to check the report against the context of rules, standards, and guidelines that had matured in the meantime (including the new RDA Toolkit Restructure and Redesign 3R project), and to update it with respect to comparison with an extended community of librarians. As anticipated, the new version of the report takes a more drastic stance with respect to the issue, indicating the removal of the 375 tag from authority records and the provision of operational systems and training tools that prevent the use of this tag. Unstructured information (thus, not from controlled vocabularies) with respect to the person's gender may continue to be recorded in MARC 21 Authority tag 670:[263] 'However, avoid outing, misgendering, or deadnaming[264] the person, or recording details about a person's gender transition. Respect requests from the person to remove or update information pertaining to the person's gender or name gender' (PCC Ad Hoc Task Group on Gender in Name Authority Records, 2022).

What is interesting in this new version of the report is the reminder of how careful the recording of data must be to avoid hurting the sensibilities and wishes of the person described. It acknowledges that gender identity is a complex issue, related to the personal sphere but with a public visibility, subject to change over time, and closely related to different cultural and social contexts.

There is, however, one element that is likely to prove weak in this report and which should perhaps be reinforced regarding the different contexts of using authority records in entity modelling procedures. The weak points, or rather those very much related to the more traditional view of cataloguing, are those in which it is defined as the main role of authority data to disambiguate entities, not to provide biographical information about the person. And the next point is the one that asserts it is not the cataloguer's job to determine and record personally identifiable information. The weakness of these assertions is in defining the activity of cataloguing within the specific limitation of identifying the person for the purpose of linking with the work produced, thus in the narrow bibliographical realm. We know, however, that entity modelling tends instead to create 'objects' that can be reused in contexts very different from the ones limited to the bibliographic sphere. In this sense, it is clear that the more elements useful for identifying the object, the more the reuse of that data in different contexts is guaranteed. However, the issue posed by the Task Group in the next two reports is too sensitive and close to the personal sphere to be assimilated into the practices of assigning the various attributes useful in identifying people. It is clearly a hot-button issue, so much so that the discussion extends to other bibliographic communities, and in October 2022 ISNI agencies receive a note from the ISNI Library Sector Consultation Group to take a look at the draft ISNI Gender Identities policy document and provide suggestions and thoughts. An August 2021 press release by the ISNI International Agency (ISNI-IA) announced the draft report entitled 'Representation of Gender Identities in ISNI Records and the ISNI Database,'[265] which recalled the traditional use of the gender attribute in cataloguing for the purposes of disambiguation of identities and enhancement of search functionality. It also announced the formation of an advisory group to review the gender assignment policy previously adopted by ISNI and to share the results of their reflections on the topic with the broader community.

In October 2022, the ISNI-IA distributed the draft of the new policy to the ISNI Library Sector Consultation Group[266] (and other consultative groups under ISNI), aiming to share its content with a wider community and receive feedback, prior to finalising and officially publishing the new policy. The new policy regarding the registration of gender identity for individuals was aligned with that of the PCC and shared with the consultation group of librarians with a clear reference to the central point from which ISNI's reflections and subsequent position arose:

> After months of research and consultation with industry- and thought-leaders, ISNI has come to the conclusion that while gender information is important for some purposes (including those which contribute to gender equity), it does not facilitate disambiguation, and the risks to individuals in some regions are too great to include this information in ISNI records.[267]

In July 2023, ISNI-IA formalised its position regarding the registration of gender in the profile of agents with a press release published on the website. The official position of ISNI-IA is to remove data relating to the gender of persons, from the ISNI database, feeds, portal and any source. Subsequently, the data editing or creation templates that the various ISNI agencies use for data entry will also be modified, so as to completely inhibit the possibility of registering data on gender.[268]

These two examples, the one from the PCC Ad Hoc Task Group on Gender in Authority Records and this one from the ISNI-IA,[269] provide clear evidence of how the international community deliberates and expresses itself on issues related to entity identification, which in the past we would not have imagined that we should or could question. And this opens up reflection on other horizons, including how difficult it is in classificatory systems to give evidence of the richness, complexity and changeability of real-life things.

Conclusions on change and persistence

The idea that intrinsic properties pertain to physicality, or at any rate to *objective* properties of an entity, and that in the name of this objectivity they can have more value or more weight in identification processes, does not seem to work. What I would argue instead is that *intrinsic properties*, understood as *essential* (hence *core*) are those that, *in a given context*, qualify or better express the thing, its essence, according to the profile we want to give it. We would never have imagined, when the first theoretical data models were introduced into the cataloguing discipline, that we would question certain intrinsic elements of an entity, mistakenly considered highly significant for the identification of the thing itself. Returning to our example of the banknote on p. 117, we have perhaps shown that it is not its *physicality* (a certain paper, with a certain watermark, with a certain effigy, of a certain colour, elements in any case relevant to that object) but *the attributed value* (the purchasing power, in this case), which the object possessed by unanimous consent at a certain time. The relational property of purchasing power in a given context is so strong that, once that diminishes, inevitably the object changes. Or at any rate it changes in our perception or in its function, acquiring, for example, only historical or artistic value. More traditional cataloguing practice, however, tends to fix intrinsic and extrinsic or relational properties in a rigid way, classifying schematically and especially categorically the profiles of the entities that are part of the bibliographic universe. And this classificatory approach works well as long as the models remain theoretical: the FRBR relational model has been an excellent data model as long as it is useful for soliciting thought. The shift to cataloguing practice (or even its use in search retrieval systems to enhance the search capabilities of end-users) immediately exposed its frailties, including that of grasping with difficulty the element of change, essential instead in the concreteness of reality. The definition of the translations of a work as different entities (expressions), instead of as different ways of presenting the same thing (and therefore as different identities of the same entity) generates that proliferation of entities from which the bibliographic universe suffers. It also creates a difficulty for those who concretely have to define the profile of the entity in order to describe it, and in identifying the boundaries, that 'entity boundary' introduced by Official RDA, or 'ontological break', as defined in this study. Again, we are supported here by Weberman, who seems to identify clearly this risk of entity multiplication when he writes:

> Still, to talk too loosely of emergent entities could lead to an ontologically overcrowded universe – one in which entities are multiplied ad infinitum by their multifarious relations to other things. For this reason, I have framed my argument as being about 'entities identified and individuated in terms of their emergent properties' rather than as being about distinct 'emergent entities.'
>
> (Weberman, 1999, 146)

When, regarding the outdated banknote, we say that its emergent property is in its purchase value, we do not mean that its physical characteristics are unimportant, but that the declaration of being out-of-date affects those particular characteristics that made it exchangeable currency, and not the fact that it is an object of a certain material, decorated in a certain way, of a certain size. And so, if we look at the banknote before and after its being declared out of circulation and try to answer the question, 'Is it the same object?', we must first answer the question, 'The same what?' That piece of decorated paper is the same sort as the decorated, watermarked pieces of paper produced by the State Mint, but it is not the same thing as those objects that, because of their purchasing power, allow for the exchange of goods:

> Why do we care about objects and not just the stuff? Because objects are stuff with extra properties, properties that often persist and are often useful to know about even if the stuff changes.[270]
>
> (Grandy and Freund, 2021)

The use of ontological models to classify objects in the bibliographic universe addresses the need to define a *reference* (reference model) and *identify* what we intend to include in our inventory. Philosophy supports us in this, through the suggestion of the *sortal* concept that provides an answer to the ontological question 'What is this?' as well as criteria for the identification of an object in a given time or across time (thus in its changes). When we classify objects, when we construct ontologies as reference models for everything that we then, participating in one class or another, recognise to be 'sort of' something, we are doing nothing more than defining a model to help us locate and identify things in the real world. In the article 'È un uccello, è un aereo, è Superman! Visione e identificazione sortale' , the authors attempt to answer the question of whether every time we refer to an object it is necessary to identify it by sortal qualifications (Soavi, Carrara and Giaretta, 2008). We are not interested here in getting to the bottom of their investigation, but the reference to possible notions of 'sortal' supports us in arriving at a conclusion to the research path I have explored in this chapter. Three notions of sortal can be found in philosophical literature:

1 A sortal provides criteria for identifying and counting particulars that fall under it, and tells us when something continues to exist and when it ceases to exist. This definition is found in Peter F. Strawson's work and uses the sortal criterion primarily for the *identification* of things (Strawson, 1959).
2 A sortal provides criteria for counting in a determinate way the objects that fall under it. In this sense, clear reference to a concept (and thus a clear profile) is what makes questions such as 'how many are there?' meaningful. The Stanford Encyclopedia of Philosophy defines this position more explicitly: 'a sortal . . . tells us how to count things of that kind, which requires knowing which things are different and which are the same.' This notion, which we might call *accountancy*, is attributable to Spinoza and also to Gottlob Frege, but it is the one that least supports our understanding of the extent to which even cataloguing (ontological) categorisations rely on the sortal criterion.[271]
3 A sortal makes it possible to answer the Aristotelian question 'What is this?' and provides both identification criteria and persistence criteria concerning the nature of the objects that fall under it. This *identification* criterion is formulated by David Wiggins and involves not only the identification of an object in a given time but also the ability to keep track of it through time (Wiggins, 1980, 2001).

The interpretation of the sortal criterion in terms of identification is perhaps the approach that best explains the classificatory need that cataloguing practice has always expressed. The construction of data models and ontologies is functional to the identification of those elements (be they properties or relationships) necessary to design the models with which to compare each thing and to be able to say, 'it's a sort of' even in its evolution over time.

> The possibility of reidentifying an object correctly depends precisely on knowing what properties characterise its nature. A sortal *S* tells us what these properties are, that is, which properties the objects that fall under *S* can change without it leading to the end of their existence. Therefore, it is argued, a sortal provides us with persistence criteria necessary for identification.
>
> (Soavi, Carrara and Giaretta, 2008)

Fixing models, classes, comparison profiles is the starting point for entity modelling processes to then identify the entities that fill the complex world that cataloguing processes are supposed to represent. Yet, we have seen how reality, the things of the real world, can be more complex in their continuous becoming than the models to which they are supposed to refer. The Hegelian duality between the intellect that thinks things in the abstract (from *ab-trahere,* to pull out, to extract) and reason that thinks concretely (from *cum-crescere,* to grow together, to develop) perhaps helps us express the distance between theoretical models and practical realisation. I opened this chapter with a famous quote from Hegel's *Phenomenology of Spirit*: 'The bud disappears when the blossom breaks through, and we might say that the former is refuted by the latter. In the same way when the fruit comes, the blossom may be explained to be a false form of the plant's existence, for the fruit appears as its true nature in place of the blossom.' The intellect, in its fixing things in the abstract, in a static, rigid way, specifies entities by isolating them. The bud is the bud, the flower is the flower, the fruit is the fruit. And this, as mentioned, multiplies entities by freezing each state or each mode of presentation into many different entities. Hegelian reason operates differently. It brings the fixed concepts of the intellect back into a single conceptual movement, to a thought process that shows us, if we return to the example given, that the bud, the flower, the fruit are moments of the same reality. Just as, to return to an example used in the first chapter, that little girl pictured in the school photo 40 years ago and the woman of today are still me.

'*Speaking to the world* is its identity.' With these words Pope Paul VI, who had to write to the Red Brigade to ask for the release of Aldo Moro, addresses Monsignor Cesare Curioni, head of the prison chaplains, in a scene from Marco Bellocchio's television series *Esterno Notte,* asking for help in using language that is more understandable to the recipients of the letter. A truly significant example of what we might consider to be an emerging property.

CHAPTER 4

O Romeo, Romeo, Wherefore Art Thou Romeo?

Or Romeo, Romeo, wherefore art thou Romeo?
Deny thy father and refuse thy name.
Or if thou wilt not, be but sworn my love
And I'll no longer be a Capulet.
'Tis but thy name that is my enemy:
Thou art thyself, though not a Montague.
What's Montague? It is nor hand nor foot
Nor arm nor face nor any other part
Belonging to a man. Or be some other name.
What's in a name? That which we call a rose
By any other name would smell as sweet.

William Shakespeare, *Romeo and Juliet*

Introduction

The entity *agent*, in its various forms proposed by cataloguing tradition (person, corporate body and family) is certainly one of the most fascinating entities to investigate in terms of entity modelling. The primary role played by the agent in the complex articulation of the bibliographic universe is demonstrated by the attention paid to this entity in cataloguing rules, data models and ontologies. This entity is of central importance in the various bibliographic models: in FRBR, the Agent (person, entity) occupies the second group of entities analysed in the model, closely related to the first group (Work, Expression, Manifestation, Item); the Agent class[272] is a fundamental component of the BIBFRAME model and represents any entity or organisation involved in the creation, production, distribution or consumption of a resource and can be modelled as a person, family, organisation, jurisdiction or meeting. The relationships between a resource and anyone with a role connected to it are, therefore, central to any data model related to the bibliographic field, and more generally, the broader web.

The shift in focus from the record (understood as a surrogate of the resource) to the complex network of entities that make up the bibliographic universe is well illustrated in the analysis of one of the central and relevant entities in this domain: using the agent (understood in its various meanings) to demonstrate the importance of this shift in focus is a choice suggested by the concrete, and therefore easily profiled, nature of this entity. Added to this consideration is also the certainty that the agent is one of the most cross-domain entities that can be analysed. There is no archival document, work of art, book, administrative act, post, film, musical work, video, any product of human and other activity that is not relatable to an agent. It is therefore particularly easy to demonstrate how approaching the entity instead of the record opens bridges of collaboration between different domains. The analysis of the terminology used in some cataloguing standards and ontological models that start from the *name* and arrive at the definition of the *agent* is intended to demonstrate the evolution of the approach to information processing, which is less and less focused on string construction and more oriented toward entity identification. The study of a complex cataloguing case – such as that of the popes, which, as seen in Chapter 3, expresses an entity articulated in terms of defining the ontological and identity profile – will demonstrate how much the change in approach from name strings to the identification of agent-type entities can impact the ability to transmit knowledge in historical terms as well. The perspective of *clusters* and the possibility of identifying an entity and its possible, multiple identities offers a new scenario in cataloguing. The chapter closes with a proposal for the concrete realisation of this new scenario.

The agent in cataloguing tradition[273]

Name, author, agent: not only an issue of terminology

The term *agent*, found in several ontological models of the GLAM sector and referring to someone whose deliberate action determines or influences a creative expression, is a recent addition to bibliographic terminology. The website Librarianship Studies & Information Technology adopts the definition for the term 'agent' from IFLA LRM: 'Here agent refers to an entity who is capable of deliberate actions, of being granted rights, and of being held accountable for its actions. An agent includes a collective agent and a person.'[274] The term agent is defined in the meaning indicated previously in close relation to the concept of entity, and its use is indicative of a change not only in terminology but in cataloguing perspective. In the bibliographic tradition, the terms most widely used to define an equivalent role are those of *name* (of person, entity etc.), *heading, access point* or *author*. The focus is on the identification and construction of a *string* and thus of a set of encoded or uncoded characters that in some way represent an entity, primarily aimed at ensuring the searchability of a resource. The gradual abandonment of the term *header* in favour of the term *access point* reflects a shift from the vision still centred on the paper record (albeit digitised), which allowed only one entry point and thus one header, to a new dimension. This new dimension has been fostered by the evolution of cataloguing systems that enhance the possibilities of indexing the metadata present in bibliographic description by introducing multiple access points to the same description.

As early as 2009 IFLA ICP Statement had devoted paragraph 6 entirely to Access Points, defined according to the searchability of the bibliographic or authority record: 'Access points for bibliographic and authority data retrieval should be formulated following general principles (see 2. General Principles). They can be controlled or uncontrolled' (Tillett and Cristán, 2009). Despite the now-established tradition of entity-relationship models (already referred to in the 2009 edition, with reference to the FRBR and FRAD models) the 2016 edition of the Principles does not change the definition of access point, but maintains the focus on a mechanism for pointing to bibliographic or authority records. A further telltale sign of how attention was shifting toward entity–relationship models can be found in the Original RDA's existing treatment of relationship designators, which, as defined in Appendix I of the Original RDA Toolkit, are used to specify the relationship between a resource and a person, family or entity associated with that resource.[275] The Official RDA suggests consistent and widespread use of relationship designators, even in the case of structuring the main access point (tag 1xx), despite the apparent unambiguity of the relationship between this access point and the described resource. The definition of access point in the Original RDA Toolkit already shifts the focus to the entity – 'Name, term, code, etc. that represents a specific entity' – and this view is later reaffirmed in the Official RDA.[276] Meanwhile, the reference landscape had changed, extending to different domains, and the need arose to introduce a term that immediately refers not to one of the possible elements of describing a resource, but to something that calls attention to someone who deliberately performs an action with some influence on the described entity.

The agent in AACR2

The *Anglo-American Cataloguing Rules,* in their second edition,[277] became the most widely used code in the world, constituting the first international cataloguing code.

AACR2 has a still very traditional, record-oriented general framework. Much of the guidance related to persons or entities responsible to some extent for a work in some manner is recorded in Part II, dedicated to headings, uniform titles, and references. It also deals, of course, with headings for persons (Chapter 22) and corporate bodies (Chapter 24). It is fully consistent, then, with the approach focused on selecting elements necessary to construct a record, whether bibliographic or authority-related. The AACR2 Glossary offers, however, an initial definition of a *personal author*[278] and a *corporate body,*[279] hinting at the need to identify an entity responsible for a described resource beyond the practical necessity to define how to choose an access point to a description and how to structure its string.

The agent in the Regole italiane di catalogazione (Italian Cataloguing Rules) (REICAT)

New *Regole italiane di catalogazione*[280] prepared by the Commissione permanente per l'adeguamento e le eventuali semplificazioni delle RICA were published in 2009 as an update of the previous rules. The Commission had been established by the Direzione generale per i beni librari, gli istituti culturali e il diritto d'autore (Directorate General for Libraries, Cultural Institutes and Copyright) at the end of 1996 'with the aim of updating the current Italian Cataloguing Code' (Commissione permanente per la revisione delle regole italiane di catalogazione and ICCU, 2009, Ch. VII).

REICAT does not define the entity responsible to some extent for the resource as an *author* nor as an *agent*. It does not offer a definition of this entity. We are in the realm of traditional cataloguing and the context is that of the bibliographic or authority record. Persons and entities (the two categories under which an agent is specified) are spoken of with reference to the elements of access to records and selection of access, depending on the different cases. The names of persons and entities that can be attributable to the production of a work, expression or publication are treated in the context of access elements as headings. Specifically, it is emphasised that 'In the rules, the term *heading* is used to refer to the expression that identifies a *person* or entity in the catalogue' (Commissione permanente per la revisione delle regole italiane di catalogazione and ICCU, 2009, par. 0.4.3.2, p. 9).

Again, people and entities are discussed in Part III of the *Regole,* focusing on *responsibility relationships* and the selection and structuring of headings. The reference to author in some places is clear, but the focus is constantly kept on the bibliographic record, and thus on how to choose a record header based on the responsibility of a person or entity with respect to the document described.[281] From the definition of authorship responsibility given in the footnote we can certainly derive some sort of definition of what or who is an author, but the perspective, even of this definition, is naturally that of the cataloguer faced with the traditional bibliographic record. And all this is certainly legitimate, considering that the rules are still a long way from an entity modelling approach. The following chapters of this Part III are devoted, in fact, to the choice of *name* when creating a heading and its structuring into the different elements that constitute the name itself. If we wanted to venture an anachronistic parallelism, we could say that the analyses made around the person or entity as the header of a record in REICAT are much closer to the investigations that we would make around the *Nomen* and its construction in the IFLA LRM framework, than around the agent and its identification.

The agent in the Original RDA Toolkit

The RDA, published in 2010 and proposed as the successor to AACR2, was created as a set of data elements, guidelines, and instructions for creating metadata, especially in the digital domain[282] (Joint Steering Committee for the Development of RDA, 2010a). RDA Toolkit is deliberately designed as a website rather than a printed guide,[283] with a series of links between sections and pages that make it more challenging to identify and cite specific points in the guide, especially in the Official version, where numerical references to instructions disappear altogether.

The Original RDA clearly distinguishes, in the instructions contained in 8.1, Terminology, the elements of *person, family, entity* (as searchable and identifiable entities), *name*[284] and *access point*.[285] The description of the terms *person, family* and *entity* provides precise definitions for each of these agent types:

- The term *person* refers to an individual or identity established by an individual (alone or in collaboration with other individuals).
- The term *family* refers to two or more persons related by birth, marriage, adoption, civil union or similar legal status, or who present themselves as a family.
- The term *entity* refers to an organisation or group of people and/or organisations identified by a particular name, which acts, or may act, as a unit.

Evident in this structure is reference to the FRBR conceptual model, which the Original RDA absorbs along with FRAD and around which it builds the set of cataloguing rules and instructions. In fact, the second group of entities modelled in FRBR refers to the entities that are involved in various ways in the creation, realisation, distribution and management of the entities in the first group (Work, Expression, Manifestation and Item), and that can be declined as person or corporate body.

The person, family and corporate body entities are modelled in the Original RDA Toolkit through the definition of attributes and relationships. Until AACR2 the name string had constituted the access point to the representation of the resource and therefore the element on which to focus attention in cataloguing analysis, but now it loses prominence, becoming one of the possible attributes (name of the person or corporate body) useful for identifying the agent, that class of entities capable of acting with different responsibilities in the construction or management of a resource. Figure 4.1 outlines the core properties of the Person entity, which result from the combination of attributes provided by FRBR and FRAD for this entity:

- identifier for the person
- name of the person (attribute linked to the preferred name of the person)
- fuller form of the name
- title of the person
- field of activity of the person
- profession or occupation
- other designation associated with the person.

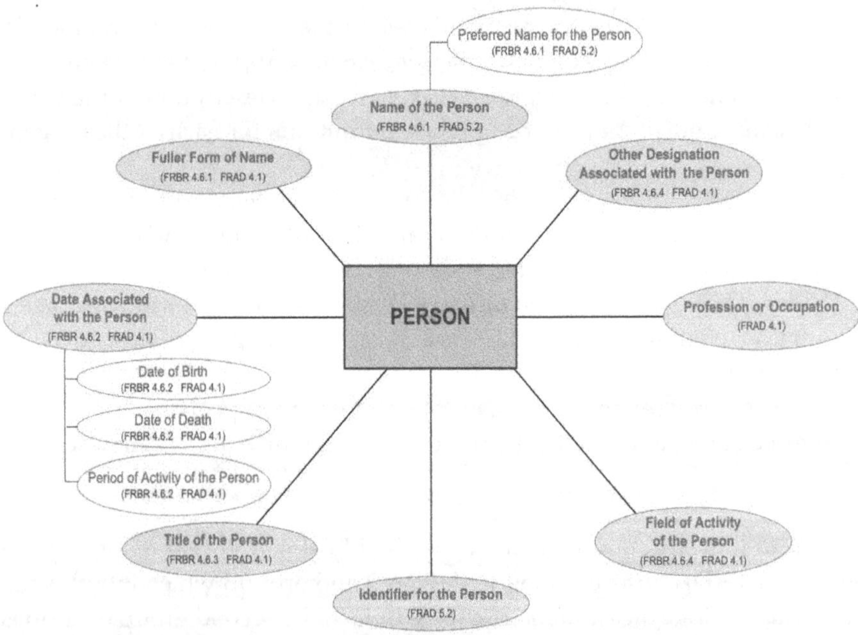

Figure 4.1 *Person: Core elements in Original RDA Toolkit.* Image from the RDA Toolkit (www.rdatoolkit.org) used by permission of the copyright holders for RDA (American Library Association, Canadian Federation of Library Associations, and CILIP: Chartered Institute of Library and Information Professionals)

The entity person is then enhanced with a number of other properties, ranging from places of birth, death and residence, affiliation, language used and gender. What had been, in traditional cataloguing regulations, a string of names, has evolved into an object, modelled into an actual entity, with a kind of concrete physicality. The focus is no longer on how to compose a *string* so that it refers unequivocally, where possible, to an agent that can be associated with the resource, but rather on the agent itself, on its characteristics profiled in terms of attributes and relationships.

Yet, we haven't quite arrived at the point we can say we are distant from the record approach. The transition from the record to the entity is not yet complete, and traces of the old approach are still evident even in the Original RDA Toolkit. To illustrate this immaturity, it is interesting to look at the *status of identification* attribute not inherited from the FRBR and FRAD models but added in the Original RDA Toolkit as an *attribute of the Person entity*, and therefore, present in the roster of other attributes referable to the entity. The definition that is given of this attribute in instruction 8.10.1.1 would seem to confirm this assumption. 'Identification status is an indication of the level of authentication of the data identifying an entity.' Therefore, I describe an entity with a set of data (attributes and relationships) and express the level of authentication of these data, to give evidence of how reliable the entity's identification is. Yet there is an element of fragility in the explanation of the different levels of authentication that can be applied, because while the cataloguer's focus is now on the entity person, the explanation of the different levels invokes the traditional concept of authorised access referable to a character string constructed to grant access to a description.

The terms listed apply as follows:

1 'completed' is recorded if the data is sufficient to establish definitively an authorised access point representing the person, family, or corporate body;
2 'provisional' is recorded if the data is insufficient to establish satisfactorily an authorised access point representing the person, family or corporate body;
3 'preliminary' is recorded if the data is inferred from the description of a resource when the resource itself is not available.

Regardless of the identification status of the data, these refer to the string constructed to give access to the record and not to the entity as a whole; therefore, they refer to the degree of completeness of the authorised access point, defined in the Glossary of the Original RDA Toolkit as a standardised access point representing an entity. In the Official RDA Toolkit, the *status of identification* element is defined as 'an indication of a level of authentication of the nomen of an entity.' The introduction of the *Nomen* entity linking an RDA entity with its corresponding identifying string allows the boundaries of this element to be at least fixed. It is used not to express the degree of authority of all attributes referable to an object (thus to the set of attributes and relationships that, together, shape that entity) but to the nomen element alone and thus to that label (defined just so in RDA, *label*) that references the entity to which it is linked. The confusion generated in the Original RDA Toolkit by defining the status of identification element as a property of the person is definitively clarified in the Official RDA Toolkit, where it is unequivocally linked to the *nomen* class.

The same modelling of the entity *person* is presented in the Original RDA Toolkit for the entities *family* and *corporate body*.

Core property associated with the *family* entity:

- name of the family
- type of family
- date associated with the family
- place associated with the family
- identifier for the family
- prominent member of the family.

Core property associated to the *collective* entity:

- name of the corporate body
- associated institution
- date associated with the corporate body
- identifier for the corporate body
- place associated with the corporate body
- other designation associated with the corporate body.

The proposed relationships for the three entities – person, family, corporate body – are reciprocal, and thus:

- related person
- related family
- related corporate body.

The Original RDA Toolkit represents, therefore, an important innovation in the field of cataloguing rules, because it absorbs a conceptual model, theoretical in nature, oriented toward entities and relationships (ER model) and translates it into instructions, practices and guidelines for identifying and describing the bibliographic universe, modelled precisely in entities. Elements of immaturity with respect to a fully entity-oriented approach are still evident, but the distance of the framework from traditional cataloguing rules is significant.

The agent in Encoded Archival Description

Encoded Archival Description (EAD) is an international standard for the management and transmission of hierarchical archival field descriptions.[286]

The development of EAD has made possible the creation of electronic finding aids with archival data structuring specifications that are fully compatible with the General International Standard Archival Description. As stated on the standard's description page, this development has facilitated the move of archival descriptions from local contexts to the web, and has also encouraged the rapid dissemination of national archival descriptive content standards[287] and the emergence of a broad professional consensus toward the idea of shared archival knowledge that is not confined to local domains.

The EAD standard has a traditional, description-oriented matrix of elements, and the concept of entities is completely alien, as is also evident from the terminology used. The definition of the relator element, for example, uses terms clearly that refer to the traditional approach to description and cataloguing, such as *controlled access term*:

> A contextual role or relationship that a controlled access term has with the materials described. For example, {persname} may have a relator value of 'creator' or 'photographer.' EAD does not supply a controlled list of values for this attribute, but use of some other controlled vocabulary (e.g., MARC relator codes), is encouraged.[288]

The language is the same as that used in MARC's definitions and cataloguing regulations. Among the elements described we find Agent, but with a completely different meaning from what the term will assume in the context of entity modelling: 'A required child element of {maintenanceevent} that provides the name of a person, institution, or system responsible for the creation, modification, or deletion of an EAD instance.'[289] The term Agent, then, is not related to the resource described but to the EAD instance, thus to the description itself. It is used with the {maintenanceevent} element that clearly refers to an EAD management action:

> Use {maintenanceevent} to record an activity in the creation and ongoing maintenance of an EAD instance, including revisions, updates, deletions, etc. There will always be at least one maintenance event for each instance, which will typically be its creation.[290]

Along the lines of the more traditional perspective we find the {persname} Personal Name element which is defined as follows:

> Identifies a name, including any or all forenames, surnames, honorific titles and added names, of a person who is related to the materials being described as either a source, creator, or subject.[291]

The perspective is that of the string and its construction, with only indirect reference to an entity, referred to as the subject identified by that name.

The treatment of the agent in MARC

The reference to the treatment of the agent in MARC is outside the main focus of the chapter. MARC, in fact, is not configured as a set of cataloguing rules or standards, nor does it rank among the conceptual modelling of the bibliographical domain, since it is exclusively a format devoted to the exchange of data (bibliographical, authority, local). Its distance from any standards for the selection and formulation of data is clearly stated in the third element that makes up the basic setting of the format, namely the so-called content, the actual information content 'defined by standards outside the formats.'[292]

Despite this distance from the cataloguing rules examined thus far, it will nonetheless prove useful to reflect briefly on the terminological evolution addressed by the MARC format, through which it is possible to trace the transition from a focus on headings and strings to entity modelling.

Leaving aside the details of the birth and spread of MARC, now widely known, and focusing specifically on the two most popular formats (MARC 21 and UNIMARC), the first and perhaps obvious element of reasoning is offered by the fact that the MARC format, despite being historically linked to an electronic context, in fact re-proposes the same articulation provided in paper records. For the purposes of the present analysis, this is of essential importance, since everything related to agents in MARC is managed as simple strings with very few identifying elements and is used for simple access and retrieval of the record. Agents are not treated as entities then, but as headings or headings expressed through specific fields, following an approach that fully reflects more traditional cataloguing rules such as AACR2 or REICAT.

It is no accident that both formats do not even provide an Agent definition, limiting themselves to a few words of explanation about the individual field, mainly to clarify its practical applicability and usage context. As an example, see the description provided for field 100 MARC 21, which reads, 'Personal name used as a main entry in a bibliographic record.' Notably, the emphasis here is on the name, specifically on formulating the name string, and on its nature as a *main entry*, to emphasise its role as an element placed, not materially but logically, at the head of the record.

This approach does not imply, however, that the MARC format has remained insensitive to the intervening changes. Some evolution in terminology has certainly taken place following the publication of FRBR, from which there has been a gradual adaptation to the model, either through the formulation of fields developed from scratch or through the reinterpretation of existing fields.[293] Such impact has been most notable at the level of the MARC authority format, where there has been a clear shift towards the use of dedicated fields, used not so much to express strings as to provide additional information about the object (entity) described by the record; it is no coincidence that the fields that make up the 3XX block in the MARC 21 authority are almost all subsequent to the late 1990s.

Even more impactful, however, has been the dissemination of principles related to the semantic web and the subsequent establishment of entity modelling in the treatment of bibliographic data as well, both of which have led to a rethinking in the flat structure of the MARC record.

Going into a little more detail, one can speak of a dual condition that brought about this change. First, the need to make MARC closer to – or rather more convertible and usable than – linked open data technology, in which the monolithic nature of the record constitutes a strong obstacle to any reuse. The second condition was the desire to make the most of the vast amount of data made available with the emergence of the first large international authority files such as VIAF and ISNI. It is in relation to these needs that the work of the PCC Task Group on URIs in MARC[294] came into play, thanks to which it is currently possible to introduce URIs, i.e. universally valid IDs mainly from authoritative external sources, into specific subfields. Such insertion is ensured by the presence of special subfields associated with heading fields, with the aim of making the entity expressed by that precise heading more identifiable – a practice that, it must be emphasised, is now gaining more and more ground and assumes central importance within all the automatic processes of conversion of MARC records into linked open data.[295]

Agent modelling in the semantic web

The semantic web opens a new perspective with respect to the identification of an agent that somehow operates in the different contexts of the network. The way we interact in the cybernetic space, whither we have shifted much of our lives, compels us to identify in an increasingly precise way the things of the real world, not necessarily related to or referable to a specific context. The concept of agent, which transcends the human boundary to embrace mechanical and software agents, becomes common domain and enters ontological modelling, often as a central entity. Following are some examples of agent definitions in domain ontologies.

The agent in IFLA LRM

This is the definition of the entity *agent* provided by IFLA LRM: 'An entity capable of deliberate actions, of being granted rights, and of being held accountable for its actions' (IFLA LRM, 2017, 28).

The modelling proposed by IFLA LRM has entailed a profound reflection upon, and questioning of, now-established models. Defined by one of its creators as a 'reference model',[296] IFLA LRM has taken the modelling of the bibliographic universe to a level of abstraction clearly superior not only to the relational models from which it comes (FRBR, FRAD and FRSAD), but to the same ontological modelling that emerged within a context linked to the semantic web, such as BIBFRAME. A necessary starting point for reasoning is the presence of a specific Agent class, which is in fact absent in both FRBR and FRAD. In fact, in both previous models the emphasis was on the concept of responsibility, intellectual or material, towards the so-called 'entities of the first group', which were treated in their singularity, thus differentiating by person, corporate body and family.[297] In IFLA LRM, however, the path taken was one towards not only greater abstraction but also rationalisation of the model. The choice to include an apex super-class that groups any subclasses allows for what is called inheritance of attributes and relationships, on the basis of which everything defined for a class is automatically inherited by its subclasses, thus avoiding unnecessary redundancy of information. In addition to this basic assumption, which is valid for the entire model and constitutes one of the most novel aspects of IFLA LRM, substantial differences are also noticeable in terms of the entity definition itself. As will also be pointed out for BIBFRAME, the emphasis is on agency, on performing an activity of some kind, in a deliberate and responsible manner. The terms *deliberate* and *responsible* are of great conceptual importance, in that for the first time greater emphasis is placed on the voluntariness in the roles assumed by the agent, who acts rather than merely being acted upon. Also interesting are the comparisons that can be made in the more specific definitions assumed by the Person and Corporate body subclasses with respect to FRBR and FRAD:

- Person in FRBR: 'An individual'
- Person in FRAD: 'An individual or identity established or adopted by an individual or group'
- Person in IFLA LRM 'An individual human being'.

The conceptual distance appears significant. While FRBR and FRAD still show some confusion between entity and identity, in IFLA LRM the reification of agents is complete, following an approach similar to that proposed by Wikidata. While less obvious, this is also evident in the definition of corporate bodies:

- Corporate body in FRBR: 'An organisation or group of individuals and/or organisations acting as a unit'
- Corporate body in FRAD: 'An organisation or group of persons and/or organisations identified by a particular name acting as a unit'
- Corporate body in IFLA LRM: 'A gathering or organisation of persons bearing a particular name and capable of acting as a unit'.

However, unlike Wikidata, which emerged from practical needs related to the creation of an open, cross-domain, encyclopaedic information source, the approach of IFLA LRM takes on the contours of a 'real abstraction'. This is because it is a high-level model deeply rooted in the domain from which it originates. It is no coincidence that IFLA LRM repeatedly states that both attributes and relationships do not constitute an exhaustive list. This is not due to an inability to identify and relate the model's entities to each other, but rather to ensure greater applicability of the model. The attributes and relationships explicitly declared in the model, although limited in number, still allow for the correct entity identification in any case:

Subtypes
Person, Collective agent
Attributes
Contact information
Field of activity
Language
Main relationships
With the main entities of the model (Work, Expression, Instance):
Created
Manufactured
Distributes
Owns
Modified
With the other entities in the model (Nomen, Place, Timespan):
Has appellation
Has association with[298]
Assigned

The agent in BIBFRAME

The Agent class in BIBFRAME 2.0 is defined as 'entity having a role in a resource, such as a person or organisation'[299] and is explained in the model overview as 'agents are people, organisations, jurisdictions, etc., associated with a Work or Instance through roles such as author, editor, artist, photographer, composer, illustrator, etc.'.

Unlike IFLA LRM, which maintains a more generic and abstract approach with respect to the Agent entity before detailing it in specific subclasses, BIBFRAME proposes a more empirical definition of the Agent entity. This is not indicative of the genesis of BIBFRAME, which flows directly from practical requirements and needs[300] that have conditioned its modelling.

Looking back at the early history of BIBFRAME, in the initial version 1.0, the modelling was focused on identifying those entities capable of expressing the multiple layers underlying bibliographic resources in the strictest sense, the entity Work and the entity Instance. The Agent entity, unrecognised as such, was instead relegated to the far more ambiguous Authority class,[301] generically denoting anything that could be expressible through authority data, be it names of persons and organisations or subjects. This Authority class demonstrates how, at least in its earliest formulation, entity modelling in BIBFRAME was affected by a still somewhat traditional approach, in which importance was not given to the entity itself, but rather to the formulation of the name strings and the source of origin of those strings (bibliographic *v.* authority record).

This approach has largely survived in the MADS ontology,[302] used by the Library of Congress for the RDF conversion of authority records produced in the various sources (LCNAF, LCSH, LCGFT, etc.). In fact, entity modelling appears to be absent in MADS, as it is a mere reproduction in RDF language of a setup still tied to headings and their formulation. The concept of Agent is ignored in favour of the class Name,[303] then divided into the various subclasses ConferenceName, CorporateName, FamilyName, PersonalName.

Unlike the MADS ontology, in its version 2.0 BIBFRAME has made a decisive leap towards true entity modelling by also recognising agents as entities in their own right. Referring to the initial definition, BIBFRAME clarifies first and foremost that the Agent entity should be attributed to specific types ('people, organisations, jurisdictions, etc.'), whose relevance is directly related to their relationship with the main entities of the model (Work and Instance). In the context expressed by BIBFRAME, even more than in IFL LRM, the nature of the agent emerges as an entity whose active role is recognised and by whose action the other entities of the model are in fact generated (by authors, creators, artists, etc.) or are modified in their substance and/or materiality (by illustrators, curators, printers, etc.).

This view of the Agent, on the other hand, implies a certain vagueness in the profiling of the entity, which takes on a dimension only in relation to other entities. In BIBFRAME, the agent still appears too ill-defined, especially if one looks at the list of attributes and relationships provided by the model. What are the factors that have determined and still determine this limited approach of BIBFRAME? To a large extent, one can speak of a vision still conditioned by MARC 21, and especially the Format for Bibliographic Data, from which the MARC21–BIBFRAME conversion effectively originates. But it is no coincidence that, among the agent attributes extended by the Library of Congress to facilitate retroconversion to MARC 21,[304] there is the bflc:marcKey, with which an attempt is made to compensate for the inability to identify correctly the main attributes associated with agents by repurposing the string of the MARC21 record. One could speak of a true preservation of the MARC21 structure, currently unreachable in its granularity:

Subtypes
Person, Family, Organisation, Jurisdiction, Meeting
Metadata Licensor (extension of BIBFRAME)
Attributes
identifiedBy
marcKey (extension of BIBFRAME)
Main relationships
agentOf
contributionOf

The agent in Wikidata

The modelling of 'Agents' in Wikidata appears profoundly different from the data models already seen, and also from those that will be analysed later.

While far removed from a record-centric approach such as that discerned in MARC formats or more traditional cataloguing rules, in both IFLA LRM and BIBFRAME the very essence of agents is closely related to the idea of action. Taking a definition from the Treccani dictionary, the Agent (*Agente* in Italian) is one 'who acts, who causes a certain effect', and therefore exists only to the extent that they perform a well-defined action, on the basis of which it is also possible to define the specific role performed. While such a perspective is consistent with models more properly related to the bibliographic universe, in which modelling revolves around resources (*core* entities), conversely it proves unsuitable in application to a broader context.

This is the case with Wikidata, an open, collaborative, multilingual dataset based on data structured according to linked open data technologies.

Although widely used in international projects related to the library sphere and more generally GLAM, Wikidata differs from projects like VIAF and ISNI in that it did not originate from needs related to authority control or bibliographic purposes. Instead, Wikidata serves as a centralised core for the management of data from projects in the Wiki world, such as Wikipedia, Wikisource, etc.

Thus, the goal of Wikidata is not to provide identification of entities related to a specific domain of knowledge, but to propose a set of structured data about any real-world entities of interest (cultural and/or scientific, informative, encyclopaedic, etc.). Placed in such a context, the agent in fact loses substance to be articulated and identified in its most real and concrete essence. What are the agents of the Person subtype if not people and therefore human beings? And are the agents of the Organisation subtype not responsive to a multiplicity of different institutional realities and therefore manifest as universities, municipalities, hospitals, research centres, etc.? In other words, Wikidata aims to offer an identification of entities (or items) based not on what these entities have accomplished vis-à-vis other entities, but on their actual, tangible essence. Any intellectual responsibilities towards Works, Expressions, Manifestations, etc. are declared through specific properties that in this case express their role as agents. The relationship between the author and their work, for example, is made explicit by property P50[305] ('main creator(s) of written works'), while the relationship between the publisher and a specific publication by property P123[306] ('organisation or person responsible for publishing books, periodicals, printed music, podcasts, games or software').

After this long but necessary introduction, the following are some definitions related to entities that more frequently have intellectual and material responsibilities to other entities:

Human (Q5): 'common name of Homo sapiens, unique extant species of the genus Homo, from embryo to adult'.[307]

Items of the human type (persons) can be associated with a large number of properties aimed at expressing both attributes and relationships with other entities. Their use depends on what information can and will be provided and on their actual applicability: for example, for people from contemporary times, the P97 *noble title* property[308] is certainly more difficult to apply than for people from other historical periods, while the P1853 *blood type* property data[309] might be difficult to know and considered irrelevant except in reference to specific people.

To facilitate the choice of properties, the Wikidata community provides several tables, which are continuously being updated with the properties considered most important, including:[310]

- Wikidata:List_of_properties[311]
- Template:Bibliographic_properties[312]

Family (Q8436): 'group of people affiliated by consanguinity, affinity, or co-residence'.[313]
Since this is an entity less present in Wikidata, it was not possible to retrieve a well-defined list of properties associated with entities of type Family. Similarly for People, properties are retrievable through the query: https://w.wiki/6Szc.

Organisation (Q43229): 'social entity established to meet needs or pursue goals'[314]

Institution (Q178706): 'structure or mechanism of social order and cooperation governing the behaviour of a set of individuals within a given community'.[315]

Unlike People or Families, Wikidata entities are almost never directly classified as Organisations or Institutions, because these types are too generic. It is generally good practice to use the numerous relevant subclasses for which it is not easy to get an exhaustive list of properties. Some examples include university, library, hospital, chamber of commerce, etc.[316]

Even in the case of organisations/institutions, there are various lists of properties defined by specific communities interested in their management. These include, for example, the special tables formulated by the archival community operating in Wikidata: Describing_Organisations.[317]

For a more comprehensive examination of managing agents, it is necessary to briefly discuss the treatment of pseudonyms, which due to their complex nature, have always been the subject of detailed cataloguing reflections.

In Wikidata, first and foremost, there is a significant distinction between pseudonyms referring to single entities and collective pseudonyms. Starting with pseudonyms referring to single entities, and thus referring to a single person, Wikidata's modelling focuses on the identification of the entity itself, on the person as a real object therefore, and not on the multiple identities that this person may have assumed in the course of their existence. This therefore leads to the presence of a single, human-type item to which all the different labels are attributed whether they are variant forms of the name or actual pseudonyms.

One example among many is the item referring to the person Samuel Langhorne Clemens, better known as Mark Twain, who, in his uniqueness as an individual, corresponds to a single item (www.wikidata.org/entity/Q7245). The pseudonym is not only listed as a simple label (in the case of Mark Twain, even preferred over the given name) but also through the specific property P742 *pseudonym*.[318] The disadvantage of such an approach is the loss of the relationship between works and the pseudonym under which they were created. In fact, as already widely stated, often the use of a pseudonym implies the intention not to associate certain works with one's given name, deeming them unsuitable for one's public or institutional reputation, or as a result of assuming certain types of offices, such as the papal one. By not managing identities separately from entities, Wikidata effectively does not guarantee such associations, except in part by the use of the property P1932 *object named as*.[319] Shifting attention to items of the type Edition, thus on a more concrete level than that of 'Work', the property P50 *author*[320] can indeed be qualified with the property P1932, useful to indicate the name of that same author as originally expressed in the source, or in that very specific edition.

Quite different is the treatment of collective pseudonyms. Because they cannot be attributed to an individual, they themselves become entities to which individual components are then appropriately linked via the P527 *has part(s)* property.[321]

To better clarify this distinction between pseudonyms and collective pseudonyms, a schematic summary is offered below:

PSEUDONYMS

Item *instance* of	human
pseudonym	string value
Item *instance of*	version, edition or translation
author	author item
object named as	string value

COLLECTIVE PSEUDONYMS

Item *instance of*	group of authors
has part(s)	member(s) item

The agent in the Official RDA

In order to analyse the interpretation of agent within the scope of the Official RDA and the changes this revision introduces by absorbing IFLA LRM, it is perhaps interesting to present a list of terms related to agent found in the glossary (RDA Steering Committee, 2021), indicating where the term refers to a new version of a term already in the Original RDA, to a version identical to the previous one, or whether it is a new entry. For each term, the corresponding definition is provided, again taken from the glossary.

The Official RDA Toolkit therefore:

- maintains and specifies *access point* (Official RDA Toolkit, 'Access point for agent'): 'An appellation of an entity in natural language that is selected from a vocabulary encoding scheme or constructed using a string encoding scheme by an agent who creates metadata.' The access point is specified for different types of entities, and thus also for different subtypes of agent (example: access point for agent defined as 'A nomen that is an appellation of agent in natural language that is taken from a vocabulary encoding scheme or is constructed using a string encoding scheme')

- maintains and specifies *Person*[322] ('An agent who is an individual human being who lives or is assumed to have lived.'), *Corporate Body*[323] ('A collective agent who is composed of persons who are organised for a common purpose or activity.'), *Family* (Official RDA Toolkit, 'Entities – Family') ('A collective agent who is composed of persons who are related by birth, marriage, adoption, civil union or similar legal status, or who otherwise present themselves as a family.') Corporate body and Family become subclasses of Collective agent.
- *redirects* the *author* entry to the *Author agent* (Official RDA Toolkit, 'Entities – Work – Author agent'): 'An agent who is responsible for creating a textual work. Creation of a new work by paraphrasing, rewriting or adapting works by another creator, if the modification has substantially changed the nature and content of the original or changed the medium of expression, is included.'
- inserts the term *Agent*:[324] 'An entity who is capable of deliberate actions, of being granted rights, and of being held accountable for its actions. An agent includes a collective agent and a person.'
- introduces *Collective Agent*:[325] 'An agent who is a gathering or organisation of two or more persons that bears a particular name and that is capable of acting as a unit. A collective agent includes a corporate body and a family.'
- introduces *Nomen*:[326] 'A label for any RDA entity except a nomen. A label includes a name, title, access point or identifier.'

Many of these entities are included in the *RDA Entity* class:[327] 'An abstract class of key conceptual objects in the universe of human discourse that are a focus of interest to users of RDA metadata in a system for resource discovery. An RDA entity includes an agent, collective agent, corporate body, expression, family, item, manifestation, nomen, person, place, timespan, and work.'

The list of terms taken from the Glossary demonstrates the maturity of this new version with respect to a clearer differentiation between an object of a string-type, such as an access point, and an object understood as an entity, such as the agent with its person, entity or family specification. The introduction of the *nomen* class, in compliance with IFLA LRM, is perhaps the most significant new element with respect to the profound shift in perspective that we are outlining. The entity 'nomen', much discussed in the library community due to the difficulty in understanding and practically implementing it in the cataloguing workflow, represents a kind of missing link between the name string – constructed with all its artifices in order to be increasingly 'dense' with identifying elements – and the entity itself, that agent who, with various roles, *acts* deliberately, creating, or in some way exerting, an influence on the resource. The nomen[328] is defined as a label (thus as a tag and as a string) but at the same time it is modelled as a class, as an entity, and is linked to an entity. In the implementation scenario in linked data,[329] 'nomen' is defined as: 'a reification of the generic triple or *metadata statement* RDA entity – has [the] appellation of RDA entity – "nomen string".'[330]

In the report *Introducing RDA: A Guide to the Basics After 3R* Chris Oliver dedicates Chapter Five to what is new in RDA and gives both a historical and conceptual overview of the nomen entity, perhaps useful in clarifying its scope. The nomen, which, as mentioned, seems to add complexity to the model, in fact responds to that natural need to name things, especially when we need to identify things. In defining the conceptual model, IFLA LRM follows the historical approach of FRAD and FRSAD, which models naming as a separate entity from the named thing, as opposed to FRBR, which instead defines naming as an attribute of the entity. The Original RDA followed FRBR's approach by considering the name as the attribute of the entity (person, family, corporate body). The introduction of nomen in the Official RDA does not seem to change, in practice, the outcome of data modelling, but it expresses exactly that change in perspective that we are trying to trace. To illustrate this change in perspective, Chris Oliver uses the example of the terminology used for the naming of things in the Original and Official RDA Toolkit:

> *RDA in the original Toolkit*
> Record the name chosen as a preferred name for person by applying the general guidelines
> *RDA in the new Toolkit*
> Record this element as a value of a Nomen: nomen string or as an instance of a Nomen
>
> (Oliver, 2021, 127)

Nomen, then, is a broad entity, including a name, a title, an access point, an identifier, a subject, a classification or even just a heading.

In the same report, Oliver devotes Chapter Three to presenting the IFLA LRM conceptual model that underpins RDA and focuses a specific section on modelling Agents.[331] Describing the hierarchical structure of IFLA LRM, with the superclass *Res* as the apex element, she presents the agent entity as an additional hierarchical level introduced with the harmonisation of previous models. The agent is a subclass of *Res* and, at the same time, a superclass, encompassing any entity capable of deliberate actions, that can be granted rights and can be held accountable for its actions (with wording taken from LRM E-6). The agent, therefore, includes those entities that have a deliberate relationship with bibliographic entities (works, expressions, manifestations and items) (Oliver, 2021, 50–3). The agent conceptually includes the three entities defined in FR models (persons, families and entities).

However, in the IFLA LRM definition, a new entity (*collective agent)* is introduced that serves as a higher entity by including families and corporate bodies. In this way, the IFLA LRM agent is modelled with only two subclasses, that of persons and that of collective agents. But IFLA LRM does not define families and corporate bodies as subclasses; it simply includes them as collective agents. Official RDA, on the other hand, with its more practical modelling requirement, defines hierarchical structures that, through the mechanism of property inheritance from the higher class, guarantee a more streamlined (and usable) model and a greater ability to extend subclasses where necessary. For this reason, the Official RDA, which we can consider in its function as a practical implementation of IFLA LRM, models *family* and *corporate bodies* as subclasses of *collective agents.* And here, in fact, we find the most relevant difference in the modelling of agent in the Original RDA and the Official RDA: the Original RDA, even before the alignment of FR models in IFLA LRM, had adopted the term 'agent' more for practical convenience. This allowed for the avoidance of repeated phrases in instructions and elements referring to persons, families and corporate bodies. The term 'agent' had been introduced to refer to the three types of entities without having to describe repeatedly each entity individually. But the entity 'agent', in terms of entities, did not exist. Only the Official RDA, in continuity with Original RDA in adopting the term 'agent', actually models it as an entity, along the lines of IFLA LRM, linking it to the RDA *entity* which is the corresponding (but narrower) superclass to IFLA LRM's *Res,* and specifying it in the two subclasses of 'person' and 'collective agent'. The latter class is then concretely modelled with the 'family' and 'corporate body' extensions or subclasses. Following the criteria and principles of object-oriented and ontological architectures, a subclass is introduced into a hierarchical structure when it is deemed necessary to define properties (attributes or relationships) that pertain only to the subclass and not to the higher class (thus not to all members of the superclass). Those who analysed the IFLA LRM model to concretise it in the Official RDA deemed it necessary to achieve a higher level of granularity in the modelling of family and corporate body entities by presenting these, evidently, differently in the attributions of their respective properties (Oliver, 2021, 98).

The concept of *person* also changes in the update from Original to Official RDA Toolkit: the Original RDA absorbed the definition of 'person' from FRAD, thus including pseudonyms, fictitious entities and non-human entities. IFLA LRM changes the approach and excludes fictitious and non-human entities from the 'person' entity. The Official RDA must change the definition of person to align with IFLA LRM: instances of fictitious entities such as Geronimo Stilton, Snoopy or Miss Piggy risk being somewhat 'downgraded' from the body of a person entity referable to a real individual. And this risk seems to materialise in the definition given for these entities in the section *Fictitious and non-human appellations*:[332]

> An appellation of a fictitious entity that is included in a statement in a manifestation that assigns responsibility to an agent is assumed to be a pseudonymous appellation of an Agent, Collective Agent, Corporate Body, Family or Person.

Already here the change of perspective is evident. We are back in the realm of designations and thus names and not entities. To explain this choice Oliver points out that, with a fictitious entity, what matters to an end-user is the name, and not the entity with which that name claims to be associated (Oliver, 2021, 132). The nomen, then, steps in to solve a problem of relationship between a somewhat hidden entity and the name string with which that entity is associated. Official RDA's starting point for solving these cases is the assumption that there is nevertheless a real entity behind a fictitious identity. The instructions provided for managing these fictitious entities (or rather identities) then change depending on whether the hidden entity, hence the agent, is known or unknown. In the case of a known identity, the scenarios are akin to those of pseudonyms and the choice of nomen (that of the fictitious identity or the birth identity) is at the discretion of the cataloguing agency. In the case of the unknown entity, the name (and nomen) of the fictitious identity can certainly be chosen to identify this type of agent.

Literary, legendary and otherwise non-human figures are treated differently, which is ontologically coherent but complicated to understand in practice. The instruction for non-human entities says: 'A non-human entity that is associated with a statement in a manifestation that assigns responsibility to an agent is treated as an entity that is external to RDA.'

From an ontological perspective, it is not possible to define this entity as a subclass of the agent entity, since an agent is defined as 'a person or two or more persons acting as a unit'. And on the other hand, the hypothesis of defining this entity as a subclass of the more general RDA entity does not work from an ontological viewpoint either. The RDA entity is an entity that specifies the IFLA LRM *res*. To include a subclass of res other than agent would have meant a substantial change to the IFLA model, which would then have been absorbed by RDA. Clearly, this was not deemed feasible, so the final decision with respect to modelling non-human entities is perhaps, with many misgivings, functional for cataloguing implementation but quite incomprehensible from a modelling point of view – to exclude this entity from RDA, relying on something 'external', to allow registration of relationships with an unspecified non-RDA entity. It is too early to make a substantive judgement on this choice, which at first analysis seems truly difficult to understand and share.

Another noteworthy element in the Official RDA is the introduction of the definitions of *real identity of a person* (a person who has an appellation of person that is a real identity) and *alternate identity of a person* (a nomen that is a pseudonym or other appellation used by a person). The RDA Metadata Guidance Documentation (MGDs),[333] used by the PCC along with the Official RDA Toolkit devotes an entire section to instructions for dealing with the alternate identity of a person.[334]

As is perhaps evident from this brief examination of the agent in the Official RDA, several changes have been made, partly resulting from choices that IFLA LRM had to make by harmonising the entity profiles originally defined in FRBR and FRAD, and partly due to RDA-specific choices. The aim, in some cases successful and in others less agreeable, was to make modelling instructions more practical in cataloguing terms.

To close this analysis of the treatment of the agent in Official RDA, it is worth mentioning again the concept of 'entity boundary', which I have already discussed in Chapter 3 and which is so strongly functional to the entity modelling with which this entire research is concerned. In the Official RDA instruction section 18.17.07.55, devoted to Person (which I quote here as an example, but which is equally present in all RDA entities), entity boundary is defined as follows:

> The absolute boundary of the entity is determined by characteristics of the entity that reflect the physical world.
> Record a new instance of the entity when the following occurs:
> There is a significant difference in a value of one or more of the elements:
> – Person: date of birth
> – Person: date of death
> – Person: place of birth
> – Person: place of death

For general guidance on entity boundaries, see Guidance: Entity boundaries.
A significant difference in a value of one or more other elements may indicate a boundary of the entity.

The agent in CIDOC CRM

The CIDOC Conceptual Reference Model (CIDOC CRM)[335] provides a flexible ontology for modelling cultural heritage concepts and information with reference to the entire GLAM domain. It is an international standard (ISO 21127:2014)[336] and has the overall goal of providing a reference model and information standard that museums (especially) and other cultural institutions can use to describe their collections and promote them, facilitating information sharing.

The CIDOC CRM[337] consists of 81 classes and 160 properties. The E1 CRM Entity superclass encompasses all things in the discourse universe that CIDOC CRM considers its domain.

Of particular interest for this agent analysis is the *E39 Actor*, defined as follows: 'This class comprises people, either individually or in groups, who have the potential to perform intentional actions of kinds for which someone may be held responsible.'[338] The term *Agent* is used as an alternative label for this class in some languages, including French and Portuguese.

Actor is a subclass of the class E77 Persistent item,[339] which includes objects that have persistent characteristics of a structural nature that are substantially related to their identity and integrity. Persistent items can be physical entities such as people, animals or things, conceptual entities such as ideas, concepts and products of the imagination, or even names.

It has as subclasses:

- *E21 Person*: this class includes real people who are living or presumed to have lived.
  Legendary figures who may have existed, such as Ulysses and King Arthur, fall into this class if documentation refers to them as historical figures.[340]
- *E74 Group*: this class includes all ensembles (gatherings, meetings, conventions, etc.) or organisations of individuals or human groups acting collectively or similarly through any form of aggregation relationship. Of interest is what follows in the later part of the definition: broadly speaking, this class also includes official roles held by individuals but with public or community significance, such as the president of a country. In these cases, the entity is considered a 'group' even if it is represented by only one member.

A collection of people becomes an instance of the class E74 Group when it is united by something, which could be a project, a common idea, the creation of an artifact, a study project, or a cultural, religious or sports activity. Common nationality can also define a group and thus an instance of this class, as can the family, which is considered a particular example of a group.341

The Persistent item, of which E21 Person and E74 Group are subclasses, is itself a subclass of E1 CRM Entity, which includes all things in the universe of discourse of the CIDOC CRM. The E1 CRM Entity is an abstract concept with three general properties:

- identification by *name or appellation*, and particularly by preferred identifier
- classification by *types*, which allows further refinement of the specific subclass to which an instance belongs
- the ability to associate free text and other unstructured data to express anything not captured by formal properties.

All other classes within CIDOC CRM are directly or indirectly specialisations of the E1 CRM Entity.[342]

Summarising the hierarchical structure of the segment of our interest in this ontology, starting from the top-level CRM Entity element we have:

E1 CRM Entity
  subclass: E77 Persistent Item
    subclass: E39 Actor
        subclasses: E21 Person

To identify any instance of the CRM Entity class, the E41 Appellation class is used, which provides a sequence of signs that are used or can be used to refer to and identify a specific instance of a certain class or category within a certain context. All things must have a name, and this class includes precisely those instances which, associated with any of the entities provided in this domain, serve to identify it. It is interesting to note the specifications regarding this class, which once again, in the context of ontological models as opposed to traditional cataloguing norms, underscores a shift in focus to the entity as opposed to the string that identifies that entity (boundaries not clearly defined in cataloguing codes). With regard to this class, it is specified that:

> E41 Appellation class instances do not identify things by their meaning, but on the basis of conventions, traditions or agreements. Instances of the E41 class are *cultural constructs;* as such, they are placed in relation to a context, history, and use in time and space by a group of users. A given instance of

> E41 Appellation can have *alternative forms*, that is, other instances of the same class that are considered equivalent regardless of what they denote.[343]

Although declared to be a cross-domain ontology (for the GLAM domain), the CIDOC CRM ontology is heavily influenced by the museum domain. This influence is also noted by looking at the properties that the E39 Actor class either has associated directly or inherits as a subclass of Persistent item and thus CRM Entity. Some examples are:

- E5 Event – P11 participated in (has participant): E39 Actor
- E7 Activity – P14 carried out by (performed): E39 Actor
- E24 Physical Man-Made Thing – P62 depicts (is depicted by): E1 CRM Entity
- E18 Physical Object – P51 has former or current owner (is former or current owner of): E39 Actor
- E18 Physical Object – P52 has current owner (is current owner of): E39 Actor
- E18 Physical Object – P50 has current keeper (is current keeper of): E39 Actor
- E36 Visual Item – P138 represents (has representation): E1 CRM Entity
- E32 Authority Document – P71 lists (is listed in): E1 CRM Entity.

The actor or agent is a creator of a physical object (thus acting as a producer) but is also, and above all, the subject of a network of relationships inherent in the broader GLAM world, as a rights holder, a party to events, an owner or custodian of objects or a performer of activities. The role of the agent is less centred on the realisation of a resource but is nevertheless well delineated in the ontology, with a central role in the universe shaped by this ontology.

The agent in Schema.org

Unlike the models examined above, Schema.org does not aim to define domains of knowledge of bibliographic or cultural topics. As stated on the same presentation page, 'Schema.org is a collaborative, community activity with a mission to create, maintain and promote schemas for structured data on the internet, on web pages, in email messages, and beyond.'[344]

The main focus of Schema.org is the internet, with the primary objective of making web data indexed by major search engines more structured and, therefore, usable and machine-readable. Although it is also used in contexts closer to the library field, which will be discussed later, it is important to start from this premise in order to understand the proposed ontological modelling, centred to a large extent on classes related to economics and business, the communicative forms typical of the internet, and the agents operating in this context.

The term 'agents' is actually used rather loosely here, as it has a significantly different meaning in Schema.org.

First, as will be better seen in subsequent descriptions, the classes assimilated to Agents, namely Person and Organisation, express categories of users to whom a service is addressed, rather than entities capable of affecting the others present. This approach is then further confirmed by the list of attributes and relationships provided, for the most part, aimed at providing descriptive information, contact details or highlighting work and/or family relationships, similar to the Friend of a Friend (FOAF) approach.

If we focus on these two classes, the term agent or even author is never actually mentioned; it is necessary to shift attention to all those properties for which Person or Organisation constitute the range, hence the 'destination' class of a certain property. Starting from the superclass Thing, the concept of agent appears in various properties, including Agent, Author and Creator. The different origins of Schema.org thus become explicit in this shift of focus for the Agent, understood as an expression of relationships between various entities in the model rather than as a standalone object or a central element with which to group increasingly 'concrete' entities.

Similar to the conception offered by Wikidata, Person and Organisation in Schema.org are identified by their foundational and identifying characteristics, as entities that hold certain importance in the multifaceted context of the internet, but that do not necessarily play active roles. Indeed, in some cases their importance is linked to a passive approach, as beneficiaries of certain services (for an example, see the definition of the only subclass of the entity Person). Hence, the consistent choice to delegate the action capacity of these classes to specific properties, both of a more general nature (Creator, Author, etc.) and aimed at indicating a more precise role (Actor, Artist, Athlete, etc.).

Additionally, it is interesting to note that even in the absence of an Agent class that groups any subclasses with similar characteristics, this does not result in redundancy of attributes and relationships, since all classes in the model are derived from the one Thing superclass.

Before moving on to a quick analysis of the Person and Organisation classes, it is worth concluding this discussion by emphasising that despite its distance from the bibliographic context, Schema.org has also been variously used in library sector projects, including some projects carried out by OCLC.[345]

Here follows a brief analysis of the two aforementioned classes:

***Person:* 'a person (alive, dead, undead, or fictional)'**[346] Several considerations can be made regarding the definition proposed by Schema.org for the class Person. The first is that such a definition certainly aims to be as comprehensive as possible, addressing a wide range of people who are currently alive or have existed in the past or are fictional. Consequently, the second consideration that emerges is that, in attempting to be broad, the Person class is actually ambiguous, as it does not clarify the most important point, what is meant by a person?

Schema.org does not explicitly state what a person is, thus leaving open to interpretation a concept that may seem obvious but actually isn't. This concept can take on different meanings depending on each user's cultural background. For example, in the Treccani encyclopaedia, the term 'person' is initially defined as 'an individual of the human species, without distinction of sex, age, social condition, etc., considered either as a standalone element or as part of a group or community.' But later, 'In philosophical language, the human individual as a being that exists, that understands and wills, that experiences and creates, desires and loves, rejoices and suffers, and through self-awareness and self-realisation constitutes a unique manifestation of what can be considered the essence of humanity, in its intellectual and creative entirety, and as a conscious subject of various specified activities'.[347]

It goes without saying that the second definition proposed by Treccani would certainly not be applicable to an imaginary person, which is instead included in the brief description by Schema.org. The ambiguity becomes even more evident when considering 'people' (or alleged people) that fall under imaginary cases. Would Sauron, the dark threat of Middle-earth, fall under the category of Person as defined here?

Subtypes

Patient ('A patient is any person recipient of health care services.')

Attributes

additionalName; address; award; birthDate; callSign; deathDate; duns; email; familyName; faxNumber; gender; givenName; globalLocationNumber; honorificPrefix; honorificSuffix; isicV4; jobTitle; knowsAbout; knowsLanguage; naics; taxID; telephone; vatID.

Main relationships[348]

With other Person entities:

children; colleague; follows; knows; parent; relatedTo; sibling; sponsor; spouse

With the Organisation entity:

affiliation; alumniOf; brand; funder; memberOf; sponsor; worksFor
With the CreativeWork entity:
publishingPrinciples
With the Place entity:
birthPlace; deathPlace; homeLocation; nationality; workLocation
With the Event entity:
performerIn

***Organisation*: 'an organisation such as a school, NGO, corporation, club, etc.'**[349] Similarly to the concept of Person, the concept of Organisation remains rather vague and poorly defined, limited to a brief list of organisation types intended to clarify what is meant by organisation. Here too, the potential for semantic ambiguity is very high, and probably even more so than for the concept of person; the meaning of the term Organisation is subject to significant variations. More defined, however, are the specific subclasses, which are dedicated to precise types of organisations.

Subtypes
Airline; Consortium; Corporation; EducationalOrganisation; FundingScheme; GovernmentOrganisation; LibrarySystem; LocalBusiness; MedicalOrganisation; NGO; NewsMediaOrganisation; OnlineBusiness; PerformingGroup; Project; ResearchOrganisation; SearchRescueOrganisation; SportsOrganisation; WorkersUnion
Attributes
address; award; dissolutionDate; duns; email; faxNumber; foundingDate; globalLocationNumber; isicV4; iso6523Code; keywords; knowsAbout; knowsLanguage; legalName; leiCode; naics; slogan; taxID; telephone; vatID
Main relationships
With other Organisation entities:
brand; department; funder; member; memberOf; parentOrganisation; sponsor; subOrganisation
With the Person person:
alumni; employee; founder; funder; member; sponsor
With the CreativeWork entity:
correctionsPolicy; actionableFeedbackPolicy; diversityPolicy; ethicsPolicy; ownershipFundingInfo; publishingPrinciples; unnamedSourcesPolicy
With the Place entity:
areaServed; foundingLocation; hasPOS; location
With the entity Event:
Event

The agent in Dublin Core

Despite its bibliographic origins, the Dublin Core did not originate as an attempt to model the description of any type of resource but was specifically aimed at digital objects. In fact, the birth of the Dublin Core can be traced back to the conference held in 1995 in the city of Dublin, Ohio, during which a broad community made up of both professionals in the field (librarians, archivists) and more cross-disciplinary figures, such as computer scientists and developers, expressed the need to ensure easier access to digital resources through a specially dedicated set of metadata.

From this conference emerged the differences between Dublin Core and the models seen previously, summarised as follows:

- *Metadata set*: The Dublin Core is not typically defined as an ontology, model or similar terms seen previously, but rather as a metadata set. This is because its primary purpose is not so much to define a context ontologically as to provide a description of objects, primarily of a digital nature. However, Dublin Core cannot be associated with the MARC format either, whose primary goal is related to the exchange and reuse of data across different systems. It could be said that in Dublin Core, the possibility of exchange occurs as a consequence of a very different intent, namely to achieve a common definition of certain types of digital resources through the use of a limited but satisfactory and agreed-upon number of elements.
- *Ample community*: the development and maintenance of the Dublin Core is entrusted to a rather large international community, which includes librarians, publishers, museum workers and representatives of some important organisations such as OCLC. This aspect allowed the set not to be set exclusively on bibliographic elements but, indeed, applicable and responsive to the needs of a variety of different contexts. As a negative consequence, the elements expressed by the Dublin Core are often ill-defined as well as numerically limited, which makes the Dublin Core scarcely applicable in situations that require greater detail and complexity.
- *Access v. identification*: As previously mentioned, Dublin Core was born from the impetus of various professional communities, united by a single goal – to make digital resources more accessible to their users. The aim is thus quite different from what we have seen in previous modelling efforts. It does not clearly identify entities but rather facilitates the use of a certain type of objects. This results in a set of elements that are less abstract, oriented towards the concrete description of specific aspects and services.

Originally there were only 15 elements in the Dublin Core, later appropriately extended into additional terms, properties and controlled vocabularies. Referring to the entire set in its extended form, there are both classes and specific elements dedicated to the Agent.

Agent Class:[350] 'A resource that acts or has the power to act.' In a more explicit manner than seen in BIBFRAME and IFLA LRM, in the Dublin Core's Agent class the nature of the Agent is entirely placed under its capacity for action. An Agent is precisely someone who acts or has the power to act, an expression crucial for including in this group even those who do not act directly but potentially have the capabilities to do so. Nothing else suggests a different aspect in identifying the Agent, as there are no specific subclasses or properties associated with it, further demonstrating Dublin Core's distance from anything deemed non-utilitarian. However, it is interesting to note the presence of an Agent Class (http://purl.org/dc/terms/AgentClass) that functions for expressing groupings of Agents.

Lastly, it's worth noting the choice of the term 'resource' instead of 'entity', which dominates the usage in other models.

Within the range of Agent, the following properties are found:

- *Contributor* Property:[351] 'An entity responsible for making contributions to the resource'
- *Creator* Property:[352] 'An entity responsible for making the resource'
- *Publisher* Property:[353] 'An entity responsible for making the resource available'
- *Rights Holder* Property:[354] 'A person or organisation owning or managing rights over the resource'.

The agent in RiC-O – Record in Context Ontology

The International Council on Archives (ICA) commissioned the Experts Group on Archival Description (EGAD) to develop a conceptual model, Records in Contexts (RiC-CM) and an ontology, Records in Contexts-Ontology (RiC-O)[355] based on the four existing ICA standards of the International Council on Archives: the General International Standard Archival Description (ISAD (G))[356], the International Standard Archival Authority Record for Corporate Bodies, Persons and Families (ISAAR),[357] the International Standard for Describing Functions (ISDF)[358] and the International Standard for Describing Institutions with Archival Holdings (ISDIAH[359]), in order to form a comprehensive model for archival description, harmonising and extending these four standards.

RiC-CM is the conceptual model that defines the main archival entities, their properties and the relationships between them. RiC-O is the OWL ontology that forms the second part of the RiC-CM standard, providing formal representation of that conceptual model. RiC-O offers a generic vocabulary and formal rules for creating RDF datasets (or generating them from existing archival metadata) that consistently describe any type of archival resource record.[360] The ontology is modelled in 106 classes, 62 datatype properties and 423 objects properties.

The choice of this ontology among the several available in the archival domain[361] is aimed at creating a bridge that will lead us to the second part of this chapter, dedicated to the analysis of some special cases of cataloguing treatments in the traditional domain, to demonstrate the value of entity modelling with respect to the cataloguing record approach. The opportunity to create this bridge is provided not so much by the definition of the Agent class[362] in this ontology ('A Person, or Group, or an entity created by a Person or Group (Mechanism), or a Position that acts in the world') as by the scope note that best defines this entity:

> An Agent may have one or more identities; an identity is a constellation of properties or relations that together 'identify' the Agent. A Person or Group commonly has one identity, though each also may have one or more alternative identities. Such alternative identities may be shared by more than one Person or Group. Alternative identities include but are not limited to pseudonyms, heteronyms, DBA (Doing Business As), and trade identities. An alternative identity should not be confused with a Position in a Group, for example, presidents, prime ministers, governors, popes, royalty, or bishops. Nor should an alternative identity be confused with a variant name or identifier of the same identity. Agent also includes entities created by a Person or Group that act on behalf of the creating Agent in an autonomous or semi-autonomous manner. Examples of a Mechanism include software agents, robots, and space and underwater probes that generate data (records) in the course of Activity assigned to and in conformance with the instructions given to them by the creating Person or Group.[363]

We must stop and review this note carefully because it introduces some new elements that recall the concepts of entity and identity that we have already dealt with in the earlier chapters of this book. First of all, an agent can have more than one identity, and each identity consists of a constellation of properties or relations that together express that entity or one of that entity's ways of being. This definition immediately makes us think of the prism, that representation of complex entity we have already discussed, and the set of faces that make this figure articulate. A person, a group, can have one identity or alternative identities, which could be a pseudonym, a heteronym, a professional profile. The note then continues by specifying an element. An identity should not be confused with a position in a group, and thus with a role that a person may assume with respect to a group or community, such as a president, a prime minister, a governor, a pope a royal or a bishop. This discussion brings us back to what was said in Chapter 3 regarding emerging properties and functions, such as that of pope, which is something more than just a role assumed within a group. The rest of this chapter will take up exactly the case of the pope in the cataloguing tradition to try to show how complicated it is, with respect to the statement made in this scope note, to agree without seeing another way of understanding certain roles. But let's stay on the note a bit longer, to isolate some other interesting elements, very consistent with the analysis done so far.

The phrase 'Nor should an alternative identity be confused with a variant name or identifier of the same identity' clearly defines a confusion of levels that is apparent not so much in cataloguing codes, but in the application of cataloguing codes overlapping with the adoption of a first approach to entity modelling. A variant of a name is not a different identity of an entity, but only a different formulation of the name, a different way of expressing the same identity of an entity. A name or title formulated in a script other than Latin is not a different identity of that entity, but only a different formulation of the same entity. MARC formats glimpse this boundary between two different concepts, structuring redirects or references into two different tag blocks of the authority record:

- Block 4xx: referring to a different formulation of the same identity (thus structuring the variant forms of a name)
- Block 5xx: referring instead to a different identity of the same entity
- Tag 663: to explain the type of relationship between the name tracked in tag 1xx and the access points tracked in block 5xx, which are usually themselves recorded in different authority files. In subfield $a, a phrase is recorded that specifically explains this relationship, often one of pseudonymity.

This substantial difference is not formulated as clearly as in this scope note. The time to define this double meaning, each profoundly different from the other, had not yet come. Obviously, even though entity modelling has finally clarified this element theoretically (more clearly in some ontologies than in others, but always glimpsing the boundary), the application in the daily practice of these concepts is more complex, as we will see later in this chapter.

The RiC-O Agent class has as subclasses:

1 *rico:Group*:[364] 'Two or more Agents that act together as an Agent'. A Group is a type of agent. A Group has a socially recognised identity. Each member of the Group plays a particular role or roles, thus holding a specific position in the co-ordinated activity of the Group. Entities and families are types of Groups, but of course they are not the only possible types: the electorate (all voters in a given election round) is an example of a different type of Group. Subclasses of the Group class are *rico:CorporateBody; rico:Family*
2 *rico:Mechanism*:[365] 'A process or system created by a Person or Group that performs an Activity'. Again the scope note clarifies what is meant by this type of Agent: Mechanism is a kind of agent; it can have both mechanical and software components, or it can be exclusively software. A Mechanism acts in the world by producing physical or social effects, and frequently generates or modifies records.
3 *rico:Person*:[366] 'An individual human being'. Already in the definition there is an interesting element, with the introduction of the term *person* being synonymous with the terms *character, personality* or *identity*. A human being (person) is presented with a social identity or personality. Drawn here, though not explicitly stated, is that boundary between entity and identity that is instead totally absent in traditional cataloguing codes. The scope note of this class is indeed significant and leads us back to certain concepts, such as that of synchronous identity, which we have also extensively discussed.

The entity *person* is explained in this way: a person is a type of agent. Most commonly, a human being (biological person) has a unique contemporaneous social identity or personality. In everyday discourse, this identity is what we call a *real person*. Less common but not uncommon, different personalities in addition to the coeval (or original) personality, may be associated with the human being over the course of a lifetime. Such alternative personalities are often created by the original person for specific purposes. In some circumstances, an alternative person might eclipse or replace the original person, just as Mark Twain eclipses Samuel Clemens and John Wayne eclipses Marion Mitchell Morrison.[367] The social (shared) alternative identity becomes the predominant identity. Less common is the case where two or more people collaborate to create a shared personality. The shared personalities of two or more people constitute a type of Group. Within the archival context, for example, the original person will generally be at the centre of the description, with alternative persons noted.

Exceptionally, an alternative persona may replace coeval personalities.

4 *rico:Position*:[368] 'The functional role of a Person within a Group'. Our analysis is not focused on this subclass of Agent, as it is not relevant to our discussion. Certainly, the decision to model this entity as a subclass of Agent causes some perplexity, whereas in many ontologies it becomes an independent class, connected to Agent but still autonomous or a property of Agent. In any case, ontology modelling choices take into account various factors, and it is not pertinent in this context to investigate the specific choice made for this particular class.

The RiC-O ontology now has clearly defined the boundaries between an agent and a name. The *rico:AgentName* class[369] defined as a label, title or term that designates an Agent in order to make it distinguishable from other similar entities, used with the *rico:isOrWasAgentNameOf* property, definitively clarifies the principle that everything has a name, but that the thing *is not the name itself*, although it helps to express its identity. Another useful element to underscore the maturity expressed by this ontology in terms of entity modelling, is the reference to the *rico:Record* class,[370] where the sharp distinction between the 'record' object and the 'agent' object (for example) described within that record, or simply referenced, becomes evident.

The ability of entity modelling to identify things in the world

In the second part of this study, I will address a particular and complex case of cataloguing, such as that of the pope, which, as seen in Chapter 3, represents an entity articulated in terms of ontological and identity profiling. By analysing some of the traditional approaches to handling the agent (or the name or the author, as we will see later), and referring to concrete cases of managing this type of entity, we will see how the information transmitted in this manner can even be misleading. This case will demonstrate how entity modelling, by placing the real-world object and not the mode in which it is represented in a particular context at the centre of its inquiry, can revolutionise the way information is constructed and shared.

The treatment of popes in cataloguing tradition

As anticipated in Chapter 3, we will use the complex case of agent-type 'pope' to examine how some cataloguing rules handled this type of access, and then to formulate some treatment hypotheses in entity modelling. The reference is to the specific paragraphs of each rule, in which cataloguers are given instructions for choosing the heading or access point and structuring the access.

Cataloguing rules usually devote some sections to the treatment of access points to works written by popes or other entities who, in the course of their lives, change their names while also assuming a representative function of a community. These two elements, the change of name together with the assumption of a representative role or function of a community, with the related powers, determine that element of deepening and reflection around the form to be given to this type of entity in the entity modelling processes. Name change in certain historical traditions, and particularly in the context of the Holy Scriptures, has a very deep meaning: 'In the Bible to change one's name means to take possession of someone, to give a new direction to life. . . . At the moment of reception into a religious community and assumption of the throne, the change of name recalls the profound change of being.'[371] Examples of name changes from the Holy Scriptures are numerous and always refer to significant changes occurring in the individual; one example among all: 'no longer will you be called Abram but you shall be called Abraham, for father of a multitude of peoples I will make you'.[372]

A reflection should be made, then, on the name change within the Catholic tradition, which, based on usage derived from the Holy Scriptures, suggests a profound change in the entity, at least in some situations. Can we identify this change as symptomatic of a change in identity, or should we classify the assignment (or self-assignment) of a new name as not at all challenging and significant in terms of identity shift?

The attribution of a role or function in relation to a context can carry significant weight in profiling an identity. We have already emphasised this in reflections on the Real-World Objects and in the approach of Object-Oriented Programming, which models the entity always from a certain perspective, one of the many possible profiles that an entity can have. But the element of role or function is not automatically indicative of significant change and thus relevant property. The relationship of function or role that exists, for example, between an agent and work (translator of, illustrator of, editor of, co-author of, etc.) does not affect the entity to the point of qualifying a new identity, but it does better specify the type of responsibility with respect to an object. In the case of the popes, which we are analysing as an expression of a certain type of complex entity, that *emergent property* that is identifiable precisely in the assumption of a role (in this case, before a community) we have seen to be particularly profound, so much so that even on its own, apart from the element of name change, it could be defined as an *identity break*.

But let us see how much this was perceived or even intuited in the cataloguing tradition.

Cataloguing norms for the treatment of popes

Norme per il catalogo degli stampati della Biblioteca Apostolica Vaticana (NV) (Standards for cataloguing printed books of the Vatican Library)

These 'originated from the decision, made in the second half of 1927, to create a new general catalogue of the printed books of the Vatican Library', and 'arose from the collaboration of librarians from different nations, aiming at a cosmopolitan public' (Biblioteca Apostolica Vaticana, 1949, v–vi).

The *Norme* devote paragraph 61 to the choice of name for popes.

> *Popes*:
> Popes are filed under the assumed name in the Latin form, followed by the abbreviation PP., the ordinal number in Roman numerals, and the dates of birth and death. Reference is made to the family surname and, if appropriate, the given name.
>
> Benedictus PP. XIV, 1675–1758
> Clemens PP. XIV, 1705–1774
> Innocentius PP. III, 1161–1216
> Leo PP. XIII, 1819–1903
> Pius PP. XI, 1857–1939

In Section IV on Corporate Bodies as Authors, paragraph *169. Catholic Church* states:

> The various publications issued by the Church and ecclesiastical bodies are filed according to different rules. *Acts of pontiffs*, bulls, briefs, constitutions, etc., are filed under the heading 'Popes', followed by the date of pontificate, and, in parentheses, the pope's name in Latin.

And again, paragraph *170. Popes* (again referring to the treatment of Corporate Bodies as authors) states:

> a) Individual writings and 'collected works' of popes are filed under the pontiff's name in Latin.
> *Clemens PP. XIV*, 1705–1774.
> b) Official and governmental acts published under the name of a pope, and collections comprising the acts of a pontificate, are filed under the designation 'Popes', followed by the date of the pontificate and the pope's Latin name between round parentheses; secondary files are made under the pontiff's name.
> *Popes.* 1621–1623 *(Gregorius XV).*

c) A general collection of bulls, briefs, etc. due to more than three pontiffs is tabulated under Papi. *Atti.*
   Papi. Atti

d) A collection comprising the acts of various pontiffs belonging to a defined historical period is tabulated under 'Popes' but with added chronological determination, according to this pattern.
   Papi. *Sino al 1305*
   Popes. *Sino al 590*

e) In the case of a single bull or encyclical, the introductory words with which the bull is cited are added to the heading.
   Papi. 1922–1939 *(Pius XI). Studiorum ducem.*

RICA – Regole italiane di catalogazione per autori (Italian Rules for Cataloguing Authors)

The Regole italiane di catalogazione per autori (RICA) were published in 1976 by the Istituto centrale per il catalogo unico delle biblioteche italiane e per le informazioni bibliografiche (ICCU) and constitute a code of rules for the compilation of the alphabetical catalogue by authors.

Paragraph *40. Writings of religious community leaders,* dedicated to the choice of header, states:

1. The writings, including official ones, of the heads of religious communities are headed under their names, if the head of the collectivity is presented as the author of the writing and not simply as the signatory of an administrative act. Such works are encyclicals, bulls, pastoral letters and similar documents.
   Humani generis. Lettera enciclica di sua santità Pio XII sulle false opinioni che minacciano l'integrità della dottrina cattolica. 1964.
   i.p. Pius XII, *papa*
   Vantaggi e pericoli della televisione. Lettera di s.s. Pio XII all'episcopato cattolico italiano. 1961.
   i.p. Pius XII, *papa*

Paragraph *62. Religious Dignitaries* is devoted to the form of heading for this type of agent and says:

Individuals who, upon assuming a religious office, change their name are always catalogued under the name adopted for that office. The names of popes (or antipopes) are given in Latin.

Gregorius I, *papa*
x Gregorius Magnus, *santo*

Pius XI, *papa*

x Ratti, Achille (Commissione permanente per la revisione delle regole italiane di catalogazione and ICCU, 1995, 92–3).

A header under the pope's official name, with deferral from the birth or registry form (here one could say baptismal name, but once again I avoid using this terminology to detach the analysis as much as possible from specific definitions applicable only to certain contexts).

REICAT – Regole italiane di catalogazione (Italian Cataloguing Rules)

In REICAT – Regole italiane di catalogazione (Italian Cataloguing Rules), Section 15, *Uniform Person Headings*, Section 15.1.2.2 *Sovereigns, Popes and Heads of Religious Groups* in Item E, with references to popes and heads of religious groups, it says:

> For popes and leaders of other religious groups, the name assumed with the office is adopted as the heading, accompanied by the relative ordinal number and the appropriate title, which is given in Italian if possible. The names of popes and antipopes are recorded in the Latin form. From the names used before taking office and any Italian forms are referred to.
>
> *Gregorius I*, papa
> { Gregorio I, papa
> { Gregorius Magnus, santo
> { Gregorio Magno, santo
>
> *Pius II*, papa
> { Piccolomini, Enea Silvio
> { Pio II, papa
>
> *Ioannes XXIII*, antipapa
> { Cossa, Baldassarre
> { John XXIII, antipapal
>
> *Ioannes Paulus II*, papa
> { Wojtyła, Karol
> { Giovanni Paolo II, santo
>
> (Commissione permanente per la revisione delle regole italiane di catalogazione and ICCU, 2009, 416)

Chapter 17, *Responsibility for the Work*, Section 17.4.1.3 *Popes and other persons holding religious offices* is devoted to precisely this type of agent:

17.4.1.3 A. Writings, speeches, and other works by popes or other persons holding offices or roles in religious bodies have the person's name as their main heading, even if they have official value, as they are generally known and cited in this way. This includes encyclicals and papal bulls, bishops' pastoral letters and instructions, rules dictated by a person for a religious order, works by founders of religious groups or sects customarily published under the author's name, even if they are considered sacred texts by the group itself.[373]

Il lavoro umano : testo dell'encliclica [i.e. enciclica] / Giovanni Paolo II
t.u. Laborem exercens
i.p. Ioannes Paulus II, pope
Bolla di scomunica di papa Pio VII gloriosamente regnante contro Buonaparte ed i suoi ministri
(papal brief generally known by the initial words Quum memoranda*)*
t.u. Quum memoranda
i.p. Pius VII, pope
Lettera a Maometto II = Epistola ad Mahumetem / Pio II (Enea Silvio Piccolomini)
t.u. Epistola ad Mahumetem
i.p. Pius II, pope

AACR2 – Anglo-American Cataloguing Rules (2nd edition)

In AACR2, the reference to the access points created for the pope in his official role and to the pope in his personal profile is recorded repeatedly, in several paragraphs of the code. Here are some excerpts which have significant relevance to our discussion:

21.4D1. Official communications. Enter a work that falls into one of the following categories under the corporate heading for the official (see 24.20 and 24.27B):
(a) an official communication of a head of state, head of government, or head of an international body (e.g. a message to a legislature, a proclamation, an executive order other than one covered by 21.31)
(b) an official communication of a pope, patriarch, bishop, etc. (e.g. an order, decree, pastoral letter, bull, encyclical, constitution, or an official message to a council, synod, etc.).

21.4D2. Other works. Enter all other works of such a person under the personal heading. Make an explanatory reference from the corporate heading to the personal heading (see 26.3C1).

Science and the existence of God ; and, Science and philosophy : two addresses / Pope Pius XII
Main entry under the personal heading for Pius XII.

21.4D3. Collections of official communications and other works. Enter a collection of official communications and other works by one person under the personal heading. Make an added entry under the corporate heading.

Discorsi, messaggi, colloqui del Santo Padre Giovanni XXIII : 28 ottobre 1958-3 giugno 1963 *Main entry under personal heading for John XXIII.*

Added entry under the corporate heading for John XXIII as Pope.

24.27B2. Popes. Enter a pope acting in an official capacity (see 21.4D1) under *Catholic Church* followed by *Pope.* Add the year or inclusive years of the reign, and the pontifical name in its catalogue entry form.

Catholic Church. *Pope* (1878–1903 : Leo XIII)

Catholic Church. *Pope* (1978 : John Paul I)

If the heading applies to more than one pope (see 21.4D1), do not add the dates and names.

Catholic Church. *Pope*

If a heading is established for a pope as a person in addition to the heading as a religious official, make an explanatory reference under the heading for the official (see 26.3C1).

25.24A. Use as the uniform title for an individual work entered under the official heading for a pope (see 21.4D1) the short title (generally the first word or words of the text) by which it is generally known and cited in the original language (usually Latin).

Catholic Church. *Pope* (1963–1978 : Paul VI)

[Populorum progressio]

List of local variations to AACR2/RDA cataloguing rules allowed in URBE Network catalogues

The list of local variations in use in URBE (Unione Romana Biblioteche Ecclesiastiche) to define specific uses that deviate from the AACR2/RDA cataloguing rules, otherwise followed for the selection and construction of access points to cataloguing descriptions, also refers to the Norme per il catalogo degli stampati della Biblioteca Apostolica Vaticana (NV) where the local variant coincides.[374]

The list deals with access points to popes and antipopes in local variant 2:

VL2. Papi ed antipapi (NV § 61–62, 170 deviating from AACR2 21.4D1, 22.1, 22.16B, 24.27B/2)

Popes are indexed under the name assumed in the Latin form, followed by the abbreviation 'PP.', the ordinal number in Roman numerals and the dates of birth and death. A cross-reference is made from the family surname and, where appropriate, the given name, e.g. 'Leo PP. XIII, 1819–1903'.

Antipopes are similarly indexed under the name they adopted as pontiffs, but without the abbreviation PP., and with the ordinal number in Roman numerals, followed by the appellation 'antipope' and the date of birth and death. A cross-reference is made from the surname and if necessary from the first name:

Benedictus XIII, antitpapa, m. 1424
Cross-reference from: Pietro di Luna
and from: Petrus de Luna
and also: Luna, Pedro de

For official and governing acts of only one pope (e.g. encyclicals, briefs, constitutions, etc.), the heading is formulated according to the following scheme:

Papi (pontificate year beginning-ending : formulation of Pope's name in Latin).
Papi (1958–1963 : Iohannes PP. XXIII)
For official and governing acts of more than three popes: Papi. Atti.

RDA – Resource Description and Access

The change in perspective in RDA from previous cataloguing rules is evident, and the goal of structuring metadata in a way that makes it compatible with web technologies is equally explicit. The reference to entities (those of FRBR and FRAD first and of IFLA LRM later) already positions this guide in the direction of entity modelling, so much so that the organisation of the toolkit refers to entities identified as those needed to model the bibliographic universe, with the indication of properties and relationships useful for identification and description. And in the Official RDA Toolkit, in the section 'Objectives and principles governing RDA', reference is made to the goal of *differentiation*, emphasising the need for metadata to distinguish not only one entity from another entity, but also different identities attributable to the same entity: 'The metadata describing an entity should differentiate that entity from other entities, and from other identities used by the same entity if differentiation is needed in the context of a specific agent who creates the metadata.'[375] Regarding the *pope* entity under discussion, the instructions inherit those given in the previous AACR2, with clear reference to the pontifical name acquired by election to the papal throne (personal access point) and the pope's role as the official representative of the Catholic Church (entity access point).

Instruction *11.2.2.26.2 Popes* of Original RDA Toolkit says:

> Record the title of a pope who is acting in an official capacity (see 6.31.1) as a subdivision of the Catholic Church. Record the title in the form of a subdivision of the authorized access point representing the Catholic Church. Record the title in a language preferred by the agency creating the data
> Catholic Church. Pope
> If the official being identified is a specific incumbent of the office, add, in parentheses (in this order):
>
> a) the inclusive years of the reign
> b) the pontifical name of the incumbent (see 9.2.2.18).
>
> Separate the years of the reign from the pontifical name using a space, colon, space.
> Example:
>
> Catholic Church. Pope (1878–1903 : Leo XIII)
> Catholic Church. Pope (1978–2005 : John Paul II)
> Catholic Church. Pope (2013– : Francis)
> Record the relationships between the office and the person by applying the instructions in chapters 30 (related persons) and 32 (related corporate bodies).

It is not straightforward, however, to pinpoint the section of the guide where indications regarding the treatment of popes as authors of works not connected to the institution of the Catholic Church[376] can be found. RDA perhaps prompts a reflection that goes beyond just the selection and structuring of an access point and moves towards entity modelling. Referring to the Original RDA Toolkit (where instructions are easier to identify), Section 9, dedicated to the identification of persons, refers to three different situations related to name changes, albeit without any direct reference to the case we are analysing:

> – *9.2.2.6 Different names for the same person*: if a person is known by more than one name, the name most commonly used to refer to the person is chosen.
> – *9.2.2.7 Name change:* if a person has changed his or her name, the most recent name or form of the name is chosen as preferred. The same instructions apply to a person who has acquired a title of nobility and is known by that title. An exception is made when there is reason to believe that a previous name will persist as the name by which the person is best known; in this case this is chosen as the preferred name.

- *9.2.2.8 Individuals with multiple identities*: if an individual has multiple identities, the name associated with each identity is chosen as the preferred name for that identity. If an individual uses one or more pseudonyms (including joint pseudonyms), they are considered to have multiple identities. If an individual uses their real name as well as multiple pseudonyms, they are considered an individual with multiple identities. An exception is when an individual uses only a pseudonym and does not use his or her real name as a creator or contributor: in this case, the pseudonym is chosen as the preferred name. In the case of an individual with multiple identities, the relationship between the distinct identities is recorded.

Paragraph 9.2.2.8, therefore, introduces the possibility of identifying an entity through its different identities, to which different works can be attributed depending on the context. The case of birth identity (the baptismal name of an individual who later becomes pope) and the pope (name change upon election to the pontificate) is not specifically mentioned as an example. Indeed, even libraries that have officially adopted RDA choose to create access points for the pope's unofficial works, both before and after election, using the pontifical name rather than the baptismal name; but we will discuss this shortly.

Comparison of cataloguing standards

For a more general reference framework, let's try to outline in Table 4.1 opposite the choices made by each cataloguing standard mentioned above, based on two parameters: the identity profile defined by the role or function assumed by the entity in relation to the work, and the type of work associated with the entity. To simplify the table, we will use abbreviations to identify the different cataloguing rules:

- NV: Vatican Standards
- RI: RICA
- RE: REICAT
- UR: URBE – Local Variants
- AA: AACR2
- RDA: Original RDA

Table 4.1 *Summary of the choices made by some of the cataloguing rules analysed*

	Birth Identity (given/baptism name) (GN)	**Acquired Individual Identity (papal name) (PN)**	**Collective Identity (Catholic Church or Popes) (CN)**
Official Acts of the Catholic Church		RI – RE	NV – AA – UR – RDA
Non-official Writings (as pope)		NV – RI – RE – AA – UR – RDA	
Individual writings	RDA[377]	NV – RI – RE – AA – UR – RDA	

The analysis conducted on these cataloguing regulations with respect to the treatment of the name change that is needed by an individual with the election as pope has highlighted some elements to keep in mind, including:

- focus on the choice of heading or access point and its formal structuring
- the identification of a *function* or *role* that the name change entails and signifies
- the definition of a preferred form of the name in relation to variant forms, linked by a referral mechanism that would seem to resolve any doubt about attribution.

Looking at cataloguing standards, it is perhaps more evident in the Anglo-American tradition, which also includes the Vatican tradition, the tendency to assign an identity to the role of the pope as the official spokesperson of the institution he represents, in this case, the Catholic Church. The same entity is expressed and exists also with the identity given by the election and the corresponding name change (from the personal name to the papal name). In all the codes, with a possible exception of Original RDA, although not explicitly stated, the personal profile seems to disappear completely, dissolved into the acquired identity. This dissolution of the birth identity occurs even for works that are entirely unrelated to the institution the pope represents and that were produced even before the election to the papacy. We have, therefore, at the same time a loss of identity (the personal name) but also the intuition of a different entity (the official one) that connects us to those entities that Weberman identifies as emergent. The role of pope is assigned by a community through a voluntary act and creates a profile that associates the individual with a power (the power to make decisions that otherwise, outside that role, the same person could not make), that primatial power that is not assigned by episcopal consecration 'but directly by Christ through the acceptance of the legitimate election' (Ghirlanda, 2013).

This interpretation certainly reminds us of that economic power, that purchasing ability that a simple piece of paper (say, a €10 banknote) is assigned by a community through the European Central Bank, to become something different from the piece of paper itself. Having purchasing power is that *emergent property* we mentioned and is remarkably analogous to assuming *a role and decision-making power* that the election as pope confers on a person. Thus, a pope expresses a complex entity that can be profiled with at least three identities, of which one, if not two, qualify as emergent.

1 *Karol Józef Wojtyła* (birth identity)
2 *John Paul II* (individual identity acquired with the papal name)
3 *Catholic Church. Pope (1978–2005 : John Paul II)* (collective or corporate body identity).

In the case of Karol Józef Wojtyła, a fourth identity would be added, that of the pseudonym Andrzej Jawień,[378] under which we have also selected a work. However, we do not include it here as a fourth possible identity due to the limited data found, which is insufficient to define its profile. Nonetheless, we will provide some indications and take this pseudonym into account when reviewing cataloguing practices.

The change that happened to Karol Józef Wojtyła on 16 October 1978 and led him to assume the role, the robes, and the name of Pope John Paul II, however *relational* and *non-substantial*, cannot but be identified as a change *profound* enough to generate another identity (defining, therefore, that *identity break* we are talking about).[379] We can certainly agree here that nothing physical has changed in the intrinsic properties of the individual Karol Wojtyła. Yet we simultaneously recognise that his election to the papal throne – and thus the acquisition of a relational and therefore extrinsic property (between himself and the community of the Catholic Church) – has generated a profound change in the entity, defining an identity, that of pope. Certain cataloguing traditions further split this identity (pope on the one hand and referent and representative of the entire Catholic Church on the other).

> We can say that the dollar bill changes, when the piece of paper does not, because the dollar bill and the piece of paper do not stand in a relation of strict identity. The dollar bill is materially embodied in but not strictly identical with the piece of paper just as an artwork is materially embodied in but not strictly identical with the stone from which it is carved.
>
> (Weberman, 1999, 146)

How the theoretical norm has been implemented in cataloguing practice is another matter, and the confusion in the choice and structuring of access points for a work related to a complex entity, such as the one we are discussing, first and foremost reveals an immaturity, albeit legitimate, regarding a real *identification of* the entity, in favour of the practice of 'choosing the preferred or authorised form of the name'. Let's look at some cases of application of the aforementioned cataloguing rules to verify, first of all, what the potential starting point of entity modelling processes could be.

Cataloguing and the risk of historical falsehoods

To analyse the different ways in which an entity of the *pope*-type is treated, we will use examples related to two different popes: Karol Józef Wojtyła (John Paul II) and Joseph Ratzinger (Benedict XVI). Both individuals experienced changes in status that we can understand as significant in terms of identity. Let's see which ones, and review the cataloguing choices of some institutions.

Karol Józef Wojtyła, 1920–2005

- 6 October 1978: under the name John Paul II he is elected 264th Pope of the Catholic Church, Bishop of Rome and sixth sovereign of the Vatican City State.
- From 6 October to 2 April 2005, the day of his death, he exercised his mandate as pope.
- 27 April 2014: canonised as a *saint* by Pope Francis, after being beatified on 1May 2011.

Joseph Aloisius Ratzinger, 1927–2022

- 19 April 2005: under the name Benedict XVI is elected 265th Pope of the Catholic Church, Bishop of Rome and seventh sovereign of the Vatican City State.
- On 11 February 2013, Benedict XVI announced his resignation from the Petrine ministry. As of 8 p.m. 28 February 2013, he ceased his pontificate, assuming the official title Supreme Pontiff Emeritus or Pope Emeritus

For Karol Wojtyła/John Paul II let's consider four different works that could potentially be related to the three profiles defined earlier:

1. *Persona e atto* (original title *Osoba i czyn*)
2. *La bottega dell'orefice* (original title *Przed sklepem jubilera*)
3. *Varcare la soglia della speranza*
4. *Redemptor Hominis.*

For Joseph Ratzinger we will analyse:

5 *Le omelie di Pentling*
6 *Gesù di Nazareth* (original title *Jesus von Nazareth. Von der Taufe im Jordan bis zur Verklärung*)
7 *Deus Caritas Est* (in English 'God is Love').

The treatment of these works has been analysed in several catalogues:

A Italian National Library System catalogue (Sistema Bibliotecario Nazionale) (SBN)[380]
B The Library of Congress catalogue, in the linked data version (LOC);[381]
C Catalogue of the Deutsche Nationalbibliothek (DNB); [382]
D The general catalogue of the Bibliothèque nationale de France (BnF);[383]
E Catalogue of the Library of the Pontifical Gregorian University (GRE);[384]
F The general catalogue of the Vatican Apostolic Library (VatLib).[385]

The examples used for this analysis do not focus on specific details (records for works or publications, original language version or translation) because the objective of this outline is not to analyse the cataloguing performed in different institutions, but rather to choose the access point for the work. The selected works exemplify:

- a work written before the person was elected pope
- a work written after his election as pontiff, but not considered an official work
- a work written in the name and on behalf of the institution Catholic Church.

For Karol Wojtyła one of the works written before his election as pope – but under the pseudonym Andrzej Jawień, which was used for the writing of some plays – was also selected. The names are reported in the Italian or Latin formulation found in the catalogues, in compliance with the instructions defined in each standard. To summarise and simplify the choices made by each cited institution, Tables 4.2 to 4.8 present the data identified in the different catalogues for each significant title.

The Heading/Access column uses an abbreviation to indicate the type of access preferred by each institution for each work, as follows:

- personal access by given/baptism name: GN (given name)
- access by papal name: PN (papal name)

- entity access: CN (corporate body name).

The analysis will continue (with a summary shown in Tables 4.2–4.9) by relating this data to those *significant moments* identified earlier for the two entities, to verify if the choices made by individual institutions are consistent and in line with the profiles defined through the identification of an ontological or identity break:

1 *Persona e atto* (original title *Osoba i czyn*), published in 1969 by Karol Wojtyła, then professor of ethics at the Catholic University of Lublin.

Table 4.2 *The cataloguing of the work* Persona e atto *in the different catalogues analysed*

	Source	Work	Access by Agent	URI/URL	Header/Access
A	SBN	Persona e atto / Karol Wojtyła ; testo definitivo stabilito in collaborazione con l'autore da Anna-Teresa Tymieniecka	Ioannes Paulus II {papa}	http://id.sbn.it/bid/SBL0602906	PN
B	LOC	Osoba i czyn, oraz inne studia antropologiczne/Karol Wojtyła ; redakcja Tadeusz Styczeń [et al].	John Paul II, Pope, 1920–2005	https://lccn.loc.gov/95141091	PN
C	DNB	Osoba i czyn	Johannes Paul II., Papst.	https://d-nb.info/gnd/4694506-4	PN
D	BnF	Personne et acte [Texte imprimé] / Karol Wojtyła ; traduction française, Gwendolyne Jarczyk ; avertissement, introduction et notes sur la traduction, Aude Suramy	Jean-Paul II (1920–2005; pape)	https://catalogue.bnf.fr/ark:/12148/cb42412034f	PN
E	GRE	Persona e atto : testo definitivo stabilito in collaborazione con l'autore / Joannes Paulus PP. II. ; Anna-Teresa Tymieniecka. Introduzione all'edizione italiana di Armando Rigobello	Iohannes Paulus PP. II, santo 1920–2005	https://oseegenius.unigre.it/pug/resource?uri=77855BIB&v=l	PN
F	Vatlib			Not present	

2 *La bottega dell'orefice,* original title *Przed sklepem jubilera,* a play written in 1960 by Andrzej Jawień, pseudonym of the then Bishop of Krakow (and therefore not yet Pope) Karol Wojtyła.

Table 4.3 *The cataloguing of the work* La bottega dell'orefice *in the different catalogues analysed*

	Source	Opera	Access by Agent	URI/URL	Header/Access
A	SBN	La bottega dell'orefice / Karol Wojtyła	Ioannes Paulus II {pope}	http://id.sbn.it/bid/RMS1811454	PN
B	LOC	The jeweller's shop : a meditation on the sacrament of matrimony passing on occasion into a drama / Karol Wojtyła ; translated from the Polish by Boleslaw Taborski.	John Paul II, Pope, 1920–2005	https://lccn.loc.gov/79005543	PN
C	DNB	Der Laden des Goldschmieds : Meditationen über d. Sakrament d. Ehe, d. sich vorübergehend zum Drama wandeln / Andrzej Jawień	Johannes Paul II., Papst.	https://d-nb.info/810297744	PN
D	BnF	La Boutique de l'orfèvre [Texte imprimé] : méditations sur le sacrement du mariage se transformant, de temps à autre, en drame / Andrzej Jawień (Karol Wojtyła) ; texte français de Koukou Chanska	Jean-Paul II (1920–2005; pape)	https://catalogue.bnf.fr/ark:/12148/cb346526991	PN
E	GRE	La bottega dell'orafo : meditazioni sul sacramento del matrimonio che assumono a volte la forma d'un dramma / Joannes Paulus PP. II ; traduzione di Renzo Panzone	Iohannes Paulus PP. II, santo1920–2005	https://oseegenius.unigre.it/pug/resource?uri=77736BIB&v=l	PN

Continued

Table 4.3 *Continued*

	Source	Opera	Access by Agent	URI/URL	Header/Access
F	Vatlib	La bottega dell'orefice (Meditazioni sul sacramento del matrimonio che di tanto in tanto si trasformano in dramma) ...	Iohannes Paulus PP. II, s., 1920–2005	https://opac.vatlib.it/stp/detail/10428503	PN

3 *Varcare la soglia della speranza,* an essay written by Pope John Paul II and Italian writer and journalist Vittorio Messori, published in 1994.

Table 4.4 *The cataloguing of the work* Varcare la soglia della speranza *in the different catalogues analysed*

	Source	Opera	Access by Agent	URI/URL	Header/Access
A	SBN	Varcare la soglia della speranza / Giovanni Paolo 2. ; con Vittorio Messori	Ioannes Paulus II {pope}	http://id.sbn.it/bid/VIA0174989	PN
B	LOC	Da prekrachish praga na nadezhdata / Ĭoan Pavel II otgovaria na vŭprosi na Vitorio Mesori.	John Paul II, Pope, 1920–2005	https://lccn.loc.gov/2019432008	PN
C	DNB	Die Schwelle der Hoffnung überschreiten / Johannes Paul II. Aus dem Ital. von Irene Este	Johannes Paul II., Papst.	https://d-nb.info/947577661	PN
D	BnF	Entrez dans l'espérance [Texte imprimé] / Jean-Paul II ; avec la collab. de Vittorio Messori	Jean-Paul II (1920–2005; pape)	https://catalogue.bnf.fr/ark:/12148/cb35830131m	PN
E	GRE	Varcare la soglia della speranza / Giovanni Paolo II con Vittorio Messori	Iohannes Paulus PP. II, santo 1920–2005	https://oseegenius.unigre.it/pug/resource?uri=402526BIB&v=l	PN
F	Vatlib	Cruzando el umbral de la esperanza / Juan Pablo II ; editado por Vittorio Messori ; traducción de Pedro Antonio Urbina	Iohannes Paulus PP. II, s., 1920–2005	https://opac.vatlib.it/stp/detail/10741349	PN

4 *Redemtor hominis*, the first encyclical written by Pope John Paul II, published 4 March 1979.

Table 4.5 *The cataloguing of the work* Redemptor Hominis *in the different catalogues analysed*

	Source	Opera	Access by Agent	URI/URL	Header/Access
A	SBN	Redentor Hominis : lettera enciclica del Sommo Pontefice Giovanni Paolo 2. ai venerati Fratelli ...	Woityła, Karol[386]	http://id.sbn.it/bid/MIL0591301	GN
B	LOC	Encyclical Redemptor hominis of the Supreme Pontiff John Paul II.	Catholic Church. Pope (1978–2005 : John Paul II)	https://lccn.loc.gov/81153830	CN
C	DNB	Redemptor Hominis : Enzyklika Papst Johannes Pauls II. ; dt. Übers.	Johannes Paul II., Papst.	https://d-nb.info/800426983	PN
D	BnF	Le Rédempteur de l'homme [Texte imprimé] : lettre encyclique 'Redemptor hominis' : mars 1979 / Jean-Paul II ; présentation de Jean Potin	1 Église catholique 2 Jean-Paul II (1920–2005; pape)	https://catalogue.bnf.fr/ark:/12148/cb34625607n	CN-PN
E	GRE	Redemptor hominis / Joannes Paulus PP. II ; commento di Bernhard Häring	Iohannes Paulus PP. II, s., 1920–2005	https://oseegenius.unigre.it/pug/resource?uri=77801BIB&v=l	PN
F	Vatlib	Redemptor Hominis : encyklika	Papi (1978–2005 : Iohannes Paulus II)	https://opac.vatlib.it/stp/detail/10946897	CN

5 *Le omelie di Pentling*: The work brings together the recordings of ten homilies given by Ratzinger extemporaneously between 1986 and 1999, well before his election to the papal throne, in the little church of Pentling. Transcribed by Christian Schaller, of the Institut Benedikt XVI, they were sent to the *pope emeritus* for review. First published in the German original (Joseph Ratzinger, *Pentlinger Predigten*, Regensburg, Schnell & Steiner, 2015), the unpublished collection was also published in Italian by Libreria Editrice Vaticana, with a preface by Benedict XVI, pope emeritus (*Le omelie di Pentling*, Città del Vaticano, Libreria Editrice Vaticana, 2015).

Table 4.6 *The cataloguing of the work* Le omelie di Pentling *in the different catalogues analysed*

	Source	Opera	Access by Agent	URI/URL	Header/Access
1	SBN	Le omelie di Pentling / Joseph Ratzinger, Benedetto 16. ; con una prefazione del papa emerito	Benedictus XVI {pope}	http://id.sbn.it/bid/TO01963393	PN
2	LOC	Pentlinger Predigten / Joseph Ratzinger.	Benedict XVI, Pope, 1927–2022	https://lccn.loc.gov/2015457402	PN
3	DNB	Pentlinger Predigten / Joseph Ratzinger	Benedikt XVI., Papst[387]	https://d-nb.info/1069551708	PN
4	BnF			Not present	
5	GRE	Le omelia di Pentling / Joseph Ratzinger – Benedetto XVI ; con una prefazione del Papa emerito	Benedictus PP. XVI 1927–2022	https://oseegenius.unigre.it/pug/resource?uri=422878BIB&found=1	PN
6	Vatlib			Not present	

As evident from the title of the event listed, for example in the row related to the SBN OPAC, the publication details do not aid in identifying the agent, because they simultaneously cite Joseph Ratzinger, Benedict XVI, and the Pope Emeritus as the author of the preface. We have already addressed the delicate issue of the designation 'Pope Emeritus' and how this change in status affects the entity.

6 *Gesù di Nazareth*, (original title *Jesus von Nazareth. Von der Taufe im Jordan bis zur Verklärung*, is the first book published by Pope Benedict XVI (Joseph Ratzinger) after his election as pontiff. It is an essay on the historical figure of Jesus Christ. The cover bears two signatures: Joseph Ratzinger and Benedict XVI, a feature absent from the books of his predecessors, intended to emphasise that the volume is not an act of magisterium, as reiterated both before and after its publication, but merely the viewpoint of 'believer Joseph Ratzinger' on the figure of Christ.[388]

Table 4.7 *The cataloguing of the work* Gesù di Nazareth *in the different catalogues analysed*

	Source	Opera	Access by Agent	URI/URL	Header/Access
A	SBN	Jesus of Nazareth : from the Baptizm in the Jordan to the Transfiguration / by Joseph Ratzinger pope Benedict XVI	Benedictus XVI {pope}	http://id.sbn.it/bid/PBE0160964	PN
B	LOC	Jesus of Nazareth / by Joseph Ratzinger (Pope Benedict XVI) ; translated from the German by Adrian J. Walker.	Benedict XVI, Pope, 1927–2022	https://lccn.loc.gov/2007022357	PN
C	DNB	Jezus z Nazaretu : od chrztu w Jordanie do Przemienienia / Benedykt XVI (Joseph Ratzinger) ; przekład Wiesław Szymona	Benedikt XVI., Papst	https://d-nb.info/1155183533	PN
D	BnF	Jésus de Nazareth. 1, Du baptême dans le Jourdain à la Transfiguration [Texte imprimé] / Joseph Ratzinger ; [...]	Benoît XVI (1927–2022; pape)	https://catalogue.bnf.fr/ark:/12148/cb41338641x	PN
E	GRE	Gesù di Nazaret. [Prima parte], [Dal Battesimo nel Giordano alla Trasfigurazione] / Joseph Ratzinger – Benedetto XVI ; edizione integrale illustrata ; prefazione di Gianfranco Ravasi	Benedictus PP. XVI 1927–2022	https://oseegenius.unigre.it/pug/resource?uri=58601BIB&v=l	PN
F	Vatlib	Gesù di Nazaret / Joseph Ratzinger Benedetto XVI ; prefazione di Gianfranco Ravasi.	Benedictus PP. XVI, 1927–2022	https://opac.vatlib.it/stp/detail/20013083	PN

7 *Deus caritas est* is the first encyclical letter published by Pope Benedict XVI. Announced during his general audience on 18 January 2006, it was officially released on 25 January of that year. The encyclical bears the date 25 December 2005, the day it was signed.[389]

Table 4.8 *Cataloguing of the work* Deus caritas est *in the different catalogues analysed*

	Source	Opera	Access by Agent	URI/URL	Header/Access
A	SBN	Deus Caritas Est / Benedetto XVI - Lettera enciclica sull'amore cristiano	Benedictus XVI {papa}	http://id.sbn.it/bid/BRI0490015	PN
B	LOC	God is love : Deus caritas est, Encyclical letter of the Supreme Pontiff Benedict XVI to the bishops, priests, and deacons, men and women religious, and all the lay faithful, on Christian love.	Catholic Church. Pope (2005–2013 : Benedict XVI)	https://lccn.loc.gov/2006923028	CN
C	DNB	[Deus caritas est] Gott ist die Liebe : 1. Enzyklika = Deus caritas est / Papst Benedikt XVI. In den Rollen: Erzählerin Annette Gunkel ; Erzähler Ingo Pfeiffer ; Bibelzitate Achim Beck ...	Benedikt XVI., Papst	https://d-nb.info/1192264967	PN
D	BnF	Lettre encyclique 'Deus caritas est' du souverain pontife Benoît XVI aux évêques, aux prêtres et aux diacres, aux personnes consacrées, et à tous les fidèles laïcs sur l'amour chrétien [Texte imprimé] / Benoît XVI	1) Église catholique 2) Benoît XVI (1927–2022; pape)	https://catalogue.bnf.fr/ark:/12148/cb40172610j	CN – PN
E	GRE	Lettera enciclica 'Deus caritas est' del sommo pontefice Benedetto XVI ai vescovi, ai presbiteri e ai diaconi, alle persone consacrate e a tutti i fedeli laici sull'amore cristiano	Papi (2005–2013 : Benedictus PP. XVI)	https://oseegenius.unigre.it/pug/resource?uri=346817BIB&v=l	CN

Continued

Table 4.8 *Continued*

	Source	Opera	Access by Agent	URI/URL	Header/Access
F	Vatlib	Deus caritas est : lettera enciclica del sommo pontefice Benedetto XVI ai vescovi, ai presbiteri e ai diaconi, alle persone consacrate e a tutti i fedeli laici sull'amore cristiano	Papi (2005–2013 : Benedictus XVI)	https://opac.vatlib.it/stp/detail/10967079	CN

Identifying the ontological and identity breaks

The recorded temporal segments for each of the two Popes, delimited by specific events, can generate profound changes in the individual, and therefore may be identified with the ontological or identity breaks discussed in Chapter 3, presented here in Table 4.9.

Table 4.9 *The ontological and identity breaks for the pope-type entity*

Identity type	Event	Ontological/identity break[390]	Evidence of identity break
Individual (birth identity)	Birth. Enrolment at the civil registry	yes (I)	Assignment of the registry name[391]
Pope	Acceptance of election to the papal throne	yes (I)	Papal name assumption
Pope Emeritus	Renunciation of the Petrine ministry	yes (I)	Assumption of the title Pope Emeritus

In the case of synchronous identities, such as that of the Pope who is simultaneously an individual (with his own birth identity) and the Pope, or who uses both his personal name and a pseudonym concurrently, the ontological or identity break cannot be determined solely by a chronological event, something that happens over time to modify the entity's profile. For the correct identification of this significant change, the *diachronic element* (the occurrence of an event at a certain time) must be accompanied by the *synchronic profile* (the capacity to write works under a personal name or pseudonym while simultaneously writing official works in the name and on behalf of an institution). From the intersection of these two parameters, we manage to establish the *identity breaks* that are useful in identifying different profiles and associating each work, or each type of work, with the correct identity (Table 4.10 and 4.11).

Table 4.10 *Identification of ontological or identity breaks in the individual Karol Józef Wojtyła*

Karol Józef Wojtyła, 1920–2005				
Dates	**Type of work**	**Type of Identity**	**Name Identity**	**Identity type abbreviation**
18.05.1920–6.10.1978	Works written before becoming pope	Birth identity	Karol Józef Wojtyła	BI
1960–??	Theatrical Dramas	Pseudonym	Andrzej Jawień	PS
6.10.1978– 2 April 2005	Works written as pope	Personal identity as pope	John Paul II	PI
6.10.1978– 2 April 2005	Works written in the period coinciding with the papacy but as private	Birth identity or Personal identity as pope[392]	Karol Józef Wojtyła / John Paul II	BI
6.10.1978 – 2 April 2005	Official works	Corporate Body-identity	Catholic Church. Pope	CI

Table 4.11 *Identification of ontological or identity breaks in the individual Joseph Aloisius Ratzinger*

Joseph Aloisius Ratzinger, 1927–2022				
Dates	**Type of work**	**Type of Identity**	**Name Identity**	**Identity type abbreviation**
17.04.1927–19.04.2005	Works written before becoming pope	Birth identity	Joseph Aloisius Ratzinger	BI
19.04.2005–28.02.2013	Works written as pope	Personal identity as pope	Benedict XVI	PI
19.04.2005–28.02.2013	Official works	Corporate Body-identity	Catholic Church. Pope	CI
19.04.2005–28.02.2013	Works written in the period coinciding with the papacy but as private	Birth identity or Personal identity as pope	Joseph Aloisius Ratzinger /Benedict XVI	BI/PI
28.02.2013–31.12.2022	Works written after the end of the term	Personal identity as pope emeritus	Benedict XVI, pope emeritus	PI

For Pope Wojtyła, we have identified a personal profile as the author of works written under the name Karol Józef Wojtyła before his election as pope, and the pseudonym Andrzej Jawień, which would fully constitute a second identity encompassing his theatrical works and poems. We have also established the identity acquired through his election as pope, whose emergent property is derived from the *primatial authority* received upon his election.

A significant question arises from profiling the pope when enhanced by the responsibility to represent an entire community, that of the Catholic

Church. The difference here is exceedingly subtle, as primatial authority is received upon election to the papal throne, which, in our analysis of significant events, marks the transition from baptismal name to pontifical name. Yet even traditional cataloguing practices, particularly those of Anglo-American origin, feel the need for further distinction by qualifying the pope in metadata structuring as 'personal access' in his individual capacity and 'institutional access' in his official and in his collective capacity as the Catholic Church. It is the Catholic Church that, under the pontificate of such a pope but as a Church entity, issues an act.[393] In this case, is it sufficient to speak of an *identity break*, or is this a scenario where it becomes necessary to discuss an *ontological break*, profiling the Catholic Church as an entity distinct from the pope who represents it? Tables 4.10 and 4.11 illustrated respectively the ontological breaks for Karol Józef Wojtyła and Joseph Aloisius Ratzinger.

How entity modelling addresses this type of entity, constructed with various profiles in relation to the role that each identity has in relation to something else (such as a community or a work), is an interesting consideration. In practice, we will see how it reveals a general confusion that, in my opinion, still needs resolution between the application of a norm to guide the choice and structure access points to a resource (inherited from more traditional cataloguing practices) and the perception of something different and deeper, pertaining precisely to the entity and identity of the individual.

The tables that follow (Tables 4.12–4.18), summarise the cataloguing choices made by the institutions being analysed, of the preferred access points for each work. Here, we are still largely within the framework of traditional cataloguing (regardless of how the data is ultimately presented to the public or on the web), so it is preferable to refer to the authors of the various works

Table 4.12 *Summary of cataloguing choices recorded in the sources consulted for the work* Persona e atto, *with entity modelling exercise*

1. Persona e atto (original title *Osoba i czyn*)				
	Source	**Birth name/baptismal name (GN)**	**Pontifical name (PN)**	**Corporate Body name (Catholic Church or Popes) (CN)**
A	SBN		x	
B	LOC		x	
C	DNB		x	
D	BnF		x	
E	GRE		x	
F	Vatlib		–	
G	Entity modelling	Birth identity (BI)		

as access points rather than identities. In the same summary tables of cataloguing choices, we also propose assigning each work to each entity or identity defined in Table 4.10, identified through the tracing of that 'boundary' or rather that ontological or identity break delimited by some significant events that occur in a person's life (refer here to row G – Entity modelling). The 'x' in the table indicates the choice made for each institution reported.

Table 4.13 *Summary of cataloguing choices recorded in the sources consulted for the work* La bottega dell'orefice, *with entity modelling exercise*

2. *La bottega dell'orefice* (original title *Przed sklepem jubilera*)				
	Source	**Birth name/baptismal name (GN)**	**Pontifical name (PN)**	**Corporate Body name (Catholic Church or Popes) (CN)**
A	SBN		x	
B	LOC		x	
C	DNB		x	
D	BnF		x	
E	GRE		x	
F	Vatlib		x	
G	Entity modelling	Pseudonym (PS)		

Table 4.14 *Summary of cataloguing choices recorded in the sources consulted for the work* Varcare la soglia della speranza, *with entity modelling exercise*

3. *Varcare la soglia della speranza*				
	Source	**Birth name/baptismal name (GN)**	**Pontifical name (PN)**	**Corporate Body name (Catholic Church or Popes) (CN)**
A	SBN		x	
B	LOC		x	
C	DNB		x	
D	BnF		x	
E	GRE		x	
F	Vatlib		x	
G	Entity modelling		Acquired individual identity (PI)	

Table 4.15 *Summary of cataloguing choices recorded in the sources consulted for the work* Redemptor Hominis, *with entity modelling exercise*

4. *Redemptor Hominis*				
	Source	**Birth name/baptismal name (GN)**	**Pontifical name (PN)**	**Corporate Body name (Catholic Church or Popes) (CN)**
A	SBN	x		
B	LOC			x
C	DNB		x	
D	BnF		x	x
E	GRE		x	
F	Vatlib			x
G	Entity modelling			Corporate Body-identity (CI)

Table 4.16 *Summary of cataloguing choices recorded in the sources consulted for the work* Le omelie di Pentling, *with entity modelling exercise*

5. *Le omelie di Pentling*				
	Source	**Birth name/baptismal name (GN)**	**Pontifical name (PN)**	**Corporate Body name (Catholic Church or Popes) (CN)**
A	SBN		x	
B	LOC		x	
C	DNB		x	
D	BnF	-		
E	GRE		x	
F	Vatlib	-		
G	Entity modelling		Acquired individual identity (PI)[394]	

Table 4.17 *Summary of cataloguing choices recorded in the sources consulted for the work* Gesù di Nazareth, *with entity modelling exercise*

6. *Gesù di Nazareth*				
	Source	**Birth name/baptismal name (GN)**	**Pontifical name (PN)**	**Corporate Body name (Catholic Church or Popes) (CN)**
A	SBN		x	
B	LOC		x	
C	DNB		x	
D	BnF		x	
E	GRE		x	
F	Vatlib		x	
G	Entity modelling	BI/PI[395]		

Table 4.18 *Summary of cataloguing choices recorded in the sources consulted for the work* Deus caritas est, *with entity modelling exercise*

7. *Deus caritas est*, in English 'God is Love'				
	Source	**Birth name/baptismal name (GN)**	**Pontifical name (PN)**	**Corporate Body name (Catholic Church or Popes) (CN)**
A	SBN		x	
B	LOC			x
C	DNB		x	
D	BnF		x	x
E	GRE			x
F	Vatlib			x
G	Entity modelling			Corporate Body-identity (CI)

The cataloguing rules are quite clear regarding the choice and structuring of access points, but they are far from useful in guiding the cataloguer in entity modelling. The indications focus primarily on constructing the access point to be used in different cases, largely based on the type of work being catalogued, with a specific emphasis on string construction. The Official RDA Toolkit, which strengthens its entity modelling-oriented approach through the absorption of IFLA LRM, includes in each section on each entity a paragraph called *Prerecording*,[396] where guidance is given on the reflections to be accrued around the entity in order to identify it before beginning to record the metadata necessary to represent it. In this same section are the directions for *entity boundary*, which, as mentioned earlier, express exactly that concept of ontological profile or identity break. The association of a possible identity to the works above is, however, a pure exercise, because the entity modelling mechanism does not require the choice of a name or identity associated with the work, but resolves doubts about complex entities by the mechanism of clusters (or entity as a prism).

Identifying entities and identities through URIs

I have already emphasised how the perspective of clusters and the possibility of identifying an entity and its possible, multiple identities offer a new scenario even in the field of cataloguing. In Chapter 2, in the section 'The prism and its facets in synchronous and diachronic identities', I presented examples of synchronous and diachronic identity entities in prism representation. Each facet can express a different mode of representing an entity or can express a different identity. In the two cases of Popes that I have analysed above, we would therefore have:

1 entity: person Karol Józef Wojtyła:
   - *identity 1*: Karol Józef Wojtyła, Wadowice 18 May 1920 – Vatican City, 2 April 2005 (registry or birth identity)
   - *identity 2*: Andrzej Jawień, a pseudonym of Karol Józef Wojtyła used in the writing of some plays (pseudonymous identity)
   - *identity 3*: Pope John Paul II, 264th Bishop of Rome and Pope of the Catholic Church from 16 October 1978 to 2 April 2005 (personal identity as Pope)

2 entity: person Joseph Ratzinger:
   - *identity 1:* Joseph Aloisius Ratzinger, Marktl, 16 April 1927 – Vatican City, 31 December 2022 (registry or birth identity)
   - *identity 2:* Pope Benedict XVI, 265th Bishop of Rome and Pope of the Catholic Church from 19 April 2005 to 28 February 2013 (personal identity as Pope)
   - *identity 3:* Pope Emeritus, 28 February 2013 to 31 December 2022.

In the cases of complex entities that we are examining, where identities, except in the case of pseudonyms, are more difficult to profile, the international sources consulted show minimal differences in treatment. A different case is the management of pseudonyms, where the lines of entity and identity modelling are sometimes more clearly delineated, as we will see shortly.

Entity and identity distinction in the popes

The two entities used for this study of traditional cataloguing approach versus entity modelling are treated quite uniformly in the various sources consulted, with almost complete reconciliation of different identities into a single entity, and with very uniform choices regarding the treatment given to different denominations (whether they are true variants of the name or identifiers of different identities). Let's look at some examples.

Database data.bnf.fr:

- John Paul II.[397] The preferred form for display is *Jean-Paul II (pape, 1920–2005)* (*nom en religion)*; all different identities (the pseudonym, birth identity, pope identity) are presented as *variant forms of the name*, introduced by the property {www.w3.org/2004/02/skos/core#altLabel} which expresses an alternative label to the one chosen as preferred. All works are associated with the entity ID. There are no direct references to the entity Catholic Church (during the pontificate of Pope John Paul II), as is the case in other sources.

- Benedict XVI.[398] The same observations apply as for John Paul II. The preferred form is that of the papal name, in the French form *Benoît XVI (pape, 1927–2022)*; all identities are reconciled into the single personal identity as pope just as all works are associated with the descriptor of this identity. The property used to handle variant forms is, of course, the same one cited for John Paul II.

ISNI database:

- John Paul II:[399] Here too, diverse identities are grouped under the heading *Name*, considered all variants of the name, without any distinction between a variant that is such because it is expressed as a formulation of the name in other scripts (variants in Arabic, Chinese, Cyrillic etc.) and a variant understood as the pseudonym of an entity (and therefore a different identity). Several pseudonyms used by Karol Wojtyła are listed, including *Andrzej Gruda, Piotr Jasień* and *Andrzej Jawień*, but on the list of names these pseudonyms are also associated with the term 'pope' in different languages, such as: *Gruda, Stanisław Andrzej (Pope)* or *Jawień, Andrzej (Papst)*. The variant forms of the name are introduced by the Schema.org property https://schema.org/alternateName, so again indicating a different wording of the name without any reference to a different identity. The name, or rather the different forms of the name, structured as access to the entity (Catholic Church) are grouped under *Related names* but refer to the general entry *Catholic Church Pope*.[400]
- Benedict XVI:[401] In this entry there is a new element, missing in the entry for John Paul II. The label *Related identities* is, in fact, introduced and the values associated with this label are *Benedictus (XVI; paavi; pseud)* and *Ratzinger, Joseph (real name)* where, therefore, beyond the wording of the names (already present as variants) the two different identities are declared, the one of the papal name here defined as pseudonymous and the real one. It is not possible to give any indication of the property used in the RDF format to structure this datum because it is not presented in the RDF/XML and JavaScript Object Notation for Linked Data (JSON-LD) serialisations proposed in the record download function. The *Related identities* element could be the result of a datum coming from the operational database and therefore resolved with a simple html label. However, it is interesting to note the insight into a different identity to be distinguished somehow from a pure linguistic or spelling variant of a name.

VIAF database:
The mechanism of managing clusters from authority records from various bibliographic agencies is certainly the main insight of this database. The structure of the authority record in MARC greatly influences the presentation of data, which indeed distinguishes the 4xx block (Alternate Name Forms) for 'see' references, intended in MARC to manage variant forms of a name, from the 5xx block (Related Names) for 'see also' references, and thus for entities or identities different from those treated in the 100 block (the person John Paul II or the person Benedict XVI, in our case) but related to it. This presentation in logically distinct blocks in MARC, which would greatly help in identifying a variant form of a name from a different entity, actually helps very little in the cases examined here. Analysing the two blocks, we see a considerable confusion in the presentation of the various entries, often reported in both the 4xx and 5xx blocks, evidently in relation to the source (the original authority record) from which the entries come and which contribute to creating the cluster. Regarding the examples analysed:

- John Paul II.[402] The cluster already presents both the variant forms of the papal name and the personal (birth) name Karol Wojtyła in the *Preferred Forms* section. Pseudonyms, e.g. *Jawień, Andrzej* are equally present in the three name blocks provided by VIAF, thus as Preferred forms, as Alternate Names Forms and as Related Names. In the latter block, by the way, the names presented as related to the entity represented by the cluster have no particular qualifiers to help distinguish what the underlying relationship is. The intention is, therefore, the right one; the cluster creation algorithms suffer, however, from the too-divergent cataloguing choices expressed by the different participating agencies. The result, then, is a very meaty cluster, expressing more the summation of the many choices expressed upstream than a rationalisation and classification of them. Some of the forms present in block 5xx, e.g., the pseudonym name *Jawień, Andrzej*[403] generated their own cluster, which would go in the right intuition of a different identity but, as already pointed out, being also present as a variant form of the same papal name, it is difficult to really determine the conceptual choices made by VIAF. There are also several clusters created for the Catholic Church entity (with association of the Pope's name)[404] present in the Related Names section.
- Benedict XVI.[405] This situation mirrors that which was registered for John Paul II. Again, there are several duplications of clusters,[406] as well as several duplications of name forms in the three sections on Preferred forms, Alternate Names Forms, and Related Names mentioned above.

Again, accesses to the entity Catholic Church (in different linguistic or syntactic formulations) are reported in the Related Names section, and again with different duplications of clusters.

VIAF's situation in handling these cases (and in general, all cases of complex entities with multiple entities) is ambiguous, and certainly reflects a framework that long predates the idea of entity modelling. The assignment of a URI for each entity or identity is mostly influenced by the cataloguing choices that are upstream of the clustering processes and that can be summarised as one URI for each entity (that is one for the person/people and one for the entity) and duplication of clusters (with duplication of URIs) in cases where entities are not clustered.[407]

LC Name Authority File (LCNAF):

- John Paul II.[408] The preferred form for presentation on the web page is in the English language declension *(John Paul II, Pope, 1920–2005)* and in this case too the choices made are perfectly aligned with the positions already mentioned above. There is no distinction between another identity and a variant form of a name, and the properties used to handle variants are either the same as those mentioned above or similar properties taken from other ontologies or languages, for example: *madsRDF:variantLabel*[409] or even *skosxl:altLabel;*[410] the property used for Related agent is *skos:related*[411] and it links the *John Paul II* entity to the *Catholic Church* entity. *Pope (1978–2005 : John Paul II).*[412]
- Benedict XVI.[413] The preferred form is the English form *(Benedict XVI, Pope, 1927–2022)*, and otherwise the entry is structured in the same way as that for John Paul II.

The situation in these clusters is certainly cleaner and more straightforward than that in VIAF, but this is normal, since we are dealing with the catalogue of a library – albeit a central and massive one like that of the Library of Congress – as opposed to the set of catalogues covered in VIAF and with different cultural origins and cataloguing traditions.

The last example I will give is that of **Wikidata**, which, because of its particular nature as a collaborative and cross-domain tool, and also because it is the result not of the conversion of traditional catalogues but of a different approach already oriented to the identification of real-world things, does not seem to be burdened by a data structure oriented to the cataloguing record. The two entities (or 'items' in Wikidata) we are analysing[414] represent the person in his or her complexity, modelled with a relevant number of properties, ranging from biographical data to family and historical data, educational and professional records and many other identifying elements. The different forms of names associated with the entity are treated as *aliases*. For the entity John Paul II, there is also a *Pseudonym* property[415] that links the item to the name Andrzej Jawień. Obviously, there is no reference to different identities nor descriptor for identities. Wikidata is not a bibliographic catalogue and does not, therefore, have as one of its informational purposes the linking of each person-type entity to the work, if any. It does not, therefore, have to deal with entity modelling problems in relation to the correct identification and attribution of works. There is, however, the property *object named as*[416] related to the edition (which in Wikidata roughly corresponds to the publication). According to the Italian definition associated with the property, this is used as a qualifier to indicate how the value of the property is indicated in the source. Examples associated with this property include the wording of the name as expressed on the resource:

Before the Embers
author Léon Barracand
object named as Léon Grandet

While referring to the edition, this property would help to disambiguate to some extent some of the cases we analysed earlier. For example, the case of the work *Jesus von Nazareth: von der Taufe im Jordan bis zur Verklärung* which, as mentioned, is intended to express the perspective of believer Joseph Ratzinger and not an act of magisterium by Pope Benedict XVI.

Entity modelling and identity management

The examination of how popes are treated in various authoritative international sources shows a certain uniformity in handling these cases. They are not managed as complex entities but are mostly 'flattened' into either a personal or papal profile. The treatment of complex entities can certainly differ in cases of pseudonyms, especially when pseudonymous profiles are clear and recognised. The identification and attribution of URIs in the case of pseudonyms in the sources we have considered here, could be summarised as follows:

- Wikidata assigns a URI to the entity (to the real person, mostly), associating all the different identities with the same entity. A different treatment is reserved for collective pseudonyms, which are assigned a specific URI linked to the personal single entity. An example of a collective pseudonym treated in this way is that of Wu Ming[417] linked through the *has part(s)* property[418] to the individual members of the collective, including Wu Ming 5.[419]

- LCNAF, where possible, assigns a URI to each identity. For example, in the case of Lewis Carroll a URI is assigned for this identity[420] but also a URI for Charles Lutwidge Dodgson,[421] and the two identities are linked through the property *Related Terms*.
- VIAF: Here too there is a glimpse of a desire to distinguish between the different identities (the personal and the pseudonymous), but with considerable confusion, because the pseudonym is often also reported as a variant form of the name, and conversely, the birth name is also reported as a variant form of the pseudonym. Where possible, two different identifiers are still assigned, but more often cases of multiple entities (traceable to the same entity) are found.[422]
- ISNI: The theme of pseudonyms is very well handled,[423] although entity and identity modelling practices do not always replicate this clarity. In the case of clearly recognised and identified pseudonyms, such as the case we are now using as an example of Carroll-Dodgson, two specific URIs for the two entities are given.[424] The two identities are linked through the previously mentioned *Related identities* property.

The expert community has been questioning for some time now the issue of identity management with particular reference to issues related to digital identity and the themes of sharing or privacy rights that are linked to these identities. Noteworthy is the study being conducted by Charlene Chou, of New York University, presented in December 2022 as part of a series of webinars organised by the Dublin Core Metadata Initiative.[425] The study focuses on the treatment of pseudonymous identities; it was still ongoing at the time I checked it, but it is interesting to share here, in Figure 4.2 on the following pages, the two summary tables on the terminology used in the different sources analysed to identify identities/pseudonyms in different contexts. Particular attention is paid to the data dissemination policies related to pseudonymous identities, and its reference therefore, to digital identity management policies on the web.[426]

This study is closely related to what is being discussed here, although it concentrates on the treatment of pseudonyms. However, let's see how to reach conclusions regarding the entity cases that have been used as examples, based on the ongoing practical experience of the SVDE community.

Term	Wikipedia	RDA	Privacy-enhanced identity management
Pseudonym	A name that a person or group assumes for a particular purpose, which can differ from their first or true name.	A name used by a person, either alone or *in collaboration with others**, that is not the person's real name (*also called: *joint pseudonym*)	-An identifier of a subject other than one of the subject's real name -Regarding the degree of linkability, various kinds of pseudonyms may be distinguished: *person pseudonym, role pseudonym, relationship pseudonym, role pseudonym, role-relationship pseudonym* and *transaction pseudonym* -Might be an identifier for a partial identity
Alternate identity	N/A	A pseudonymous or other identity assumed by a person	Related terms: pseudonyms, partial identities, etc.
Real identity	N/A	A real person who assumes an alternate identity	The holders' civil identity; one of its real name
Person	A being that has certain capacities or attributes such as reason …; about *personal identity* and *self*: both about what makes any particular person that particular person instead of another…"	An individual or an identity established by an individual, either alone or in collaboration with one or more other individuals.	The holder's name
Identity	Identity (social science), individuality, personal identity, social identity, and cultural identity in psychology, sociology, and philosophy	N/A	An identity is any subset of attribute values of an individual person which sufficiently identifies this individual person within any set of persons.
Individuals with more than one identity	N/A	An individual uses his or her real name as well as one or more pseudonyms (9.2.2.8)	

Figure 4.2 *Comparative table of terminology: pseudonyms and/or Identity Management. Courtesy of Charlene Chou* (New York University)

Term	Wikipedia	RDA	Privacy-enhanced identity management
Collective identity	The shared sense of belonging to a group	Joint pseudonym	N/A
Partial identity	N/A	N/A	An identity of an individual person may comprise many partial identities which each represents the person in a specific context or role. It is a subset of attribute values of a complete identity
Complete identity	N/A	N/A	The union of all attribute values of all identities of this person
Anonyms or anonymity	Without a name or namelessness	N/A	Anonymity of a subject means that the subject is not identifiable within a set of subjects, the anonymity set
Digital identity	Information on an entity used by computer systems to represent an external agent. That agent may be a person, organization, application	N/A	Attribution of attribute values to an individual person, which are immediately operational accessible by technical means; the identifier of a digital partial identity can be a simple e-mail address in a news group or …
Identity management	Also known as identity and access management (IAM) is, in computer security, the security and business discipline that "enables the right individuals to access the right resources at the right times and for the right reasons".	N/A	Managing various partial identities (usually denoted by pseudonyms) of an individual person …)

Figure 4.2 *Continued*

A proposal for identity management in SVDE

The opportunity for the proposal of entity modelling that concludes this study arises from the ongoing practical experience within the Share Family, the community of libraries I have mentioned before, where many of the reflections reported here are prompted and matured. The Share Family organises participating libraries in various *tenants*[427] or hubs (Figure 4.3 opposite), based on different criteria (nature of the library, scope of interest, a specific project), each entirely autonomous from the others. This means that each tenant manages its own entity database, resulting from the conversion of catalogues or the creation of new entities, uses its own tool to enhance the quality of clustering results (the entity editor JCricket), and has its own portal for publishing and enabling data access. Consequently, each entity identified in the entity resolution processes described in Chapter 2 will be constructed as a cluster (or prism) and will have its own unique identifier. In the very common case where the same entity exists in different tenants, it will assume a domain URI in each tenant. However, the libraries' goal is to create a network of relationships that allows tracking the presence of the same entity across different tenants, to build upon this network a series of services, such as being able to correct a cluster present in one hub and reflect the correction onto the same entity (constructed with a different cluster) in a different hub.

From here stems the idea of integrating an identity manager into the Share Family's tenant architecture, the Share Family Index. This component functions to assign a unique URI to each entity present in one or more Share Family tenants (the Share Family Identifier), linking this URI to each entity's URI within the individual tenant. If the entity Karol Wojtyła were present, for example, in both the SVDE and Parsifal tenants, we would link to the URI present in the Share Family Index both the URI assigned to the entity within the SVDE tenant and the URI assigned to the entity within the Parsifal tenant. The Share Family Identifier serves as a centralised indicator that references the various entities across different tenants. The Share Family Identifier does not have any attributes, not even the attribute of the entity's name, as its role is solely to indicate the same entities catalogued and modelled, which themselves have all the identifying properties, across different tenants.

Therefore, the Share Family Index's role is to construct a map of entities within the Share Family and to enable the orchestration of services, such as entity updates. The Share Family Index has, therefore, the role of building a map of entities within the Share Family and enabling orchestration of services: for example, those for updating entities.

This entity tracking solution could be extended to track different identities, thus creating a far more granular lattice network of relationships and thus extending entity modelling to the concept of identity management.

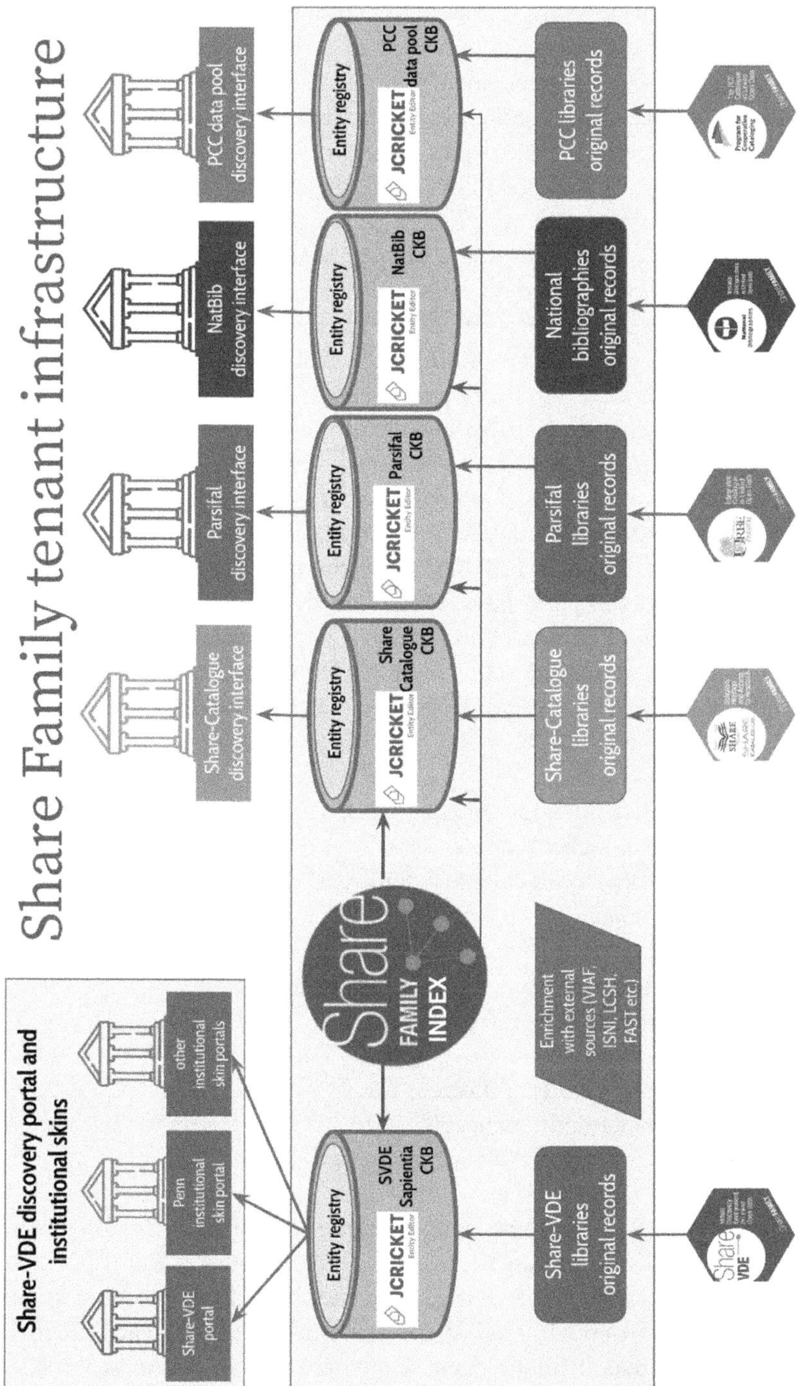

Figure 4.3 *The architecture for individual tenants or library hubs in the Share Family*

I would like to start from the representation of the two entities we discussed to express graphically what we assumed in terms of entity and identity modelling. Figure 4.4 opposite shows the representation of the entity Karol Wojtyła. The entity, in its entirety, is expressed in the birth identity, pseudonymous identities and the papal identity (which we might call role, or context, or function). As Pope John Paul II, this entity is part or member of a collective entity (in this case, specifically a corporate body entity), which we identify with the Catholic Church, and specifically in the identity we can profile with the specific period of the pontificate (1978–2005).

The diagram in Figure 4.5 on page 224 depicts the entity Joseph Ratzinger, with a grid similar to that seen for Karol Wojtyła and with the addition of the identity we have identified in the title of Pope Emeritus.

In order to construct this lattice, specific properties must be identified or defined that express the different entity–entity or entity–identity relationships. The SEI WG is developing an extension of the BIBFRAME ontology for the Share community, which would accommodate certain classes and properties not found in BIBFRAME or the other ontologies used but useful in entity modelling processes. These extensions will include, precisely, the properties needed to model an Agent in its complex articulation into entities and identities. Looking at the diagrams in Figures 4.4 and 4.5 we could derive some possible classes and properties that then, formally structured, will be proposed to the SEI WG:

- Entity A *has identity* Birth identity
- Birth identity *has* Real/birth name
- Entity A *has identity* Papal (context) identity.
- Papal identity *has name* Papal name
- Entity A *has* pseudonym Pseudonymous identity
- Pseudonymous identity *has* name Pseudonymous name
- Entity A *related to* Entity B
- Entity B *is of type* Entity
- Entity B *has time segment* Pontificate x
- Pontificate x *includes* Pontificate 2005–2013
- Papal identity *member of* pontificate x.

In Figure 4.6 on page 225, I show how, from the Share Family Identifier, the lattice of entities and identities is developed for the person Karol Wojtyła, present in two different tenants of the Share Family. Also represented in this diagram are the works mentioned earlier and associated with each identity. The URIs are, of course, fictitious, constructed here only as examples. Looking at the figure, we can derive other useful assertions, including:

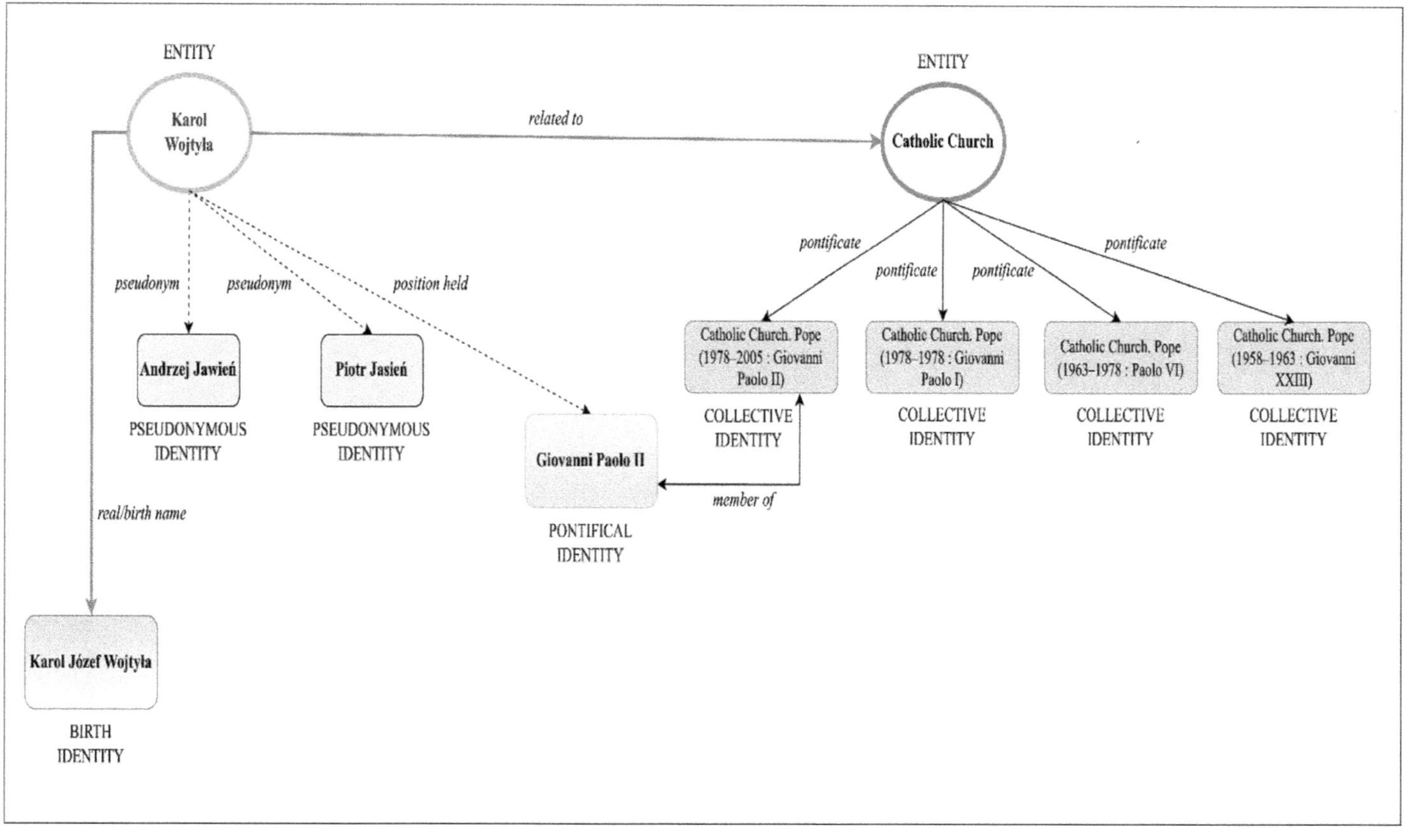

Figure 4.4 *The Karol Wojtyła entity with links to its identities and the Catholic Church entity*

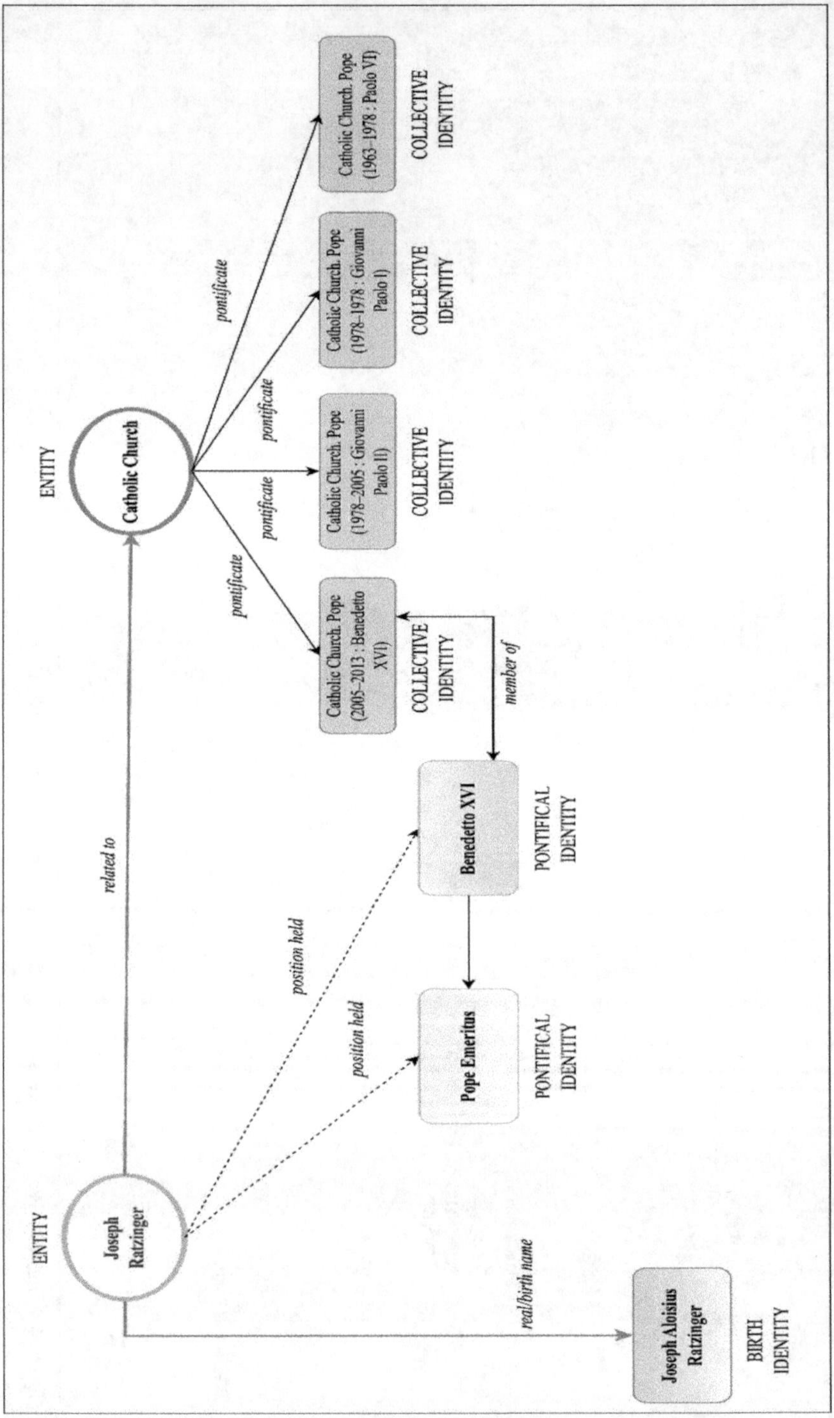

Figure 4.5 *The Joseph Ratzinger entity with links to its identities and the Catholic Church entity*

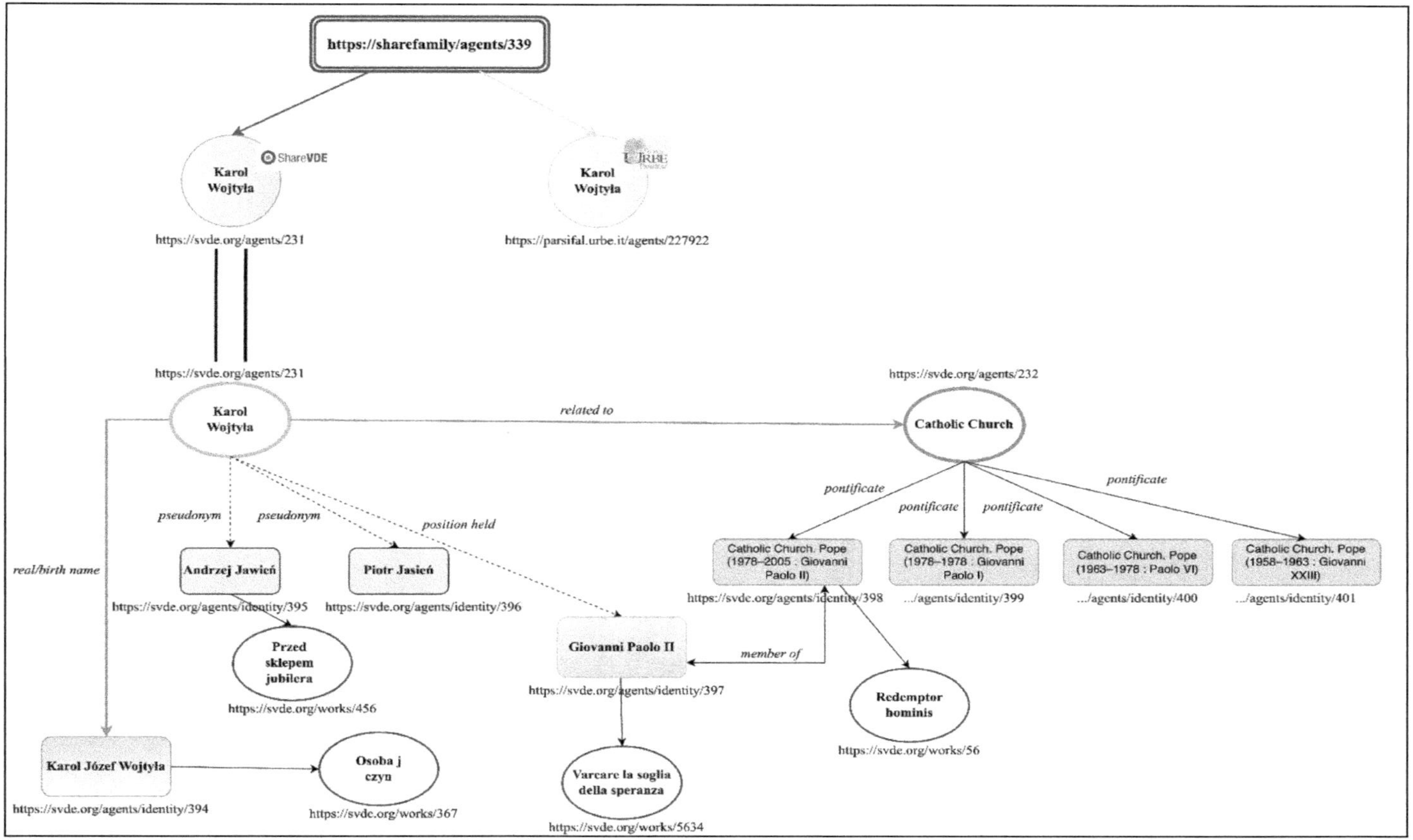

Figure 4.6 *The diagram of entities and identities for Karol Wojtyła with indication of URIs and association of works with each identity*

- Birth Identity (Karol Józef Wojtyła) *author of* Opera 1 (Osoba i czyn)
- Pseudonymic identity (Andrzej Jawień) *author of* Opera 2 (*Przed sklepem jubilera*)
- Pontifical Identity (John Paul II) *author of* Opera 3 (*Crossing the Threshold of Hope*)
- Pontifical identity *member of* Collective Entity (Catholic Church. Pope (1978–2005 : John Paul II)) *author of* Opera 4 (*Redemptor Hominis*).

These assertions illustrate a historical-bibliographical framework that restores to each significant identity the authorship of the work. At the same time, the definition of such specific properties avoids the risk of disintegration of the complex entity, favouring the grouping of the rich to varied artistic expression under the single entity constituted by that specific and unrepeatable real-world object that is the agent with its many facets.

Conclusions on entity modelling and the significance of changing collective mindsets

This chapter has been inspired by the studies on the Agent-type entity and the modelling of these entities that are under way, especially within the Parsifal project, the project to create a single catalogue and central authority file in linked open data of the ecclesiastical academic libraries of the URBE network. The cataloguing community has always paid great attention to the logic of disambiguation of the entities we now call agents, even if, as we have seen, this terminology had not yet entered the cataloguing lexicon. Problems of homonymy, pseudonymy, and collective identities versus individual identities have been the subject of extensive discussion and debate since the birth of cataloguing. But the conflation of the descriptive and syntactic levels (how do I construct a string of names so that it is identifiable?) with the semantic level (who exactly do I want to identify behind this string, what is the profile to which this string refers?) has accompanied and continues to accompany much cataloguing regulation. And this framework has conditioned whole generations of cataloguers. However, something new and different is happening in the new generations of future cataloguers, who have not yet crystallised and assumed as an irrefutable notion the idea of constructing a string (an access point) as a second skin that in itself constitutes the author or curator of a work. The new generation of cataloguers has a background born on and from the web, where certain issues of 'identity', starting with the different digital identities used to access social networks, are common and widely shared.

In a recent course on Linked Data, part of the Level II Master's Program in Organisation and Management of Archives, Cataloguing and Metadata of

Manuscript, Printed and Digital Resources at the University of Florence, I had the opportunity to share with the students some thoughts on entity and identity in cases of pseudonymity. When asked, 'How do you think these cases can be handled in the linked data environment?' the almost unanimous response was 'By assigning an identifier to the entity and an identifier to each identity.' Instead, this seemingly minor event is symptomatic of how much a mindset is changing, and how new generations of cataloguers are starting from the idea that it does not make much sense to have, within the same library domain, separate repositories for personal names used as the preferred access point for cataloguing description of a work, and personal names used to construct a subject string. Once I get past the idea that the role or function performed by an agent (author or subject of a work) should generate a different set of metadata, I come without too much difficulty to understand that modelling the Joseph Ratzinger entity, in its fullness and richness, is irrespective of the domain in which this 'object' is used (I can reuse that object in different domains, to denote the author of a work as well as the producing subject of an archive) and also prescinds from the role that this object assumes with respect to a work (thus being able to be used equally as the author or as the subject of the work).

This is one of the most significant achievements of these new web technologies applied to cultural domains: to produce a collective mindset change that understands the value of data reuse and breaks down the barriers that for years have kept different knowledge domains isolated.

Final Reflections

The topics analysed in this publication are part of a journey that is recent in comparison to the long cataloguing tradition. The purpose of the study was to tell a part of this journey. One of the elements that we can perhaps call mature is the realisation of how much traditional cataloguing is distancing itself and gradually being replaced by entity and identity modelling. This initial point of arrival is necessarily also the starting point for a series of further reflections and experiences. For example, the awareness of the urgency for libraries and all cultural institutions to think about a new way of looking at and describing the world suggests the hypothesis that entity reasoning is really the only way to build inter-domain bridges (or cross-domains, as it is often called in the literature).[428] To identify and model the profile of an entity, to the extent that this is necessary to enable its expression in a given context, is to think about modelling objects in a way that completely ignores the construction format of the attributes that identify it, the standard or cataloguing rule that determines its information content, and a host of other constraints and structures that, over time, have created almost impregnable silos between domains. And very often even within the same domain. I am reminded of the words of Pierluigi Feliciati, who writes:

> In a given historical context, dynamic, changeable and imperfect by definition, the same people, in the same places and at the same times, alone or gathered in more or less formal families or organisations, drafted and received documents, read and wrote literary or scientific works, produced or acquired artistic objects, of which they may also have been the subject, built and inhabited walls, houses and palaces, and contributed and breathed their own intangible culture.
>
> (Feliciati, 2022, 147)

As well as:

> A virtuous and practicable action in which our disciplinary communities could engage – together – would be to identify possible semantic integrations between

> the entities envisaged by the conceptual models that the different disciplinary communities have given themselves. . .. It seems to the writer that there could be at least three scenarios of cooperation, not necessarily alternative to each other. The first strategy, seemingly the easiest to deal with, would be to make conceptual models talk to each other, that is, to verify the potential convergence on the same concepts (entities) and to define their possible relationships.
>
> (Feliciati, 2022, 149)

One of the strategies for semantic co-operation between archivists and librarians advocated by Feliciati profiles entity modelling that is usable in different contexts and domains. We could, therefore, say that identifying and marking boundaries is, paradoxically, the most direct way to destroy barriers.

Among the results of this research is also the definition of a clear distinction between the entity, in its richness and complexity, and each identity proposed by the entity. The agent-type entity modelling exercise, in a case as complex and ill-defined in terms of profiles as that of the pope, has given us the opportunity to hypothesise a data model that, once again stepping out of the cataloguing tradition of string structuring, puts the entity at the centre, represented even if only by an identifier, and the different identities in relation to each other and to the context of expression. Data models should and could accommodate an extension toward properties related to a whole range of articulated ways for the entity to present itself, as demonstrated in the presentation of the lattice for the pope and related entities and identities. This would open other scenarios for analysis aimed at a possible reduction of the number of entities that make up the bibliographic universe in favour of a multiplication of identities. The FRBR model itself, with the four main entities – Work, Expression, Manifestation and Item – could be simplified by considering the entity in its entirety (the Work) and the different, many identities with which, crossing different times and cultures, it could present itself.

The reference to Work suggests another reflection, centered on what was lacking in this discussion. Work and Opus were discussed in Chapter 2, with reference to an example of entity modelling in the context of the Share Family. This topic could have occupied a more expansive discussion, and in the initial plan was the idea of continuing the analysis of Work which Richard Smiraglia had ended with his definition, 'A signifying, concrete set of ideational conceptions realised through semantic or symbolic expression' (Smiraglia, 2001). Analysis of continuing discussion in the SEI WG around Opus, in the Library of Congress around the Hub and what is being explored in the applicability of IFLA LRM Work and Official RDA, convinced me of the impossibility of defining a modelling proposal for this entity. SEI WG's work of extending the BIBFRAME ontology and drawing a bridge spanning IFLA LRM, as anticipated, will go on until at least summer 2025. It is likely that the results of these Work and related entity modelling activities will then be documented elsewhere. But the suggestion of adding more specific elements into a discussion, such as the current one, that is so general has been set aside.

I must account for another major absence. I have not mentioned here the topic of modelling conceptual entities such as those referable to the category of subjects. On this issue, which the Share community too, is investigating, there are still many unexplored areas related to the various processes of entity shaping, starting with clustering criteria. On the other hand, identification processes, which are effective on some kinds of things, show all their fragilities when the boundaries of the object become uncertain or even changeable: semantic indexing becomes a slippery terrain in this sense, being largely influenced by cultural contexts, linguistic variants and the different political and social approaches of the responsible institutions. The problem of using the owl:sameAs property[429] to link individuals with the same identity but in different datasets, which is not new in the field of AI and the semantic web, becomes enormous when the entities to be linked are difficult to place in a precise semantic boundary. To conclude and to illustrate how complex entity modelling processes are when transferred to certain domains, I would like to reference an example of semantics closely linked to cultural context that Matias Frosterus, Information Systems Manager at the National Library of Finland, related in a recent conversation about analysis and disciplinary studies in a multilingual and multicultural context for the construction of Finto[430] and general Finnish ontology. The example given by Frosterus is that of terminology used in Scandinavia to identify a river in relation to terms derived from other vocabularies (for the construction of a Finnish vocabulary, with references to equivalent concepts in French and Swedish):

- in French:
  fleuve: a river that flows into the sea
  rivière: a river that flows into a lake or other river
- in Swedish there are three terms whose semantic differences are rather vague:
  Älv: a large river in Sweden, Norway or Finland
  flod: a great river elsewhere
  å: everything else referable to rivers (a smaller stream would be called a *bäck*).

Also, in Finnish culture, when naming rivers, the convention is that rivers north of Götaälv (a river located in Sweden) are called *älv* and rivers to the south are *å* and finally rivers outside Scandinavia are *flod*.

This intriguing example renders very well the complexity of defining clear and unambiguous boundaries in contexts (such as semantic contexts, i.e. subjectification) that are conditioned by different linguistic, cultural, and geographical traditions. The field is indeed vast and this analysis explores just a portion of it. The hope, however, is that these reflections and insights will generate new ideas for future exploration.

Appendix
Attributes of the Entity svde:Opus and svde:Work

The following is the list of properties that in the BIBFRAME model are applicable to the bf:Work entity and that the SEI WG has divided by attributing them to the svde:Opus and svde:Work entities. To facilitate comparison between entities, the bf:Hub referable properties are also shown. These are derived from the analysis of the MARC to BIBFRAME conversion specifications published on the Library of Congress website (www.loc.gov/bibframe/mtbf).

A. Properties referable to the entity svde:Opus

Preferred Title
Main Title
Part Number
Part Name
SVDE URI
Variant Title
Abbreviated Title
Collective Title
Key Title
Portion Variant Title
Former Variant Title
Running Variant Title
Caption Variant Title
Added Page Variant Title
Distinctive Variant Title
Year
Genre
Intended Audience
Target Audience
Intended Audience Note
Identifiers/s
ISSN-L
EIDR
Geographic Coverage
Geographic Coverage Note
Temporal Coverage
Legal Date
Music Medium
Music Key
Cartographic Attributes
Dissertation
Creator Characteristics
Issuance
Hierarchical Place
Series Analysis
Series Provider
Series Numbering
Series Numbering Peculiarities

Series Classification
Series Tracing
Serial Sequential Designation

B. Properties applicable to the entity svde:Work

Version
SVDE URI
Content
Language
Origin Date
Color Content
Music Format
Supplementary Content
Notation
Duration
Capture
Stairs
Scale Notes
Geographic Coverage
Cartographic Attributes
Arrangement
Arranged Statement Music
Credits
Place of Origin
Language Note
Awards
Summary
Table of Content
Content Accessibility
Moving Image Technique
Serial Pub Type
Government Pub Type
Relief
Notes
Illustrative Content
Category of Material
Aspect Ratio
Sound Content
Projection
Genre
Data Source
LOC Call Number
LOC Copy Statement
Geographic Classification
NML Call Number
NML Copy Statement
LAC Classification
NAL Call Number
NAL Copy Statement
UDC Number
DDC Number
Additional DDC Number
Other Classification Number
Government Document
Classification Number

Endnotes

1 With this work, the so-called 'change' occurs in Heidegger's thought, in which he shifts from a phenomenological approach to one based on language in the reflection on being.

2 In this regard, we recall the seminar 'Modelling Knowledge, Archival and Bibliographic Standards in Comparison. 1st JLIS.it Seminar,' held in Florence on 19 May 2022, the proceedings of which are available at ('Modelling Knowledge, Archival and Bibliographic Standards in Comparison. 1st JLIS.It Seminar – May 19th 2022).

3 See, for example, Knautz and Stock (2011) and Savolainen (2014).

4 The essay by Philip Schreur, presented at the European RDA Interest Group 2017, was later published in 2018 (Schreur, 2018).

5 https://en.wikipedia.org/wiki/Adolphe_Quetelet.

6 'When MARC was created, the Beatles were a hot new group and those of us alive at the time wore really embarrassing clothes and hairstyles. Computers were so large, complex, and expensive that it was ludicrous to think that you would one day have one in your home, let alone hold one in the palm of your hand. Although age by itself is not necessarily a sign of technological obsolescence (how much has the wooden pencil improved in the last 40 years?), when it comes to computer standards it is generally not a good thing.

The very nature of the MARC (machine-readable cataloging) record is, to some degree, an anachronism. It was developed in an age when memory, storage, and processing power were all rare and expensive commodities. Now they are ubiquitous and cheap' (Tennant, 2002).

7 'However, in recent years the Web has evolved from a global information space of linked documents to one where both documents and data are linked. Underpinning this evolution is a set of best practices for publishing and connecting structured data on the Web known as Linked Data. The adoption of the Linked Data best practices has lead to the extension of the Web with a global data space connecting data from diverse domains such as people, companies, books, scientific publications, films, music, television and radio

programmes, genes, proteins, drugs and clinical trials, online communities, statistical and scientific data, and reviews' (Bizer, Heath and Berners-Lee, 2009).

8 https://wiki.share-vde.org/wiki/ShareFamily:Main_Page.

9 https://en.wikipedia.org/wiki/Real_world_object.

10 http://kcoyle.blogspot.com/2015/01/real-world-objects.html.

11 For an overview of the Share Virtual Discovery Environment (SVDE) project, which will be discussed extensively in later chapters of this book, see the Wiki page, available at https://wiki.share-vde.org/wiki/Main_Page.

12 See, for an overview of the change in terminology introduced by RDA from the previous AACR2 standards, what Magda El-Sherbini reported in *RDA: Strategies for Implementation* (El-Sherbini, 2013, 17).

13 IFLA Study Group on the Functional Requirements for Bibliographic Records, *Functional Requirements for Bibliographic Records: Final Report*, (IFLA FRBR Study Group, 1998 and 2009).

14 www.sparontologies.net/ontologies/frbr.

15 www.cidoc-crm.org/frbroo.

16 www.iflastandards.info/fr/frbr/frbrer.

17 https://vocab.org/frbr/core#.

18 http://purl.org/spar/fabio.

19 http://purl.org/spar/biro.

20 www.ifla.org/files/assets/cataloguing/frbr/frbr.pdf.

21 http://purl.org/vocab/frbr/core#Expression.

22 www.iflastandards.info/fr/frbr/frbrer#C1002.

23 www.cidoc-crm.org/f2-expression.

24 http://purl.org/spar/fabio/Expression.

25 'Already when FRAD and Functional requirements for subject authority data (FRSAD) were on the verge of completion, in 2009 and 2010 respectively, it became clear that there was a need to combine or consolidate the FR family into a single coherent model that would clarify its overall meaning and remove obstacles to its adoption . . . The resulting model definition was approved by the FRBR Review Group (November 2016) and then submitted for comments to the Standing Committees of the Cataloguing and Subject Analysis & Access sections, as well as the International Standard Bibliographic Description (ISBD) Review Group, in December 2016. The final document was approved by the IFLA Committee on Standards and adopted by the IFLA Professional Committee on August 18, 2017' (IFLA LRM, 2017, 6).

26 The use of the terms 'Entity detection' and 'Entity identification' is rather ambiguous in the NLP (Natural Language Processing) field, because the two expressions seem to refer to essentially equivalent concepts. I think that this is not the case and that the first expression Entity *detection* refers to the activity of identifying the entities present in a resource (a text, an audio, a video, etc.),

through different algorithms: through text analysis, entities of the type by which people, places, subjects and so on are identified. Entity *identification* is, on the other hand, an activity more focused on identifying the identity of an entity, through the assignment of qualifying attributes and relationships with other entities. We could perhaps simplify by saying that entity detection identifies the entity while entity identification dresses it and sews the dress on it so that it is uniquely identifiable. 'The task of Entity Detection and Tracking (EDT) is suggested by the Automatic Content Extraction (ACE) project [National Institute of Standards and Technology (NIST), 2003]. The goal is to detect all entities in a given text and track all mentions that refer to the same entity. The task is a fundamental to many Natural Language Processing (NLP) applications, such as information retrieval and extraction, text classification, summarisation, question answering, and machine translation' (Zhou et al., 2021, 232). 'The objective of entity identification to determine the correspondence between objective instances from more than one database' (Lim et al., 1993, 294).

27 https://en.wikipedia.org/wiki/Shakespeare_(disambiguation).

28 https://en.wikipedia.org/wiki/William_Shakespeare_(disambiguation).

29 In this case we speak serenely of 'first name' because we know with certainty that William Shakespeare was baptised (on 26 April 1564), the event in which he must have officially received the personal name William.

30 As Varzi makes clear in his article (Varzi, 2007, 285–303), this conception of ontology is generally attributed to Willard Van Orman Quine (1948) while the inventory metaphor goes back to C. D. Broad, (Broad, 1923, 242). The definition of ontology and metaphysics reported by Francesco Franda is even clearer because it also specifies the nature of the objects that are part of this inventory: 'Ontology is that branch of philosophy that deals with answering the question "what exists?", that is, to draw up an inventory of the objects that are part of the world, whether physical or ideal, while metaphysics answers the question "what is", and thus investigates the ultimate nature of what there is' (Franda, 2014).

31 Interesting is Edmund Runggaldier and Christian Kanzian's use of Venus as *evening star* and *morning star* to distinguish extensional properties from the intensional properties associated with an entity and used to identify its identity: 'If one speaks of coincidence in properties as a necessary and sufficient condition of identity, in the sense of Leibniz's principle, then clearly one means only extensional properties, i.e. to the exclusion of intensional properties . . . A thing, for example, may be distressing or calming; but whether such a property agrees with a thing depends on how the latter is perceived by human beings and how they relate to it. The evening star may arouse romantic feelings, while the morning star may bring to mind work; and yet the two stars are identical'

(Runggaldier and Kanzian, 2002, 99). It may also be interesting to go further and talk about the function of naming things: it was Pythagoras who identified both *Lucifer*, the morning star, and *Vesperus*, the evening star, in the planet Venus. (For a history of the naming of this planet in the various peoples and through the centuries see: www.marsilioparolini.com/esperienze/astronomia/Montepiano/Stelle22alta.pdf).

32 The themes discussed in this study have since been taken up in different articles, both by Tillett and other authors. See only Bean and Green, 2001, which also includes Tillett, 1987.

33 As Alan Danskin points out in a commentary to one of the papers under discussion in the Sapientia Entity Identification Working Group (SEI WG) of SVDE, regarding the relationship between an anthology and the contained works: 'RSC [RDA Steering Committee] Aggregates Working Group concluded that the relationship between an anthology and the contained works is not a whole-part relationship. The contained works are embodied by a manifestation.' The text reproduces the comment added by Danskin on one of the working papers under discussion within the group, entitled 'Relationships Between Entities: Management of Tags 76X-78X.'

34 We will return extensively in later chapters of this book to the question of how the most widely used bibliographic models consider certain entities, for example the Agent.

35 We will return to the concept of identity between entities by referring to the theory of the identity of indiscernibles in Leibniz. In the context of the relations drawn by Tillett, the discussion is simpler because it refers mainly to resources considered copies of each other, such as an original and its reproductions, facsimile publication of a resource, etc.

36 We will not go into the history of Einstein's pre- and post-Theory of Relativity concepts of space and time: we will settle for the moment to think about the three dimensions of space (length, width and depth) and the dimension of time, 'the component that constitutes the unified 4-dimensional space-time in which all events in our universe occur and exist' (from Wikipedia: https://en.wikipedia.org/wiki/Four-dimensional_space).

37 Do not confuse 'being' with 'entity' and 'identity' with 'equality'. In the assertion 'x is', 'being' is the 'is' of the thing that is, and 'entity' is the thing that is. Referring to the binomial identity and equality, we can say that identity is the sexiness of the being, while equality is the property whereby the attributes and characteristics of one being correspond to the characteristics of a second being in such a way as to make them in all respects superimposable except that one is not the other. For there to be equality there need to be at least two entities between which to establish a relation of equality; for there to be identity there needs to be at most one entity.

38 https://en.wikipedia.org/wiki/Alter_ego. One of the meanings of alter ego is one that defines it as 'another self, a second personality within one and the same person, with characteristics clearly distinct from the first'.

39 https://en.wikipedia.org/wiki/Heteronym_(literature).

40 www.treccani.it/vocabolario/pseudonimo.

41 https://en.wikipedia.org/wiki/Lewis_Carroll.

42 https://it.starsinsider.com/celebrita/203021/da-beyonce-a-david-bowie-gli-alter-ego-piu-famosi-nella-storia-della-musica.

43 https://en.wikipedia.org/wiki/Heteronym_(literature).

44 Andrea Zanzotto, interviewed by Antonio Tabucchi about the 'patient' Pessoa and what connotes the Portuguese poet's quadruple, says: 'One thinks of the dark anguish but also of the subtle perfidy of not wanting nor being able to call these signs pseudonyms. For, in fact, it seems that everything comes to play precisely around the name, the names. In Pessoa a divided self, which cannot even suspect the pseudonym, goes hand in hand with a superlogical fingidor. And, on the other hand, in the countless authors who gave themselves pseudonyms . . . how much false consciousness was there precisely in accepting this term?' (Tabucchi, 2019).

45 Letter to Adolfo Casais Monteiro on the genesis of heteronyms, published in Tabucchi (2019). In the Note that anticipates the work, Antonio Tabucchi writes: 'It seems almost pleonastic to say that in the immense and mysterious Book that Pessoa has left us the most reposed, and certainly the most imperious, centre is heteronymy. Heteronymy understood not so much as a metaphorical theatre dressing room in which the actor Pessoa hides in order to assume his literary-stylistic disguises; but precisely as a free zone, as a terrain vague, as a magical line through which Pessoa became an "other than himself" without ceasing to be himself.'

46 For an in-depth discussion of Pessoa's theory of heteronymy, and how it is explained and argued by the author himself, refer to Pessoa (2020). The Note to the texts states, 'This volume collects for the first time all the prose fragments that Fernando Pessoa, within his oeuvre, dedicated to the theme of heteronymy, the literary project of creating works for fictitious authors endowed with autonomous personalities and biographies.'

47 The Family of Works scheme, in its entirety, is explained by Tillett as follows: 'Content relationships can be viewed as a continuum from works/expressions/manifestations/items. Moving left to right along this continuum we start with some original works and related works and expressions and manifestations that can be considered "equivalent", that is, they share the same intellectual or artistic content as realized through the same mode of expression. Next, we come to works/expressions/manifestations that are related through a "derivative" relationship. These comprise a range of new

expressions, such as translations, different performances, slight modifications and editions that move along the continuum across a magic line where they become a new work yet still related to some original work. To the far right on this continuum we find "descriptive" relationships that involve new works describing some original work' (Tillett, 2005).

48 We will see, in the chapters that follow, how this discourse of the original one that then manifests itself in so many different identities – and indeed, does not manifest itself except in the identities that express it – will strongly influence the ontological model within the SVDE project, with the introduction of the Opus entity that has exactly the purpose of identifying that original work from which the 'family' derives.

49 The data in this ranking, updated to 2019, refer to works other than the Bible and the Koran, which remain the absolute most translated works in the world, www.eurotrad.com/classifica-10-libri-piu-tradotti-al-mondo.

50 The growing argument (*auxanómenos logos*) has been attributed to Epicarmus of Syracuse (5th century BCE) but has since had several versions and reinterpretations.

51 The example of numbers was given by the Academics as proof that addition or subtraction can cause a total change in identity. The response adopted by Chrysippus to this assertion is expressed by the principle of nonidentity between the qualified individual and the material substratum of which the individual itself is composed.

52 Substance in Aristotle is *synolus* of matter and form, essence of being and being of essence: the essence of being, is what Aristotle says is the fundamental part of the *synolus*, the form, that by which a thing is what it is; the being of essence, or matter, is the 'support' that allows the essence of being to make itself explicit. https://it.wikipedia.org/wiki/Metafisica_aristotelica.

53 Principle of 'non-identity' between the qualified individual and the material substratum of which the individual is made.

54 Chrysippus's answer to the question of who survives between Dion and Theon is that Dion survives, because, to the question 'Whose foot was amputated?' the only possible answer is 'Dion's foot', who was the only one to have one, while in Theon there was no mutation since he already had an amputated foot. Chrysippus's solution therefore wants to overturn the growing argument by arguing that the processes of increase and decrease of matter are not processes of generation and corruption in which one entity transforms into another, but on the contrary, they are a condition of identity over time. In this argument, the will to safeguard the individual identity (Dion) whose permanence is demonstrated by the mutation is clear: if this were not the case, every mutation would have to produce a destruction and a generation of another entity. The same theme is also present in Aristotle, especially in the work *De Generatione et*

Corruptione (321a 10 ff.), where it is demonstrated that an object that increases or decreases is not destroyed if it maintains its identity. In order for there to be generation and destruction, in fact, it is necessary that the thing changes in its entirety from one state to another (Alesse, 2007, 167 ff.).

55 The term endurantism comes from the English 'to endure' which means 'to persist'.

56 The term comes from the English 'to perdure', which means to continue to exist, to endure over a period of time, or to last permanently despite changes or challenges.

57 https://en.wikipedia.org/wiki/Transgender.

58 https://en.wikipedia.org/wiki/Elliot_Page.

59 www.wikidata.org/entity/Q173399.

60 http://viaf.org/viaf/107713968.

61 https://isni.org/isni/0000000120324422.

62 www.worldcat.org/identities/lccn-no2005031915.

63 With redirection from The Wachowskis.

64 https://en.wikipedia.org/wiki/The_Wachowskis.

65 www.wikidata.org/entity/Q195719.

66 Incidentally, in VIAF there are two identifiers for the same duo: https://viaf.org/viaf/311287582/ and https://viaf.org/viaf/312946357/ both referring to the Wachowski Brothers form.

67 https://id.loc.gov/authorities/names/n2012071391.html.

68 https://isni.org/isni/0000000121014610.

69 https://isni.org/isni/0000000456088515.

70 Official RDA Toolkit, section Corporate Body. All links to the Official RDA Toolkit pages are accessible only after authentication with a username and password. For this reason, the quotations refer to the specific sections of the Official RDA Toolkit without including links or instruction numbers.

71 https://en.wikipedia.org/wiki/Italian_Institute_for_Africa_and_the_Orient.

72 Wikipedia was last accessed, for this entry, on 3 August 2024.

73 http://viaf.org/viaf/136882721.

74 https://isni.org/isni/0000000121656605.

75 www.oclc.org/research/areas/data-science/identities.html. The analysis of the WorldCat Identities prototype project was conducted at the time of its publication at that address. As announced later on the same page, the experimental research project has concluded, and the information still visible is provided for historical purposes only. It is no longer possible, therefore, to verify the examples used in the study phase. Also on the same page is cited the link to the WorldCat Entities project, the project on the publication of entities in linked data resulting from the results achieved with the previous research project, https://entities.oclc.org/worldcat/entity.

76 https://it.wikipedia.org/wiki/Istituto_italiano_per_il_Medio_ed_Estremo_Oriente.
77 www.wikidata.org/entity/Q3803624.
78 https://viaf.org/viaf/140988904.
79 https://isni.org/isni/0000000122931218.
80 Name that IsMEO must have assumed in the years between 1936 and 1943 due to some change in the name or even some change in the very nature of the institution.
81 https://id.oclc.org/worldcat/entity/E39QH7JmtdXkdTRRhHjkrrhMJt. On this page, the Related identities section, still present in 2021, is no longer detectable in the August 2024 consultation.
82 www.wikidata.org/entity/Q1132827.
83 https://viaf.org/viaf/130260303.
84 https://isni.org/isni/0000000122688959.
85 https://id.oclc.org/worldcat/entity/E39QH7JmpYCJ7TPcwR6cHr33GR.
86 There is currently an International Association for Mediterranean and Oriental Studies – ISMEO, which draws inspiration from the three aforementioned institutes but should not be confused with any of the three: www.ismeo.eu/chi-siamo.
87 www.wikidata.org/entity/Q102070188.
88 www.wikidata.org/entity/Q104701272.
89 www.wikidata.org/entity/Q102069715.
90 www.wikidata.org/entity/Q3600960.
91 The use of this dual property to link the two journal titles helps complicate the process of identifying the respective entities. In Wikidata the property 'followed by' (P156) has this meaning 'immediately following item in a series of which the subject is a part [if the subject has been replaced, e.g. political offices, use 'replaced by' (P1366)],' while the property 'replaced by' (P1366) has this different meaning: 'other person or item which continues the item by replacing it in its role. Use P156 (followed by) if the item is not replaced (e.g. books in a series), nor identical, but adds to the series without dropping the role of this item in that series.' Using both properties to link the same, identical resources does not help to understand the real relationship between these two titles.
92 Below are links to view the files of the two journals in ANCP, in print and digital formats:
- Bollettino AIB (printed text): ID 914566
  https://acnpsearch.unibo.it/journal/915466.
- Bollettino AIB (Online): ID 2244681
  https://acnpsearch.unibo.it/journal/2244681.
- AIB Studi (Printed text): ID 2882869
  https://acnpsearch.unibo.it/journal/2882869.
- AIB Studi (Online): journal of library and information science: ID 2859319
  https://acnpsearch.unibo.it/journal/2859319.

93 www.sacredspace.ie. The project is defined as follows in the source notes recorded on the authority page of the Library of Congress id.loc.gov service: 'Sacred Space is a joint apostolate of the Irish Province of the Society of Jesus – the Jesuits, and Loyola Press. The site originated in the offices of the Jesuit Communication Centre in Ireland in 1999.' http://id.loc.gov/authorities/names/no2011007966.

94 http://viaf.org/viaf/185796361.

95 http://id.loc.gov/authorities/names/no2011007966.

96 Jesuits. Irish Province. Sacred Space.

97 https://archive.org.

98 https://en.wikipedia.org/wiki/Internet_Archive.

99 For a definition of the discipline that studies, within ontology, the part–whole relation, see the entry 'Mereologia' reported by Maurizio Ferraris (Ferraris, 2003): 'In contemporary ontology, it is the discipline that studies, within ontology, the part–whole relation. The relation can be applied to concrete objects, spatiotemporal regions, events and processes (temporal parts) and also to abstract objects. The essential parts of an object are those without which it ceases to exist (see ontological dependence), while the accidental parts are those that it can also do without. For Peter Simon (*Parts:* a *Study in Ontology*, 1987), the minimal formal properties of the part–integer relation are: 1. It is not reflexive (nothing is a proper part of itself); 2. It is asymmetrical (if a is part of b, b is not part of a); 3. It is transitive: that is, if a is part of b and b is part of c, then a is part of c [see Husserl].'

100 It's a pity that the Wikidata dataset related to the *Divine Comedy* proposes, in the case of unauthenticated access, the title in English, *The Divine Comedy*, as the preferred form, reporting the variants *Divina Commedia, Commedia, Comedìa* (Italian forms), under the label 'Also known as'. The mechanism of proposing the language by which the name of an entity (a title, in this case) is presented in Wikidata, in the case of unauthenticated access, does not involve the identification of a language proper to that entity (Italian, in the case of the *Divine Comedy*) but uses the default language, which is English www.wikidata.org/wiki/Q40185.

101 www.wikidata.org/entity/Q4509219.

102 www.wikidata.org/entity/Q605018.

103 www.wikidata.org/entity/Q2713307.

104 https://en.wikipedia.org/wiki/Sorites_paradox.

105 These words are quoted from one of the conversations I had with Mennato Tedino, Professor of Philosophy at the Liceo Scientifico 'G. Rummo' in Benevento and author of several philosophical and musical works, who had, for the spring and summer of 2021, the patience to help me retrace and rediscover the thread of certain philosophical reasoning that I had practised many years

ago and now abandoned. To him, I hope to have conveyed a curiosity for a world, that of the bibliographic universe and the various forms of shaping the entities that constitute it, not at all distant from the terrains he holds dear.

106 The syntax used for this term is not homogeneous: Real-World Object, real-world object and real world object are the different syntactic formulations most frequently used in the different sources consulted. Although the Real-World Object formulation simplifies the understanding of the abbreviation RWO, I will use the lowercase formulation here for both the terms real-world object and real-world entity, unless otherwise formulated in literal citations.

107 www.loc.gov/bibliographic-future/news/lcwg-ontherecord-jan08-final.pdf.

108 The semantic web isn't just about putting data on the web. It is about making links, so that a person or machine can explore the web of data. With linked data, when you have some of it, you can find other, related, data.
1. Uniform Resource Identifiers (URIs) should be used to name and identify individual things.
2. HTTP URIs should be used to allow these things to be looked up, interpreted and subsequently 'dereferenced'.
3. Useful information about what a name identifies should be provided through open standards such as RDF, Protocol and RDF Query Language (SPARQL).

109 In the same article Fiander cites a talk given by Dick R. Miller and other speakers (Miller et al., 1999) at the 1999 Medical Library Association (MLA) annual meeting. In this talk the authors point out that the MARC proposes as many as five different fields for recording a personal name, each with about seven subfields but, despite this, it is not possible to distinguish in coded form the surname field from the first name field.

110 'To create standards that are both adequate for present needs and flexible enough to offer new opportunities, we should begin with the requirements of bibliographic descriptions (see Functional Requirements for Bibliographic Records, for example) and devise an encoded standard that provides power and flexibility' (Tennant, 2002).

111 See, for example, Mary Finn's article (Finn, 2004), in which she reports on a discussion between Roy Tennant and Rebecca Guenther (Senior Networking and Standards Specialist for the Network Development and MARC Standards Office of the Library of Congress) on the subject at the 39th Annual Potomac Technical Processing Librarians (PTPL) Meeting. On this occasion the two speakers discussed each other's positions and with reference to the articles 'MARC Must Die' and 'MARC Exit Strategies', published by Tennant in 2002 in *Library Journal* to which Guenther responded with a letter to the editor, 'MARC: Not Dead Yet', published in *Library Journal* in January 2003.

112 *LC21: A Digital Strategy for the Library of Congress* (National Research Council (US), 2000).

113 The AACRs were first published in 1967 and then in a second revised edition in 1978 (AACR2) with regular updates. The work leads to the definition of the new RDA rules, 'being developed as a new standard for resource description and access designed for the digital world'.

It is worth quoting a text that gives a broader picture of the genesis of RDA: 'Work on the new standard began in 2004, and in the same year the Committee of Principals for AACR (CoP) appointed Tom Delsey as the Editor. In December 2004 a draft of part I of AACR3 was made available to the constituencies for review. In 2005 a new approach was agreed on, and the decision made to adopt the title: "RDA: Resource Description and Access". In December 2005, the draft of RDA part I was made available for review. Further drafts of RDA chapters were issued in 2006 and 2007. At the October 2007 meeting, the Joint Steering Committee for Development (JSC) agreed on a new organisation for RDA, see "A New Organisation for RDA". A full draft of RDA was issued in November 2008. JSC discussed the responses to the full draft at its meeting in April 2009 and the revised text was delivered to the publishers in June 2009. RDA was published in the RDA Toolkit in June 2010.' (www.rda-rsc.org/archivedsite/rda.html).

114 www.w3.org/TR/1998/WD-rdf-syntax-19980720.

115 www.w3.org/TR/2004/REC-rdf-primer-20040210.

116 www.w3.org/TR/rdf-concepts.

117 www.w3.org/TR/2004/REC-owl-guide-20040210.

118 www.w3.org/TR/owl-ref.

119 www.w3.org/TR/sw-oosd-primer/#comparison.

120 www.w3.org/TR/2008/NOTE-cooluris-20081203/#semweb.

121 www.w3.org/TR/rdf11-concepts/#resources-and-statements.

122 In sequential or unstructured programming, the program consists of a single block of code called main, within which data are manipulated sequentially.

123 In procedural programming, the basic concept is to group repeated pieces of program into usable and callable portions of code whenever the need arises.

124 In modular programming, a further step is taken toward software reuse and interoperability: in order to be able to reuse the procedures made available by one program so that other programs can also benefit from them. It is decided at some point to group procedures having a common domain into separate modules, called bookshelves, which can be reused in different programs.

125 For example, domain models consist of classes, properties and instances/individuals. Classes can be organised in a hierarchy of subclasses with inheritance mechanisms that facilitate the definition and modelling of an object by defining it in specific characteristics without also repeating the characteristics inherited from the class to which it belongs; properties can consist of objects or primitive/letter values.

126 'This final report of the Incubator Group examines how Semantic Web standards and Linked Data principles can be used to make the valuable information assets that libraries create and curate – resources such as bibliographic data, authorities and concept schemes – more visible and reusable outside of their original library context on the wider Web.': www.w3.org/2005/Incubator/lld/XGR-lld-20111025

127 In library classification systems, realia are three-dimensional objects from real life such as coins, tools and textiles, that do not fit into the traditional categories of library material: https://en.wikipedia.org/wiki/Realia_(library_science).

128 https://en.wikipedia.org/wiki/Real_world_object.

129 For a clear and comprehensive discussion of the work of the PCC Task Group on URIs in MARC, please refer to Jackie Shieh's article (Shieh, 2019).

130 Representatives from the SVDE community are participating in the PCC Task Group on URIs in MARC, to work with the group of metadata experts to define how to use URIs in the RDF/BIBFRAME dataset produced through the conversion of the millions of bibliographic and authority records from libraries participating in the initiative.

131 The $0 subfield for recording URIs that can be associated with different MARC fields had already been introduced in 2007, and was the subject of several subsequent updates. For a detail on this see MARC 21 Bibliographic Format – Appendix A – Control Subfields, which traces, in the Content Designator History section, the editorial history of this data element:

$0 – Authority record control number [NEW, 2007]
$0 – Authority record control number [REDEFINED, 2010]
$0 – Authority record control number or standard number [REDESCRIBED, 2016]
In 2016, the requirement to precede a dereferenceable URI (such as an HTTP URI) in subfield $0 with the parenthetical prefix code '(uri)' was removed.
$0 – Authority record control number or standard number [REDESCRIBED, 2017]
In 2017, the scope of subfield $0 was broadened to include classification record control number: www.loc.gov/marc/bibliographic/ecbdcntf.html.

132 www.loc.gov/aba/pcc/resources/poco.html.

133 Again, the syntactic formulation can change to real world entity, real-world entity and similar forms.

134 www.gabormelli.com/RKB/Real-World_Entity.

135 The choice to underline the two formulations in the text is mine, to better highlight the point of interest discussed.

136 www.isi.edu. The precise bibliographic references are not given in this part of the research, except in a few specific cases, due to the number of different pages and resources consulted on the topic in order to create one's own idea with respect to the subject matter.

137 The Semantic Web – ISWC 2016: 15th International Semantic Web Conference, Kobe, Japan, October 17–21, 2016, Proceedings, Part I, Springer International Publishing, 2016.

138 Be it that of databases, OOP, semantic web, AI.

139 For everything related to OOP, reference is made to Bertrand Meyer's work *Object-oriented Software Construction* (Meyer, 1997). Special thanks go to Andrea Gazzarini, a long-time colleague who describes himself as an inquisitive software engineer, focused mainly on Java technology, a lover of programming, who likes to be considered a developer: www.linkedin.com/in/andreagazzarini. Andrea, with whom I have worked and collaborated for many years and who is responsible for the back-end development of the Share projects' technology platform, resolved many of my informational and logical doubts about what this kind of programming is, but above all, he revealed to me the 'methodological' foundation that underlies my explorations and conclusions around the relationship between real-world entity and real-world object. A programmer does not have the ambition to describe an entity in its complexity; therefore he builds 'objects' that are nothing but that entity in a certain, determined and limited context. To Andrea I owe also the conception of the choice of the term 'prism,' which we will discuss later, to express the multi-faceted characteristic of entities.

140 To remove any criticism with respect to the 'behaviour' or 'doing' of everything that constitutes the real world, I will point out that even a knick-knack has a behaviour, namely to sit on top of a piece of furniture to beautify it!

141 In searching for a definition or even a clear answer to the question 'Why does a software object not represent a real-world entity?' I came across Quora (www.quora.com/about), a site that defines as its mission to share and extend world knowledge. Among the many responses to the question posed, I was struck, perhaps because it was clearly in the direction of my own research, by the response of Keith Bentley (BA Computer Science, UC Berkeley) who says 'Two main reasons. First, real-world entities are incredibly complex. Any software application that needs to represent a real-world entity will really only have the information needed for the application to work properly. Modelling any extra data would be needless work. For example, I'm a 6′ 3″ white male with grey hair and weigh about 225 lbs. For an application that is modelling passenger weight distribution on an airplane, I'm a 225 lb blob. Nothing else really matters. An application that models airplane seating would need to know that I'm 225 lbs and 6′ 3″. Nothing else really matters. I'm also part of a clinical trial for a cancer treatment. 6′ 3″ white male weighing 225 lbs is just the start. They also needed information about my skeleton, my heart function, blood measurements and bone marrow samples. The grey hair doesn't seem to be important though.

'Second, software objects don't have to represent real-world entities at all. There's no real-world entity that corresponds to a node in a linked list, for example. In this case, the software object is just being used as a way of organising the program's code and data.'

142 www.c-sharpcorner.com/article/polymorphism-concept-in-object-oriented-programming. See also www.c-sharpcorner.com/UploadFile/cda5ba/object-oriented-programming-with-real-world-scenario.

143 Even in the case of the terms entity resolution and entity modelling, the formulations used in the literature are different (upper- or lower-case formulation, with or without hyphen). The form Entity Resolution, often preferred in the literature, more clearly explains the origin of the abbreviation ER. Here I will use the lower-case wording without hyphen (entity resolution and entity modelling) except in quoted texts.

144 It is interesting to see how the lively mind of a software programmer, who concretely undertakes the experience of building 'objects' representing real-world objects, is also able to explain in a clear and exemplary way what this approach means. Precisely because of the clarity of ideas and expository synthesis that a young software developer named Salakha Gawas demonstrates, I have decided to quote his post, significantly titled 'God is an OOPS Programmer', which can be found at this link: https://medium.com/@salakhagawas/god-is-an-oops-programmer-123b14389228. The post explains well the role of the programmer in constructing objects that represent the real world.

145 On the general topic of entity reconciliation, I have dedicated some of my studies, which have then been transformed into various conference presentations and some articles. Among them are: Possemato (2018; 2022) and Schreur and Possemato (2019).

146 www.ibm.com/docs/en/iii/9.0.0?topic=insight-core-concepts.

147 The Cluster Knowledge Base (CKB) of the SVDE project, called Sapientia, brings together all the entities (of type agent, opus, work, instances etc.) produced through the entity resolution processes designed for this project and applied to the data coming from the bibliographic and authority catalogues of the libraries that join the initiative. We will return in this study to the CKB of Share-VDE and other Share Family projects, but some additional information can be found in the meantime at https://wiki.share-vde.org/wiki/Main_Page.

148 In the identification of entities in the bibliographic universe, which we will discuss in later chapters, a relevant relationship for identifying an author-type agent is to its work, and conversely, a relevant relationship for identifying the work is to its author (or other contributing agents).

149 This definition seems to shuffle the cards a bit in what has been fixed so far with respect to what an entity is as opposed to a real-world object, but this is only because, as we have said, there is no clear and unequivocal definition of these terms. It is enough for us to fixate on the concept that an entity, in its entirety, is too complex for anyone to have the ambition to describe it completely. When we talk about real-world objects we are, therefore, talking about entities but in a way that is 'relative' to the whole.

150 In the work *The Four Generations of Entity Resolution* (Papadakis et al., 2021), the authors classify ER into four successive generations, identified with four 'Vs' understood as the goals achieved:

1. generation: Veracity: first generation entity resolution processes are mainly concerned with analysing and transforming the profiles received as input into objects as close as possible to the real-world object or entity to which the profiles refer, operating mainly on textual analysis.
2. generation: Volume: In this second generation of ER processes, the main focus is on processing large amounts of data to optimise resolution processes. The techniques for process optimisation are diverse and mainly involve machine processes.
3. generation: Variety: the extension of data sources and the explosion of data produced especially by web-generated content force an extension of processes to increasingly less structured or completely unstructured formats. As the information universe becomes more complicated, ER processes also become more challenging and articulated as a result.
4. generation: Velocity: the increase in sources and therefore information profiles, and the increasingly evident diversification of formats, pose a problem for performance, especially related to the speed of processes, which are the subject of the attention of all the improvements made in the fourth generation of ER.

Each of these generations represents a step up from the previous one and each new generation contains the goals of the previous generation.

151 https://parsifal.urbe.it.

152 www.urbe.it.

153 https://data.bnf.fr/en/12102838/gilles_d_assise.

154 www.ifla.org/wp-content/uploads/2019/05/assets/cataloguing/frbr-lrm/ifla-lrm-august-2017.pdf.

155 https://id.loc.gov/ontologies/bibframe.html.

156 The concept of 'super record' does not then find its way with this designation into the cataloguing rules. The concept, however, is closely related to the Name/Title heading of MARC and the grouping under what was called Uniform Title.

157 'Super records for works are in effect a device for incorporating the concept of "super works", i.e. the totality of a work, its different editions and manifestations and the relationships among them' (Fattahi, 1996, 23).

158 'Superwork is not an entity by itself. It is a concept which may be applied to the totality of a work, i.e. its different expressions and manifestations and other related works. Svenonius (1992: 6) defines superwork as: "The set of all manifestations of an original work and all manifestations derived from it." Superworks also encompass new works, such as reviews, criticisms, indexes and bibliographies, which are based on the same work. In this context, many bibliographies (for example, of writers, philosophers, etc.) have a superwork approach in bringing together all expressions and manifestations of a work and also other related works' (Fattahi, 1997, ch. 4).

159 The Library of Congress, after an initial period of practical experimentation with the Hub as a subclass of bf:Work, decided to remodel this entity as a separate class, as discussed later in this book.

160 The Hub's identification processes analyse, in particular, authority records for titles, tags 130 and 240 of the bibliographic record, for uniform titles, as well as tag blocks dedicated, in MARC 21, to recording relationships between records (and between entities), including block 76x–78x, Linking entries, block 700–740, added entry fields, the series access block, then 800–830, series added entries and those for subjects 6xx, subject access fields (McCallum, 2022).

161 https://wiki.share-vde.org/wiki/Main_Page. SVDE has gradually expanded its reach by embracing a community of authoritative institutions in different fields and establishing the Share Family: https://wiki.share-vde.org/wiki/ShareFamily:Main_Page. The initiative is promoted by Casalini Libri, an international bibliographic agency and member of the Program for Cooperative Cataloging, @Cult, a provider of ILS and semantic web solutions, with input and active participation from an international group of libraries, including national and research libraries, and influenced by the vision of the LD4P (Linked Data for Production) project. After two research and development phases initiated in 2016 with the collaboration of the Library of Congress, SVDE and the Share Family are now moving to a production phase by connecting library catalogues in the USA, Canada and Europe.

162 The initiative has as its main areas of focus:

- The analysis of data in MARC (MARC 21 format) produced by participating libraries and the definition of rules for conversion to RDF.
- The development of data analysis criteria for identifying the entities and relationships in them, even if poorly expressed by the 'flat' format constituted by MARC and Universal Machine
- Readable Cataloguing (UNIMARC).
- Data processing in a mode that is still traditional (in MARC) but enriched

with all the URIs useful for marking the entities identified in them and preparing the conversion process.

- The analysis of the data model, among those available in the catalography field (RDA, BIBFRAME, IFLA-LRM – successor to FRBR, FRAD and FRSAD) to be applied in the process of conversion to linked data.
- The construction of the entities provided by the selected data model, starting from the set of bibliographic and authority records of the participating libraries and enriched through the association of information and identifiers from external authoritative sources (VIAF, ISNI, Integrated Authority File (GND) of the Deutsche Nationalbibliothek Library (DNB), LC etc.).
- Conversion to an RDF dataset according to the selected or processed model and publishing it on the web for activation of new services for end users and professionals.
- The creation of a dataset of entities (Agent, Work, Instance, Item, Event, Subject) called Sapientia: an authoritative CKB that expresses the informational contribution made to the web by the successful co-operation of libraries from broad cataloguing traditions and from different geographical and cultural areas.
- The conception and development of an entity editor to allow the community of librarians to review and correct, in a shared and collaborative manner, what has been automatically produced by machines during the processes of identification and reconciliation of entities contained in the CKB in different formats (including RDF).

163 https://wiki.share-vde.org/wiki/ShareVDE:Members/Share-VDE_working_groups.

164 The Sapientia Entity Identification Working Group (SEI WG) has articulated its mandate in several points:

1. Analyse the use of Cluster Knowledge Base Sapientia entities and identifiers and the associated data model.
2. Review and refine processes for clustering CKB Sapientia entities and creating open and permanent URIs associated with these entities, accessible by the library community and the broader web space.
3. Review the rules for conversion from MARC 21 to BIBFRAME and from BIBFRAME to MARC 21 of items related to entities in CKB Sapientia.
4. Engage with the library community to identify and develop best practices for the use of Sapientia entity identifiers in BIBFRAME and MARC 21 data.

More detailed information on the activities of this working group can be found on the Wiki page: https://wiki.share-vde.org/wiki/ShareVDE:Members/Share-VDE_working_groups#SVDE-AC_Sapientia_Entity_Identification_working_group_.28SEI.29.

165 www.rdatoolkit.org.

166 RDA's main objective is to ensure the description of and access to all kinds of resources, regardless of content and format, and to structure the data in a way that can be shared with the broader information space of the Web. RDA also proposes specific element sets and controlled vocabularies already available in RDF, known as RDA element sets and RDA value vocabularies, which are useful for expressing the entities Work, Expression, Manifestation, Item, Agent, Collective Agent, Corporate Body and Family. The attributes of each of these classes, as well as the relationships between the different entities, are represented as properties.

167 The project to publish the British Library's National Bibliography (BNB) in linked open data, for example, in its first version, used a rich set of ontologies and vocabularies, including those made available by RDA on the RDA Registry, http://rdaregistry.info. With reference to the first version of the BNB in linked open data, a view of the data model designed for modelling resources of the book type can be found at the link: https://web.archive.org/web/20230519034438/www.bl.uk/bibliographic/pdfs/bldatamodelbook.pdf. The original links to the pages on the British Library website are not available due to the cyberattack suffered in October 2023, but this Wayback Machine PDF provides the links to the same pages. In April 2022, the British Library closed the first project of publishing the BNB in linked data to join the Share Family initiative, thus creating the first hub of National Bibliographies in linked data t.ly/CJ5OU. See the post published on the British Library's Digital Scholarship Blog page regarding this transition of the national bibliography to the Share Family platform (British Library, 2023).

168 In reality, the North American initiative was inspired by an all-Italian project, that of university libraries in southern Italy, called Share Catalogue, which had already made a definite choice to adopt BIBFRAME (https://sharecatalogue-lod.org). Information on the Share Catalogue project can be found in several sources, including Forziati and Lo Castro, 2018 or Possemato and Delle Donne, 2017.

169 Described as Work or Hub that is an expression of a described Work or Hub. Use to relate Works and/or Hubs under LRM/RDA guidelines or similar implementations (https://id.loc.gov/ontologies/bibframe.html#p_hasExpression).

170 Described as Work or Hub that the described Work or Hub is an expression of. Use to connect Works and/or Hubs under LRM/RDA guidelines or similar implementations (https://id.loc.gov/ontologies/bibframe/expressionOf).

171 For example, an English translation of *Pinocchio* from an Italian version.

172 For example, a Japanese translation of *Pinocchio* might be derived not from an Italian version of Collodi's work but from an English translation of the same work.

173 www.loc.gov/bibframe/news/bibframe-update-an2019.html. At the time of Sally McCallum's presentation, the Hub had not yet been officially declared a new

entity. The proposal assigned this entity the function of a container – hence the name – to group together diverse works wherever possible. The Hub's application to LC data converted to linked open data is already visible on the site https://id.loc.gov.

174 www.bfwe.eu/stockholm_2019. The presentation of the new Hub entity was later repeated by the same author at the ALA Midwinter 2020 held in Philadelphia in January 2020, as part of the session on Bibliographic Conceptual Models (Ford, 2020).

175 Recall that we are talking about RDF entities created through conversion processes from traditional MARC 21 data, specifically from the tag blocks:
– MARC Auth 1XX with $t MARC
– MARC Auth 130 MARC Bib 1XX + 240
– MARC Bib 130
– MARC Bib 600, 610, 611 + $t;
– MARC Bib 630 (if $v, $x, $y, or $z not present)
– MARC Bib 700, 710, 711 + $t; 730

176 'They are aggregators, basically. They provide a point to collect like or related Things' (Ford, 2019).

177 'Hubs perform three functions as aggregators, just as would be expected given their MARC Bib source fields: as subjects, as related works and as Works in the RDA sense' (Ford, 2019).

178 http://id.loc.gov/ontologies/bibframe/Hub.

179 The proposal for the new Hub class was published on GitHub on 24 June 2021, as follows:
'Experimentation with bf:Hub began (at LC) more than three years ago, first becoming instantiated publicly in June 2019. Hubs, which are defined as a subclass of Work, are abstract resources that function as a bridge between two Works. In this way, they function as aggregation and collocation resources. They make it possible, for example, to gather all of the Spanish translations of Mark Twain's *Tom Sawyer* or to capture in which other BF Works Francisco Tarrega's *Capricho árabe* is included. In LC's experimentation, Hubs perform three functions as aggregators: as subjects, as related works and as Works in the RDA sense. Hubs, being BF Works, can be used as Subjects to describe other Works.'
Expected/recommended changes:
– bf:Hub – new class
– Label: Hub
– Definition: An abstract resource that functions as a bridge between two Works.
– SubClassOf: Work
It is available at https://github.com/lcnetdev/bibframe-ontology/issues/75.

180 The proposal for the new modelling of the Hub as 'a basic model class instead of a subclass of bf' is published on Github at the link https://github.com/lcnetdev/bibframe-ontology/issues/108. The BIBFRAME ontology accepted and published this proposal on 30 November 2023: https://id.loc.gov/ontologies/bibframe.html#c_Hub.

181 In slides presented at the European BIBFRAME Workshop (later replicated at the ALA Midwinter in Philadelphia) Kevin Ford presents the Hub 'as an RDA Work . . . But not always an RDA Work' (Ford, 2019).

182 It is worth quoting the original text of IFLA's reasons for modelling this type of entity, the Representative Expression, because it really best expresses the user need that mostly drove the SEI WG Share Working Group to consider the Original Work: 'In a strictly formal sense, in the model all expressions of a work are equivalent as realisations of the work. However, research with end users indicates that they regard certain features as inherent in the works and that expressions that reflect these features are felt to best represent the intention of the creators of the work. The perceived "distance" between a given expression and the image of the "ideal" expression is often indicative and can be used as a criterion for expression selection. In many respects, end users specifically look for expressions with the "original" characteristics and are particularly interested in the manifestations of these expressions.

'In many cases the representative or ''canonical'' features are easily identified as those fixed in the work's first or original expression, which in turn materialises in the work's first manifestation. The other expressions, if the entire history of the work is known, can be considered to be shaped by a network of derivations and transformations from an original expression' (IFLA LRM, 2017, 91).

183 To reflect on the challenges of interoperability of what have been termed different 'flavours' of BIBFRAME, the PCC organised a meeting, in September 2021, of libraries, project groups and bibliographic data providers to discuss the topic of data exchange between different BIBFRAME systems and implementations. There are a number of different projects in the works experimenting with or implementing BIBFRAME and linked data. An essential question now is to ensure that we can all talk to each other in the end: www.loc.gov/aba/pcc/bibframe/PCC-BIBFRAME-Data-Exchange-Summary.pdf.

During the meeting, two temporary working groups were formed:

- the Use Cases Working Group, led by Philip E. Schreur (Stanford University), which released the 'Use Case Working Group Final Report' (a document for internal community use) in December 2021

– the Data Exchange Working Group, led by Nathan Putnam (OCLC). This second temporary group later merged into the permanent PCC BIBFRAME Interoperability Group (BIG) founded by PCC and whose role and functions are summarised in the 15 April 2022 document called 'Terms or References': www.loc.gov/aba/pcc/bibframe/TaskGroups/BIG/BIG-TOR.pdf.

184 Definition of the Work entity (LRM-E2) in IFLA LRM (2017): 'The intellectual or artistic content of a given creation. A work is an abstract entity for the grouping of expressions that are considered functional equivalents or near functional equivalents. A work is a conceptual object: no single material object can be identified as the work. The essence of the work is the constellation of concepts and ideas that form the shared content of what we call expressions of the same work. A work is perceived through the identification of the commonality of content among various expressions. However, the mere similarity of factual or thematic content is not sufficient to group multiple expressions as realisations of the same instance of work. For example, two textbooks that both feature an introduction to calculus or two oil paintings of the same landscape (even if painted by the same artist) are considered distinct works if their creation involved independent intellectual or artistic effort' (IFLA LRM, 2017, 21).

185 Extensive consideration was given to the analysis of the more specifically semantic attributes (subjects, classifications), which are linked in BIBFRAME to Work, as well as in the IFLA LRM model, and thus should more naturally be associated with Opus. Doubt about this stemmed from the desire to make the data modelled in SVDE as compatible and interchangeable as possible with data produced according to other data models and this extended the discussion and analysis. The same is true for the attribute derived from the genre/form field: the vocabulary of terms to express the genre and form of a resource contains values more specifically related to the content of a resource and values related to its form, which makes the attribution to svde:Opus or svde:Work rather ambiguous.

186 https://protege.stanford.edu.

187 In an interesting article (Dadalto et al., 2024, 1) on the importance of distinguishing and appropriately applying the concepts of types and individuals in dataset modelling the authors use the example of words to clarify the boundaries between the two concepts: how many words do we count in the sentence 'The book is on the table'? The answer is six if we count the two occurrences of 'the' as distinct words (tokens), or five if we count the types of words used in the sentence. When we say, 'they drive the same car', do we mean the same type of car (qualitative identity) or the same specific car (numerical identity)? In some practical experiences, such as in the case of Wikidata, a confused application of these concepts generates quite a few issues of identification and representation of entities.

188 For the comparative study, the following sources were used: Opus types, RDA categories, RDA content types, BF Work types, DCMI types and MARC 21 record types.

189 Libraries are increasingly designing systems to publish their catalogues in linked open data with the aim of making their data available in an open and linked manner or to enhance the ways in which resources can be searched and accessed.

190 See, as an example, the mighty training plan for the use of BIBFRAME organised and delivered by the Policy, Training, and Cooperative Programs Division of the Library of Congress for in-house library cataloguers: www.loc.gov/catworkshop/bibframe/index.html

191 For a general overview of the MARVA tool, visit the page www.loc.gov/bibframe/implementation/index.html. One can also try out the MARVA editor on the Library of Congress page available at https://bibframe.org/marva/editor.

192 A brief overview of the JCricket editor can be found at https://wild.share-vde.org/wiki/ShareDoc:PublicDocumentation/LODPlatform/EntityEditor.

193 https://metadataetc.org/metadatabasics/overview.htm.

194 One cannot fail to mention here the very effective visual map of the metadata landscape of metadata proposed by Jenn Riley, in 'Seeing Standards: a Visualization of the Metadata Universe' (Riley, 2018).

195 I have had several opportunities to discuss the value of data reuse on the web facilitated by the linked data paradigm and the practice of entity modelling. See for this specific topic Possemato (2023b).

196 Since this example aims not to identify the apartment but to illustrate a way of looking at the world, the floor plan, the cadastral map and the Google Maps image for geolocation are, intentionally, not related; that is, they do not really represent the same object.

197 Michael K. Buchland's (1997) essay questions the term 'document' and what should be considered a document in an ever-expanding and varied landscape. It offers an examination of the different interpretations given to this term over time, from Paul Otlet to Suzanne Briet to the most modern digital technologies that have revived old questions on the subject.

198 The definition of 'resource' found in one of the W3C pages is interesting: 'A "resource" is a conceptual entity . . . a resource may be generic in that as a concept it is well specified but not so specifically specified that it can only be represented by a single bit stream.': www.w3.org/DesignIssues/Generic.html. See also the definition proposed by the W3C Recommendation 21 March 2013 for the term *Resource*: 'Per [RDF-MT], the referents of RDF URI references are called *resources* but no assumptions are made about their nature. For the sake of this protocol, the [RFC2616] definition is used (unless the term *RDF Resource* is

used explicitly): a network-accessible data object or service identified by an IRI'. www.w3.org/TR/sparql11-http-rdf-update.

In the above definition, *RDF-MT* refers to RDF Semantics, P. Hayes, Editor, W3C Recommendation, 10 February 2004, www.w3.org/TR/2004/REC-rdf-mt-20040210/; while *RFC2616* refers to Hypertext Transfer Protocol – HTTP/1.1. J. Gettys, J. Mogul, H. Frystyk, L. Masinter, P. Leach, T. Berners-Lee, June 1999, www.ietf.org/rfc/rfc2616.txt.

199 Still on the subject of terminology, Zeng and Qin point out that different communities often refer to the same metadata elements with different terminology:

> For instance, in computer science metadata is information about database objects and/or program objects, such as tables and stored procedures. A database may call metadata elements 'data fields' instead of 'elements.' Other terms such as 'properties' and 'attributes' are also frequently used in metadata literature, but their meanings change as the context in which these terms are used changes. An ontological view of metadata, for example, treats Person as a class with 'name,' 'age,' 'gender,' and 'education level' as *properties* of the Person class. Meanwhile, an entity-relationship model calls Person an *entity* with 'name,' 'age,' 'gender,' and 'educational level' as *attributes* of the Person entity. In a schema encoded with an encoding language (e.g. Extensible Markup Language), an *attribute* has yet another meaning: it is an integral part of an XML element that defines the features of that element.
>
> (Zeng and Qin, 2016, 12–13)

200 Here we point to the Bad Meets Evil duo as another identity of Marshall Mathers, but we will see later that in this case it may be more appropriate to speak of it as another entity of which Marshall Mathers is a part.

201 Fernando Pessoa defines Bernardo Soares in a letter as his semi-heteronym 'because although his personality is not mine, it is not different from mine, but is a mere mutation of it: it is me without the reasoning and affection.' From the letter on the genesis of heteronymy sent to Adolfo Casais Monteiro, dated 13 January 1935 (Pessoa, 1987, Vol. I:133).

202 This example introduces the topic of event entity modelling already under discussion within the international bibliographic community and defined in BIBFRAME as 'Something that happens at a certain time and location, such as a performance, speech, or athletic event': https://id.loc.gov/ontologies/bibframe.html#c_Event. In a 2017 study by the Library of Congress, the event is even more precisely defined as 'An event is something that takes place – a musical performance, football game, battle, radio interview, press conference, meeting/conference, etc. It occurs at a specific

location and on a specific date or time or over a specific date/time interval.': www.loc.gov/bibframe/docs/pdf/bf2-eventmodel-march2017.pdf. The Share Family community is also analysing the event entity and its relationships with other entities in BIBFRAME and the SVDE ontology, but these analyses are not yet developed enough to be publicly shared in this study.

203 Incorrectly published under the title *Summer*, and available at www.youtube.com/watch?v=q9R_P3EooAE.

204 https://en.wikipedia.org/wiki/Elena_Ferrante.

205 https://en.wikipedia.org/wiki/Bad_Meets_Evil.

206 The reference here is to Chapter 1, the section 'The paradoxes of identity over time'.

207 As examples referring to this idea of change Lombard cites: Plato, *Theaetetus*, 155a3–5 'Socrates: And as we consider them, I shall say, I think, first, that nothing can ever become more or less in size or number, so long as it remains equal to itself. Is it not so? Theaetetus: Yes. Socrates: And secondly, that anything to which nothing is added and from which nothing is subtracted, is neither increased nor diminished, but is always equal.' (Plato, 2011, 264–5) and Aristotle, *Physics*, Book I, Chapter 7, 191a3–7 'It has, thus, been established how many are the principles of natural things subject to becoming, and in what sense they are many; and it is clear that necessarily something is subject to contraries, and that the contraries are two. But, in another sense, this is not necessary, since even one of the contraries will be sufficient to produce the change by its absence or presence.' (Aristotele, 2007, 49:21)

208 https://en.wikipedia.org/wiki/John_Ellis_McTaggart. On the subject of change in McTaggart, see Luigi Cimmino's article, 'John Ellis McTaggart' (Cimmino, 2016), in which he says: 'In fact, one might think that even in the B-series a certain kind of change is allowed. Suppose that a given poker is red-hot at time t1 and then cold at time t2, where t1 is 'before' t2. Since a necessary condition of change is that the same event possesses different properties at different times, even within a time consisting only of succession relations this condition seems to be satisfied. From Russell onward this is called the at conception of change, set forth in *Principles of Mathematics*. Although necessary, this condition is not sufficient, however. To the Russellian proposal McTaggart objects that in time consisting of B relations an event certainly possesses different properties at different times without, however, losing one property in taking on another. In short, change implies that an event, as such, no longer possesses one property in possessing another, not that it possesses both even if at different times.'

209 https://en.wikipedia.org/wiki/Bertrand_Russell.

210 The philosophical discussion of intrinsic properties versus extrinsic properties, relational and nonrelational predicates is extremely rich, and a detailed analysis of the different positions, though complex, would take us in a completely

different direction from the study we are undertaking. However, I find the study of Gottfried Wilhelm Leibniz's positions conducted by Hidé Ishiguro in the aforementioned work Leibniz's Philosophy of Logic and Language particularly relevant, with specific reference to Chapter VI 'Subject and Predicates (Relational and Non-Relational)' and Chapter VII 'Monads, Attributes, Accidents, and Relations' (Ishiguro, 1990).

211 The Italian translation of 'core' with the term *essenziale* (essential) is perhaps significant of this idea of elements that qualify the substance of the thing. In one of its possible meanings in the Treccani dictionary, the term *essenziale* is described as follows: 'adj. a. Constituting or containing the essence of a thing; substantial, indispensable (as opposed to accidental, accessory)' (www.treccani.it/vocabolario/essenziale), and even better in Dante's *Encyclopedia Treccani* (www.treccani.it/enciclopedia/essenziale_%28Enciclopedia-Dantesca%29), where it says: 'In the sense of "precisely the essence, nature, substance" of a thing, occurs twice in Dante. Synonymous with "substantial" (cf. Latin *essentialis*) and opposed to "accidental", the term denotes all that is naturally connected to the essence (cf. Tomm. Verit. 25 1 ob. 3 "*quidquid convenit alicui inquantum huiusmodi, est ei essentialis*")'. About essentials in RDA see Guerrini (2016).

In *Convivio* III XI 7 essential passions indicate the 'affections' of substance or essence (see ESSENCE). In *Convivio* IV XVI 9 the essential principles are those notions which, falling within the definition, identify the ontological foundations of the essence of a species, according to genus and diversity (in the case of man: the being he 'animal', i.e. genus, and 'rational', i.e. differentia, which coincides with the specific form or essence of the species).

212 www.librarianshipstudies.com/2016/03/rda-core-elements.html.

213 See Carlo Bianchini's reflections on the IFLA LRM model, and in particular what is reported in 'Osservazioni sul modello IFLA Library Reference Model':

> A novelty of the IFLA LRM model is that for all attributes that can be represented as URIs, it has always been preferred to establish a relationship (instead of defining an attribute). The number of attributes in the new model is drastically decreased (there are 37 in all), because properties of a given entity are declared as attributes of that entity only if the property is not an instance of any other entity in the model. In this way, all attributes (e.g., place of. . . or date of. . .) that can be reformulated as relationships between model entities (in this example, the Place and Time Interval entities), are replaced with a mechanism that, starting from a single definition of a general relationship between an entity and a Place or between an entity and a Time Interval, associates the entities concerned.
>
> (Bianchini, 2017, 92)

214 Examples used here are in part adapted to a more familiar context.

215 'And he would understand then that the death of her husband had caused her to feel the death of her girlhood as well; she was mourning the loss of the only herself she had ever known – gone now, to this new, bewildered young widow.' This sentence, from Elizabeth Strout's *Olive Kitteridge*, confirmed my idea of a widespread and shared perception of certain relational changes as significant in terms of identity profiles, even at the level of mere and common feeling, without any need for theoretical support to substantiate it. And if it is true that the world is as I perceive it, and not the mere objective realisation of a model, it is clear that even only the perception of something has its own value, especially when applied to a reproduction, made to communicate with machines, of that same world. Perceiving a relations change as significant, such as becoming a parent or losing an important person in one's life, is not something that can be classified as unimportant by definition, and therefore requires to be taken into account in certain situations of entity identification and modelling.

216 The *Stanford Encyclopaedia of Philosophy* website provides a lucid definition of emergent properties, using the example of a tornado. It explains that a tornado's existence is dependent on dust and debris, and its properties and behaviours are similarly reliant on the interacting properties and behaviours of its fundamental components. However, the tornado's identity is not tied to any specific micro-entity or configuration that composes it. This is evident in the fact that one can have a good understanding of how tornadoes work without delving into the physics of the particles from which they are formed. 'The general notion of emergence is meant to conjoin these twin characteristics of dependence and autonomy.': https://plato.stanford.edu/entries/properties-emergent.

One clear example of emergent properties is that often used to explain systems:

Emergent properties (or behaviours) can appear when a number of subsystems, properties, components, and elements operate together, giving rise to more complex behaviours that go beyond the simplistic logic of the whole being . . . Suppose we take blocks of iron, wood, nails, and bolts. Placed all together as a whole, 'piled up,' they would sink in the sea. If, instead, we 'compose' them in such a way as to create a boat, the same objects will be able to float and carry other objects. This is a very simple example of an emergent property: the sum of the parts does not suffice to arrive at the end product; rather in order to have a boat, the objects must be 'composed', that is, 'nonlinearly added together'. Nonlinear means just this, that it is not enough to add them up . . . but something more has to be done with them. Scientifically, an emergent property is said to occur when the components interact with each other giving rise to a property that, looking at the parts individually, is unexpected and inexplicable: in our case, buoyancy.

https://istitutoprogettouomo.it
(no longer available)

A clear definition of emergent properties is also given by Wikipedia, in the entry Emergent behaviour https://en.wikipedia.org/wiki/Emergence.

217 For those who have not had the opportunity to read Barbara Tillett's doctoral dissertation, I recommend an article that provides a summary of the main concepts explored in the dissertation: Tillett (2001).

218 The reasons behind FRBR are well summarised by Carlo Bianchini: 'The need to analyse the objects of cataloguing and their attributes, to further clarify the relationships between them and the functions of the catalogue, in order to reduce the costs of cataloguing and more effectively meet the needs of users, is at the origin of FRBR' (Bianchini, 2005, 54).

219 As an example, see the Content Designator History section of MARC 21 tag block 760–787:

Fields 760–787 originally were defined only in the serials specifications and contained information describing relationships between bibliographic items that did not necessarily facilitate indexing or provide a machine link to the record for the related item. In 1977, subfield $w (Record control number) was defined in these fields to facilitate linkage among records within a given system and across systems.

In 1981, the following fields were validated for the books specifications and subfield $r was defined to permit linkage through report numbers of technical report materials: 765, 767, 770, 772, 775, 776, 780, 785, and 787.

When the record-linking technique was fully developed in 1982, field 773 (Host Item Entry) was defined for all MARC specifications to accommodate the cataloguing of component parts. The definitions of several other subfields were either broadened or more narrowly defined at that time.

www.loc.gov/marc/bibliographic/bd760787.html.

220 Here I intentionally use header terminology to indicate the main access to the card, referring to a pre-RDA cataloguing framework, which has since revised some of the cataloguing terminology.

221 www.vatican.va/archive/cod-iuris-canonici/ita/documents/cic_libroII_330_it.html#SEZIONE_I.

222 www.vatican.va/archive/cod-iuris-canonici/ita/documents/cic_libroII_331-335_it.html.

223 I denote by (O) an ontological break (change of entity) and by (I) an identity break (change of identity).

224 Benedict XVI, *Declaratio*, 11 February 2013 (Benedict XVI, 2013).

225 An interesting reconstruction on the historical precedents of renunciation is provided by Stefano Violi (Violi, 2013).

226 Monsignor Georg Gänswein, Archbishop, Prefect of the Papal Household and a figure close to Pope Benedict XVI, speaks about an 'expanded ministry' in an interview with *Aci Stampa* on 21 May 2016: 'Since the election of his successor, Francis, on 13 March 2013, there are not two popes, but *de facto* an expanded ministry – with an active member and a contemplative member. That is why Benedict XVI has not renounced either his name or the white cassock.': www.acistampa.com/story/bendetto-xvi-la-fine-del-vecchio-linizio-del-nuovo-lanalisi-di-georg-ganswein-3369.

227 The question of the Pope Emeritus in the context of cataloguing would probably not have arisen if Benedict XVI had not clearly expressed the intention to assume the title Emeritus and if he had not expressed himself (through interviews and writings) on this issue. His experience after his resignation was historically unique, as was his handling of that last, particular phase of his life, especially in terms of communication. In this regard see Muolo (2023). The cataloguing question of the Pope Emeritus had already been raised on 12 July 2019 by Mauro Guerrini at a workshop organised by Barbara Tillett at the Library of Congress to analyse some aspects of RDA. The example of Pope Benedict XVI was given among the examples of the RDA cataloguing guide, and Mauro Guerrini posed the question of a new function referable to the Pope after his resignation, which required special cataloguing attention. Discussion at the meeting did not yield an immediate result, but in any case the example of Pope Benedict XVI was later removed from RDA.

228 *Lumen Gentium* is the second of the four constitutions of the Second Vatican Ecumenical Council, issued on 21 November 1964, and promulgated by Pope Paul VI on the same day. The full text of *Lumen Gentium* can be found at www.vatican.va/archive/hist_councils/ii_vatican_council/documents/vat-ii_const_19641121_lumen-gentium_it.html.

229 The text of the missive I have quoted here is from an article by Andrea Tornielli (Tornielli, 2018).

230 See Andrea Tornielli's earlier article (Tornielli, 2016).

231 www.vatican.va/content/benedict-xvi/it/audiences/2013/documents/hf_ben-xvi_aud_20130227.html.

232 www.treccani.it/enciclopedia/beatificazione/

233 www.treccani.it/enciclopedia/canonizzazione

234 See *Sanctorum Mater* – Instruction for Conducting Diocesan or Eparchial Inquiries in the Causes of Saints, Part I – Causes of Beatification and

Canonization, Title II – Reputation of Holiness or of Martyrdom and of Intercessory Power, Art. 4 – § 1.The cause of beatification and canonisation regards a Catholic who in life, in death and after death has enjoyed a reputation of holiness by living all the Christian virtues in a heroic manner or enjoys a reputation of martyrdom because, having followed Christ more closely, he has sacrificed his life in an act of martyrdom: www.vatican.va/roman_curia/congregations/csaints/documents/rc_con_csaints_doc_20070517_sanctorum-mater_en.html#Reputation_of_Holiness_or_of_Martyrdom_and_of_Intercessory_Power.

235 The following are some points extracted from various cataloguing standards regarding the treatment of titles of blessed or saint:

- NV, paragraph 60. Saints. a) The names of saints are written in the Latin form . . . The appellation 'sanctus' is abbreviated and placed after the name, in lower case. References are made from vernacular forms.
- REICAT: 15.2.3B Noble titles and the term saint are retained even when the name consists of more than one element, if they routinely accompany it in publications. They are omitted, however, if the person appears predominantly without them.
- AACR2: 22.13A. The word saint is added after the name of a Christian saint, unless the person is a pope, emperor, businesswoman, king, or queen . . . 22.13B. Any other suitable words or expressions that are necessary to distinguish between two saints shall be added.
- Original RDA Toolkit: 9.6 Other designation associated with the person. Essential element.
  The other designation associated with the person is an essential element for a Christian saint, spirit, person mentioned in a sacred scripture or apocryphal book, fictitious or legendary character, or real non-human entity. For other persons, the other designation associated with the person is an essential element only when it is necessary to distinguish one person from another. 9.6.1.4 Saints: For a Christian saint is registered Saint.
- Official RDA Toolkit: here it says, 'Include the term Saint unless the person is a pope, emperor, empress, king, or queen.'

236 Some of these examples are taken from AACR2, 2nd edn, 2002 Revision, 2004 Update.

237 This statement, taken from a video presented by Jacquie Samples, Head of Metadata & Discovery Strategy Department at Duke University Libraries, gives an idea of the complexity of the issue, where a decisive criterion for distinguishing one type of resource from another is left to the will or intention of the publisher, who is responsible for shaping the work (ALCTS, 2012).

238 A change in the mode of issuance is one of those changes for which RDA requires the creation of a new record and thus, evidently, the identification of a

new entity (see Original RDA Toolkit 1.6.3.1. Change in the issuance mode of an integrative resource).

239 MARC Tag 008 position 21 (a type of continuing resource) lists the different types of resources that can fall into this category, including databases being updated, magazines, blogs, planners, loose-leaf resources, monograph series, newspapers, periodicals, repositories or depositories, newsletters, address book, updated websites (www.loc.gov/marc/bibliographic/bd008s.html).

240 www.loc.gov/catworkshop/courses/cataloginginternet/pdf/ceig1_IM-FINAL.pdf (Miller, 2008, 26).

241 For an examination of some useful sources and the most recent interventions available on the web regarding this topic, see the following references:

- For the ALCTS – Association for Library Collection & Technical Services, a division of the American Library Association (ALA), merged in 2020 into the new ALA Core division (https://en.wikipedia.org/wiki/Association_for_Library_Collections_and_Technical_Services), webinar co-ordinated by Regina R. Reynolds: ALCTS (2015).
- Very useful, also in terms of updates, is the record of the Continuing Resources Cataloging Committee (CRCC) Forum, posted on the Core's News page: Leadership, Infrastructure, Futures on 28 February 2022: Levine (2022)
- The section of the Yale University Library website devoted to cataloguing education publishes an interesting summary of the guidelines adopted by the library, referring mainly to the policies defined within the RDA/LC PCC Policy Statements in the RDA Toolkit and the Cooperative Online Serials Program (CONSER): https://web.library.yale.edu/cataloging/e-resources/updating-websites.
- For a comparison of the treatment of continuing resources in the Original RDA Toolkit and the Official RDA Toolkit see the LC PCC Metadata Guidance Document (MGD) with particular reference to the Serial Work and Integrating Work Decisions section: Library of Congress and PCC (2022).

242 In December 2020, the news page of the RDA Toolkit published the announcement of the official transition from the 'Beta' version of the new Toolkit to the 'Official' version: www.rdatoolkit.org/December2020release. As Gordon Dunsire emphasised in a personal conversation with me, it is important to note that Original RDA is based on an incomplete implementation of FRBR and FRAD, with only FRBR Groups 1 and 2 fully implemented. In contrast, Official RDA is based on the LRM, which amends and consolidates the FR family. Consequently, Official and Original RDA are distinct standards built on different data models.

243 'Neologisms in RDA: RDA creates terminology for new concepts and processes that are not covered by the LRM, such as diachronic work'. Citation in Official RDA Toolkit, section Guidance – Terminology.

244 Freely adapted from the Official RDA Toolkit, section titled 'Diachronic works' (Official RDA Toolkit, section Guidance – Diachronic works).

245 'A transformation boundary is an entity boundary for a diachronic work' (Official RDA Toolkit, section Guidance – Diachronic works).

246 I had the opportunity to address the topic of the entity boundary in the Official RDA and how the introduction of this term is significant in expressing a profound change in the approach to cataloguing resources in terms of entity modelling, in my contribution to the festschrift in honour of Mauro Guerrini (Possemato, 2023a).

247 Freely adapted from the Official RDA Toolkit, section titled 'Entity boundaries' (Official RDA Toolkit, section Guidance – Entity boundaries).

248 Official RDA Toolkit, section Guidance – Diachronic works.

249 https://en.wikipedia.org/wiki/ISSN.

250 https://github.com/OpenMetadataRegistry/marc21rdf.info.

251 Freely adapted from the Official RDA Toolkit (section Guidance – Diachronic works). See also the Official RDA Toolkit, section Resources – Glossary, item 'WEM lock'.

252 The interest in this type of resource is also related to the particular, complex experience of metadata conversion of continuing resources under the Share initiative I have already mentioned. The database now hosting linked open data from the PCC will soon also receive data from CONSER, and thus these issues are under discussion and analysis.

253 The examples used are taken from Parsifal, the single catalogue project in linked open data by URBE and are presented in MARC 21, which is the data format used in the analysis phase for the regeneration and flattening of clusters. The URIs of the clusters obtained in the entity resolution processes are not indicated because, at the time of writing this publication in summer 2024, the project had not yet officially gone into production, and therefore the URIs were not yet permanent. For more information on the project see Danieli (2024). The Parsifal website can be found at https://parsifal.urbe.it/parsifal/home.

254 The occupation qualifications in these examples are taken from the P106 property of the Wikidata data model (www.wikidata.org/entity/P106).

255 I have already mentioned ISNI at several points in this study. It is worthwhile here to report the purpose of this project, which aligns exactly with the aim of entity identification for cross-domain reuse of data associated with each entity, facilitated by the assignment of a unique identifier. From the ISNI website, I have quoted the useful text for explaining the mission of this project:

ISNI is the ISO certified global standard number for identifying the millions of contributors to creative works and those active in their distribution, including researchers, inventors, writers, artists, visual creators, performers, producers, publishers, aggregators, and more.

The mission of the ISNI International Agency (ISNI-IA) is to assign to the public name(s) of a researcher, inventor, writer, artist, performer, publisher, etc. a persistent unique identifying number in order to resolve the problem of name ambiguity in search and discovery, and to diffuse each assigned ISNI across all repertoires in the global supply chain so that every published work can be unambiguously attributed to its creator wherever that work is described.

(https://isni.org)

256 I did not indicate the source of this document as it is part of internal regulations distributed to national agencies actively collaborating in the creation of new data on the platform.

257 Here we talk about gender including the topic of biological sex, knowing full well that they are two different yet complementary areas. The topic is however more closely linked to gender identity, that is, to the perception that each person has of themselves as female, male or non-binary, and therefore to the way in which the person identifies or perceives themselves. We are talking about a sense of belonging to a gender that may not correspond with the biological sex assigned at birth.

258 www.loc.gov/aba/pcc/documents/Gender_375%20field_RecommendationReport.pdf.

259 www.loc.gov/aba/pcc/documents/gender-in-NARs-revised-report.pdf.

260 www.loc.gov/marc/authority/ad375.html.

261 The results of the work are then absorbed into several functional documents for librarian training or third-party use: in the aforementioned Library of Congress DCM Z1 training programme document, from the Library of Congress Program for Cooperative Cataloging Policy Statements (www.loc.gov/aba/rda/lcps_access.html) and the Library of Congress Demographic Group Terms (LCDGT), (www.loc.gov/aba/publications/FreeLCDGT/freelcdgt.html).

262 The PCC Advisory Committee DEI, whose mandate is outlined in the document available at www.loc.gov/aba/pcc/taskgroup/DEI-Advisory-Committee-charge.pdf, then evolved in 2023 with a renewed operational plan, which is also reflected in its name change to PCC Advisory Committee on Equity, Diversity, Inclusion, Belonging, and Accessibility (EDIBA), www.loc.gov/aba/pcc/advisory/EDIBA-Advisory-Committee-charge.pdf.

263 www.loc.gov/marc/authority/ad670.html.

264 Notes on the meaning of these neologisms are mine and not included in the original text of the report.

- Outing: the English word 'outing' means the practice of making a person's sexual orientation or gender identity public in the absence of his or her consent, https://en.wikipedia.org/wiki/Outing.
- Misgendering: the dictionary defines misgendering as the act of referring to a transgender person by their biological sex rather than their gender identity, whether intentionally or unintentionally: www.wikidata.org/entity/Q64737957.
- Deadnaming is a neologism that originated in the LGBT community and refers to the act of addressing a transgender person using the name and gender they had before their gender identity change. Deadnaming can be unintentional or used intentionally to disregard a person's gender identity. Transgender individuals who are victims of deadnaming feel hurt by this practice because the birth name belongs to the gender opposite to the one they perceive and desire: https://en.wikipedia.org/wiki/Deadnaming.

265 https://isni.org/page/article-detail/isni-press-release-august-2021-representation-of-gender-identities-in-isni-records-and-the-isni-database.

266 As a member of Casalini Libri, which is an official ISNI agency, I received the draft. The invitation to everyone is to provide feedback on the draft without sharing its content externally until the official publication of the text. For this reason, I provide only a general reference to the policy without disclosing detailed elements of it.

267 The text is taken from the e-mail sent to cataloguing agencies participating in ISNI, including Casalini Libri.

268 'ISNI data recipients, Registration Agencies and Members are asked to ensure, so far as is feasible, that gender-related information gathered by the ISNI-IA or its affiliates and suppliers in the past is not further distributed (except via anonymised statistics).': https://isni.org/page/gender-policy.

269 The discussion that has been opened on the same topic within the Wikidata project is also very interesting. The research project Wikidata Gender Diversity (WiGeDi) studies gender diversity in Wikidata, focusing particularly on the gender identities most at risk of marginalisation ('focusing in particular on the marginalised identities of trans, non-binary, and gender non-conforming people'). It examines how Wikidata's current ontological model represents gender and the extent to which this representation is accurate and inclusive. The project analyses data stored in the knowledge base to gather insights and identify possible gaps. Finally, it examines how the community has managed the transition towards the inclusion of a broader spectrum of gender identities: https://meta.wikimedia.org/wiki/Research:Wikidata_Gender_Diversity.

270 https://plato.stanford.edu/entries/sortals.

271 Although this definition of a sortal seems the furthest from our way of understanding the concept with the aim of explaining the reasons for our

ontological categorisations, the example given by the authors, related to this property of 'countability', is interesting. Imagine being in front of a set table and having to count the glasses on it. We can count the glasses one by one, two by two, or in groups of three – or in any other way we choose. Each of these methods presupposes unique criteria for identifying the glasses and our count will be based on this criterion (Soavi, Carrara and Giaretta, 2008, 3). This sortal criterion is less familiar in the bibliographic universe, perhaps due to a resistance to circumscribing entities useful for representing this world into always somehow 'countable' objects. The bibliographic universe is rich in entities (or perhaps in this case, it is better to say concepts) that are not easily reducible to something necessarily accountable. But the idea that to count something one must define its boundaries is a concept that, by now, at this point in the book, we should be aware of.

272 https://id.loc.gov/ontologies/bibframe.html#c_Agent.

273 Thanks to Alessandra Moi for her assistance in writing some parts of this chapter, at a time when fatigue had taken over.

274 www.librarianshipstudies.com/2020/07/pseudonym.html.

275 Relation designators were already covered in AACR2 (AACR2 21.0D) and structured in the MARC ($e relator term and $4 relator code, then became relationship), but with a level of use limited only to specific cases.

276 'An appellation of an entity in natural language that is selected from a vocabulary encoding scheme or constructed using a string encoding scheme by an agent who creates metadata' (Official RDA Toolkit, Resources – Vocabulary Encoding Schemes – RDA Terms).

277 The quotations are taken from: Anglo-American Cataloguing Rules 2nd edn, 2002 Revision, 2004 Update, published by ALA, CLA, CILIP. The second edition of the AACR2 replaced the 1967 code of the same name in 1978, under the direction and care of the Joint Steering Committee for Revision of AACR (JSC AACR), which after 1978, circulated a series of revisions and amendments.

278 Person who is primarily responsible for creating the intellectual or artistic content of a work.

279 Organisation or group of people identified by a particular name and acting, or likely to act, as an entity.

280 Abbreviated REICAT. The references here are to the 2009 edition (Commissione permanente per la revisione delle regole italiane di catalogazione and ICCU, 2009).

281 See, for example, § 14.2.2. 'Author and other type of responsibility', where it says: 'The persons or entities who conceived and composed or performed the work itself in its original form, or assumed these functions, have authorial responsibilities. Author responsibilities may relate to the entire work or its component parts or contributions (e.g. chapters of a textual work, text and

music, or text and images)' (Commissione permanente per la revisione delle regole italiane di catalogazione and ICCU (2009), para. 14.2.2, p. 409).

282 RDA first absorbs FRBR, FRAD and ICP, and then, with the Official RDA, as an update of the previous Toolkit, it absorbs IFLA LRM.

283 The full text of the RDA was nevertheless published in print format (Joint Steering Committee for Development of RDA, 2011).

284 'The term name refers to a word, character, or series of words and/or characters by which a person, family or entity is known.'

285 'The term access point refers to a name, term, code, etc., that represents a specific person, family or entity. Access points include both authorised access points and variant access points.'

286 Developed by the EAD Working Group of the Society of American Archivists and first published in 1998, EAD is an XML format used by the global archival community. A second version, with more international scope, was published in 2002, first as DTD www.loc.gov/ead/ead2002a.html and in 2007 as Relax NG (https://relaxng.org) and as a W3C schema. The EAD3 version (1.1.1) was published in 2019 by the Technical Subcommittee for Encoded Archival Standards of the Society of American Archivists.

287 https://saa-ts-dacs.github.io/about.html.

288 www.loc.gov/ead/EAD3taglib/EAD3-TL-eng.html#attr-relator.

289 www.loc.gov/ead/EAD3taglib/EAD3-TL-eng.html#elem-agent.

290 www.loc.gov/ead/EAD3taglib/EAD3-TL-eng.html#elem-maintenanceevent.

291 www.loc.gov/ead/EAD3taglib/EAD3-TL-eng.html#elem-persname.

292 www.loc.gov/marc/96principl.html.

293 In the MARC 21 Bibliographic Format, for example, the presence of field 046, concerning the creation date of a Work, Expression or Manifestation entity, depending on the selected indicator. In UNIMARC, on the other hand, an interesting example is represented by field 101 (Language of the Resource), where subfields are explicitly linked to the entities of the FRBR model (Permanent UNIMARC Committee (PUC), 2023).

294 www.loc.gov/aba/pcc/pilots/URIs-in-MARC-Pilot.html.

295 Among the elements of MARC that we have already mentioned in this study are the blocks of cross-references or references.

296 'This is a specific term describing an abstract high-level model, and it is distinct from implementation models or data models' (Riva, 2018, 9).

297 It should be noted that in the initial version of FRBR, the entity Family was not included. It was a later addition derived from FRAD.

298 Both this and the previous relationship are not explicitly stated for the Agent, but for the entity Res. However, since Res is the super entity of the entire model and by virtue of that inheritance mentioned earlier, the two relationships also apply to Agent, a subclass of Res.

299 http://id.loc.gov/ontologies/bibframe/Agent.
300 First of all, the need to convert data from MARC 21 to RDF. The starting point for the definition of the model, although oriented by FRBR, is MARC 21 and the bibliographic record (minus the authority record).
301 'BIBFRAME Authority is used to identify the following that may be associated with a Work or Instance.'
302 www.loc.gov/standards/mads/rdf.
303 'Describes a resource whose label represents a name, especially when a more precise Name cannot be identified.': https://id.loc.gov/ontologies/madsrdf/v1.html#Name.
304 The Library of Congress defines with the namespace http://id.loc.gov/ontologies/bflc an extension of the BIBFRAME ontology that expands the original data model with a set of classes and properties aimed primarily at ensuring greater adherence to MARC 21 and the traditional sequence of information in tags and subfields. https://id.loc.gov/ontologies/bflc.html.
305 www.wikidata.org/entity/P50.
306 www.wikidata.org/entity/P123.
307 www.wikidata.org/entity/Q5.
308 www.wikidata.org/entity/P97.
309 www.wikidata.org/entity/P1853.
310 It turns out, however, that it is possible to extrapolate the properties used in human-type entities through an appropriate query: https://w.wiki/6SzT.
311 www.wikidata.org/wiki/Wikidata:List_of_properties.
312 www.wikidata.org/wiki/Template:Bibliographic_properties.
313 www.wikidata.org/entity/Q8436.
314 www.wikidata.org/entity/Q43229.
315 www.wikidata.org/entity/Q178706.
316 Subclasses of the class Organisation: https://w.wiki/6Szf. Subclasses of the Institution class: https://w.wiki/6Szj.
317 www.wikidata.org/wiki/Wikidata:WikiProject_Archives_Linked_Data_Interest_Group/Describing_Organisations.
318 www.wikidata.org/entity/P742.
319 www.wikidata.org/entity/P1932.
320 www.wikidata.org/entity/P50.
321 www.wikidata.org/entity/P527.
322 Official RDA Toolkit, section Entities – Person.
323 Official RDA Toolkit, section Entities – Corporate Body.
324 Official RDA Toolkit, section Entities – Agent.
325 Official RDA Toolkit, section Entities – Collective Agent.
326 Official RDA Toolkit, section Entities – Nomen.

327 Official RDA Toolkit, section Entities – RDA Entity.

328 Definition of nomen in the Official RDA Toolkit: 'An instance of Nomen associates an RDA entity, excluding Nomen itself, with an appellation of the entity. An appellation is a string or combination of signs that is used to refer to an entity. Any entity that is referred to in an RDA context is named through at least one Nomen. A nomen associates a string with an RDA entity on the basis of cultural or linguistic conventions for naming and referencing an entity'. The quotation is taken from the Guidance section of the Official RDA, under the entry 'Nomens and appellations'.

329 In 2009 Tom Delsey defined for the Joint Steering Committee for Development of RDA three possible scenarios (www.rdatoolkit.org/archivedsite/docs/5editor2rev.pdf), representing some of the potential implementations of RDA data in various database structures. The three scenarios express varying degrees of implementation of cataloguing systems that would want to adopt the RDA guidelines and range from the most elaborate and complex (scenario 1) to the most simple (scenario 3):

- Scenario 1: Relational/object-oriented database structure
- Scenario 2: Linked bibliographic and authority records
- Scenario 3: 'Flat file' database structure (no links).

In 2019, Gordon Dunsire, RSC (RDA Steering Committee) Technical Team Liaison Officer, updated these implementation scenarios based on the new version of the RDA Toolkit being developed, adding a scenario dedicated to implementation in the linked data environment: www.rdatoolkit.org/sites/default/files/rsc/Implementation%20scenarios%20briefing%20paper.pdf.

The four scenarios thus reformulated are:

- Scenario A: Linked open data
- Scenario B: Relational or object-oriented data
- Scenario C: Bibliographic/authority data
- Scenario D: Flat file data.

330 RDA Toolkit, section Guidance – Nomens and appellations.

331 'The FRBR Group 2 entities are the entities responsible for the creation of a work, the realisation of an expression, the production or dissemination of a manifestation, or the ownership of an item. The FRBR model identified two Group 2 entities: person and corporate bodies. The FRAD model expanded the Group 2 entities to include also family. These entities were never collectively identified as subclasses of agent. This occurred only in IFLA LRM, but in putting them together as Group 2, FRBR was already setting the groundwork for this move.'

(Oliver, 2021, 45).

332 See also the LC-PCC Metadata Guidance Document regarding Fictitious and Non-Human Entities available at https://www.loc.gov/aba/rda/mgd/mg-fictitiousNonHumanEntities.pdf.

333 www.loc.gov/aba/rda/mgd.

334 www.loc.gov/aba/rda/mgd/person/mg-p-alternateIdentityOfPerson-01.pdf.

335 www.cidoc-crm.org.

336 ISO 21127:2014: Information and Documentation – a Reference Ontology for the Interchange of Cultural Heritage Information, version 3, 2023, is available at the link www.iso.org/standard/85100.html.

337 The reference is to version 7.1.2 published in June 2022: www.cidoc-crm.org/html/cidoc_crm_v7.1.2.html#E74.

338 www.cidoc-crm.org/html/cidoc_crm_v7.1.2.html#E39.

339 www.cidoc-crm.org/html/cidoc_crm_v7.1.2.html#E77.

340 www.cidoc-crm.org/html/cidoc_crm_v7.1.2.html#E21. About disambiguation of identities, the ontology says of Persons: in cases where there is doubt as to whether multiple persons are actually identical, multiple instances can be created and linked to indicate their relationship. CIDOC CRM does not provide a specific module to support entity identification processes. In a bibliographic context, a name structured following the conventions usually employed for person names will be assumed to correspond to a real person (an instance of Person E21), unless evidence indicates otherwise.

341 www.cidoc-crm.org/html/cidoc_crm_v7.1.2.html#E74.

342 www.cidoc-crm.org/html/cidoc_crm_v7.1.2.html#E1.

343 'Instances of E41 Appellation are cultural constructs; as such, they have a context, a history, and a use in time and space by some group of users. A given instance of E41 Appellation can have alternative forms, i.e., other instances of E41 Appellation that are always regarded as equivalent independent from the thing it denotes.': www.cidoc-crm.org/html/cidoc_crm_v7.1.2.html#E41.

344 https://schema.org.

345 See for example the development of a controlled vocabulary for describing texts and dissertations, based on Schema.org: www.oclc.org/research/publications/2014/describing-theses-using-schema.html. Further references can also be found at: http://openbiblio.net/2012/06/23/linked-data-in-worldcat-org/index.html.

346 https://schema.org/Person.

347 www.treccani.it/vocabolario/persona.

348 Relationships that the Agent class has with other entities in the model that are in some way assimilable to the other models selected here. Therefore, relationships with entities completely unknown to the bibliographic domain, such as ContactPoint or Grant, have been excluded.

349 https://schema.org/Organization.

350 http://purl.org/dc/terms/Agent.
351 http://purl.org/dc/terms/contributor.
352 http://purl.org/dc/terms/creator.
353 http://purl.org/dc/terms/publisher .
354 http://purl.org/dc/terms/rightsHolder.
355 www.ica.org/standards/RiC/ontology.
356 General International Standard Archival Description (ISAD(G)) 2nd edition: www.ica.org/resource/isadg-general-international-standard-archival-description-second-edition.
357 (ISAAR(CP)): www.ica.org/resource/isaar-cpf-international-standard-archival-authority-record-for-corporate-bodies-persons-and-families-2nd-edition.
358 ISDF: International Standard for Describing Functions: www.ica.org/resource/isdf-international-standard-for-describing-functions.
359 International Standard for Describing Institutions with Archival Holdings (ISDIAH): www.ica.org/resource/isdiah-international-standard-for-describing-institutions-with-archival-holdings.
360 RiC-O can support publishing RDF datasets as Linked Data, query them using SPARQL, and make inferences using ontology logic. Between 2018 and 2021 both the RiC-CM conceptual model and the related RiC-O ontology were updated (including textual definitions of many entities, specifications of many attributes and designations of many relationships). The official RiC-O 0.2 version was released in 2021, a few weeks before the full draft of RiC-CM 0.2, and is fully compatible with the conceptual model. Special attention has been paid to handling alignments and cross-mapping (recorded through the use of the rico:closeTo property) with other models, including CIDOC CRM, IFLA LRM, Preservation Metadata Implementation Strategies (PREMIS), Provenance Ontology (PROV-O), Wikidata, and Schema.org.
361 In the very least it is worth mentioning:
- Encoded Archival Context-Corporate Bodies, Persons, and Families (EAC-CPF) Ontology: carried out in 2010 as part of an experimental project conducted by the Institute for Cultural and Natural Artistic Heritage of the Emilia-Romagna region (IBC) on descriptions of subjects (archival-producing entities, persons and families produced in XML format and conforming to the EAC-CPF (Encoded Archival Context-Corporate Bodies, Persons, and Families) standard: http://culturalis.org/eac-cpf.
- OAD – Ontology of Archival Description: https://labs.regesta.com/progettoReload/oad-ontology. The ontology of archival description, published in 2013, aims to represent the descriptive elements of individual units of description – understood as objects of their own archival descriptions. Specifically, OAD aims to make explicit only those information elements deemed necessary for display in the web of data of

archival description units to ensure integration with other datasets also published in linked open data format. It consists of 23 classes, 28 object properties and 18 datatype properties and materialises equivalences and semantic relationships with the National Archives System (SAN), FOAF [Friend of a Friend] and GeoNames (Veninata, 2019, 111).

- National Archives System (SAN) Ontologies: Ontologies developed in 2015 by the Italian Central Institute for Archives (ICAR) to represent the conceptual schema of the information structure expressed by the Catalogue of Archival Resources (CATexchange formats – data representation standards within the SAN) related to producer entities, conservator entities, archival complexes and research tools in OWL format. The ontology comprises 40 classes, 34 object properties and 50 datatype properties and establishes equivalences and semantic relationships with OAD, ORG, EAC-CPF, GeoNames, SKOS (Veninata, 2019, 109).

362 www.ica.org/standards/RiC/ontology#Agent.

363 www.ica.org/standards/RiC-O_1-1.html#Agent.

364 www.ica.org/standards/RiC/ontology#Group.

365 www.ica.org/standards/RiC/ontology#Mechanism.

366 www.ica.org/standards/RiC/ontology#Person.

367 Known also as Marion Robert Morrison and Marion Michael Morrison.

368 www.ica.org/standards/RiC/ontology#Position.

369 www.ica.org/standards/RiC/ontology#AgentName .

370 The Record class is defined as follows: information inscribed at least once by any method on any physical medium in any persistent form and retrievable by an Agent during the lifetime or Work Activity www.ica.org/standards/RiC/ontology#Record.

371 www.giureta.unipa.it/2003/diritto_al_nome.htm#:~:text=Per%20questo%20motivo%20nel%20giudaismo,tuo%2C%20ma%20%C3%A8%20mio%E2%80%9D.

372 Genesis 17:5.

373 In truth, the rule here isn't entirely clear and leaves some room for interpretation. Point 17.4.1.3 B., following the one mentioned above, states: 'Acts of normative or administrative character signed or issued by a person in their office and those that present themselves with the name of the entity to which they refer have the main entry under the appropriate religious entity name, according to previous norms.' However, the examples provided refer to congregations, religious orders, monasteries and archdioceses, but never to the Catholic Church. Should we therefore conclude that no normative or administrative acts are issued by the Catholic Church, that the Catholic

Church is an exception, or that these are only partial examples but implicitly refer to this type of act being applicable to the Catholic Church as well?

(Commissione permanente per la revisione delle regole italiane di catalogazione and ICCU, 2009, 515)

374 The bibliographic description and rules for compiling headings in URBE catalogues follow the set of standards established by AACR2/RDA. However, due to the nature of URBE catalogues and the need to preserve the peculiar forms of certain categories of headings, the use of local variants is allowed for the cases listed below. These variants constitute an adaptation, in whole or in part (mainly linguistic in nature), to the corresponding standards of the cataloguing code adopted by the Network. These variations take into account primarily the reality of URBE catalogues, as revealed by the responses to the questionnaires completed at the time.

Where the local variant (LV) effectively corresponds to the Vatican Norms (*Norme per il Catalogo degli Stampati* (NV, 1949), the reference and description of the paragraphs of these Norms are faithfully maintained.

The text is extracted from the List of Local Variants to AACR2/RDA Cataloguing Rules allowed in the URBE network catalogues, approved at the librarians' assembly on 10 November 2009.

375 Official RDA Toolkit, section Guidance – Introduction to RDA – Objectives and principles governing RDA.

376 A useful reference might be to people with two or more preferred names: Official RDA Toolkit, section Entities – Person – authorized access point for person, 'Persons with two or more preferred names'.

377 In the case of RDA, I have included in Table 4.1 the reference to both birth identity and papal identity for individual works not clearly referable to the Pope in his official capacity, because, as seen, RDA introduces the concept of individuals with multiple identities, thus leaving open the hypothesis that certain writings may be related to birth identity (e.g., works written before election as Pope), although not explicitly stating so.

378 Under the pseudonym Andrzej Jawień, poems, the dramas *Przed sklepem jubilera* and *Promieniowanie ojcostwa*, a philosophical monograph on anthropology and a book on the Second Vatican Council were published: https://encyklopedia.interia.pl/slownik-jezyka-polskiego/news-wojtyla-karol-pseud-andrzej-jawien-stanislaw-a-gruda-piotr-j,nId,2070865.

379 Access to the Catholic Church (or the entry for Popes) defined for official acts opens up, in truth, another possible scenario, even more extreme in ontological terms. This is the hypothesis that there are two entities: the person (the Pope) and the entity (the Catholic Church). In this case, if we want to consider the

different nature of a person compared to an entity as a relevant element, it is difficult to stop at the entity expressing itself in different identities; instead, we must consider the scenario of different entities.

380 https://opac.sbn.it/web/opacsbn.

381 https://id.loc.gov.

382 www.dnb.de/DE/Benutzung/Katalog/katalogDNB_node.html.

383 https://catalogue.bnf.fr/index.do.

384 https://oseegenius.unigre.it/pug/home.

385 https://opac.vatlib.it/all/?ling=it.

386 The error of accessing the baptismal name of the Pope in this case, and not the pontifical name as we would expect, is in my opinion produced by an ambiguity in the definition of rule 17.4.1.3 A of REICAT, which refers to the name of the person to whom the writings, speeches, and other works of the popes are attributed, even if they have official value. What does 'name of the person' mean in this case? Baptismal or birth name (which is a person's name) or pontifical name (which is the Pope's personal name)? The subsequent examples leave no doubt that it refers to the Pope's name, but upon a first reading of the rule, the misunderstanding is possible (Commissione permanente per la revisione delle regole italiane di catalogazione and ICCU, 2009, 515).

387 It is interesting to note that in the label view of the record the author is indicated as Benedikt XVI., Papst; in the RDF download available as a service associated with the record, the responsibility is associated with Joseph Ratzinger, which we can see is more consistent with the concept of entity modelling. However, expressed with the RDA property www.rdaregistry.info/Elements/u/#P60327, the statement of responsibility relates to the title proper.

388 https://en.wikipedia.org/wiki/Jesus_of_Nazareth:_From_the_Baptism_in_the_Jordan_to_the_Transfiguration. This statement from Wikipedia precisely reflects what we are investigating: the hypothesis that a single complex entity, such as that of the popes, can express itself in different ways (thus, with different identities) depending on the context and the type of work produced.

389 https://en.wikipedia.org/wiki/Deus_caritas_est.

390 I denote an ontological break (change of entity) with (O) and an identity break (change of identity) with (I).

391 Here I use personal name and not baptismal name to avoid further limiting the applicability of this table to other cases of identity. In the case of the Pope, we know that he certainly received baptism as a sacrament and therefore we can assume this is the moment of name assumption, but I preferred to refer to the act of registration at a registry office or similar, knowing that even this practice, which Westerners consider universal, is instead limited to certain cultures and certain administrations and therefore not universally recognised.

392 The decision to sign with the papal name or with the civil name on personal works, therefore not strictly related to the papal function (such as a novel, poems or historical works), is correlated to personal choice and expressed individually, as in the case of the aforementioned work by Joseph Ratzinger titled *Jesus of Nazareth: From Baptism in the Jordan to the Transfiguration*.

393 This distinction is instead very clear in MARC formats: in MARC 21, a pope as the principal author of an individual work is recorded in tag 100–Main entry-Personal name (example: 100 0#$aJohn Paul$bII,$cpope,$d1920–2005), while the Pope in his official capacity is recorded in tag 110–Main entry-Corporate name (example: 110 2# $aCatholic Church. $bPope (1978–2005 : John Paul II)).

394 The title of Pope Emeritus could be added to the personal identity of Pope Benedict XVI as a necessary qualifier to define the identity subsequent to his resignation from the pontifical throne, yet no longer referable to his civil identity, in accordance with what Ratzinger himself, as cited in Chapter 3, declared in the *Declaratio* of 10 February 2013.

395 This attribution is quite questionable, as this is a work published after the election to the pontifical throne had already occurred. However, in accordance with the Pope's wishes, as mentioned in the brief description of the work previously stated, he reaffirms that the volume is not an act of teaching but merely the viewpoint of 'believer Joseph Ratzinger' on the figure of Christ.

396 Example of Prerecording section for Agent entity: Official RDA Toolkit, section Entities – Agent, 'Prerecording'.

397 https://data.bnf.fr/12079078/jean-paul_2.

398 https://data.bnf.fr/11921205/benoit_16.

399 https://isni.org/isni/0000000120981449.

400 https://isni.org/isni/0000000107419005.

401 https://isni.org/isni/0000000121458385.

402 http://viaf.org/viaf/35605.

403 http://viaf.org/viaf/89614729.

404 http://viaf.org/viaf/121540659, http://viaf.org/viaf/121007399, http://viaf.org/viaf/305862611 just to offer some examples.

405 http://viaf.org/viaf/102167198.

406 In addition to the above URI a further example is at http://viaf.org/viaf/257054839.

407 An interesting study on the challenges to the clustering processes of VIAF is that of Thomas B. Hickey and Jenny A. Toves, 'Managing Ambiguity in VIAF'(Hickey and Toves, 2014), where they discuss the most problematic cases in VIAF, those in which different entities have been merged into a single cluster or, conversely, the same entity has been managed with several clusters. In the article, Hickey and Toves advocate a different approach from that of classical automated clustering mechanisms: 'Extrapolating from our experience we

expect that naïve uses of linked data will run into many of the same problems, resulting in very strange inferences. This can be especially difficult across domains (we see a rather manageable slice of this problem dealing with relationships between different types of names), and suspect that resolving these issues will be very difficult without deep domain knowledge.' The suggested approach is certainly to deal with data for specific domains, primarily using the expertise that professionals can offer in these particular domains. The Share Family community, which we have already mentioned, is also moving in this direction: the JCricket editor aims precisely at creating a tool for use by cataloguers, in a shared and participatory manner, designed to correct errors arising from entity identification/clustering processes.

408 http://id.loc.gov/authorities/names/n78078345.

409 www.loc.gov/mads/rdf/v1#variantLabel.

410 www.w3.org/2008/05/skos-xl#altLabel.

411 www.w3.org/2004/02/skos/core#related.

412 http://id.loc.gov/authorities/names/n80055818. The LCNAF source is displayed in the Library of Congress site section id.loc.gov in several formats, including multiple RDF serialisations. This is, however, essentially a conversion of the authority file, so much so that each item is considered an instance of MADS/RDF PersonalName, www.loc.gov/mads/rdf/v1#PersonalName, and MADS/RDF Authority, www.loc.gov/mads/rdf/v1#Authority, thus maintaining a strong approach to the concept of 'person name management'. Under the label Additional information, which is quite generic, a link is created to the same 'person' treated as Agent and therefore as a real-world object (the equivalent treated as RWO can be viewed at the link http://id.loc.gov/rwo/agents/n78078345). This section of the site displays information derived from a process of transformation of authority records into entities, which – albeit still incompletely and with all the shortcomings resulting from a conversion process – represents this evolution from the record as a description of an entity, to entity modelling.

413 http://id.loc.gov/authorities/names/n79106175.

414 Karol Wojtyła, www.wikidata.org/entity/Q989, and Joseph Ratzinger, www.wikidata.org/entity/Q2494.

415 Property P742, www.wikidata.org/entity/P742. This property encompasses various types of identities, including: pseudonym, stage name, code name, username, known professionally as, heteronym, ring name, alias, battle name, war name, artistic name.

416 Property P1932, www.wikidata.org/entity/P1932: 'use as qualifier to indicate how the object's value was given in the source'.

417 www.wikidata.org/entity/Q1752976.

418 www.wikidata.org/entity/P527.

419 www.wikidata.org/entity/Q16623548: I point to this and not to other components because it is the one with the most complete profile in Wikidata, including an indication of the pseudonym.

420 http://id.loc.gov/authorities/names/n79056546.

421 http://id.loc.gov/authorities/names/nr96015884.

422 To refer again to the rather simple Carroll-Dodgson case, in VIAF we find at least two URIs for Lewis Carroll: https://viaf.org/viaf/66462036 and http://viaf.org/viaf/32144928665654441241 and no specific URI for Dodgson.

423 Of interest is the paper 'Pseudonyms: an ISNI Policy Paper' available on the ISNI website at https://isni.org/resources/pdfs/isni-pseudonyms.pdf.

424 URI for Carroll, https://isni.org/isni/000000012137136X, and URI for Dodgson, https://isni.org/isni/0000000456215596.

425 The link to the webinar recording is available at the DCMI page: www.dublincore.org/webinars/2022/linking-challenges-for-pseudonyms.

426 To better understand what is meant by Privacy-Enhancing Identity Management the article by Marit Hansen et al. is recommended.

> In an online world, it is in principle still possible for users to manually manage their identities; however, this is a cumbersome process defying the surplus value of speed and convenience offered by online transactions and processes. We assume that the majority of users will prefer an automated solution for managing their roles and identities, a so-called Identity Management System (IMS). In this context, the meaning of 'Identity Management' is determined by the respective support for 'administration of information subjects' versus 'active management of personal information'. Systems supporting the latter are called 'Privacy-Enhancing Identity Management Systems' (PE-IMS)
>
> (Hansen et al., 2004)

427 https://wiki.share-vde.org/wiki/ShareFamily:Main_Page#The_Share_Family_branches_.28tenants.29.

428 The theme of entities as a meeting point between different domains of culture was discussed in depth during the online conference organised by Giovanni Michetti (Michetti and Biblioteca nazionale centrale di Roma, 2020).

429 On this topic, see the articles by Joe Raad et al. (2019) and the article by Harry Halpin et al. (2010).

430 Centralised service for interoperable thesauri, ontologies and classification schemes for different subject areas: https://finto.fi/en.

Bibliography

ALCTS (2012) What the Heck is a Continuing Resource Anyhow?, www.youtube.com/watch?v=AbVnJBG1LCc.

ALCTS (2015) Cataloging Continuing Resources in a Changing Landscape, www.youtube.com/watch?v=7zjjXTQ7OoU.

Alesse, F. (2007) Il concetto di ousia nel pensiero metafisico e cosmologico di Posidonio. In Ioppolo, A. M. and Sedley, D. S. (eds), *Pyrrhonists, Patricians, Platonizers: Hellenistic Philosophy in the Period 155–86 BCE* (Tenth Symposium Hellenisticum), Bibliopolis, 143–85, Bibliopolis.

Aristotele (2007) *Opere. Vol. 3: Fisica–Del cielo*, Laterza (Biblioteca universale Laterza; 49).

Bean, C. A. and Green, R. (eds) (2001) *Relationships in the Organization of Knowledge*, Kluwer Academic Publishers (Information Science and Knowledge Management; 2).

Benedict XVI (2013) *Declaratio* (11 February), | Benedetto XVI, www.vatican.va/content/benedict-xvi/it/speeches/2013/february/documents/hf_ben-xvi_spe_20130211_declaratio.html.

Berners-Lee, T. (2001) *L'Architettura del nuovo web. Dall'inventore della rete il progetto di una comunicazione democratica, interattiva e intercreativa*, Feltrinelli.

Berners-Lee, T. (2006) Linked Data – Design Issues, www.w3.org/DesignIssues/LinkedData.html.

Berners-Lee, T., Hendler, J. and Lassila, O. (2001) The Semantic Web: a New Form of Web Content that is Meaningful to Computers will Unleash a Revolution of New Possibilities, *Scientific American Magazine*, **284** (5), https://lassila.org/publications/2001/SciAm.pdf.

Bianchini, C. (2005) *Riflessioni sull'universo bibliografico: funzioni, oggetti e modelli della catalogazione per autore e titolo*, Ed. Sylvestre Bonnard (Studi bibliografici).

Bianchini, C. (2017) Osservazioni sul modello IFLA Library Reference Model, *JLIS.it*, **8** (3), 86–99, https://doi.org/10.4403/jlis.it-12416.

Biblioteca Apostolica Vaticana (1949) *Norme per il catalogo degli stampati*, 3rd edn.

Billey, A., Drabinski, E. and Roberto, K. R. (2014) What's Gender Got to Do with It?

A Critique of RDA 9.7., *Cataloging & Classification Quarterly*, **52** (4), 412–21, https://doi.org/10.1080/01639374.2014.882465.

Bizer, C., Heath, T. and Berners-Lee, T. (2009) Linked Data: The Story So Far, *International Journal on Semantic Web and Information Systems (IJSWIS)*, **5**, 1–22, https://doi.org/10.4018/978-1-60960-593-3.ch008.

British Library (2023) Share Family: British National Bibliography (Beta) Service is Live, *Digital Scholarship Blog*, 14 July, https://blogs.bl.uk/digital-scholarship/2023/07/share-family-british-national-bibliography.html.

Broad, C. D. (1923) *Scientific Thought*, Routledge & Kegan Paul.

Buckland, M. K. (1997) What is a 'Document'?, *Journal of the American Society for Information Science*, **48** (9), 804–9, https://doi.org/10.1002/(SICI)1097-4571(199709)48:9<804::AID-ASI5>3.0.CO;2-V.

Cimmino, L. (2016) John Ellis McTaggart, *APhEx: Rivista Italiana di Filosofia Analitica*, **13** (January).

Codice di Diritto canonico (n.d.a) Libro II: Il Popolo di Dio, Parte II: La Costituzione Gerarchica della Chiesa; Sez. I: La Suprema Autorità della Chiesa; cap. I: Il Romano Pontefice e il Collegio dei Vescovi (Can. 330), s.d., *Codice di Diritto canonico*, www.vatican.va/ archive/cod-iuris-canonici/ita/documents/cic_libroII_330_it.html#SEZIONE_I.

Codice di Diritto canonico (n.d.b.) Libro II: Il Popolo di Dio, Parte II; Sez. I; cap. I; Art. 1: Il Romano Pontefice (Can. 331–335), s.d., *Codice di Diritto canonico*, www.vatican.va/archive/cod-iuris-canonici/ita/documents/cic_libroII_331-335_it.html.

Commissione permanente per la revisione delle regole italiane di catalogazione and ICCU (eds) (1995) *Regole italiane di catalogazione per autori, reprint of the 1979 edition – REICAT*, ICCU.

Commissione permanente per la revisione delle regole italiane di catalogazione and ICCU (eds) (2009) *Regole italiane di catalogazione – REICAT*, ICCU.

Coyle, K. (2015a) Coyle's InFormation: Real World Objects, *Coyle's InFormation* (blog), 16 January, http://kcoyle.blogspot.com/2015/01/real-world-objects.html.

Coyle, K. (2015b) LISTSERV 16.0 - BIBFRAME Archives, 2015, https://listserv.loc.gov/cgi-bin/wa?A2=ind1501&L=BIBFRAME&P=42216.

Cutter, C. A. (1876) *Rules for a Dictionary Catalogue*, US Government Printing Office, http://archive.org/details/cu31924029519026.

Dadalto, A. A., Almeida, J. P. A., Fonseca, C. M. and Guizzardi, G. (2024) Evidence of Large-Scale Conceptual Disarray in Multi-Level Taxonomies in Wikidata, *Semantic Web*, **15** (6), 2253–70, https://doi.org/10.3233/SW-243562.

Danieli, S. (ed.) (2024) *Parsifal: un modello di collaborazione bibliotecaria per condividere la conoscenza registrata*, Firenze University Press, https://doi.org/10.36253/979-12-215-0356-2.

El-Sherbini, M. (2013) *RDA: Strategies for Implementation*, ALA Editions.

Fattahi, R. (1996) Super Records: an Approach Towards the Description of Works Appearing in Various Manifestations, *Library Review*, **45** (June), 19–29, https://doi.org/10.1108/EUM0000000004129.

Fattahi, R. (1997) The Relevance of Cataloguing Principles to the Online Environment: an Historical and Analytical Study, PhD dissertation, University of New South Wales, https://profsite.um.ac.ir/~fattahi/thesis1.htm.

Feliciati, P. (2022) Name, Things, Places: Towards a Semantic, Sustainable, Usable Integration?, *JLIS.It*, **13** (3), 145–53, https://doi.org/10.36253/jlis.it-480.

Ferrante, E. (2016) *Frantumaglia: a Writer's Journey*, Europa Editions.

Ferraris, M. (2003) *Ontologia*, Guida.

Ferraris, M. (2022) La biblioteca di Abele, *AIB studi*, **62** (1), 105–12, https://doi.org/10.2426/aibstudi-13403.

Fiander, D. J. (2002) Applying XML to the Bibliographic Description, *Cataloging & Classification Quarterly*, **33** (2), 17–28, https://doi.org/10.1300/J104v33n02_02.

Finn, M. (2004) The Future of MARC: R.I.P. or Let Her Rip?, *Virginia Libraries*, **50** (1), https://doi.org/10.21061/valib.v50i1.927.

Ford, K. (2019) Concerning Relationships: Hubs Part II, paper presented at the European BIBFRAME Workshop, Kungliga Biblioteket Stockholm, Sweden, 17–18 September, www.kb.se/download/18.d0e4d5b16cd18f600eafb/1569324367132/2019-kefo-relationships.pdf.

Ford, K. (2020) On Bibframe Hubs, paper presented at the Bibliographic Conceptual Models IG, ALAMW Philadelphia PA, 26 January, https://wiki.share-vde.org/w/images/7/7b/ALA2020_Midwinter_BCMIG_On_BIBFRAME_Hubs.pdf.

Forziati, C. and Lo Castro, V. (2018) La connessione tra i dati delle biblioteche e il coinvolgimento della comunità: il progetto SHARE Catalogue-Wikidata, *JLIS.it*, **9** (3), https://doi.org/10.4403/jlis.it-12488.

Franda, F. (2014) L'identità diacronica fra ontologia e metafisica, *Rivista Italiana di Filosofia Analitica Junior*, **5** (2), https://doi.org/10.13130/2037-4445/4431.

Geach, P. T. (1969) *God and the Soul*, Schocken Books.

Ghiringhelli, L. and Guerrini, M. (2018) Entità, attributi e relazioni bibliografiche: rileggendo la tesi PhD di Barbara B. Tillett trent'anni dopo, *AIB studi*, **58** (3), https://doi.org/10.2426/aibstudi-11868.

Ghirlanda, G. (2013) Cessazione dall'ufficio di Romano Pontefice, *La Civiltà cattolica*, **3905** (March), 445–62.

Gorman, M. (2015) *Our Enduring Values Revisited: Librarianship in an Ever-changing World*, ALA Editions.

Gorman, M. (2018) *I nostri valori, rivisti: la biblioteconomia in un mondo in trasformazione*, ed. by M. Guerrini, trs. by G. Genetasio, Firenze University Press.

Grandy, R. E. and Freund, M. A. (2021) Sortals. In Zalta, E. N. (ed.) *The Stanford Encyclopedia of Philosophy*, Summer 2021, Metaphysics Research Lab, Stanford University, https://plato.stanford.edu/archives/sum2021/entries/sortals.

Guerrini, M. (2020) *Dalla catalogazione alla metadatazione: tracce di un percorso*, Associazione italiana biblioteche (Percorsi AIB 5).

Guerrini, M. (2022a) *Metadatazione: la catalogazione in era digitale*, Editrice Bibliografica (Biblioteconomia e scienza dell'informazione 42).

Guerrini, M. (ed.) (2022b) La metadatazione: cos'è?, *Biblioteche oggi*, **40** (3), 21–50, https://doi.org/10.3302/0392-8586-202203-021-1.

Guerrini, M. and Bianchini, C. (2016) *RDA Handbook: the Metadata Standard for the Digital Age*, Editrice Bibliografica, 60–3.

Hahn, J. and Possemato, T. (2023) The Share-VDE Ontology: a BIBFRAME Extension for Linked Data Discovery, Zenodo, https://doi.org/10.5281/ZENODO.8414627.

Halpin, H., Hayes, P., McCusker, J., McGuinness, D. and Thompson, H. S. (2010) When owl:sameAs isn't the Same: An Analysis of Identity in Linked Data. In *The Semantic Web – ISWC 2010*, 305–20, https://doi.org/10.1007/978-3-642-17746-0_20.

Hansen, M., Berlich, P., Camenisch, J., Clauß, S., Pfitzmann, A. and Waidner, M. (2004) Privacy-Enhancing Identity Management, *Information Security Technical Report*, **9** (1), 35–44, https://doi.org/10.1016/ S1363-4127(04)00014-7.

Harman, G. (2018) *Object-Oriented Ontology: a New Theory of Everything*, Penguin.

Heath, T. and Bizer, C. (2011) *Linked Data: Evolving the Web into a Global Data Space*,. Morgan & Claypool, Publishers (Synthesis lectures on the semantic web: theory and technology 1).

Heidegger, M. (1968) *Sentieri interrotti*, La nuova Italia (Pensatori del nostro tempo).

Hickey, T. B. and Toves, J. A. (2014) Managing Ambiguity in VIAF, *D-Lib Magazine*, **20** (7/8), https://doi.org/10.1045/july2014-hickey.

Hobbes, T. (1972) *Elementi di Filosofia: il Corpo, l'Uomo*, ed. by A. Negri, Unione tipografico-editrice torinese.

HTML.it (2022) Tecniche di Programmazione, www.html.it/pag/15586/tecniche-di-programmazione.

IFLA FRBR Study Group (1998 and 2009) *Functional Requirements for Bibliographic Records: Final Report*, K.G. Saur, https://repository.ifla.org/handle/20.500.14598/811.

IFLA LRM (2017) *IFLA Library Reference Model: a conceptual model for bibliographic information*. In Riva, P., Le Boeuf, P. and Žumer M. (eds), Consolidation Editorial Group of the IFLA FRBR Review Group, IFLA, https://origin-www.ifla.org/files/assets/cataloguing/frbr-lrm/ifla-lrm-august-2017_rev201712.pdf.

Ishiguro, H. (1990) *Leibniz's Philosophy of Logic and Language*, 2nd edn, Cambridge University Press.

ISSN International Centre (2020) ISSN Linked Data Application Profile, www.issn.org/wp-content/ uploads/2020/09/ISSN-LinkedDataApplicationProfile-v2_0.pdf.

JLIS.It (2022) Modeling Knowledge, Archival and Bibliographic Standards in Comparison: 1st JLIS.It Seminar, 19 May 2022, *JLIS.It*, **13** (3), I-III, https://doi.org/10.36253/jlis.it-493.

Joint Steering Committee for Revision of AACR (2004) *Anglo-American Cataloguing Rules*, 2nd edn, 2002 Revision, 2004 Update, ALA, CLA and CILIP.

Joint Steering Committee for Development of RDA (2010a) *Original RDA Toolkit: Resource Description & Access*, ALA, https://original.rdatoolkit.org.

Joint Steering Committee for Development of RDA (2010b) *Resource Description & Access: RDA*, ALA.

Joint Steering Committee for Development of RDA (2011) *Resource Description & Access: RDA*, ALA.

Joint Steering Committee for Development of RDA (2014) *Resource Description & Access: RDA*, 2014 Revision, ALA, CLA and CILIP.

Knautz, K. and Stock, W. (2011) Collective Indexing of Emotions in Videos, *Journal of Documentation*, **67** (October), 975–94, https://doi. org/10.1108/00220411111183555.

Levine, J. (2022) CRCC Update Forum on Continuing Resources Recording Now Available, *Core News*, 28 February, https://alacorenews.org/2022/02/28/crcc-update-forum-on-continuing-resources-recording-now-available.

Lewis, D. K. (1983) Extrinsic Properties, *Philosophical Studies*, **44** (2), 197–200, https://doi.org/10.1007/BF00354100.

Lewis, D. K. (1986) *On the Plurality of Worlds*, Blackwell.

Library of Congress (2008) *On the Record: Report of The Library of Congress Working Group on the Future of Bibliographic Control*, www.loc.gov/bibliographic-future/news/lcwg-ontherecord-jan08-final.pdf.

Library of Congress (2016) BIBFRAME: Bibliographic Framework Initiative, www.loc.gov/bibframe.

Library of Congress and PCC (eds) (2022) *LC-PCC Metadata Guidance Document – Serial Work and Integrating Work Decisions*, www.loc.gov/aba/rda/mgd/mg-serialsDecisions.pdf.

Lim, E.-P., Prabhakar, S., Srivastava, J. and Richardson, J. (1993) Entity Identification in Database Integration. In *Proceedings of the Ninth International Conference on Data Engineering*, IEEE Computer Society Press, 294–301.

Lombard, L. B. (1978) Relational Change and Relational Changes, *Philosophical Studies: an International Journal for Philosophy in the Analytic Tradition*, **34** (1), 63–79.

Lubetzky, S. (1960) *Code of Cataloging Rules: Author and Title Entry. An Unfinished Draft for a New Edition of Cataloging Rules*, ALA.

McCallum, S. (2022) Collocation and Hubs. Fundamental and New Version, *JLIS.It*, **13** (1), 45–52, https://doi.org/10.4403/jlis.it-12760.

Meyer, B. (1997) *Object-oriented Software Construction*, 2nd edn, Prentice-Hall PTR.

Michetti, G. and BNCR (eds) (2020) *Ritrovarsi nel Contestocontesto: le entità come luogo di incontro fra discipline*, online conference, 5 November, https://youtube.com/playlist?list=PL-iQNAYlNN_GQ-xuV9svNA3MACSaA4xTl.

Miller, R. R., Buttner, M., Murnane, P. M., Li, Y., Feng, M., Woelfel, R., Dharma, P. and Grappone, T. C. (1999) Restructuring Serial, Circulation and Traditional Bibliographic Data for Deployment in Changing Digital Environments, paper given at MLA Chicago.

Miller, S. J. (ed.) (2008) *Rules and Tools for Cataloging Internet Resources: Instructor Manual: Cataloging for the 21st Century*, Course 1, Cataloger's Learning Workshop Washington DC, February 2008, Library of Congress, and ALCTS, www.loc.gov/catworkshop/courses/catalinginternet/pdf/ceig1_IM-FINAL.pdf.

Morton, T. (2018) *Iperoggetti*, trs.by V. Santarcangelo, Produzioni Nero.

Muolo, M. (2023) Il Magistero. L'ultima Cattedra del Silenzio del Papa e Teologo della Parola, *Avvenire.it*, 1 March, www.avvenire.it/opinioni/pagine/lultima-cattedra-del-silenzio-del-papa-e-teologo-della-parola.

National Institute of Standards and Technology (NIST) (2003) *The ACE Evaluation Plan*, www.nist.gov/speech/tests/ace/index.htm.

Nelson, D. (2018) What are Emergent Properties? Definition and Examples, *Science Trends*, 29 October, https://sciencetrends.com/what-are-emergent-properties-definition-and-examples.

NIST (2003) The ACE Evaluation Plan, www.nist.gov/speech/tests/ace/index.htm.

NRC (2000) *LC21: a Digital Strategy for the Library of Congress*, National Academy Press, https://doi. org/10.17226/9940.

Oliver, C. (2021) *Introducing RDA: a Guide to the Basics after 3R*, 2nd edn, ALA Editions (special report).

Panizzi, A. (1841) *Rules for the Compilation of the Catalogue.* Vol. 1, printed by order of the Trustees.

Papadakis, G., Ioannou, E., Thanos, E. and Palpanas, T. (2021) *The Four Generations of Entity Resolution*, Morgan & Claypool Publishers (Synthesis Lectures on Data Management 65).

PCC Ad Hoc Task Group on Gender in Name Authority Records (2022) *Revised Report on Recording Gender in Personal Name Authority Records*, 7 April, www.loc.gov/aba/pcc/documents/gender-in-NARs-revised-report.pdf.

Permanent UNIMARC Committee (PUC) (2023) *UNIMARC Bibliographic Format Manual*, Version 1.0.0, IFLA, www.ifla.org/ unimarc-updates/unimarc-bibliographic-format-manual-online-ed.

Pessoa, F. (1987) *Una sola moltitudine*, Vol. 1, ed. by A. Tabucchi, Adelphi.

Pessoa, F. (2020) *Teoria dell'eteronimia*, ed. by V. Russo, Quodlibet.

Pessoa, F. (2021) *Una sola moltitudine*, ed. by A. Tabucchi, Adelphi.

Plato (2011) *Theaetetus*, ed. by F. Ferrari, Greek facing text, Rizzoli (Classici greci e latini).

Plutarco (1996) *Vite parallele*, ed. by A. Traglia, UTET.

Possemato, T. (2018) How RDA is Essential in the Reconciliation and Conversion Processes for Quality Linked Data, *JLIS.It*, **9** (1), 48–60, https://doi.org/10.4403/jlis.it-12447.

Possemato, T. (2022) Universal Bibliographic Control in the Semantic Web. Opportunities and Challenges for the Reconciliation of Bibliographic Data Models, *JLIS.It*, **13** (1), 53–66, https://doi.org/10.4403/jlis.it-12748.

Possemato, T. (2023a) Il concetto di entity boundary nell'Official RDA. In Bergamin, G. and Possemato, T. (eds), *Guardando oltre i confini: partire dalla tradizione per costruire il futuro delle biblioteche: studi e testimonianze per i 70 anni di Mauro Guerrini*, 303–14, Associazione italiana biblioteche (Bibliotecari).

Possemato, T. (2023b) Linked Data: un'opportunità per il riuso, *DigItalia*, **18** (2), 134–46, https://doi.org/10.36181/digitalia-00081.

Possemato, T. and Delle Donne, R. (2017) SHARE Catalogue: un'esperienza di cooperazione, *Biblioteche oggi*, **35** (1), https://doi.org/10.3302/0392-8586-201701-021-1.

Quine, W. V. O. (1948) On What There Is, *Review of Metaphysics*, **2**, 21–38.

Raad, J., Pernelle, N., Saïs, F., Beek, W. and van Harmelen, F. (2019) The sameAs Problem: a Survey on Identity Management in the Web of Data, *ArXiv*, https://doi.org/10.48550/arXiv.1907.10528.

RDA Steering Committee (2020) *Official RDA Toolkit: Resource Description & Access*, ALA, https://access.rdatoolkit.org.

RDA Steering Committee (2021) *RDA Glossary*, ALA, CFLA, CILIP, https://access.rdatoolkit.org/Glossary.

Riley, J. (2004) Understanding Metadata, *NISO website*, www.niso.org/publications/understanding-metadata.

Riley, J. (2018) Seeing Standards: a Visualization of the Metadata Universe, https://doi.org/10.5683/SP2/UOHPVH.

Riva, P. (2018) *The IFLA Library Reference Model: lectio magistralis in Library science*, Casalini Libri (Letture magistrali in biblioteconomia 11), https://digital.casalini.it/9788876560255.

Rose, T. (2015) *The End of Average: how We Succeed in a World that Values Sameness*, HarperOne.

Runggaldier, E. and Kanzian, C. (2002) *Problemi fondamentali dell'ontologia analitica*, Vita e Pensiero.

Saussure, F. de (2013) *Course in General Linguistics*. Translated by Roy Harris, Bloomsbury Academic.

Savolainen, R. (2014) Emotions as Motivators for Information Seeking: a Conceptual Analysis, *Library & Information Science Research*, **36** (1), 59–65, https://doi.org/10.1016/j.lisr.2013.10.004.

Schreur, P. E. (2018) RDA, Linked Data, and the End of Average, *JLIS.It*, **9** (1), 120–27, https://doi.org/10.4403/jlis.it-12448.

Schreur, P. E. (2019) Sinopia: a New Linked-Data Editing Environment Designed for Libraries. In Garoufallou, E., Fallucchi, F. and De Luca, E. W. (eds), *Metadata and Semantic Research*, Springer International Publishing (Communications in Computer and Information Science), 425–30, https://doi.org/10.1007/978-3-030-36599-8_39.

Schreur, P. E. and Possemato, T. (2019) Authify: the Reconciliation of Entities at Scale. In Garoufallou, E., Sartori, F., Siatri, R. and Zervas, M. (eds), *Metadata and Semantic Research*, Cham: Springer International Publishing (Communications in Computer and Information Science), 224–9, https://doi.org/10.1007/978-3-030-14401-2_21.

Shieh, J. (2019) PCC's Work on URIs in MARC, *Cataloging & Classification Quarterly*, **58** (3–4), 418–27, https://doi.org/10.1080/01639374.2019.1705951.

Simpson, J. (2019) Real World Objects: Conceptual Framework and University Library Consortium Study, *The Journal of Academic Librarianship*, **45** (4), 332–42, https://doi.org/10.1016/j.acalib.2019.05.003.

Smiraglia, R. P. (2001) *The Nature of 'A Work': Implications for the Organization of Knowledge*, Scarecrow Press.

Soavi, M., Carrara, M. and Giaretta, P. (2008) È un uccello, è un aereo, è Superman! Visione e identificazione sortale, *Rivista di estetica*, **39** (December), 265–80, https://doi.org/10.4000/estetica.2052.

Society of American Archivists. Technical Subcommittee for Encoded Archival Standards (2019) *Encoded Archival Description Tag Library – Version EAD3 1.1.1.*, 3rd edn, Society of American Archivists.

Stanford University (n.d.) *The Stanford Encyclopedia of Philosophy*, https://plato.stanford.edu

Strawson, P. F. (1959) *Individuals. An Essay on Descriptive Metaphysics*, London, Methuen.

Strout, E. (2008) *Olive Kitteridge*, Random.

Svenonius, E. (2008) *Il fondamento intellettuale dell'organizzazione dell'informazione*, trs. by M. L. Fabbrini, Le Lettere.

Svenonius, E. (2018) Bibliographic Entities and their Uses, *Cataloging & Classification Quarterly*, **56** (8), 711–24, https://doi.org/10.1080/01639374.2018.1524284.

Tabucchi, A. (2019) *Un baule pieno di gente: scritti su Fernando Pessoa*, Feltrinelli.

Tennant, R. (2002) MARC Must Die, *Library Journal*, October, http://soiscompsfall2007.pbworks.com/f/marc+must+die.pdf.

Tillett, B. B. (1987) Bibliographic Relationships: Toward a Conceptual Structure of Bibliographic Information Used in Cataloging, PhD dissertation, UCLA.

Tillett, B. B. (2001) Bibliographic Relationships. In Bean, C. A. and Green, R. (eds), *Relationships in the Organization of Knowledge*, Springer Netherlands (Information Science and Knowledge Management), 19–35, https://doi.org/10.1007/978-94-015-9696-1_2.

Tillett, B. B. (2005) What is FRBR? A Conceptual Model for the Bibliographic Universe, *Australian Library Journal*, **54** (1), 24–30, https://doi.org/10.1080/00049670.2005.10721710.

Tillett, B. B. and Cristán, A. L. (eds) (2009) *Statement of International Cataloguing Principles*. In IFLA Series on Bibliographic Control. Walter de Gruyter – K. G. Saur, (IFLA Series on Bibliographic Control 39), https://doi.org/10.1515/9783598441813.27.

Tillett, B. B., Gömpel, R. and Oehlschläger, S. (2004) *IFLA Cataloguing Principles: Steps Towards an International Cataloguing Code*, Report from the 1st Meeting of Experts on an International Cataloguing Code, Frankfurt, 2003 (Part 1), ed. by IFLA Cataloguing Section, K. G. Saur (IFLA Series on Bibliographic Control 26), https://repository.ifla.org/handle/123456789/847.

Tornielli, A. (2016) Sciacca: 'Non può esistere un papato condiviso', *lastampa.it*, 16 August, www.lastampa.it/vatican-insider/it/2016/08/16/news/sciacca-non-puo-esistere-un-papato-condiviso-1.34821300.

Tornielli, A. (2018) E Benedetto XVI scrisse: basta, c'è un solo Papa, e non sono io, *lastampa.it*, 21 September, www.lastampa.it/vatican-insider/it/2018/09/21/news/e-benedetto-xvi-scrisse-basta-c-e-un-solo-papa-e-non-sono- io-1.34046885.

Varzi, A. C. (2007) Sul confine tra ontologia e metafisica, *Giornale di metafisica*, **29**, 285–303, www.columbia.edu/~av72/papers/GdM_2007.pdf.

Veninata, C. (2019) Linked Open Data e ontologie per la descrizione del patrimonio culturale: criteri per la progettazione di un registro ragionato, doctoral thesis, Sapienza Università di Roma, https://iris.uniroma1.it/handle/11573/1325813.

Violi, S. (2013) La rinuncia di Benedetto XVI: tra storia, diritto e coscienza, *Rivista teologica di Lugano*, **18** (2), http://chiesa.espresso.repubblica.it/articolo/1350913.html.

Vitale, R. (2021) La rinuncia al pontificato di Benedetto XVI, per dirimere ogni dubbio, *Vox Canonica*, 6 December, www.voxcanonica.com/2021/12/06.

W3C (2006) *A Semantic Web Primer for Object-Oriented Software Developers*, http://www.w3.org/TR/sw-oosd-primer.

W3C (2011) *Library Linked Data Incubator Group Final Report*, www.w3.org/2005/ Incubator/lld/XGR-lld-20111025.

Weberman, D. (1999) Cambridge Changes Revisited: Why Certain Relational Changes are Indispensable, *Dialectica*, **53** (2), 139–49.

Wennerlund, B. and Berggren, A. (2019) Leaving Comfort Behind: a National Union Catalogue Transition to Linked Data, paper presented at IFLA World Library and Information Congress 2019, Athens, Greece, 'Libraries: dialogue for change', in Session S15 – Big Data. In *Data Intelligence in Libraries: the Actual and Artificial Perspectives,* 22–23 August 2019, Frankfurt, Germany, IFLA, https://library.ifla.org/id/eprint/2745.

Wiggins, D. (1980) *Sameness and Substance*, Blackwell.

Wiggins, D. (2001) *Sameness and Substance Renewed*, Cambridge University Press.

Wikipedia (2022) Object-oriented Programming, https://en.wikipedia.org/wiki/Object-oriented_programming.

Wittgenstein, L. (2009) *Ricerche filosofiche*. Giulio Einaudi Eeditore (Piccola Biblioteca Einaudi Ns.).

Yablo, S. (1999) Intrinsicness, *Philosophical Topics*, **26** (1), 479–505.

Yale University Library (2015) Cataloging Online Integrating Resources, https://web.library.yale.edu/cataloging/e-resources/updating-websites.

Zambrano, M. (1977) *Claros del bosque*, Seix Barral

Zapounidou, S. (2020) Study of Library Data Models in the Semantic Web Environment, PhD dissertation, Ionian University.

Zapounidou, S., Sfakakis, M. and Papatheodorou, C. (2019) Mapping Derivative Relationships from RDA to BIBFRAME 2, *Cataloging & Classification Quarterly*, **57** (5), 278–308, https://doi.org/10.1080/01639374.2019.1650152.

Zeng, M. L. and Qin, J. (2016) *Metadata,* 2nd edn, Neal-Schuman.

Zhou, Y., Huang, C., Gao, J. and Wu, L. (2021) Transformation Based Chinese Entity Detection and Tracking, August, *ACL Anthology*, https://aclanthology.org/I05-2040.

Zhu, L., Ghasemi-Gol, M., Szekely, P., Galstyan, A. and Knoblock, C. A. (2016) Unsupervised Entity Resolution on Multi-Type Graphs. In Groth, P., Simperl, E., Gray, A., Sabou, M., Krötzsch, M., Lecue, F., Flöck, F. and Gil, Y. (eds), *The Semantic Web – ISWC 2016*, Springer International Publishing (Lecture Notes of Computer Science 9981), 649–67, https://doi.org/10.1007/978-3-319-46523-4_39.

Index

(© Sathyan Rizzo)

Sathyan Rizzo, *Silicon Mirror*. Creative director, Attilio Cusani